Asian Firms

Asian Firms

History, Institutions and Management

Frank B. Tipton

University of Sydney, Australia

Edward Elgar

Cheltenham, UK • Northampton, MA, USA

Published by
Edward Elgar Publishing Limited
The Lypiatts
15 Lansdown Road
Cheltenham
Glos GL50 2JA
UK

Edward Elgar Publishing, Inc.
William Pratt House
9 Dewey Court
Northampton
Massachusetts 01060
USA

Paperback edition 2008
Paperback edition reprinted 2015

A catalogue record for this book is available from the British Library

Library of Congress Cataloguing in Publication Data
Tipton, Frank B., 1943–
  Asian firms : history, institutions, and management / Frank B. Tipton.
    p. cm.
  Includes bibliographical references and index.
  1. Industrial management—Asia. 2. Business enterprises—Asia. 3. Industrial policy—Asia. 4. Asia—Economic policy. I. Title.

HD70.A7T57 2007
338.095—dc22

2007009559

ISBN   978 1 84064 334 3 (cased)
       978 1 84720 514 8 (paperback)

Printed and bound in Great Britain by Clays Ltd, St Ives plc

Contents

List of figures and tables

FIGURES

TABLES

List of case studies

Preface

The research for this study has been supported at a number of points by the Faculty of Economics and Business in the University of Sydney. I would like to express my gratitude in particular to the Dean, Professor Peter Wolnizer, and to the Head of the School of Business, Professor Sid Gray. I have also enjoyed working with two exceptionally able research assistants, Sebastian Kevany and Attila Balogh. However, the study would not have been possible at all without the cooperation of a substantial number of people who agreed to share their experiences, some in highly informal interviews and some in more structured situations. The managers and public officials who responded to my questions are uniformly anonymous in the text, but each chapter is far better for their input. Errors and weakness in the argument are my responsibility.

The approach taken is described in the Introduction. However, there is one point about the use of sources that deserves emphasis. The text rests on secondary literature and statistical materials, supplemented by individual experiences, which, as noted already, remain anonymous. Parallel to the text there are a number of illustrative case studies. Because the firms are almost all identified by name, the material in these sections has been restricted to publicly available information, and the sources are identified at the end of each case. The analyses of these cases are mine alone, based on my judgment of these materials.

There are debts that cannot be repaid, merely acknowledged. My wife Elise and our two daughters Lee and Christine, my sister-in-law, also Christine, and my mother-in-law Daisy, all are owed far more than I can ever repay.

FBT
Sydney
March 2006

1. Introduction

So it is said that if you know others and know yourself, you will not be imperiled in a hundred battles; if you do not know others but know yourself, you will win one and lose one; if you do not know others and do not know yourself, you will be imperiled in every single battle. (Sun Tzu, *The Art of War*)

Ability to know people: knowing the character of people will ensure the soundness of your accounts. (Tao Zhu-gong, the First Business Principle)

WHO WILL WIN AND WHO WILL LOSE?

Sun Tzu and Tao Zhu-gong were Chinese who lived 2500 years ago. Sun Tzu was a master military strategist. His short book *The Art of War* rests on the shelves of military leaders around the world today. It also rests on the shelves of a great many Asian business executives. Tao Zhu-gong, an advisor to the Emperor of Yue, retired and became a fabulously successful businessman. His *12 Business Principles*, with the later addition of *12 Business Pitfalls* and *16 Business Lessons*, has also proved enduringly popular. Sun Tzu's most famous epigram reads, 'If you know others and know yourself, you will not be imperiled in a hundred battles.' And in business, Tao Zhu-gong's First Business Principle is, 'Ability to know people: knowing the character of people will ensure the soundness of your accounts.' You may know yourself, your own firm, its strengths and its weaknesses, but do you know the strengths and weaknesses of your enemy, your competitor? And, do you know the strengths and weaknesses of your supplier, your customer, your joint venture partner, or of your potential employer? Today, your competitor, supplier, customer, joint venture partner, or employer may be Asian. In the near future they almost certainly will be. Are Asian firms different? What do you need to know about them to ensure success?

Large numbers of widely distributed books warn Westerners of the pitfalls of dealing with Asian firms. Asian firms, it is said, are unreliable allies, and particularly dangerous competitors. Some say this is because Asian minds work differently from Western minds.[1] Some say it is because Asian societies work differently, because the rules of 'the ancient game of "Tilt", as practiced in Asia' are different from the West.[2] Some say it is because

1

Asian firms work differently, because Asian firms are 'natural organizations' that take advantage of the 'primary facet' of oriental philosophy, 'the idea that the universe is constantly changing'.[3] A parallel popular literature exists in Asia. Along with Sun Tzu's *Art of War* and Tao Zhu-gong's *12 Principles*, many Asian executives have read another Chinese military classic, *The 36 Stratagems*. Japanese executives may also have read the work of legendary samurai swordsman Musashi Miyamoto, *The Book of Five Rings*, and the so-called '*ninhonjinron*' books that try to identify the essence of the Japanese. Similarly, 'Neo-Confucian' works that emphasize the unique features of Asian societies are popular in Korea, Taiwan and Southeast Asia.

Globalization is having a dramatic impact on international business, and corporate governance therefore has become one of the main issues facing those who wish to succeed in the new international economy. To put it more bluntly, who will win and who will lose? Until 1997, many academic analysts agreed with the popular writers. They believed that Asian firms were winners, and that they were successful because they differed from Western firms. With the onset of the Asian crisis, opinion swung the other way, and Asian firms were accused of systematic weaknesses in their governance structures. 'Reform' of Asian corporate governance currently means movement towards a more 'Western' model.[4] Fashion changes, and we can predict that as Asian economies continue to grow there will be another shift in the wind of opinion. However, the question remains, whether it is true that Asian firms are different, and if so, why? More important, if there are differences, are the differences relevant? Is there anything Western managers can learn from Asian firms, or Asian managers from each other? A useful answer requires us to look at both the internal dynamics of Asian firms, and the external contexts in which Asian firms have found themselves.

Tao Zhu-gong's Twelfth Business Principle is the ability to be far-sighted. Sun Tzu said that a commander must adjust strategy to accord with the distinctive features of the terrain. This book revolves around a series of national studies of Asian business systems. We will examine the internal structures and operations of Asian firms, and relate them to their specific historical and cultural situations. We will ask not only how Asian firms differ from Western firms, but also how they have developed over time and how they differ from each other. We will also ask what it is in general that 'Western' managers are supposed to do to manage effectively, how Asian firms diverge from those norms, and whether the differences lead to better results for Asian firms.

We look first at the origins and development of the Japanese firm and the *keiretsu* or groups of large firms. The Japanese 'model' was often recommended both to Westerners and to other Asians during the period of

Japan's rapid growth. Over the past several years the slow growth of the Japanese economy has led many to question the effectiveness of Japan's corporate structures. What changed, and what can we learn? We then consider Korean firms and especially the large *chaebol* groups, and again look first at the period of spectacular successes, and then at the problems that emerged in the aftermath of the 1997 crisis. China will become the world's largest economy some time during the third decade of this century. We look at the variety of forms of Chinese corporate governance, the traditional 'Confucian' firm in mainland China and its successors in Hong Kong and on Taiwan, and the new forms that have emerged in the People's Republic during the period of reform and opening since 1978. Southeast Asia is a fabulous region of opportunity as well, and so finally we look at the different sorts of Southeast Asian firms in Thailand, Malaysia, Indonesia and the Philippines, as well as Singapore and the 'bamboo networks' of overseas Chinese.

In each case the specific historical background factors are set in the context of general management theory. All managers manage. All managers engage in planning and decision making to determine their firm's overall strategy. All must then organize resources in pursuit of their goals. This means they must lead, convince and inspire their employees to contribute to the firm's success. All managers must then control and monitor outcomes to ensure that assigned tasks have been completed.[5] However, not all managers manage in the same way. Managers' approaches to planning and decision making, organizing, leading and controlling, differ from one country to another. Firm structures vary. Values also differ. We need to ask for instance what role religious belief plays in management behavior.

Managerial decisions are constrained by inherited structures and present conditions. We trace the historical origins of the dominant type of firm in each country, and consider its typical internal structure. Each has its characteristic strengths and weaknesses. There typically has been one of Tao Zhu-gong's principles that seems to have led managers to success in each country, and there is frequently one of the Sixteen Lessons that appears particularly appropriate. The Korean *chaebol* groups, for example, have been led by chief executives who exemplify Tao Zhu-gong's Eleventh Business Principle, the ability to initiate and lead by example, and his Sixteenth Business Lesson, that the leader must be steady and calm. But in addition there often has been one of the Twelve Business Pitfalls that has plagued managers and led firms in that country into difficulties. In Korea, as we will see, it is the Eighth Business Pitfall, 'Do not be greedy for credit', that has been the trap into which Korean firms have fallen.

And not all managers manage exactly as they please. External operating environments differ as well. Asian states have played a large role in the

Asian firms

economy, and therefore we need to pay particular attention to the relationships between private firms and government agencies. At this strategic level
Sun Tzu's dictates seem most appropriate, and again each country seems to
have its characteristic features. 'Therefore measure in terms of five things,'
said Sun Tzu, 'the Way, the weather, the terrain, the leadership, and discipline.' And in the Korean case we find indeed that 'Leadership is a matter
of intelligence, trustworthiness, humaneness, and sternness.' But we also
will see that the most effective leadership during Korea's period of rapid
growth came from the state, and especially from President Park Chung Hee
himself, and that the absence of a strong and effective President has
significantly altered the environment.

THE HISTORICAL, INSTITUTIONAL AND MANAGEMENT GRIDS

All firms in all countries must respond to a complex and shifting environment. Sun Tzu suggested that commanders should vary the direction of
attack. We can approach the position of any firm from three directions, or
rather, we can think of the position of any firm as the intersection of three
sets of influences, or grids. The *historical grid* identifies factors inherited
from the past, including ongoing cultural patterns, but also memories, both
direct personal experience and the national histories taught in school
systems. The *institutional grid* identifies the factors impinging on the firm
in its present environment, most obviously the relations between private
firms and public agencies. The border between public and private varies
among countries and over time, and in Asia especially it can be blurred and
indistinct. The *management grid* identifies the ways in which firms respond
to opportunities. Any firm's actions will always be constrained by its
'administrative heritage', the outcome of its organizational history and its
management culture.[6] In addition, however, as we will see, a firm's actions
are further constrained by its position embedded in its nation's historical
and institutional grids.

The Historical Grid: Modernization, National Values, Stages of Development and the World Economy

Every society's history is unique, but all societies have some features in
common. Much of the discussion of Asian development rests on a
definition of 'modernization' based on the work of sociologist Talcott
Parsons.[7] Parsons believed that societies developed from 'traditional' to
'modern' along a continuum with four dimensions:

- *From* 'particularist' *to* 'universalist' in value orientation. Members of 'traditional' particularist societies assume no one outside their society is capable of being civilized, and that different groups have their own particular values, which are appropriate to their class; for instance peasants, nobles, or merchants. 'Modern' universalist societies assume a single set of values applies to all societies and to all people within all societies.
- *From* 'functionally diffuse' *to* 'functionally specific' in the degree of specialization of social roles. In a 'traditional' society, the same group of people may exercise religious, political and economic power. Or, in administration, a single official may be responsible for the entire range of government activities in a district, as in the case of Chinese scholar officials. In a 'modern' society, elites are specialized, and government officials have only one 'function', for instance tax collecting or child welfare.
- *From* 'affective' *to* 'affectively neutral' in emotional tone. Affective means you care about people you meet as persons, but in a 'traditional' society it also means you care about some people more than others, for instance whether a customer is male or female, a member of the nobility, or a member of the same ethnic group as the shop owner. Affectively neutral means you do not care about a person except insofar as they are useful to you. For a shop owner in a 'modern' society, all customers are alike, so long as they can afford the goods on display.
- *From* 'ascription' *to* 'achievement' orientation. Ascription means you 'ascribe' certain characteristics to a person, based on their membership in a class, religious, or ethnic group. Members of your own group, or members of high-prestige groups, are automatically valued more highly than members of other groups. Achievement orientation means a person is valued on the basis of individual accomplishments. This means that 'modern' organizations do not hire someone because of their race, religion, or family connections, but only because they have the best qualifications for the job.

Parsons envisaged every society as a balanced system in equilibrium. The social system adjusts to external shocks by developing new, specialized institutions, and their operation then forces additional adjustments in social structures and the accompanying social roles. Parsons, and his influential students such as Neil Smelser, considered economic change to be the main force moving societies from traditional to modern. Therefore it was their long history of dynamic economic growth that had set Western Europe and the United States apart from the rest of the world and led to their rise to dominance in the nineteenth and twentieth centuries.[8]

The most common reason advanced for the development of Western Europe and the United States was their distinctive values, and in particular religious values. Modernization theorists frequently relied on the work of German sociologist Max Weber, one of the founders of modern sociology and the pre-eminent theorist of the relation between religion and economic development, whose major works were translated into English in the 1950s. In *The Protestant Ethic and the Spirit of Capitalism*, originally published in 1904–5 and in fact translated by Parsons himself in 1958, Weber argued that the Protestant Reformation in the sixteenth century had supported the rise of capitalism and led to the subsequent higher levels of development in the predominantly Protestant countries of Northwestern Europe. In Southern Europe, in contrast, Catholic values had not supported capitalism, and development had been retarded. In *The Religion of China*, originally published in 1920–21, shortly after his death, Weber developed a parallel argument that Confucianism had hampered the emergence of capitalism in China, and therefore was responsible for China's economic backwardness.[9]

Weber has exercised an immense influence across the social sciences, and we will look at his arguments in more detail in Chapter 4, but both he and the modernization theorists were products of their times. As of 1905, all the Protestant countries of Europe were wealthy and developed capitalist societies, and the Catholic countries were mostly poor and underdeveloped. Asia appeared hopelessly backward to Western observers. A half-century later, in the 1950s and early 1960s, when Parsons and his followers produced their major works, it still made a certain amount of sense to look for underlying reasons for the disparity in development between Northwestern Europe and Southern and Eastern Europe, and between Europe and Asia. However, by the late 1960s, Southern and Eastern Europe had also become fully industrialized societies. Therefore the long-term impact of religious differences lost relevance, and discussion of the role of Protestantism disappeared from studies of European economic development. There are some management studies that continue to trace a connection between Protestantism, individualism and entrepreneurship.[10] However, it would be broadly correct to say that today no historian of Europe would argue that Protestantism caused the rise of capitalism, or that Catholicism caused Southern European backwardness.

Meanwhile, by the 1980s, the rise of Asian economies had inspired some to reverse Weber's arguments. In a famous article in 1988, Geert Hofstede argued that those teachings of Confucius that were oriented towards the future, what he called 'Confucian dynamism', explained the exceptionally rapid economic growth of certain East Asian economies over the previous two decades.[11] And, as we will see, so-called 'neo-Confucian' scholars argued in opposition to Weber that Confucian values were positively related to economic growth. Others moved even further, and began to insist that Asia's rapid economic growth rested on unique 'Asian values' that differed from 'Western' values, and therefore that there was no need for Asian societies to change in the ways predicted by modernization theorists. And if this is the case, then Asian firms may continue to differ from Western firms as well.

The Asian historical grid does possess distinctive features, and anthropologists and sociologists have indicated many ways in which cultural differences may affect behavior. In management theory this perspective underlies studies of varieties of capitalism.[12] If American, English, French, and German managers differ from each other, then we might also expect that they would differ from Asian managers, and that Asian managers would also differ from each other.[13] But we need to be careful not to overdo this. Historians today are very skeptical of explanations that rest on unchanging cultural factors, such as Asian 'tradition' or 'Asian values'. These are more likely to be myths propagated by politicians rather than factors directly influencing the managers of firms.[14] In the case of Confucian values, for example, among the Chinese students I have taught, no more than a handful have been able to name the fundamental five relationships of parent to child, husband to wife, older brother to younger brother, ruler to subject, and friend to friend.[15] In addition, as has been frequently pointed out in the discussion surrounding the work of Michael Porter, it is individual firms that compete in the marketplace, not nations.[16]

Nevertheless, it is true that what one believes about one's own national traditions can influence behavior. For example, the actual degree of concentration in large-scale industries does not in fact vary much from one highly industrialized country to another, nor does the general structure of most large organizations, and governments in all countries intervene in the economy more or less continuously. But the work of Alfred Chandler and others shows that the approaches of German, British, and American managers vary. German managers believe themselves to have a history of formal cooperation under state guidance, British managers believe themselves to cooperate informally with each other and with government officials, and American managers believe themselves to be intensely competitive and hostile to state interference, and these beliefs affect their actions, even when there is little or no objective reason for their behavior to vary.[17] Similarly, although Chinese students say for instance that they would not hire someone solely because of personal relationships (*guanxi*), they do believe that 'Chinese' firms often rely on *guanxi* to achieve their goals, and there is little doubt that this expectation will influence their own behavior.[18]

In addition, there are some historical factors that are common to all countries throughout the world. These have influenced the development of business structures both in the West and in Asia. Firstly, there is a series of stages of industrial production and exports that all developed economies have passed through in turn:

- The first stage of industrialization typically sees the expansion of textiles, clothing, consumer goods and, more recently, electronics assembly.
- In the second stage industrial expansion is led by iron, steel, basic chemicals, and heavy machinery.
- In the third stage the industrial sector shifts towards higher quality machinery, advanced chemicals and, more recently, production of electronics components for assembly elsewhere.
- In the fourth stage firms in the advanced countries concentrate on the design, coordination, and marketing of manufactured goods, and these countries also become centers for the provision of financial services such as banking, insurance, and investment.

Secondly, economic fluctuations determine the opportunities available in any period. Since the mid-nineteenth century the world economy has passed through several generation-long cycles. Buoyant upswings powered by investment in major leading sectors have been periods of relatively rapid growth in world trade, and they have also been periods of relatively rapid expansion of the supply of money. The intervening decades have been much more difficult periods of downswing or low growth. These have also typically been periods of slower growth in trade and of monetary deflation, although interspersed with episodes of inflation (the 1970s in the United States and Europe) and even hyperinflation (Germany in 1922–23). The cycles have been the following:

- 1850–1873, an upswing, a long boom driven by investment in railways, facilitated by a rapid growth of credit, and accompanied by a series of treaties that substantially reduced trade barriers.
- 1873–94, a downswing, the 'great depression' marked by slower growth in money supplies, declining prices, and new protective tariffs that hampered trade.
- 1895–1914, an upswing, the 'second industrial revolution' in machine tools, electricity, and chemicals, but also with heavy investment in urban development, aided by more rapid increases in the money supply, and rapid growth in world trade.
- 1918–39, a downswing, with postwar inflation followed by stabilization, deflation, and another 'great depression' in the 1930s, much lower levels of investment than before 1914, and competitive tariffs and quotas that choked trade.

- 1945–1973, an upswing, the 'golden age' of rapid growth, as families in the United States, Europe, and Japan acquired automobiles and other consumer durables for the first time, and world trade boomed under the General Agreement on Tariffs and Trade (GATT).
- 1973 to the mid-1990s, a downswing, with rates of growth less than half those of the golden age and periodic severe recessions, lower levels of investment, the period of 'stagflation' in the 1970s followed by increasingly restrictive monetary policies, and disputes over market access and non-tariff trade barriers.[19]

The 1990s were mixed. The United States grew more rapidly than in the previous two decades, but Europe in general did not. In Asia, China continued to expand, and South Korea and Southeast Asia boomed until the crisis of 1997, but Japan grew very slowly. The expansion of the United States in the second half of the 1990s was powered by information and communications technologies, but following the collapse of the 'dot-com boom' the economy slumped in the early 2000s, and whether the 'new technologies' will trigger another upswing remains for the future to reveal.[20]

The current situation of Asia can be placed in this perspective. Management in an era of slow world growth differs from management in an era of upswing, and Asian managers therefore face greater challenges than for instance United States managers in the 1950s and 1960s. Management also varies depending on a country's current stage of development. Asian economies differ in experiencing the difficulties of transition from one stage to the next. Japan needs to move from the third to the fourth stage, from advanced production to design and provision of services. South Korea needs to move from the second to the third stage, to more emphasis on high-end production. Southeast Asia needs to move from the first to the second stage, away from simple manufacturing based on low labor costs. China is still moving into the first industrial stage, but its sheer size means that different regions may experience very different trajectories. The problems confronting managers in each of these environments therefore will differ, and we would expect their responses to differ as well.

A final question is whether Asian firms will *ever* be able to compete in the global marketplace. Peter Nolan and his colleagues, in their encyclopedic study of large-scale enterprise in China, adopt an approach similar to that of Alfred Chandler. They argue that all industries tend towards oligopoly. Large firms force intense competition and price cutting, driving out weaker competitors. They then reinforce their position through their ability to invest in research and development. These advantages, which Chandler identified as those of 'scale and scope', lead to overall technical improvements in the quality of their products and even lower costs of production.

The resulting international oligopolies consist of only the few huge firms with sufficient economies of scale and scope to complete.[21]

We may also add that the world's leading corporations have normally enjoyed strong support from their governments, both direct and indirect. Britain maintained high tariffs and prohibited the export of machinery until the mid-nineteenth century, while refusing to allow its imperial possessions to protect their own industries. The United States subsidized strategic industries such as the railways, for over two centuries has imposed tariffs averaging 30 per cent or more, and in the current round of bilateral trade agreements has consistently refused to open its own markets to foreign competition. 'There has never been a "level playing field" in international competition, and it is doubtful whether there ever will be one.'[22]

According to Nolan the point, for China and for Asia, is the inevitable preponderance of large firms, and the overwhelming advantage of the 'first movers', the large firms of the United States and Europe. In many sectors the advantages of the major 'first mover' corporations headquartered in the United States and Europe may be insurmountable. Access to global supply chains and the massive resources they can devote to investment in research and development protect them from less well-endowed competitors. Coca-Cola may, as Nolan says, 'become more and more Asian, as East Asia's share of the global market . . . steadily rises', but the firm itself will remain American, and its Asian branches will remain dependent on decisions taken by its American headquarters.[23] Studies of the international supply chains of the 'big buyers' such as the Gap, Reebok, Price Club, and Walmart, have also suggested that Asian firms may be confined to niche roles in the global sourcing strategies of huge Western firms.[24]

These issues have not escaped the notice of Asian managers or of Asian governments. China has designated certain favored firms as 'famous Chinese brands' and in 1997 identified six that it would support in their efforts to join the group of the world's 500 largest corporations. One of them, the Haier home appliance group, fourth largest in the world, aims to produce one-third of its output in China for domestic sales, one-third in China for export, and one-third overseas for foreign sales. In 2004, a senior official at Japan's Ministry of Economy, Trade and Industry said that for Japanese firms to survive they would need an annual investment of 200 billion yen (around US$2 billion) in 'carefully chosen businesses', that 70 per cent of their sales should be overseas, and that they should command a share of at least 10 per cent of the global market in their chosen businesses. Toshiba, Sharp, Matsushita, and Canon in electronics, Daihatsu and Mazda in automobiles, and Sumitomo Metal Industries, all plan new production facilities to be located in Japan, a 'vertical integration' strategy they hope will protect their cutting-edge technologies.[25]

In addressing these challenges, Asian managers will draw on their countries' experience. History does matter, and so do inherited patterns of thought. To understand these influences in Asian business, we need to begin in the nineteenth and early twentieth centuries, with indigenous market systems, Western imperialism, and responses to the opportunities of the world economy. In the inter-war period Japanese imperialism and the depression of the 1930s had important but varying effects. The Second World War, the defeat of Japan, the Chinese Revolution and decolonization altered the environment once again. Japan, 'Asia's New Giant',[26] shared in the world upswing of the 1950s and 1960s and the following era of slow growth of the 1970s and 1980s. Much of the rest of Asia was out of phase, with very difficult conditions through the 1960s, but then followed by the beginnings of the Asian boom, and particularly the emergence of South Korea, Taiwan, Hong Kong, and Singapore, the original 'four tigers'. The 1990s saw continued difficulties in Japan, but also the spreading boom in Southeast Asia and China, the rise of new tigers and new giants.[27] The boom was followed of course by the Asian crisis, the financial collapse of 1997, and a short, sharp recession, and then by an uneven recovery.[28]

The historical grid's influence can be seen in the self-image, preconceptions, and habitual responses of individuals raised in a distinct national environment. We need to extend our imaginations a little, to get inside the skin, for instance, of someone who is born, goes to school, lives, and works in a society traumatized by European imperialism, Japanese invasion, civil war, repeated state mobilizations leading to mass famine, and ruled by a single Communist political party, but where the economy has grown by a spectacular 8 to 10 per cent on average every year since 1978. After such a history, we can well imagine that Chinese managers might be different. Just how different is difficult to say, and indeed today in China a new generation of management theorists is debating the question of whether there is a new 'Chinese' style of management.

The Institutional Grid: Strong States and Privatization

The institutional grid is the distinctive outcome of history in each country. Governments in general, and possibly Asian governments in particular, have always intervened to influence the direction of economic development. The results are disputed. International agencies tend to view development from a market-oriented neoclassical perspective. The Organization for Economic Co-operation and Development argues that the origins of Asia's rapid growth lie in 'trade liberalization' and 'an open trade regime'.[29] The World Bank argues that, when the governments of Asia's 'high performance' economies do intervene, they do so in ways that in fact cause

their economies to behave *as if* they were freely operating market economies.[30] In contrast, many see Asian development from a government-
centered or 'statist' perspective, and argue that successful export promotion
resulted from continuous and active state intervention and guidance. Asian
governments have targeted particular industries and particular firms they
believe to have special strategic significance. Japan is the archetypal 'developmental state'.[31] In addition, Taiwan and South Korea have probably been
cited most often as the Asian states in which the government agencies
responsible for economic development have possessed the characteristics
necessary to foster rapid growth.[32]

We need to understand this institutional context. It is especially important to examine the relations between government and business. Although
experts continue to debate the impact of government policy, it remains true
that the state, and the relationship between the state and the private sector,
always establish the framework for business decision making, a point
emphasized for instance in the work of Richard Whitley.[33] Many Asian
states are 'strong' states that attempt to control the direction of economic
development.[34] The Japanese 'system' has been influential as a model in a
number of other Asian countries. The essence of the Japanese system is
often taken to be the 'iron triangle' of bureaucrats, business executives, and
politicians.[35] As in the case of Asian values and cultures, the claims made
for the Japanese or other institutional systems such as 'the Korean way'
need to be subjected to a critical examination. Asian governments do not
always succeed, but their desires are a fact of business life that both local
and foreign managers must recognize. Another generalization that holds
generally across Asia is the relatively high degree of respect and prestige
enjoyed by government officials. They may not in fact be as competent or
as effective as they believe themselves to be, but these status relationships
are another aspect of the institutional environment that affect the conduct
of business.

Governments in general, and again possibly Asian governments in particular, have exercised especially strict controls over the banking sector.
Asian governments frequently direct their banks to lend to preferred
sectors, industries, or firms. The directions are often confidential, and the
relations among government officials, bankers, and borrowers are often not
transparent. Banking analysts universally disapprove of non-transparent
directed lending.[36] In contrast, numbers of economists argue that government directed lending can contribute to accelerated economic development.[37] Again, the point is to understand these crucial relationships
because they set the terms on which business can obtain working capital.
Therefore we will consider the development and structure of the banking
system in each of our studies.

Firms differ in size, but not the same way in every country. It is important to identify the role of large firms, the position of small firms, and the relations between them in each country. Japan's giant firms, for instance, sit atop dense pyramids of hundreds or even thousands of medium and small firms linked vertically and horizontally by longstanding relationships as allies, suppliers, and subcontractors. Korea's *chaebol* groups in contrast typically have attempted to provide their needs in-house or through specialized subsidiaries. The strengths and weaknesses of both systems may provide insights that can be applied more generally.

Government policy always sets the terms on which firms can operate, how large they can become, and how they interact. Asian governments in the 1950s and 1960s frequently pursued policies of 'import substitution' that favored domestic manufacturers. Foreigners were often excluded from broad sectors of the economy, and governments established large state enterprise sectors. Over the next two decades many of these same governments embraced policies of 'export orientation' that encouraged foreign manufacturing firms to settle, sometimes in special economic zones, but many restrictions on foreign investment remained. From the 1990s onward, Asian governments have pursued programs of deregulation and privatization of state enterprises. New areas have been opened to foreign investment, and domestic firms have been encouraged to 'modernize' their structures through enforced compliance with new standards of corporate governance. However, areas that governments perceive as of strategic importance may be reserved for locals, the incidence of taxation may favor them, or the legal system may support them in disputes. Alternatively, governments may encourage foreign firms to settle with special deals that in fact discriminate against local firms.

Government policy reaches over into social relations as well. In Southeast Asia we need to look at ethnic divisions among firms, especially the position of firms owned by the minority of ethnic Chinese. 'Chinese' firms dominate across broad areas of Southeast Asian economies, but their structures, and their relations with their suppliers and customers, have been conditioned by the hostility of the surrounding majority populations. Prejudice has periodically erupted in tragic violence, and has frequently been institutionalized through the legal system. Their need to adapt and protect themselves has had an ongoing influence on the conduct and structures of ethnic Chinese firms. For example, in Malaysia, ethnic Chinese believe that they will lose any court case they enter against a *bumiputra* or Malay firm, and they knew until changes announced in 2003 that 55 per cent of university places were officially reserved for *bumiputra* students. They may therefore hesitate to deal with a Malay firm, and many families send their children overseas for their education. A working knowledge of these sorts of relationships, the 'system' or 'the way things work here', is essential to success, for locals and foreigners alike.

The Management Grid: Planning and Decision Making, Organizing, Leading and Controlling

The management grid suggested here is an amalgam of approaches to firm governance. If we ask how firms are supposed to operate, it is generally accepted that the standard neoclassical model suffers from severe weaknesses. Firms do not always exist in competitive markets, and they do not always produce the economically optimum output with the economically optimum mix of inputs. Theorists have taken new approaches to address these problems, including transactions costs analysis (how much does it cost to acquire information?), agency models (how can an employer extract maximum effort from an employee?), property rights approaches (how much does it cost to enforce a contract?), and studies of firm competencies (how does the firm identify and manage its own resources?).

Management texts ask how successful firms operate. They concentrate on the four overlapping functions of management identified above, planning and decision making, organizing, leading, and controlling, and attempt to define the best or most effective approach to each.[38] However, the firms they describe are Western firms, European or, more likely, American. They do not look much like Asian firms at all.[39] Further, Asian firms differ from each other in significant ways. This is sometimes taken to mean that they should 'modernize' their structures, that is, that they should become more like Western firms. However, Asian firms have often been extremely successful. Of course it may be that these successes are merely exceptions to the general rules. But it also might be that when successful Asian firms deviate from the theoretical norms, this could mean we have to change our theory.

Most Western management texts, for instance, do not take into account the very different treatment of men and women across industries and within firms. Much of what women do does not appear in conventional economic accounts at all. Professions dominated by women are relatively poorly paid, and the 'feminization' of a profession means it will slip downward in the relative rankings. Consistently women are paid less than male colleagues in the same or similar jobs. Most women in most firms are confined to the lower levels, and women in management bump against the 'glass ceiling' when they aim for senior positions. But these factors drop from view when 'management' in general is the theme.[40] In a number of Asian countries gender differences are not only more obvious, but also explicitly defined by custom and sometimes enforced by law. Appreciation of these differences not only allows us to understand better how Asian firms operate, but also leads us to reflect on the unstated assumptions that guide much of Western management behavior.

The following chapters assume, not that there is a single 'best' way of managing, but that managers from different backgrounds will manage differently. Each of the chapters therefore asks how the functions of planning and decision making, organizing, leading, and controlling are fulfilled in each country, how this differs from the prescriptions of Western management theory, how well it works, and why. There are general principles of planning and decision making. Decision makers need to identify the problem, they need to generate alternative solutions, they need to evaluate and choose an alternative, and of course they must implement and monitor the chosen solution. However, although Sun Tzu has much to say about appropriate decisions, he is silent on the way in which a commander finally reaches a decision. Tao Zhu-gong recommends leading by example while enforcing discipline and high standards (the Eleventh Business Principle), but he too is silent on the way this goal might be achieved.

In fact there is considerable dispute over the way in which decisions are actually made in Western businesses. Decision makers may be rational, or not. Prejudice may influence decisions. Entrepreneurial 'founders' may make decisions by insight, and their successors may inherit their ability, but most likely they will not. The successful founder may leave behind a large firm. Large firms are by definition bureaucratized, but the forms vary. All suffer from problems of balance between hierarchy (top-down control) and coordination (cooperation of parallel elements). Within such firms, even if they are rational, decision makers may have their ability to be rational constrained or 'bounded' by inadequate information, search costs, time limits, or inaccurate perceptions. They may 'satisfice' rather than optimizing, making decisions that seem to be satisfactory but not searching for the best solution. They may be 'incremental' and make the smallest or least disturbing response to problems. Or indeed they may be essentially random in their response to new situations.[41]

Each of the following chapters focuses on the ways in which firms' responses may be conditioned by historical factors and by contemporary institutions, and each focuses on those aspects of firm governance that appear to be distinctive, that is, those that differ from the forms suggested by Western management theory. The structures of Asian firms have themselves sometimes generated myths, of 'systems', 'values' and 'models'. But there are differences in management, in recruitment of senior executives, and in their modes of operation, particularly the role of family and personal connections. Labor relations also differ. Although many Asian firms appear paternalistic, the forms of paternalism vary dramatically. As noted

above, within firms the gap between men and women appears especially
wide in Asia, but again the impact of gendered perceptions varies. As also
noted above, relations between large and small firms, and relations between
domestic and foreign firms, differ as well. Patterns of technology transfer
can vary, for example, depending on whether the foreign partner is from the
United States or Europe, from Japan, or from one of the newly industrializing countries within Asia itself.

We would like to know the prospects for Asian firms in an era of globalization. To judge this we need to take the broad approach to corporate governance, and not only examine owners, managers, and workers, but also
suppliers, customers, and markets, community structures, and government
involvement in the economy. Firms differ, and national traditions differ, but
times change. Tao Zhu-gong's Third Business Principle is 'Ability to focus
on the business: forgoing the old for the new is the curse of many businesses', but his Eleventh Business Pitfall is 'Do not ignore changing business conditions', and the Twelfth Business Pitfall is 'Do not over-rely on
current products.' A distinctive approach may succeed in one decade and
fail in the next. The perspectives of domestic and foreign observers also
differ. Views of Asian firms have changed over time. In addition to telling
the historical, institutional, and management stories, therefore, each of the
following chapters also considers the variety of experience in case studies
arranged as 'point and counterpoint' to highlight these changes. We need
to see both the point and the counterpoint. Only then can we begin to
appreciate how it might feel to be embedded in a different framework, and
how that framework might shape action.

FURTHER READING

Translations vary widely, and everyone has their own favorite. The quotations I include from Sun Tzu's *The Art of War* are from the translation by
Thomas Cleary (Boston and London: Shambhala, 1988), which I believe
combines clarity with literary sensitivity. Cleary emphasizes the difficulties
arising from the ambiguities of all classical Chinese texts, and *The Art of War*
is no exception. There are many points that are allusive or simply obscure.
Cleary emphasizes Sun Tzu's connection to the Taoist tradition in Chinese
philosophy, especially the idea that the highest achievement of a general is to
gain victory without fighting. Cleary also includes remarks drawn from a
standard collection of 11 commentators usually associated with the text.
There is a pocket edition (Boston and London: Shambhala, 1991).

There are a number of other translations. An older version by Samuel B.
Griffith (Oxford: Oxford University Press, 1971), with a foreword by military

specialist B.H. Liddell Hart, takes the straightforward approach that Sun Tzu's essays 'might well be termed the concentrated essence of wisdom on the conduct of war'. Griffith includes a somewhat different selection from the commentators. More recently The Denma Translation Group has produced a polished literary version (Boston and London: Shambhala, 2002). They indicate which portions of the Chinese text are rhymed couplets, for instance. Their translation embodies an explicit philosophical approach. The Sun Tzu, they say, 'invites us to enter its teachings fully. When we do so, we find we come naturally to the same insights that are contained within its text.' For them the text 'shows how we can work with conflict both within and outside ourselves'. They omit the standard commentators, including instead their own interpretive essays and directing the reader to their website, www.victoryoverwar.com, for ongoing discussion.

In addition, numerous authors have used Sun Tzu as a framework for books on business management. Donald G. Krause, *Sun Tzu: The Art of War for Executives* (London: Nicholas Brealey Publishing, 1996), for example, is not a translation, but rather a work 'designed to help the modern business reader use the material in everyday business situations'. Krause divides his text into quasi-Biblical numbered verses. There are scattered quotations, or 'insets', intended 'to give the reader a flavor for the original text', but the 'major interpretation' rests on 'the ideas of modern business thinkers'. Krause mentions Tom Peters, Peter Drucker, and Warren Bennis explicitly, and it is clearly the ideas of Western management theorists that are being presented. Other popularizations include Khoo Khen-tor, *Sun Tzu & Management* (Malaysia: Pelanduk Publications, 1997), Mark McNeilly, *Sun Tzu and the Art of Business: Six Strategic Principles for Managers* (new edition, Oxford, 2000), Gary Gagliardi, *The Art of War – Plus – The Art of Management* (Seattle: Clearbridge Publishing, 2000), and Gerald A. Michaelson, *Sun Tzu: The Art of War for Managers; 50 Strategic Rules* (Avon: Adams Media Corporation, 2001).

Tao Zhu-gong's original *12 Business Principles*, and the later additions, the *12 Business Pitfalls* and *16 Business Lessons*, are listed in full in the Appendix. Tao Zhu-gong's thought is analyzed in detail by Chow Hou Wee, *The Inspirations of Tao Zhu-gong: Modern Business Lessons from an Ancient Past* (Singapore: Prentice-Hall, 2001), and I have used Wee's translations. Wee believes that the Chinese philosophical approach is indirect and 'artistic' in contrast to the 'how to' approach of the West, but he also believes that Tao Zhu-gong's original principles are universally valid. 'It is amazing to note,' he says, 'that their applicability transcends both time, space and even the type of business or industry.'

The following chapters each have suggestions for further reading in their specialized areas. For general background on the Asian context there is my

18 *Asian firms*

own book, Frank B. Tipton, *The Rise of Asia: Economics, Society and Politics in Contemporary Asia* (Basingstoke: Macmillan, 1998). For the impact of the 1997 Asian financial crisis, see Ross H. McLeod and Ross Garnaut (eds), *East Asia in Crisis: From Being a Miracle to Needing One?* (London and New York: Routledge, 1998); Stephan Haggard, *The Political Economy of the Asian Financial Crisis* (Washington, D.C.: Institute for International Economics, 2000); Philippe F. Delhaise, *Asia in Crisis: The Implosion of the Banking and Finance Systems* (Singapore: John Wiley and Sons [Asia], 1998); Tan Kong Yam (ed.), *Asian Economic Recovery: Policy Options for Growth and Stability* (Singapore: Singapore University Press, 2002).

On the important role of Asian states in economic development, the classic statement is Chalmers Johnson, *MITI and the Japanese Miracle: The Growth of Industrial Policy, 1925-1975* (Stanford: Stanford University Press, 1982), and his more general comparative article, Chalmers Johnson, 'Political institutions and economic performance: the government–business relation in Japan, South Korea, and Taiwan', in Frederic Deyo (ed.), *The Political Economy of the New Asian Industrialism* (Ithaca and London: Cornell University Press, 1987), pp. 136–64. The most recent extended statement of the developmental state perspective is Alice H. Amsden, *The Rise of 'The Rest': Challenges to the West from Late-Industrializing Economies* (New York: Oxford University Press, 2001).

Australia, Department of Foreign Affairs and Trade, Economic Analytical Unit, *Changing Corporate Asia: What Business Needs to Know* (2 vols, Canberra: EAU, 2002) surveys the structures of Asian corporate governance from a Western perspective. Richard D. Whitley, *Business Systems in East Asia: Firms, Markets, and Societies* (London: Sage, 1992) and *Changing Capitalisms? Internationalization, Institutional Change, and Systems of Economic Organization* (Oxford: Oxford University Press, 2005) emphasizes what I have called the institutional grid. Malcolm Warner (ed.), *Culture and Management in Asia* (London: RoutledgeCurzon, 2003) contains short chapters on individual countries, tightly focused on the identification of national variations in culture, their impact on corporate cultures, and the question of convergence towards global norms. Min Chen, *Asian Management Systems* (1st edn 1995; London: International Thomson Business Press, 1997), takes a more 'Asian' perspective and is particularly good on the overseas Chinese. Henry Wai-Chung Yeung (ed.), *The Globalization of Business Firms from Emerging Economies* (Cheltenham and Northampton: Edward Elgar, 1999a) looks at the same range of issues from a different angle, the cross-border activities of non-Western firms.

On the role of women generally, see Louise Edwards and Mina Roces (eds), *Women in Asia* (St Leonards: Allen & Unwin, 2000) which contains very good survey chapters for each country. Amarjit Kaur (ed.), *Women Workers in Industrialising Asia: Costed, Not Valued* (Houndmills: Palgrave Macmillan, 2004) focuses on the gender gap that marks the institutional grids of Asian economies and the management grids of Asian firms.

There are many texts on management. The framework for the management grid as I describe it generally follows the outline presented by Kathryn Bartol, Margaret Tein, Graham Matthews and David Martin, *Management: a Pacific Rim Focus* (enhanced edn; Boston: McGraw-Hill, 2003). Charles W.L. Hill and Gareth R. Jones, *Strategic Management Theory: An Integrated Approach* (4th edn, Boston and New York: Houghton Mifflin Company, 1998) considers the problems of management at the most general level. Charles W.L. Hill, *International Business: Competing in the Global Marketplace* (5th edn, Boston: McGraw-Hill Irwin, 2005) and Arvind V. Phatak, Rabi S. Bhagat and Roger I. Kashlak, *International Management: Managing in a Diverse and Dynamic Global Environment* (Boston: McGraw-Hill Irwin, 2005) look at management in international business specifically. Philippe Lasserre and Hellmut Schuette, *Strategies for Asia Pacific: Beyond the Crisis* (South Yarra: Macmillan Education Australia, 1999), focus on the specific question of management in the Asia Pacific region. Two collections of cases that include a number of Asian firms are Paul W. Beamish, Allen J. Morrison, Andrew C. Inkpen and Philip M. Rosenzweig, *International Management: Text and Cases* (5th edn, Boston: McGraw-Hill, 2003), and Christopher A. Bartlett, Sumantra Ghoshal and Julian Birkinshaw, *Transnational Management: Texts, Cases and Readings in Cross-Border Management* (4th edn, Boston: McGraw-Hill Irwin, 2004).

The work of Geert Hofstede has been one of the important foundations for the study of the cultural origins of national variations in management practice, and remains influential despite ongoing criticism of his underlying essentialist view of culture. Two of his major works are Geert H. Hofstede, *Culture's Consequences: Comparing Values, Behaviors, Institutions and Organizations across Nations* (1st edn 1980; 2nd edn Thousand Oaks: Sage Publications, 2001) and Geert H. Hofstede and Gert Jan Hofstede, *Cultures and Organizations: Software of the Mind* (revised and expanded 2nd edn, New York: McGraw-Hill, 2005). Hofstede considered the relationship between specific Asian values and economic growth in Geert H. Hofstede and Michael H. Bond, 'The Confucius connection: from cultural roots to economic growth', *Organizational Dynamics*, **16**(4) (1988), 5–21.

There is an extensive literature on the variations among advanced capitalist economies that is relevant to the comparative study of Asian management systems as well. See Michael E. Porter, *The Competitive Advantage of Nations* (updated edn, Houndmills: Macmillan, 1998); Richard D. Whitley, *Divergent Capitalisms: The Social Structuring and Change of Business Systems* (Oxford: Oxford University Press, 1999); Richard D. Whitley (ed.), *European Business Systems: Firms and Markets in their National Contexts* (London: Sage, 1992b); Peter Hall and David Soskice (eds), *Varieties of Capitalism: The Institutional Foundations of Comparative Advantage* (New York: Oxford University Press, 2001).

NOTES

1. Chu (1995).
2. Backman and Butler (2003).
3. Krause (1996).
4. Australia, Department of Foreign Affairs and Trade, Economic Analytical Unit (2002).
5. See Bartol, Tein, Matthews and Martin (2003).
6. Bartlett, Ghoshal and Birkinshaw (2004).
7. Parsons (1954).
8. Parsons and Smelser (1956).
9. Weber (1958); Weber (1951). McClelland (1961) was an influential example of the application of Weber's ideas. See Green (1973).
10. Shane (1992), Thomas and Mueller (2000).
11. Hofstede and Bond (1988).
12. Hall and Soskice (2001).
13. Warner (2003).
14. Tipton (1998).
15. Specifically, of a total of some 600 Master of Commerce students at the University of Sydney who identified themselves as 'Chinese', approximately half from the People's Republic and the rest from Taiwan and Southeast Asia, surveyed over the three years from 1999 to 2004, only 20 could immediately name all five relationships. Of these, at least three had learned them in other university courses, and another four (all from Singapore) said they had learned them at school, not at home.
16. Porter (1998).
17. Chandler (1990).
18. Of the same 600 Chinese students noted above, four-fifths said they would not hire solely on the basis of *guanxi*, and the rest were on average 'unlikely' to do so, but over two-thirds agreed that 'Chinese' firms relied on *guanxi*.
19. Tylecote (1993); Maddison (1982); Maddison (1995).
20. Leyden, Schartz and Hyatt (2000).
21. Nolan, Sutherland and Wu (2001), ch. 1.
22. Ruigrok and Van Tulder (1995), p. 221.
23. Nolan, Sutherland and Wu (2001).
24. Gareffi (1993).
25. 'Firms look to protect sensitive technology at home', *The Japan Times*, 14 October 2004, Kyodo report.
26. Patrick and Rosovsky (1976).
27. Perkins (1986); Amsden (1989); Kulick and Wilson (1992); Hill (1996).
28. McLeod and Garnaut (1998); Bridges (2001).
29. Richards (1993); Richards (1994).
30. World Bank (1993).
31. Johnson (1982).
32. Johnson (1987); Wade (1990); Weiss and Hobson (1995); Weiss (1998).

33. Whitley (1992a).
34. Migdal (1988).
35. Trevor (2001).
36. Delhaise (1998).
37. Amsden (2001).
38. As noted above I have generally followed the outline of Bartol, Tein, Matthews and Martin (2003).
39. Hofstede (1994).
40. As an example of this blind spot, in the generally excellent text by Bartol, Tein, Matthews and Martin (2003), there are no index entries for women, gender, sex, or glass ceiling, and there are no references to the problems of women in the chapter on human resource management. The passage on 'Workforce diversity, conflict and' (p. 589) says that diversity can generate conflict, and along with older workers resenting orders from younger workers or Asians feeling singled out among a group of white workers, notes without further discussion that 'a female top manager may feel her mostly-male top-management team are ganging together when one of them disagrees with a proposal of hers'. See Waring (1988).
41. Bartol, Tein, Matthews and Martin (2003); Bazerman (1986).

2. Managing horizontal information flows in Japan

Therefore measure in terms of five things . . . the Way, the weather, the terrain, the leadership, and discipline. . . . The Way means inducing the people to have the same aim as the leadership, so that they will share death and share life, without fear of danger. (Sun Tzu, *The Art of War*)

Ability to use and deploy people: choosing the right person for the right job will ensure that he can be trusted and depended upon. (Tao Zhu-gong, the Seventh Business Principle)

Japanese firms are perhaps most famous for lifetime employment and the lifetime loyalty they command from their workers. 'The Way means inducing the people to have the same aim as the leadership', and Japanese managers appear to do this as well or better than any others in the world. In doing so, Japanese managers use and deploy their people to great effect. To understand why this is so we begin with the historical grid. Most specialists agree that the origins of the Japanese 'system' lie in the Meiji era in the late nineteenth century. However, the impact of the Meiji state, the bureaucracy, and the new legal system on the economy and structures of firm governance are all disputed. We look at the creation of the large *zaibatsu* groups, Japan's imperial expansion and changes in the *zaibatsu*, their expansion through the depression, and the war and defeat. The American occupation and reform destroyed the old *zaibatsu*, but in their place emerged the *keiretsu* groups that dominated the economy through the 1980s. During Japan's version of the postwar golden age, the 'era of high speed growth' from the 1950s into the early 1970s, the Liberal Democratic Party ruled continuously. The subsequent era of slow growth brought political instability, the Japanese system did not appear to function as it had in the past, and again the reasons are disputed.

Japan's institutional grid has been intensively examined. The controversies over the so-called developmental state have led to debate over the Japanese system from another angle, as has the discussion of the reasons for the transition from high growth to low growth. Even lower growth, the 'Heisei recession' named after the new Emperor who ascended to the throne in 1989, the 'lost decade' of the 1990s, and attempts at deregulation and reform, have dominated more recent discussion. For those favoring reform, the process has appeared excruciatingly slow. For those likely to be affected, however, 'reform' means less power, reduced market share, lower profits, and lost jobs, and therefore they have campaigned for delay and for support to cushion the impact of change.

The management grid in turn has reflected the shifting environment. The internal structures of large firms have been seen by both Japanese and foreign observers as the 'unique' product of Japanese culture, but the distinctive interlocking attributes of Japanese firms also result from a very effective system that encourages the horizontal exchange of information within the firm. This allows firms to use and deploy people effectively, as Tao Zhu-gong would put it. It also contributes to the widely-discussed system of 'lean production', but also to the relations among members of *keiretsu* groups, the role of 'lead banks', firm competencies, and relations between large firms and their subcontractors. It played a role in the 'catch up economy' of the 1960s and 1970s, and may support Japanese firms in the twenty-first century.

Finally, for the following chapters we need to remember that Japan is a crucial element in the operating environment of all other sorts of Asian firms. The Japanese model, both the relationship of firms to government and the internal structures of firms, has influenced both government officials and corporate managers throughout Asia. However, their relations with Japan are ambivalent. Memories of war and invasion linger. For the future, the prospects of other Asian countries and of other Asian firms depend in part on their ability to compete with Japan and with Japanese firms, but their ongoing success also often depends on flows of Japanese aid, Japanese foreign investment, and the expansion of Japanese firms overseas.

BOX 2.1   POINT AND COUNTERPOINT: THE
JAPANESE SYSTEM AS A SUCCESS
STORY – MAZDA, 1975

People must be handled cordially; an irritable temper and bad attitude will diminish sales greatly. (Tao Zhu-gong, the Second Business Lesson)

Japanese firms have distinctive features, and debate has concentrated on their rationality, compared to Western firms. Is it a good idea to guarantee lifetime employment to your workers, for instance? In a classic article published in 1994, Masahiko Aoki argued that the distinctive features of Japanese firms that might appear to be inefficient when viewed or implemented in isolation,

in fact act synergistically together to achieve efficiency. In addition
many have emphasized the direct role of the state. Japanese firms
sometimes appear to be embedded in a web of government
support and direction. In a book also published in 1994, Thomas
Huber argued that Japanese government officials direct the
economy in a strategic manner, targeting and protecting certain
crucial sectors and certain lead firms in those sectors.

In 1975, Toyo Kogyo, the maker of Mazda automobiles, reported
a huge loss. In the aftermath of the 1973 oil crisis new car regis-
trations fell drastically, but Mazda suffered far worse declines than
any of its major rivals. The company was hurt by its relatively heavy
dependence on the United States market, and by a decision to
maintain production, which had led to excessive inventories. In
addition Mazda was by far the least efficient Japanese auto manufacturer, but had concealed the problem by offering relatively low
dealer margins, and this in turn further weakened its dealer
network as demand plummeted.

Toyo Kogyo in fact lacked many of the attributes of a 'Japanese'
firm. An entrepreneurial company headed by the grandson of the
founder, it did not belong to one of the major groups. The incumbent president's father had decided to move the firm from its existing position as Japan's leading truck maker into the passenger car
market. He planned to leapfrog the established competition by
building a car around a redesigned version of the German rotary
engine, powerful, quiet, but also unfortunately inefficient in fuel
consumption. In 1970, after nine years of development, Mazda
launched its new model car in the United States market. In 1973,
United States sales were 117 000 cars, and exports accounted for
70 per cent of total sales. Then came the 1973 oil crisis. In 1974,
the United States Environmental Protection Agency reported that
Mazdas consumed twice as much gasoline as Toyotas or Nissans,
and sales dropped by 60 per cent.

In 1970, as well, leadership of the firm had passed to the grandson, a man who lacked the charisma and interpersonal skills of his
father and grandfather, but who inherited the tradition of centralized
decision making. As is typical of most Japanese firms, Toyo
Kogyo had a single company union. It also possessed the typical
'Japanese' network of subcontractors, 91 firms in the Hiroshima
district known as the Toyokai or Friends of Toyo Kogyo, who sold
over 50 per cent of their output to Toyo Kogyo. However, in addition
to the unaddressed problems of low productivity, the company had
not alerted the union to the sales decline or the inventory overhang,

and had agreed to a 30 per cent wage increase for 1974. In its relations with its suppliers Toyo Kogyo set prices that guaranteed their profits, but refused to accept suggestions for technical improvements. As with the union, it did not inform its suppliers of the impending crisis, and they had continued to produce at high levels.

In early 1974, Sumitomo Bank, the firm's major creditor, established offices within Toyo Kogyo; in late 1974, the bank sent a team of executives to supervise the firm's affairs, and in December it announced that it would provide any new loans required. The senior Sumitomo Bank executive referred to Toyo Kogyo as 'a backwater company, a seat-of-the-pants operation' and said in particular 'there were no management systems'. However, he did not introduce management systems as such, but rather 'looked for opportunities to drink with younger people', joined union officials 'for a cup of coffee', 'accepted a lot of invitations to dinner' and over two years 'met every manager personally and with at least 2,000 of our hourly employees'. Instead of members of the executive committee simply reporting to the president, he encouraged the leaders of each division to discuss problems together, from the dual perspective of their division and of the company as a whole.

New models were given high priority. Data on costs and expenditures were placed under the direction of one of Toyo Kogyo's existing executives, and improvements in production line efficiency were assigned to another, a long-serving engineer. The union agreed to postponement of the semiannual bonus and to the changes in production line methods (greater use of the existing quality control circles, reduced inventory, improved machine maintenance, increased automation), in return for a guarantee that there would be no layoffs. Instead a voluntary program of 'dispatched workers' placed workers as salespersons with the dealer network. Suppliers accepted price cuts, but in return Toyo Kogyo engineers worked with them to achieve even greater cost savings. Costs dropped, and sales rose in 1975. The new models, developed in record time, were successful. The dispatched workers contributed over 400 000 additional sales, and other companies in the Sumitomo group agreed to purchase a further 40 000 Mazdas. By 1980, profits were twice their pre-oil shock levels.

Toyo Kogyo, it seems, was saved by becoming more Japanese, coming to look more like Aoki's picture of interlocking attributes, becoming more integrated into a group under the guidance of a lead bank, with increased horizontal information flows, more group decision making, reaffirmed guaranteed employment, and closer relations with suppliers. In the background government played a strategic role. There were no public guarantees, as for instance the United States government made to Chrysler. However, it was strongly suggested that the Ministry of Finance had ordered Sumitomo Bank to rescue Toyo Kogyo, the major employer in the Hiroshima area. Even if not strictly true, it was certain that Sumitomo Bank and the other banks that funded Toyo Kogyo's suppliers could rely on an implicit guarantee from the MOF, insuring them against loss regardless of the outcome.

Sources: Masahiko Aoki, 'The Japanese firm as a system of attributes: a survey and research agenda', in Masahiko Aoki and Ronald Dore (eds), *The Japanese Firm: The Sources of Competitive Strength* (Oxford: Oxford University Press, 1994), pp. 11–40; Thomas M. Huber, *Strategic Economy in Japan* (Boulder: Westview Press, 1994); Richard Pascale and Thomas P. Rohlen, 'The Mazda turnaround', *Journal of Japanese Studies*, 9(2) (1983), 219–64.

BOX 2.2   POINT AND COUNTERPOINT: THE JAPANESE SYSTEM AS A FAILURE – NISSAN, 1999

Do not ignore changing business conditions. (Tao Zhu-gong, the Eleventh Business Pitfall)

Not everyone sees the Japanese system as either efficient or effective, and these critical voices have multiplied as the period of very slow growth has lengthened. Three years after the works by Aoki and Huber cited in Box 2.1, but before the Asian financial crisis, two Japanese management experts harshly criticized the existing system. Moriaki Tsuchiya and Yoshinobu Konomi insisted that 'the time for change has arrived . . . Education, politics, and government – each must now cultivate a new vision and strategies'. They noted the negative impact of the rising value of the yen, and the aftermath of the collapse of the 'bubble' economy of the late 1980s, but they focused on 'the emergence of problems inside Japanese companies – that worked to diminish firms' competitive power'. Whereas foreign firms had learned to emulate the strong points of Japanese management, 'self-centered' Japanese managers 'never seem to have pondered the risks inherent in excessive investment'.

Nissan Motor, the second largest automobile company in Japan after Toyota, has traditionally been the most prestigious company in the automotive industry in Japan. In contrast to Toyota, which had a reputation for independence, Nissan was more attentive to the desires of the Ministry of International Trade and Industry. In return, MITI regarded Nissan as one of the centerpieces of its strategic post-war industrial policy. Nissan has been known for the high level of its technology. It participated in the Japanese space development program, developing the engine to power a rocket booster. The Nissan workforce was reputed to be particularly industrious, disciplined, and motivated.

Nevertheless, Nissan suffered during the 1990s. Sales stagnated and its market share declined. Critics accused it of lacking strategic focus, with resources scattered across too many product lines and too many overseas markets. The attempt to compete with market leader Toyota in all product lines and all markets was widely seen as an error. In particular, Nissan suffered heavy losses in the United States at a time when Toyota and Honda were recording record profits. Its share price declined, and its credit rating had dropped. It was known to be seeking a partner to strengthen its weak financial position. In March 1999, it was announced that the French automobile firm Renault would acquire 36 per cent of the shares in Nissan. Renault also decided to send Carlos Ghosn to serve as Chief Operating Officer, with the intent to 'replace the bureaucratic and slow-moving management in Nissan'.

Ghosn earned his reputation as a cost-cutter from tenure as president of Michelin North America and then as executive vice-president of Renault, where in 1998 he saved FF9 billion (US$1.5 billion) by closing plants, including a politically controversial shutdown of the factory at Vilfoord in Belgium. His approach at Nissan was similar. Under the 'Nissan Revival Plan', Nissan's own plants were to be cut from seven to four, production capacity from 2.4 to 1.65 million vehicles, and employees from 148 000 to 127 000. Many of Nissan's 1394 related companies were headed by former Nissan executives. Nissan typically owned a substantial fraction of their shares, and they in turn owned shares in Nissan. Ghosn announced that Nissan would sell its shares in all but four of these firms to raise cash. Most of the firms are suppliers that provide Nissan with components, but Ghosn also announced his intention to cut the number of suppliers from 1145 to 600, and to give all of Nissan's business to the single firms that offered the best terms.

If Nissan was to succeed, it now seemed that the path was to become *less* 'Japanese'. Remarkably, the drastic proposals caused no public outcry in Japan. Ghosn became one of the most

interviewed business executives in Japan, but there was no hostility to the loss of a 'champion firm'. MITI in fact announced publicly
that it welcomed the move. Rather, Ghosn's appointment and other
mergers and alliances formed by Japanese firms have been
regarded as a sign of a shift in attitude, and as evidence of the
recognition that Japanese management practices will have to
change.

Sources: Moriaki Tsuchiya and Yoshinobu Konomi, *Shaping the Future of
Japanese Management: New Leadership to Overcome the Impending Crisis*
(Tokyo: LTCB International Library Foundation, 1997), pp. xii, 2, 12; 'Nissan revival
plan', 18 October 1999 (http://www.nissan.co.jp); N. Shirozu, 'Nissan shakes
Japan's economic structure', *The Wall Street Journal*, Interactive Edition, 19
October 1999; Risaburo Nezu, 'Carlos Ghosn: cost controller or *keiretsu* killer?',
OECD Observer, No. 220 (April 2000), pp. 17–19.

THE HISTORICAL GRID

The Meiji Origins of the Japanese 'System'

In the background of discussion of Japanese management is a larger debate
over Japanese culture. Business executives in Japan are especially avid consumers of popular books that purport to identify the traits that make
Japanese different from other peoples. The 'debate over the Japanese'
(*nihonjinron*) literature ranges from potentially plausible references to the
imprecision of the Japanese language, to claims that the Japanese are
uniquely homogeneous, to assertions that Japanese brains are physically
different.[1] Some anthropologists have argued that there is an essential core
to Japanese civilization, possibly dating from the seventh century, which
has allowed Japan to assimilate changes from outside and yet remain
the same in fundamental respects.[2] In contrast, historians have come to
emphasize the diversity of the Japanese, and tend to see Japanese identity and Japanese culture as changing in response to economic and social
development.[3]

Japan often seems a disorienting combination of traditional, modern,
and postmodern. Japanese tradition, however, is in many respects a recent
invention, and Japanese modernity is in many respects a deliberate import.
Many of the distinctive features of Japanese society date from the Meiji era,
which takes its name from the Emperor who reigned from 1868 to 1912. His
reign began with a short civil war. The victorious leaders claimed to be
restoring the direct rule of the Emperor, but in fact power lay in the hands
of a small group of men from the old *samurai* warrior class. They aimed
to defend Japan against the Western nations expanding into Asia. The

example of China's defeat in the Opium War and the Arrow War and the forced 'opening' of China, Thailand, and Japan itself to foreigners showed what would happen to countries that could not defend themselves.

The Meiji leaders adopted the slogan 'rich country, strong army'. They pushed through a broad range of reforms intended to make it easier to introduce modern Western technology. They also introduced a range of administrative and social measures intended to centralize and reinforce their power. A new army rested on conscription, and railways made it possible to move the troops around the country to suppress dissent. The legal rights of the *samurai* and the aristocratic *daimyo* were eliminated, but they were compensated with large issues of government bonds and many found employment with the new government, especially in the army and the new national police. A new law restricted the imperial succession to the male line, and new festivals celebrated the Emperor as the symbolic father of the nation.

A new centralized system of primary schools spread the new national myths. Children across the country recited the Imperial Rescript on Education daily, from its introduction in 1890 until 1945. Its opening lines are, 'Our Imperial Ancestors have founded Our Empire on a basis broad and everlasting . . . Our subjects ever united in loyalty and filial piety have from generation to generation illustrated the beauty thereof.' As we will see, the deliberate inculcation of newly created myths has been typical of emerging national states, and so has the tendency for the myths to take on a life of their own and become accepted common memories, beliefs, or clichés. Sixty years after the end of the Second World War, for instance, many Japanese continue to believe that Japan was forced to take the lead to defend Asia as well as itself against Western aggression in the 1920s and 1930s. Some members of right-wing fringe groups still believe that the Emperor is divine. Most Japanese do not, but they do echo the old Rescript in their belief that Japan is a racially pure, fully homogeneous, and essentially harmonious society. Objectively untrue, these beliefs nonetheless condition responses and in part determine the behavior of workers and managers in Japanese firms discussed below.[4]

To implement their new system the Meiji leaders established a centralized bureaucracy. An examination system that favored graduates of the new University of Tokyo was set up in the 1890s, and continues today. The University of Tokyo is one of the most selective universities in the world, and its graduates predominate among the elite few who succeed in the annual entrance exams for positions in the top-ranking ministries, especially the Ministry of Finance and the Ministry of Foreign Affairs. The Meiji leaders also introduced a new legal system and new regulations of firm governance. Along with the new Western-style corporate law, however, there remained substantial provision for government intervention. In particular new banking institutions directed funds into areas designated by the government.

Although they did not acknowledge it, the Meiji leaders built on a sophisticated national market economy already in existence. For example, rice, the basic staple food crop, was grown in specialized regions, shipped to Osaka, and then distributed throughout the country. A market in contracts for future delivery of rice grew up in the 1730s, and developed into the first commodities futures market in the world. The Meiji period opened new possibilities. Although most firms were small, manufacturing expanded rapidly in Japan's towns and villages. These firms produced consumer goods, some traditional (such as *tatami* flooring mats for sale in the expanding urban centers), and some imitations of Western goods (notably umbrellas, where metal ribs and textile covers replaced bamboo and paper). Larger private firms led the expansion of the textile industry from the 1880s onward. They built on longstanding handicraft traditions and existing inter-firm networks, and they created national industry organizations to share information on new technologies and to control their labor force. They also enjoyed support from local governments. The Kyoto municipal government, for instance, ordered examples of Jacquard looms from Europe to help local silk weavers.[5]

The expansion of consumer goods and especially textiles repeated patterns already established in Europe and the United States. As in these early industrializers, so too in Japan the new textile factories employed a labor force of young women from rural areas who often lived in dormitories built by their employers. In addition there was a large subcontracting sector of older women, especially weavers.[6] A century later, in the 1980s, the export processing zones in Korea, Philippines, Malaysia, and Thailand would also employ young female workers, migrants from rural areas who often lived in company dormitories. Again in the 1990s, young women migrants provided much of the labor for the rural industrial sector in Indonesia and the expanding coastal industrial provinces in China.

The *Zaibatsu*

Although government leaders wanted a rich country, they believed consumer goods did not help create a strong army. They preferred heavy industry and mining. The Yawata Steel Works opened in 1901 was Japan's first integrated steel-making plant. A government enterprise, it was paid for with the indemnity Japan exacted from China after the Sino-Japanese War of 1894–5. In the 1930s, the government forced mergers between Yawata and other firms to form Japan Steel, a private firm but with the government as majority shareholder.[7] Japan's first automobile firms were subsidized with contracts for trucks for the military in 1918.[8]

The government's preference for heavy industry and strategically important sectors contributed to the rise of the *zaibatsu* (literally 'financial cliques') business groups. All grew because of insider deals done with government, in particular the cheap sales of government enterprises in the early 1880s, and subsidies, especially for shipping. The close links between government and large industrial enterprises have continued to mark development both in Japan and elsewhere in Asia, so it is worth noting that these kinds of support for strategic industry and transportation are not unique to Asia. Governments in all countries, including Great Britain, Continental Europe and the United States, have subsidized 'strategic' industries in the early stages of industrialization, and they have continued to intervene in the economy to protect the interests of large firms especially. In Japan, among the 'big four' *zaibatsu*, the Yasuda group concentrated on banking, based on profits realized by the founder's dealings in government bonds. Mitsubishi relied on subsidies granted to its shipping interests and on mining concessions. The Mitsui group was based on an old commercial house and was involved in banking and in textiles. Sumitomo centered on copper mining and refining and moved into other areas of heavy industry. As the Japanese empire expanded, the *zaibatsu* grew as well. They received preferential treatment from the new colonial governments in Taiwan (1895), Korea (1910) and Manchuria (1920s and 1930s), and they became the prime contractors for the exploitation of China and Southeast Asia during the war.

The *zaibatsu* diversified away from their original sectors, and as they did so, they adopted a characteristic pattern. At the top of each *zaibatsu* stood a family-controlled holding company (Figure 2.1), which in turn controlled a range of subsidiaries. The structure formed a pyramid, since the large subsidiary companies had subsidiaries as well. The subsidiaries of each *zaibatsu* included a bank that provided finance to member firms. Here was a point of leverage for the government, for all banks were chartered and controlled by the Ministry of Finance. The MOF rescued, merged, and reorganized many banks after the crisis that swept the financial sector in 1927 following the Tokyo earthquake. In the 1930s, the government directed banks to lend to armaments firms even when they were not part of the banks' own group. The new loans were long-term, in contrast to the banks' previous preference for short-term loans, and the banks were also obligated to buy substantial amounts of government bonds. In the case of the Mitsui Bank, the resulting change in the loan and investment portfolio led in 1943 to a merger with Dai-Ichi Bank, and the new Teikoku Bank became Japan's largest bank.[9]

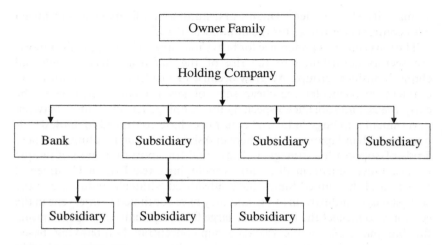

Figure 2.1 Zaibatsu *structure*

The pyramid structure did not necessarily imply direct family management of the subsidiary companies. Yasuda was the exception in that the group remained generally under the direct control of the founder and his family. The Iwasaki family owned 55.5 per cent of the Mitsubishi holding company, which in turn owned 52 per cent or more of each of the subsidiaries. One Iwasaki brother served as president and another as vice-president, but professional non-family members headed the Mitsubishi subsidiaries. The Sumitomo family had a lower share of ownership in the holding company, but owned a higher share of the subsidiary companies directly. Although the president of the group was a Sumitomo family member, this was a nominal position, and the family played no direct role in management. The Mitsui family owned 67 per cent of the Mitsui holding company, and the family also owned over 50 per cent of all of the subsidiaries. But the Mitsui family actually imposed a rule that family members were not to engage in direct management, and operational control lay in the hands of salaried executives. Some Mitsui Bank executives criticized the Mitsui family for 'damaging' the bank's interests by dictating lending policy and directing loans to specific customers.[10]

As the *zaibatsu* expanded through the 1930s, they employed increasing numbers of non-family members as managers. Is this an example of a general process of professionalization of management, and the resulting split between ownership and operational control, that characterizes many large Western corporations?[11] The answer depends in part on our definition of 'family' and what we mean by 'family' firm. In Japanese, 'family' can be either *kazoku* (those connected by blood relationship) or *ie* (the household, including those not related by blood). Historically, noble households could include retainers who were treated very much as family members. In addition it has continued to be quite common for wealthy Japanese families to adopt sons, or for a son-in-law to take his wife's family name, to preserve the *ie*. In the prewar *zaibatsu*, active managers were hired and promoted on the basis of their competence. In addition, however, as members of the company group, they were 'adopted' into the family, considered as members of the extended household. The entire group could be seen as an extended family, closed against outsiders, but willing to adopt new employees in this symbolic sense.

Labor relations in *zaibatsu* firms remained authoritarian (after all, in the view of the firms' owners and managers, the father of the family, or the senior male members of the extended family, know what is best). Confrontations with the labor movement were frequently violent. In particular, firms did not want to pay high wages or guarantee employment to their workers. The threat of instability, and the danger this might pose to strategic industries, prompted the government to intervene. On the one hand, the police repressed socialist and communist movements. However, on the other hand, the government also forced firms in strategic industries to offer improved working conditions, higher wages, and stability of employment.[12]

Government pressure therefore was one of the sources of the permanent employment system of the postwar period, and we can see this as an extension of the 'family' concept to include lower-level employees. Government officials however were only concerned with strategically important heavy industrial firms, and high wages and secure employment were granted only to 'skilled' male workers. The official ideology of the 'family state' with the Emperor as the father of the nation pictured women as wives and mothers of families in their homes, not as workers, and not as members of 'family' firms. This ignored the very large numbers of women in the labor force. Half of agricultural workers (and agriculture still employed well over half of all workers in the 1930s) were women, and over half of the workers in manufacturing industries were women as well. The labor force in the textile industry was overwhelmingly female, and the 800 000 textile workers in 1920 were twice the number of workers in the male-dominated heavy industries.[13]

THE INSTITUTIONAL GRID

The Era of High-speed Growth

After war and defeat came the occupation and reform. Politicians and industrial leaders associated with Japanese imperialism and war were forbidden to participate in public life or forced out of company leadership. The American authorities attempted to break up large firms, in order to increase competition. The *zaibatsu* were dissolved, their old names and symbols were prohibited, and members of *zaibatsu* families were forbidden to participate in management (this was irrelevant in most cases, but some wealthy family members lost their fortunes). An Antimonopoly Law based on United States antitrust legislation was also enacted.

Japanese leaders opposed these changes. Prime Minister Yoshida Shigeru said that the purge deprived Japan of its best men just when they were needed most for reconstruction. Japanese authorities allowed the reintroduction of the old *zaibatsu* names and symbols, and new groups emerged, the *keiretsu* described below. The government also rehabilitated many purged leaders in business, politics, and the bureaucracy, and began a purge of its own to eliminate leftwing elements in government. The connection between government and large firms continued to be close, and the Antimonopoly Law became a notorious 'toothless tiger'.

In the background were the Cold War between the United States and the Soviet Union, and the hot war on the Korean peninsula. The United States saw Japan as a crucial bulwark against Soviet influence in Asia. Protected by the United States' 'nuclear umbrella' and prohibited under its new constitution from possessing more than small defensive forces, Japan saved on military spending. United States spending in Japan during the Korean War benefited Japan. So too did a fixed exchange rate that generally undervalued the Japanese yen, which stimulated exports.

Japan grew at an average of 10 per cent per year from the early 1950s through the early 1970s, the longest such boom in history until the beginning of China's rapid growth in the late 1970s. Japanese economists speak of 'the era of high speed growth', but they also refer to the era of 'the catch up economy'. Japanese firms took advantage of a large backlog of American technology available at the end of the Second World War, notably in steel, nonferrous metals, the automobile, and consumer electronics. In one area after another, they improved on the originals. Japanese firm competencies concentrated on improving quality and reducing price, most spectacularly perhaps in the cases of automobiles and televisions. Japanese firms began by producing inexpensive black and white televisions for United States retailers such as Sears, and built on the skills they acquired to move to color televisions, where they eventually displaced United States producers. Some firms became genuine innovators, especially Sony and its application of transistors to consumer electronic goods.

Exports and domestic sales soared. The world economy enjoyed one of its long upswings. Within Japan a large population enjoyed rapidly rising incomes, a consumer durables revolution that saw millions of households acquiring goods for the first time – radios, refrigerators, electric rice cookers, electric fans, televisions, motorbikes, air conditioners, and auto-mobiles. In foreign markets Japanese firms priced their products aggres-sively to gain market share. In their huge and growing domestic market larger production volumes led to lower costs. Japanese firms benefited from the learning curve. As they produced more of a product, they could produce it at lower cost, even if there was no change in technology, personnel, or training.

Foreigners complained that Japanese firms dumped their goods in foreign markets, and then profited when they had driven their competitors out of business. Foreigners also complained that Japanese firms benefited from tariffs and non-tariff barriers that effectively closed the domestic market to outside competitors. Japanese automobile firms faced severe competition from imports in the 1950s, but a 'barrage of import barriers' virtually shut the Japanese market to outsiders. Imports fell from 45 per cent of the Japanese automobile market in 1950 to 1 per cent in 1960.[14] Japan turned a bland face to the external world. Southeast Asian farmers have been told that Japanese consumers prefer Japanese rice, French and American cosmetics firms that Japanese women must be protected from substandard products, and Korean steel makers that Japanese industry can only use the highest quality raw materials.

Chalmers Johnson attributed Japan's rapid growth to government policy, and extended his analysis of the structures of the 'developmental state' to other successful economies in Asia.[15] Johnson's work played an important role in the broader debates over the role of governments in economic devel-opment. In Japan, the Liberal Democratic Party controlled the Diet from 1948 to 1993. Political stability cemented ongoing relationships. Observers spoke of 'Japan, Inc.' and of the 'iron triangle' of business leaders, politi-cians, and bureaucrats. Which point of the triangle was at the top remained disputed, but many agreed with Johnson that on balance the bureaucrats and particularly the Ministry of Finance and the Ministry of International Trade and Industry played the key role in setting policy and guiding development.

There was a lot of capital available. The Japanese saved a very high per-centage of their incomes. Despite low wages and high prices compared to Western Europe or the United States, through the era of high speed growth incomes increased rapidly, and it is common to save a high fraction of incremental income. Semi-annual bonuses make up a large fraction of earnings in Japan, and again it is common to save a large fraction of irreg-ular income. Compared especially to the United States, Japan had virtually no system of consumer credit, and Japanese consumers therefore needed to save cash for large expenses. Japanese landlords require large deposits, another reason for savings. Until recently Japan's social welfare system has been poor. Relatively early retirement ages and inadequate pension plans meant that Japanese workers needed to save more to provide themselves with an income after retirement. Low levels of health insurance coverage meant that health expenses also had to be met from savings, and most Japanese doctors require payment in cash. Finally, for the middle class, there were heavy education expenses for private schools and the ubiquitous after-hours cram schools that trained students for university entrance examinations.

Until the 1970s, Japan's capital market was effectively isolated from international financial markets. The Japanese placed their money in the government postal savings system, the largest financial institution in the country, or in private banks. They were paid very low rates of interest, and the real return on savings has been negative for most of the period since the 1950s. The government segmented the capital market, controlled rates, rationed credit, and directed funds to its preferred sectors. Money for investment in housing was very limited compared for instance to West Germany, and the Japanese continue to suffer from the poor quality, small size, and very high prices of the housing stock.

The government channeled funds into industrial investment at low rates of interest. The government 'targeted' successive industries, those with high growth potential, especially for exports.[16] Certain firms were designated 'national champions' and received additional support, particularly in the acquisition of foreign technology. Foreign firms were encouraged to form joint ventures to enable their Japanese partners to acquire their technology, but foreigners were not permitted to establish subsidiaries to compete in Japan. Xerox, for instance, was allowed neither to distribute its patented copying machines nor to produce them through a subsidiary, but was instead forced to take a Japanese partner, resulting in the creation of Fuji-Xerox in 1962.[17] Foreign automobile firms were not allowed to produce in Japan and, as noted above, imports dwindled under the impact of selective prohibitions, high tariffs, and a labyrinthine system of licenses and approvals. By 1970, Toyota and Nissan, the favored national champions of the automobile industry, enjoyed a combined 65 per cent of the domestic market.[18]

The key 'pilot agency' of Japan's developmental state was the Ministry of International Trade and Industry. Following Johnson's lead, many scholars have emphasized the strategic role played by MITI in fostering and directing change, whether the introduction of new technologies or the upgrading of industries that had fallen behind in competitiveness.[19] The leaders of MITI and other agencies congratulated themselves. In 1970 Ojimi Yoshihasa, vice-minister of MITI, said,

The Ministry of International Trade and Industry decided to establish in Japan industries which require intensive employment of capital and technology . . . industries such as steel, oil refining, petro-chemicals, automobiles, aircraft, industrial machinery of all sorts, and electronics including electronic computers . . . According to Napoleon and Clausewitz, the secret of successful strategy is the concentration of fighting power on the main battle grounds; fortunately, owing to good luck and wisdom spawned by necessity, Japan has been able to concentrate its scant capital in strategic industries.

The claim that MITI had a master plan and the reference to 'scant' capital are both significant. Japanese officials preferred to emphasize how poor Japan was, because this meant that Japan could not 'afford' higher wages or better housing or more adequate health insurance. Critics also suggest that the domestic market, not exports, may have provided the crucial basis for growth. Historians have argued that Japan's officials did not in fact have a clear plan. Steel was 'targeted' early. Japan Steel, broken apart by the Allies, was re-formed into New Japan (Shin Nippon) Steel and produced 40 per cent of Japan's total steel output in the 1970s. However, MITI identified petrochemicals as a growth industry only much later.

The bureaucrats also did not agree on where the 'main battle ground' lay, and there were serious conflicts among ministries as they struggled to defend 'their' industries.[20] The bureaucrats did not always pick the winners, and there were some embarrassing lapses. Amongst several 'twilight' industries favored by the government, the attempt to prop up the coal industry failed. In the areas of emerging technologies, MITI officials also failed to recognize the importance of the transistor in electronics. Sony was a new firm, and was not the one preferred by MITI. Akio Morita overcame substantial obstacles placed in his way by the government in leading Sony to its position of leadership in consumer electronics.[21] Keeping in mind these shortcomings, it becomes less surprising that the government failed to find an easy way out of the thicket of difficulties that hampered Japan in the 1990s.

Recession, Crisis, and the Future

From the late 1960s through the early 1970s the world economy shifted to a phase of slower growth. The backlog of technology left from the 1930s was exhausted. The initial consumer durables revolution had passed. The ageing populations in industrial countries now needed higher levels of services. New competitors emerged, especially the four tigers, South Korea, Hong Kong, Taiwan, and Singapore. During the 1970s and 1980s, Japan grew at 5 per cent per year. This was still much faster than Western Europe and the United States, and this was the period when most of the works seeking the secrets of Japan's success appeared.[22] Then came the 'bubble economy', the sudden inflationary boom of the late 1980s. Japanese real estate and stock market prices rose to astronomical heights.

The bubble burst in 1989–90.[23] The Tokyo Stock Market, and Tokyo land prices, plummeted. Since 1989, Japan has grown on average only 1 per cent per year, though with some recovery beginning in 2002. The 'Heisei recession' takes its name from the new Emperor who came to the throne in 1989. Specialists across a range of disciplines refer to the 1990s as Japan's 'lost decade'. The huge non-performing debts from the 1980s posed a serious problem for Japan's banks. They attempted to recoup their losses by lending overseas and especially in Southeast Asia, and suffered further massive losses following the 1997 crisis.[24] In addition, very slow growth has been accompanied by the 'hollowing out' of Japanese industry, caused by the relocation of manufacturing to overseas locations. Slow economic growth also brought the end of LDP hegemony and political instability. The LDP re-emerged as the leading party in coalition governments, but without a clear majority in the Diet. The impact of a new electoral law, a combination of proportional representation and direct election modeled on the West German system, is difficult to see as yet.[25]

Japan's population is ageing. As had been predicted for some time, the inadequate provision for pensions meant that payments began to exceed income in 2000.[26] The gap will continue to widen, and the government faces the unpalatable choice of cutting pension entitlements, cutting spending in other areas, or substantially increasing taxes. Inherited values impose structural constraints on policies that might reinvigorate the economy. As seen below, Japanese women are still discriminated against and excluded from management. The declining birth rate has led to a labor shortage, but the government is reluctant to admit significant numbers of immigrants.[27]

Many of Japan's older people are farmers. Agriculture is very small-scale and extremely inefficient. In the 1960s, the government introduced policies intended to bring the standard of living of farmers up to the national average. As Japan moved to industry and services, farmers were supposed to disappear, but they did not. Now they are mostly part-time and they continue to enjoy huge subsidies. The high level of protection and inefficiency means that food prices have remained very high, but it is difficult to change the system because farmers' groups are highly organized, and rural areas are overrepresented in the Diet.

All three sides of the iron triangle now appear weakened. Corrupt relations among politicians, bureaucrats, and business have been widely publicized.[28] Decisive leadership has been lacking, and no Prime Minister has yet been able to push forward with comprehensive reform.[29] The potential agenda makes a depressingly long list, but eminent scholars disagree on what should be done. Michael Porter and his colleagues believe that Japan should generally deregulate its economy and introduce 'vigorous competition in a supportive business environment, free of government direction'. Their list of changes extends over the entire range of government and private sector structures, and includes toughening primary school standards and a comprehensive restructuring of the university system.[30] In contrast, Ronald Dore, after examining the consequences of 'marketization' in Britain and the United States, and its possible consequences in Japan, concludes, 'what has actually happened? . . . Not a great deal . . . Reasonably so, I would say'.[31]

As we have seen, the degree of success of government policy is disputed, even during the high-growth era. Nevertheless, the presumption that the government necessarily plays an active role in the direction of the economy is one of the crucial background factors affecting business in Japan. For instance, the Bank of Japan's estimate that Japan's 'potential growth' is limited to 2 per cent and any growth above that figure will be merely inflationary, is widely accepted as an authoritative guide to corporate planning. Similarly, Japanese firms look to the Ministry of Economy, Trade, and Industry (METI, a conglomerate ministry that exercises many of the functions of the previously independent MITI), both to protect them from foreign takeover bids and to help them defend themselves against hostile takeovers by domestic firms. In 2004, a METI survey of 62 major firms revealed that 44 feared a hostile takeover, and 49 said they needed some form of protection.[32]

THE MANAGEMENT GRID

Keiretsu Groups

The re-emergence of some of the old *zaibatsu* names did not mean the re-establishment of the *zaibatsu*. Instead there occurred a regrouping into new groups or *keiretsu*. The 'big six' *keiretsu* were Mitsubishi, Mitsui, Sumitomo, Fuyo, Sanwa, and Dai-Ichi Kangyo, but there were many others of varying size and structure. Some were horizontal groupings in a single industry or related industries, while others were vertical chains linking suppliers with customers.[33] The big six were diversified, and their structure has typically been portrayed as a 'star', as shown in Figure 2.2.

The groups did not have a hierarchical structure as the *zaibatsu* did. Instead they were linked by cross shareholdings, their connection to 'lead banks' and meetings of 'presidents' clubs'. At the top, the regular meetings of the presidents of member firms allowed exchange of information. The

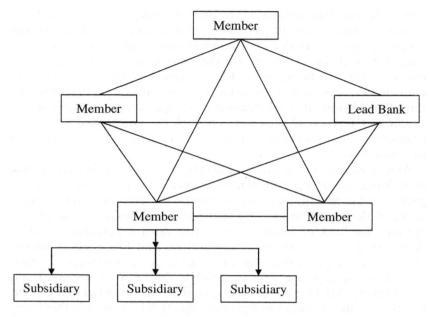

Figure 2.2   Keiretsu *'star' structure*

29 presidents of the Mitsubishi group member companies came together at the *kinyokai* or 'Friday meeting' on the second Friday of each month. Mitsui, Sumitomo, Sanwa, and Dai-Ichi Kangyo also developed a tradition of regular monthly meetings.

Large cross-shareholdings cemented these horizontal alliances. About 27 per cent of the shares of firms in the Mitsubishi group were held by other member firms. In this case they were concentrated, as Mitsubishi Bank and three other financial companies owned some three-fifths of all these group holdings. Cross-shareholdings in the other large groups ranged downward, with Dai-Ichi Kangyo the lowest at 12.5 per cent. For publicly traded companies, these levels of shareholdings virtually guarantee control, so *keiretsu* member companies were almost completely protected against potential takeover threats. In addition the government intervened to block foreign bids for control of Japanese companies.

The large groups were known by the name of their 'lead bank'. In the late 1940s and 1950s, the six largest commercial banks competed with each other to establish relationships with large firms and promising firms in emerging sectors.[34] The banks became members of the emerging groups, and although they did not directly control the others, the ongoing relationships became one of the defining characteristics of the system.[35]

Japanese firms depended on bank loans for a large fraction of their funding. During the era of high growth, bank loans sometimes reached 80 per cent of *keiretsu* members' finance. This ratio declined, but Japanese firms still typically do not raise money through new equity issues, partly because shares are issued at par value rather than at current market value. Members of each group borrowed primarily from their lead bank, and from the three government-owned long-term credit banks or smaller regional banks. They tended to borrow seldom or not at all from the lead banks of other groups.[36] In return they could rely on their lead bank for ongoing advice and assistance. As in the case of Mazda, firms in serious difficulties could come under an informal receivership, with the lead bank placing its own executives in charge and arranging further support from other group members.

The Bank of Japan and the Ministry of Finance exercised very strict control over Japanese banks until reforms beginning in the 1980s. 'Window guidance' referred to limits imposed on the amount of credit made available to commercial banks through the Bank of Japan's rediscount 'window'. Informal directions, sometimes delivered by former high school or university classmates, told the banks which industries and which firms the government wished to support. The banks could make relatively large loans compared to their capital base, and especially long-term loans to new industries, secure in the knowledge that the government would support them in case of difficulties.[37] Moral hazard, the danger that the banks would make excessively risky loans because of the government guarantee, was avoided by the close ongoing relationships between bank executives and government officials. As they retired in their early fifties, Ministry of Finance officials enjoyed the 'descent from Heaven' (*amakudari*) and took positions as members of the boards of commercial banks, reinforcing the ties among their younger colleagues.

The partial deregulation of the 1980s moved away from direct guidance and towards reliance on general measures such as the rate of interest charged by the Bank of Japan for loans to private banks. Private banks also were given greater access to foreign exchange markets. Some specialists believe that this caused the inflationary boom of the bubble economy, because competition among the banks 'led to excessive provision of long-term loans, particularly to real estate developers, and caused relatively weak players to over expand their international financing business'.[38] Others blame the incoherence of government policy, which combined expansionary low interest rates with deflationary cuts in government spending, and in effect forced the banks to seek new customers for loans. Partial deregulation also allowed for some profitable but unproductive manipulation, as those with access to credit at low regulated rates could reinvest the same funds in higher yielding securities, a maneuver known as 'financial engineering'. The bubble finally burst when the government imposed quantitative restrictions on further lending, and first the share market and then property values collapsed.[39]

The banks were severely weakened by their losses in the aftermath of the bubble. In addition, by the mid-1990s, the opening of bond markets meant that large firms relied less on bank loans than previously.[40] The 'big bang' of 1996 further deregulated financial markets and reduced the power of the Ministry of Finance by making the Bank of Japan more independent in setting financial policy and establishing a new Financial Services Agency separate from the MOF for the regulation of banks and brokers. Further proposals envisaged a division of the MOF along functional lines, with taxation and security market regulation becoming separate, for instance.

The reforms were resisted by the MOF, and then were overtaken by the 1997 crisis. As their overseas portfolios imploded, the new and more transparent accounting procedures revealed most of the banks to be insolvent. The government sponsored several mergers, some of them, such as Dai-ichi Kangyo and Fuji Bank, and the Sumitomo and Mitsui banks, between former lead banks of separate groups. Further, despite the desire to reduce the discretionary power of the MOF and move towards rule-based regulation, the government was forced to inject new capital into the system, resulting in a 'de facto nationalization of most of the largest banks'.[41] Through the early 2000s the major banks continued to report large losses, but these in part reflected the write-downs resulting from a progressive reduction in their bad loans. In other ways as well the banks began to behave more like Western corporations. In an interesting but very un-Japanese development, in 2003 and 2004, the troubled UFG Bank, under investigation by the Financial Services Agency for concealing evidence regarding the creditworthiness of its borrowers, became a takeover target for both Mitsubishi Tokyo Financial Group and Sumitomo Mitsui Financial Group. Mitsubishi Tokyo received preferred shares in UFJ Bank in return for a capital injection, but because these non-voting shares could be converted into voting shares in the event of a third-party takeover bid, they functioned as a 'poison pill' to aid UFG Bank to forestall the hostile bid by Sumitomo Mitsui.

In addition to the crisis of the lead banks, *keiretsu* groups suffered from other problems as well. The groups as such do not possess a management structure, and they do not in general interfere in the management of member firms. In fact the member firms of each group are quite highly insulated from each other. In the mid-1990s, the Mitsubishi group had several hundred senior executives. On average fewer than 10 per cent came from outside the group, but in addition only 20 per cent were from other group firms, and fully 70 per cent had spent their entire careers with their one firm. This was typical of all the large groups.

Although they are separate, members of the groups trade preferentially with each other.[42] The groups pursue a '*bento* box' strategy, like the classic Japanese lunch box with its wide variety of dishes. The large groups can almost guarantee markets for their members by encouraging employees of other group member companies to buy their products rather than those of a firm from another group. All members contribute to the assistance of member firms in difficulties. This means resources flow from strong members to weak members. The system was praised when Japan was growing rapidly, but critics have seen the defense of existing product lines, markets, and structures as a negative factor inhibiting innovation.[43]

Internal Structures of Large Firms

Japanese firms can appear mysterious, both open and closed, both egalitarian and hierarchical. Decisions seem to 'emerge' from their middle levels. No individual is 'responsible', although someone such as the president will announce decisions. The 'decision' itself may be vague, imprecise, and subject to change for unguessable reasons. For those from other corporate cultures, dealing with Japanese firms can be an exercise in frustration.

Japanese firms are known for their group decision-making processes. Internally the firm appears as an ascending tier of hierarchically organized groups. The role of each group leader is to generate consensus within the group. This has a social dimension extending beyond the formal workplace. Members of a work group drink together, and the group leader often pays the bill. When they marry, many Japanese want someone to act as a formal go-between, and it is commonly the leader of the work group who acts in this capacity.

Once a group has reached a decision the proposal is formally circulated to all groups at the same level in the firm that may be affected by the decision. All relevant groups must be persuaded, any comments or suggestions they have must be included in the proposal, and these changes in turn circulated to all other relevant groups. This process can produce difficulties and, at the next level, it is the role of a senior leader to generate consensus among these lower level groups. By the time a decision has risen to the upper levels of the firm it will be backed by a substantial consensus, but it is unlikely to be attributable to any one individual.

Group decision making has advantages and disadvantages, summarized in Table 2.1. The involvement of more people means all aspects of a problem are likely to be considered and all possible approaches examined. This can lead to superior outcomes in complex fields where there may be

Table 2.1   Group decision making

Advantages	Disadvantages
More information and knowledge is focused on the issue	It is usually more time consuming
An increased number of alternatives can be developed	Disagreements may delay decisions and cause hard feelings
Greater understanding and acceptance of the decision is likely	The discussion may be dominated by one or a few group members
Members develop knowledge skills for later use	Members may overemphasize gaining agreement
	'Groupthink' can lead to hasty adoption of an inferior decision

Source: Adapted from Kathryn Bartol, Margaret Tein, Graham Matthews and David Martin, *Management: a Pacific Rim Focus* (enhanced edition; Boston: McGraw Hill, 2003), p. 142.

multiple ways of achieving the desired goal. A group decision is also more likely to be understood and accepted by all those affected by it. On the other hand it is time consuming to consult everyone, leading to inferior outcomes where quick action is needed. In addition the desire for consensus, and indeed even the process of discussing a problem, can lead to misplaced enthusiasm. The danger of 'groupthink' means the quality of a group decision may be no better, and may be worse, than an individual decision.

Japanese labor relations have also been intensively studied. The first of the 'three jewels' of labor relations in Japan is lifetime employment. Recruits for the executive track are hired when they leave university, rotated through the firm to learn the functions of different divisions, and given additional training, before being assigned to a particular area. These are the 'salarymen', the suited 'corporate samurai' in the office from early morning to late at night, with the same firm until retirement. At the blue-collar level in the largest firms, male workers are also hired young, and they also remain until retirement.

The second jewel is promotion and pay according to seniority. Each cohort of recruits can expect to move up the corporate ladder more or less in unison, and with more or less the same salaries. This does not mean that everyone gets promoted to the top, but in general rank and salary are a function of length of service. The tradition of early retirement, typically at age 55, keeps the top from becoming clogged. Retired executives are often employed by the large firm's subcontractors.

Together the seniority system and the emphasis on group decision making mean there is little place for maverick or high-flyer types. At the

top, the profiles of company presidents look more like government bureaucrats than the Western image of corporate success. In 1990, 86.5 per cent of
the presidents of the largest 287 Japanese companies had been promoted
through the ranks of their firm. They had served an average of 34.3 years
with their firms, and they averaged 62.2 years of age when they became
president. Most firms specified a three-year term for their president, and in
addition most customarily expected their presidents to serve two terms,
after which they would either retire or take a position on the board. When
asked who selects the next president, nearly 70 per cent of presidents in a
1988 survey said 'myself', although clearly the choice was normally
restricted to the circle of senior executives already surrounding the president, and the decision was also frequently made in consultation with the
circle of 'OB' (old boys), senior board members, former presidents, or
founders.[44]

The third jewel is company unions. Every large firm has a single union.
When these are branches of national unions, they retain most of their membership dues, an arrangement that keeps the national labor movement relatively weak. Typically, all employees have been included in the union,
including the lower levels of management. The union officials have frequently been young company executives, or line supervisors about to be
promoted to executive positions, rotating through the union as one of their
assignments. The absence of any craft union tradition makes the labor force
implicitly more flexible with respect to job assignments, and the presence of
many supervisors and executives in the union makes it very difficult for the
union to represent workers' interests in opposition to management. Many
firms possess elaborate written grievance procedures, but, to the bemuse-
ment of Western observers in the 1970s, they typically had never been used.
Many other firms deny the need for formal grievance procedures. In both
cases, any difficulties are supposed to be smoothed out within groups. This
is one of the arts of being a successful group leader. Less pleasantly, as
reported in the media, when a member of a group does not fit in, they may
be browbeaten until they submit and conform, or resign.[45]

Finally there is the issue of gender. Geert Hofstede's 'masculinity' scale
measured the degree to which 'gender roles are clearly distinct', with men
'supposed to be assertive, tough, and focused on material success', while
women 'are supposed to be more modest, tender, and concerned with
quality of life'. In the original study, Japanese respondents scored exceptionally high, far higher than any other country.[46] In fact an extreme gender
bias pervades Japanese business. Large Japanese firms did not hire women
at all until recently. The only exceptions were the 'OL' (office ladies), the
secretarial positions for young women who spent most of their time making
tea for their male colleagues and then resigned when they married, ideally

before age 25. A cruel joke referred to 'Christmas cake' women, as 'perfect on the twenty-fifth, but who would want it on the twenty-sixth?'

Japan passed an Equal Employment Opportunity Law (EEOL) in 1985. However, the law was passed partly in response to international pressure, to allow Japan to ratify the United Nations Convention on the Elimination of All Forms of Discrimination against Women. The Ministry of Labor intended the law only 'to improve working women's welfare and to promote measures to enable them to harmonize work and family roles', not to recognize or support a woman's right to work. Employers were merely required to 'endeavor' to avoid discrimination. The EEOL was strengthened in 1999 with a range of identified prohibited practices, but enforcement has remained weak. For those occupations where comparative data are available, women in Japan earn a smaller fraction of male earnings than in any other Asian country, and there has been little or no improvement since the EEOL was passed. In response to the EEOL, large firms have recruited small numbers of women for executive track positions, but with no concessions in terms of the hours required and usually with little or no provision for childcare, so in effect women are forced to choose either marriage or a career. Many firms interview women applicants only after all qualified male applicants have been placed. In the mid-1990s, although 39 per cent of Japanese workers were women, only 1.2 per cent of them held positions as department head, and the majority of these worked in small and medium-sized firms.[47]

Firm Competencies and the 'Catch-up Economy'

As noted above, Japanese firms took advantage of a large backlog of American technology available at the end of the Second World War. And, however one evaluates the role of the domestic market or government policy, there is little doubt that in case after case the Japanese firms improved on the originals. The improved versions were also produced at lower cost. Successful Japanese firms developed very efficient systems for encouraging the internal flow of information. This was important at the design stage. As a German executive remarked, 'one German engineer is better than one Japanese engineer, but three hundred Japanese engineers are better than three hundred German engineers'. The reasons, according to Ikujiro Nonaka and Hirotaka Takeuchi, are that Japanese firms regard themselves as 'living organisms' and treat knowledge in a 'holistic' manner. In contrast to the Western tendency to consider only formal and systematic knowledge, Japanese firms look for ways to exploit the insights of employees at all levels, especially the 'tacit' knowledge that may not be easily communicated. Use of metaphor, analogy and schematic models allows project groups to communicate and exchange alternative ideas. The circulation of employees across divisions also encourages communication of new per-spectives. From improving foreign technologies, firms such as Honda, Canon, and Sharp moved on to the creating of genuinely new products.[48]

Knowledge management also plays an important role in reducing pro-duction costs, as in the famous 'total quality control' system, and also in savings in inventory, as in the equally famous 'just in time' management. Commonly, as a firm produces more of a product, it produces it at lower cost, even if there is no change in technology, personnel, or training. This is true everywhere, but Japanese firms have pursued the 'learning curve' approach actively. This requires very good internal flows of information. It also requires that employees have a sense of ownership and involvement. In suc-cessful Japanese firms, employees and groups are encouraged to engage in problem-solving activities, and to present the results of their approach pub-licly to the entire network of potential adopters. These presentations have a standard format, the 'quality improvement story' outlined in Table 2.2.

Japanese employees are evaluated not only on their objective perform-ance, but also subjectively on their 'commitment' to the firm and on their 'sincerity'. Participation in quality improvement exercises is evidence of commitment and sincerity, and therefore employees are motivated to par-ticipate. It is also important that managers also attend the sessions. In prin-ciple, everyone is a participant, and all need to learn continuously. It is also important that no one is punished for failure or for reporting a problem, but rather everyone is encouraged to use failure or a problem as an opportunity for learning and improvement. The precise specification of countermeasures and the resulting changes in work practices also make it easier to identify remaining problems and therefore further possibilities for improvement.[49]

Although regarded as typically Japanese, quality control circles (QCC) were based on the teachings of American management theorists Edwards Deming and Joseph Juran. In Japan, Kaoru Ishikawa and others saw QCC as a means to overcome the rigid hierarchy of Japanese firms by creating horizontal groups alongside the chain of command, where problems could be discussed in an informal, free atmosphere.[50] In the 1980s, following pub-lications celebrating their success in Japan, QCC became a management fad in the United States and Europe, but they did not always work, and dropped out of fashion. There were various reasons for this. Sometimes the circles were only discussion groups with no channel to spread ideas. Sometimes the groups were not adequately trained, or the project was not resourced but simply added on top of employees' existing duties. Sometimes the groups were simply imposed from the top, with no direct involvement of senior management. In the United States this happened because managers saw QCC as a disciplinary device to improve the perfor-mance of 'sloppy' workers. In Germany, QCC also had little impact, but in

Table 2.2   The quality improvement story

Story Step	Function	Tools
1. Select theme	Make clear why the theme is selected	'The next stages of production are our customers.' Immediate remedy v. recurrence prevention
2. Grasp the current situation	Collect data Determine key characteristics of the theme Prioritize: serious problems first	Check-sheet Frequency chart
3. Analysis	List possible causes Hypothesize relations between causes and problems Collect data on cause–effect relations	Fishbone diagram showing possible relations Scatter diagram showing possible correlations
4. Countermeasures	Devise Implement	Firm-specific technology Experience
5. Confirm the effect of the countermeasure	Collect data Before–after comparison	Entire range of tools again
6. Standardize the countermeasure	Amend existing standards and procedures	
7. Identify remaining problems		

Source: Adapted from Robert E. Cole, 'Different quality paradigms and their implications for organizational learning', in Masahiko Aoki and Ronald Dore (eds), *The Japanese Firm: The Sources of Competitive Strength* (Oxford: Oxford University Press, 1994), p. 76.

this case the failure occurred because technical improvements were seen as the responsibility of qualified technicians, not ordinary workers.[51]

However, when the system works, the result is a continuous series of seminars on problems and improvements. The seminars broadcast information about solutions to problems, and the implementation of improvements diffuses knowledge through the firm more rapidly than hierarchical top-down approach. As Nonaka and Takeuchi would put it, the firm learns to encourage the systematic move from 'tacit' knowledge to 'explicit' knowledge and back again, as the new information is absorbed by more and more employees and the process itself becomes internalized.[52] Honda Motor Company has referred to the process as 'horizontal development'. Aishin AW, a parts supplier for Toyota, has consciously sought to model itself on a school. Robert Cole contrasts this with the 'Taylorist' approach. In the mode of Frederick Taylor's classic time and motion studies, managers have to learn first by observing workers, or 'pull information out of the heads of employees'. The managers then must reorganize the observations, retain the planning elements, and then feed operational reforms back to the employees.[53]

Quality improvement was especially important for savings in inventory. 'Just in time' management means 'the next stages of production are our customers'. Japanese firms strove to have a part arrive at the production line just as it was needed. To do this each workstation only produced a part when it received an order from the next workstation. In turn each workstation would only order what it needed from the previous stage. An empty container or a card signaled the demand for the part, which was then produced and placed in the container or sent down a sub-assembly line. In such a system there was no need for stockpiles of inventory at all. There was no need for storage space. The firm saved on capital because nothing was tied up in piles of parts waiting for assembly. And, if every part and every sub-assembly is perfect, then every final product will also be perfect.

The system of 'lean production' depends on quality, because there is no backup. Each part has to be perfect. Within the system of just in time (JIT) and total quality control (TQC), the key role for workers' quality control circles is to find ways to guarantee the quality of parts produced at each stage. Working with both the preceding and following stages of production allows all workers to focus on all aspects of waste elimination. Problems are identified and solutions proposed. Quality improvement seminars then spread knowledge of improvements to the rest of the firm as well.

Quality improvement means continual upgrading, but it also means the establishment and imposition of detailed rules. Toyota's employees learn to take a certain number of steps along the production line, while turning a screw a precise number of turns. Each movement is choreographed in detail, and must be executed precisely. Every worker is expected to follow the same set of rules and to perform all operations in exactly the same manner. The system therefore depends on the willingness of workers to be governed by detailed regulations. One of the difficulties Japanese firms encounter when they expand overseas is the reluctance of American, European, Chinese, or Southeast Asian workers to submit to the discipline that Japanese firms attempt to impose. Rather than responding with a sense of ownership and involvement, foreign workers frequently regard the Japanese 'system' as merely hierarchical and authoritarian.[54]

The tendency to govern through detailed rules and regulations extends across sectors. In one case, in the late 1990s, American advisors brought in to aid in the restructuring of a troubled Japanese bank were shocked when confronted with a 300-page manual for the bank's employees, which every employee was expected to memorize. The detailed listing of rules had grown by accretion, the result of a process closely analogous to the quality improvement process in manufacturing industries. However, the result was to interfere with attempts to cope with the bank's problems, because any change would require revision of the manual, and this itself was a complex rule-driven process. The bank's culture suffered from both the weaknesses of group decision making and the memory of previous success, which had resulted in a fixed conviction that the existing system was both the 'best' and 'flexible', when in fact it was neither.[55]

Japanese firms are also known for their close relations with their subcontractors. If production depends on every part being delivered just when it is needed and if every part is required to be perfect, then it is imperative that subcontractors adopt the system as well. All large firms have a pyramid of subcontractors that supply semi-manufactures, components, parts, and services. In the automobile industry large firms may have over 1000 subcontractors. There are dangers here as well. Subcontractors are 'captive' firms in that they depend on the large firm for a major fraction or all of their business. This places them in a very risky position, subject to the good will of their major customer. At the same time, the large firms, with no stocks of inventory, must trust the efficiency and good faith of the subcontractor. These problems of asymmetric information and agency are usually avoided in the Japanese case because ongoing relationships are close, and large firms help subcontractors with technical advice and sometimes with finance. Large firms may take equity stakes in their subcontractors, and subcontractors in turn may acquire shares in the large firm, joining the circle of friendly shareholders. In addition, as noted above the executives who retire early from large firms frequently move to positions in subcontracting firms.

Subcontracting firms differ in structure from the large firms. Subcontractors do not practice lifetime employment. Their labor force is largely female, and most of these women workers are part-time: of the 39 per cent of the labor force who are women, fully 70 per cent are part-time workers. However, although technically 'part-time' workers, these women may in fact have worked full time for decades. Part-time work is defined in terms of legal status and benefits, not in terms of hours worked. Part-time workers do not qualify for paid vacations or company pensions, and they receive smaller bonuses. The 'part-time' status of their workers means that subcontractors can expand or reduce their workforce according to the demands of the large firm. Stability of employment in large firms therefore depends on instability of employment in small firms. Lifetime employment, although the norm, never applied to more than 20 or possibly 25 per cent of the labor force.[56]

Evaluating Japanese *Keiretsu*

If we reconceptualize the *keiretsu* as conglomerate firms, we may gain a clearer view of the sort of decisions they should be making, and thereby gain some insight into their problems. The Boston Consulting Group has a well-known Growth Share Matrix (Table 2.3) that compares the relative competitive position of divisions of a large firm to the growth rates of each division's market. 'Cash cows' can generate income to support potential 'stars', but a firm should consider selling or closing down its 'dogs'.

The growth share matrix is a snapshot. Table 2.4 takes another view, looking at development over time. The matrix relates each division's competitive position to the overall position of its industry. All industries pass through a series of stages that approximate a biological growth curve. An initial period of slow growth is followed by very rapid growth, but then by a period of slowdown and stagnation. A new industry's technology is still being developed, and markets are only beginning to emerge, so we find slow growth and small volumes of sales to early adopters. Then, if the product succeeds, expansion to fill the potential market leads to rapid growth and very rapidly rising volumes. At this stage small firms have difficulty adjusting to the need for larger plants, geographical expansion, and more complex organization. Most industries therefore experience a stage of competitive shakeout and consolidation. Finally comes a period of saturation when most

Table 2.3   Boston Consulting Group (BCG) growth share matrix

	High Market Share	*Low Market Share*
High Market Growth Rate	Stars	Question Marks
Low Market Growth Rate	Cash Cows	Dogs

Source: Adapted from Kathryn Bartol, Margaret Tein, Graham Matthews and David Martin, *Management: a Pacific Rim Focus* (enhanced edition; Boston: McGraw-Hill, 2003), p. 217.

Asian firms

Table 2.4   Product/market evolution matrix

	Competitive Position in Industry		
	Strong	*Average*	*Weak*
Industry Stage: *Development*	Possible Stars	Possible Stars	Question Marks
Growth	Stars	Question Marks	Question Marks
Competitive Shakeout	Stars	Question Marks	Dogs
Saturation	Cash Cows	Question Marks	Dogs
Decline	Cash Cows	Dogs	Dogs

Source: Adapted from Kathryn Bartol, Margaret Tein, Graham Matthews and David
Martin, *Management: a Pacific Rim Focus* (enhanced edition; Boston: McGraw-Hill, 2003),
p. 219.

potential customers have been satisfied. This means slower growth, but can
also mean continued large volumes. At this point the firm may act as a cash
cow to nurture newer undertakings by the group. Finally, products decline
when their market is confined to replacement of old units and supply of new
customers in line with population growth. As fashion changes, or competitive products emerge, volumes may drop.

Most members of the major *keiretsu* groups are manufacturing firms in saturated markets. They produce steel, heavy chemicals, ships, automobiles, and
basic consumer electronics. The services they supply in construction, banking,
and wholesale trade all concentrate in Japan, and the Japanese population is
ageing rapidly. The advantages of the 'Japanese system' apply to these kinds
of industries in the era of high-speed growth. *Keiretsu* firms had a stable, committed labor force, secure financial backing, support from group members,
and rapidly growing markets. Their newly constructed plants could produce
standard products with long runs, a situation where the learning curve will
reduce costs. Conversely, the strengths of the Japanese system become weaknesses in a period of generally slow growth. *Keiretsu* firms found themselves

with a 'diamond shaped' workforce with a bulge in the middle. Their workers are stable, but they are ageing, and expensive. Lower growth means less investment, which leaves relatively large shares of the firms' capital sunk in ageing plants. The banks are weak and poorly managed, and the groups are still committed to supporting their weakest members.

The disadvantages of the Japanese system may make it difficult for the *keiretsu* to identify and move into areas of growth and development, and also more difficult for Japan to move to the final stage of design, coordination, and marketing of manufactured goods and the provision of financial services. High-value products aimed at sophisticated and affluent consumers depend on fashion and marketing, or on cutting-edge scientific research. Here Japan lags badly relative to Europe and the United States. The universities are rigid and hierarchical, poorly organized for pure research. Young researchers are not encouraged.[57] Japanese design is conservative. Japanese firms pitch at the middle of the market, not at the niches. Japanese firms seem slow to react. Rapid change and shorter product life mean that the learning curve may not have time to take effect, but the classic style of group decision making is time-consuming, making it hard to change direction.

Being present in every market (the *bento* box syndrome) means that every *keiretsu* will have some dogs. In the era of high-speed growth, even dogs were pretty good cash cows. In the low growth era since the 1970s, the disparity between high and low-growth industries has widened, export markets have become more competitive, and the domestic market has opened to increased foreign competition. In this more difficult environment cash cows are not safe, and dogs are a real drag on the group. However, it is very difficult for the group to respond by divesting or shutting down a member firm, because of the structure of the *keiretsu*. There is no hierarchy, and members have a moral obligation to support each other. The firm is a community or family, including managers and workers, and the extended family includes employees of other firms in the *keiretsu* group.

Shareholders are not members of the Japanese family firm. Japanese firms pay very low dividends, and because of cross-shareholdings they cannot be punished by a decline in their share price. Cross-shareholdings protect firms, making it very difficult for an outside raider to take over a Japanese firm. In contrast, Western firms are supposed to maximize shareholder wealth. Even though management is independent of the owners of shares, the market will punish poor performance with a decline in the share price, and the firm may be taken over and the present managers lose their jobs. As argued by E.F. Fama, a well-functioning equities market operates in this way to overcome potential agency problems, in particular the potential divergence of interest between a relatively independent management and the large numbers of relatively passive investors in a modern large corporation.[58] In Japan, not only is the discipline of the market weak, but also the relatively high percentage of non-traded shares makes the market 'thin' and unstable, subject to relatively wide and sudden fluctuations.

This is not to say that Japanese managers escape responsibility. As in the United States, during the 1980s firms in Japan responded to poor results by appointing outside board members, cutting executive compensation, and dismissing chief executives. However, these responses could have a distinctive Japanese flavor. The outside directors could come from the lead bank, and the chief executive might be discreetly retired rather than publicly sacked.[59] The government's role also continued, though it might now act more as an enforcer rather than as a guide. In 2000, a tip-off led Ministry of Transport officials to search the headquarters of Mitsubishi Motors Corporation. They discovered evidence that the company had illegally concealed customer complaints. The company repeatedly denied any wrongdoing, but the investigation revealed that Mitsubishi had systematically concealed complaints from government authorities for over 20 years, using a dual set of records in its computer system, and in some cases had repaired vehicles secretly. Nearly a million vehicles were recalled, and the CEO apologized in the traditional Japanese manner with a public bow of contrition. The major shareholders, that is, other members of the Mitsubishi group, forced his resignation, and government prosecutors laid criminal charges against nine other executives, but the crisis did not lead to changes in governance structures.[60] In 2004, the new executive team was in the news again, denying responsibility for the design flaws that had led to a fatal bus crash.

Whither Japan?

In addition to the decline of the main bank system outlined above, other features of the Japanese system may be shifting as well. Examples of a weakening commitment to lifetime employment, particularly in the electronics industry, have been widely publicized, and large numbers of firms report that they have adopted management by objectives (MBO) or other performance-based systems. However, over half of firms report they intend to maintain the traditional system, and another third are mixed, introducing performance incentives while still retaining lifetime employment.[61] Between 1995 and 2005, Canon, under CEO Fujio Mitarai, shed seven loss-making divisions, greatly increased automation in production, and introduced a refined QCC system of multi-tasking groups that it calls 'cell production'. The result was to cut 45 000 jobs. However, production and sales more than doubled, and not only were the displaced workers absorbed, but the firm's total headcount rose 35 per cent. 'As long as the company keeps growing and making a profit,' said Mitarai, 'there is no conflict' between the two goals of '365-day-a-year workerless production' and 'lifetime employment in the company'.[62]

Cross-shareholdings have been declining steadily since the late 1980s, a response by firms to the low returns from cross-held shares, increased consciousness of the risks of equity holdings as the share market has declined, and divestments connected with the bank mergers and decline of the traditional main bank relationships.[63] This can be expected to continue with new accounting standards that require assets to be listed at their current value. However, cross-shareholdings by members of the big six groups remain over 20 per cent, and the proportion of 'stable' shareholdings remains very high by international standards. There were 52 takeover bids in Japan in 2003, a substantial increase on the 21 bids in each of the two previous years and a dramatic change for a country that previously had few if any takeovers at all, but this is still a very small number by American or British standards.

Those who emphasize change also point to the increased presence of foreign firms in Japan.[64] In addition to success stories such as Starbuck's now ubiquitous presence, Japanese firms with foreign partners are generally believed to be moving towards 'Western'-style corporate governance. The leading automobile firms have sought foreign partners to strengthen their financial position, but with mixed results. Following the alliance with Renault, Nissan recovered and has enjoyed particular success in the North American market. In a parallel move, Mitsubishi Motors, facing a large loss and subsequent sharp decline in its share price in 1998, launched a three-year recovery program that included finding a foreign partner willing to purchase a substantial stake in the firm. The scandal over the concealed complaints broke just as the firm was finalizing the purchase of a 34 per cent share by DaimlerChrysler, and one of the consequences was that it received several hundred million dollars less than the original price. Worse, the alliance did not bring benefits to either partner, and DaimlerChrysler first reduced its stake to 13 per cent, and eventually wrote the 'disastrous venture' down to zero on its balance sheet.[65]

Other observers continue to emphasize the continuing role of government and the remaining restrictions on competition.[66] A number of large Japanese firms, particularly in declining sunset industries, have earned the label 'zombie' corporations. Sustained by government subsidies, or by financial institutions willing to roll over their non-performing loans, these living dead, virtually bankrupt, firms continue to operate. The common argument that the zombies have caused Japan's deflationary spiral by selling below cost is almost certainly false.[67] Nevertheless, the problem was regarded as sufficiently widespread that in 2003 the government established the Industrial Revitalization Corporation of Japan (IRCJ) to provide aid and guidance to firms in need of restructuring. In one of its first actions, in 2003, the IRCJ bailed out Kanebo, Japan's second largest cosmetics company. In 2004, it began a rescue operation at conglomerate Daiei. Daiei, a group with 114 member companies, expanded across a broad range of consumer and service areas during the 1980s. Lacking focus and heavily indebted, it struggled in the 1990s, and received government aid packages in 2002 and 2003. Daiei's CEO rejected IRCJ assistance, fearing the group would be broken up. He was overruled and forced to resign by the major creditor, UFJ Bank, which, as noted above, was itself in serious difficulties and wanted to clean up its balance sheet ahead of its planned merger with the Mitsubishi Tokyo group. Observers criticized both operations. Kanebo, they said, should have been allowed to proceed with a proposed merger with Kao Corporation that would have created an internationally competitive firm, and Daiei should have accepted one of the offers made by Wal-Mart, Ripplewood Holdings, or Goldman Sachs.[68]

Japan's corporate governance structures continue to evolve. More rigorous and transparent accounting standards, arm's length relationships with their banks, increased public hostility to discretionary interference by bureaucrats, and the increasing influence of institutional investors, all will certainly work to alter the framework of decision making for Japanese executives. In addition there are proposals for more independent auditors, inclusion of independent directors on boards and oversight committees, and greater use of holding company forms of organization, which would allow for greater responsiveness to changing conditions.[69] Recent research has confirmed earlier studies in showing that the average rates of profit for *keiretsu* firms are lower than those of independent firms, and also suggests that membership has not protected firms from fluctuations in their returns.[70] Especially as capital markets continue to evolve, firms may find the costs of continued membership outweigh the benefits, and either loosen their connections with the group or exit entirely.

Nevertheless, external observers still note that 'keiretsu dominance deters competition' and worry that, although 'market forces' may become stronger, this is a slow process at best.[71] Those who criticized the Kanebo and Deiei aid packages believed politics had played a role, not only in the concern of the government for lost jobs (Daiei's Japan operations employed 40 000 workers), but also the need of the new IRCJ to justify its existence by providing government subsidies even when better options were available.[72] Within the large firms, recruitment continued as before, with male generalist graduates from the top universities preferred. In contrast, especially to Taiwan and Southeast Asia, a foreign degree or foreign experience was not valued. In addition, in contrast especially to South Korea and China, specialized management education was not valued in Japan.

Even in academic management circles, moreover, an insularity prevailed that resulted in a virtual absence of citations of foreign works. Strikingly, this was true even of those who called urgently for change in the system. For instance, the authors cited in Box 2.2, Moriaki Tsuchiya and Yoshinobu Konomi, although harshly critical of Japanese managers, simply ignored the international management literature.[73]

JAPAN AS INVESTOR AND DONOR

Despite the problems, of course, and however we may judge the necessity and speed of reform, Japan remains a dominant economic power. The obverse of the 'hollowing out' of manufacturing in Japan itself has been the massive flows of Japanese investment to other countries. The flow of Japanese foreign direct investment (FDI) peaked during the bubble economy of the late 1980s, declined in the early 1990s, rose again to the crisis in 1997, and then declined again. A recovery in the early 2000s was accompanied by a shift in the most common destination of Japanese FDI, away from the United States and towards China. Japan has also been a major source of foreign aid or official development assistance (ODA) to Asian countries. Japan is the world's second largest provider of ODA, with approximately half of its bilateral disbursements going to East and Southeast Asia. In turn, Korea in the 1960s and 1970s, Southeast Asia in the 1970s and 1980s, and China in the 1990s have been the major recipients of Japanese ODA.

Japanese FDI is a key factor in Asia's economic development, and the presence of Japanese firms is a key component of the institutional and management grids of all other Asian countries. The impact of Japanese investment has been as extensively debated as any other aspect of the Japanese system. In the 1970s, Japanese economist Kiyoshi Kojima argued strongly that Japanese investment was superior to United States investment because it was 'trade creating' and better adapted to the local environment in its business organization and factor proportions. Japanese investment, he said, concentrated in smaller enterprises, used more labor-intensive technologies, and more often took the form of joint ventures with local partners, than American investment. Japanese investment, he concluded, was essentially 'altruistic'. While Japanese investment 'plays the tutor' to developing countries, American investment 'is pursued for the sake of monopolistic or oligopolistic profit-maximization'.[74]

The Kojima hypothesis has generally been supported by Japanese scholars, and attacked by non-Japanese. The results have been mixed. Critics have generally conceded that in fact Japanese investment has differed from that of foreign investors from other countries, but they have argued that this does not reflect the 'superiority' of Japanese investment. Rather, they argue, Japanese investment patterns have reflected the stage of development of the Japanese economy, Japan's position in the product cycle in various industries, and not least the protectionist policies of the Japanese government.[75]

The initial surge of Japanese investment in Southeast Asia occurred in the late 1960s, when Japan began to lose its comparative advantage in labor-intensive manufacturing. Kojima's critics have argued that the concentration of Japanese investment in smaller-scale, more labor-intensive areas, and the greater willingness of Japanese firms to engage in joint ventures, reflected differences in economic and business conditions in Japan, compared to the home countries of other foreign investors. Japanese investors also concentrated on consumer goods because many areas of potential large-scale investment were prohibited by the host country governments. That is, Japanese foreign investment was driven by the same motives as other investors, and constrained by the same institutional factors.

More recently, it has been argued, 'Japanese-style' investment in small-scale enterprises has been undertaken by the next tier of foreign investors, firms from the newly industrializing economies, especially Taiwan and South Korea. Like Japan in previous decades, they concentrate on consumer goods or assembly of components produced elsewhere.[76] Further, in the 1990s a 'new wave' of Japanese investment began to appear in Southeast Asia, in larger-scale, more capital-intensive projects, with less likelihood that these would be joint ventures.[77]

Kojima's critics attribute these changes to the changes in the investment environment in the host countries. Deregulation and loosening of restrictions led to the spread of foreign investment into areas where foreigners were previously excluded. In the early years of their 'export-oriented' growth polices, most Southeast Asian countries confined foreign investment to consumer goods intended for export. Since the early 1990s, deregulation has opened new sectors, especially infrastructure and property development. Projects in these areas tend to be larger and longer-term than consumer goods manufacturing. Therefore, conclude the critics, the Japanese are not especially altruistic, but rather are profit seeking, more or less like all other investors.

United States scholars Walter Hatch and Kozo Yamamura have presented a much less optimistic view of Japanese investment. In their view, 'Japanese high-tech manufacturers view Asia as one integrated but technologically stratified economy, an extension of their own production base', to be developed in cooperation with government agencies through conscious control over technology licensing and capital flows.[78] In their opinion Japanese investors attempt to impose a 'flying geese' pattern on the rest of Asia. Japan will pull the rest of Asia along behind itself, but it will always be the lead goose. The flying geese thesis was first proposed by Japanese economist Kaname Akamatsu in the early 1960s, and remains something of a cliché in Japan.[79] Hatch and Yamamura quote the president of the Japanese Chamber of Commerce and Industry in Singapore: 'In my personal opinion, we should keep the control in Japan. Once you lose that control, that power, it never comes back. It never returns. All you have to do is look at what happened to England in the nineteenth century, or what is happening to the United States today.'[80]

Japanese firms control technology through licensing agreements, and critics insist they do so with government supervision to ensure that most advanced components remain in Japanese hands. Rather than 'playing the tutor' to developing countries, Japanese firms supply only mature or standardized technology, suitable only for labor-intensive assembly, not 'core' manufacturing or cutting-edge technology. Sharp's liquid crystal displays for both wide-screen televisions and personal computers, for instance, are produced at carefully guarded plants in Japan. When Japanese firms do supply technology to their foreign partners, they are accused of charging unreasonably high prices, with added fees and particularly high charges for the services of Japanese engineers. Further, because the technology is older, it will not last long before it must be upgraded. Japanese firms restrict the use of know-how, may require the purchase of specific machinery or raw materials, and may impose limits on the markets in which products can be sold.

Japanese firms are also accused of hampering the spread of technology through 'closed' regional networks of suppliers. Some arrangements that look like licensing are actually sweetheart deals with subsidiaries. This means there may be no spin-off into the local economy. The Japanese style of subcontracting reinforces these effects. Japanese firms may either import components from Japan or purchase them from other Japanese firms in the host country. These suppliers enjoy long-term relationships and stability, but host country suppliers are forced to compete with each other. In Southeast Asia particularly, Japanese firms may divide the production of components among subsidiaries in different countries so no single country has access to the entire technology.[81]

Employment and human resource management is another sore point. At senior levels, the large proportion of Japanese nationals in management positions limits the spread of skills in the host country. At lower levels, Japanese managers in foreign subsidiaries have typically brought only the less favorable aspects of Japan's labor relations with them. They have been interested only in cheap labor and unwilling to invest in raising the skill levels of their workers. The gender bias of the Japanese workplace, however, has been transferred, and female workers have been subject to additional discrimination and harassment. In China, Japanese plant managers reported no strikes and believed their labor relations to be unproblematic, but official figures report that Japanese-invested plants in fact experience substantially more labor unrest than Western-invested plants.[82]

The Japanese government has been actively involved in the investment activities of Japanese firms. Japan's negotiators have attempted to achieve the most favorable possible environment for Japanese firms. Thailand, for instance, has become a major automobile producer in Southeast Asia, and many Thai firms work as subcontractors to Japanese auto manufacturers. In 2005, the new Free Trade Agreement between Japan and Thailand mandated an end to Thai tariffs on Japanese automobile parts, although it also provided for Japanese assistance in training personnel in the Thai automobile industry. In contrast, rice, highly protected in Japan and a potential major export from Thailand to Japan, was explicitly excluded from the ongoing liberalization talks. The Japanese government has provided low-interest loans, insurance to overseas investors, and matchmaking efforts to find foreign partners. Japanese investors also benefit from administrative guidance and advice in Japan before investments are undertaken. Some is straightforward, but some is highly suspect, for instance a JETRO seminar in 1987 on techniques of bribing foreign government officials, which caused a scandal when word leaked out.[83] United States firms, especially, complained that the willingness of Japanese firms to pay bribes placed them at a competitive disadvantage in host countries, but Japan has since signed the 1997 OECD Convention on Combating Bribery.

Japan's official development assistance is also important to the development of other Asian countries and, as with Japanese FDI, the distinctive patterns of Japanese ODA have stimulated an intensive ongoing debate. In particular, compared to other OECD countries, Japanese ODA makes much greater use of bilateral loans. In 2002, a typical year, loans represented 55 per cent of Japan's total bilateral ODA. Japan's ODA has also emphasized 'hard capital' such as infrastructure projects to support industrial enterprises, rather than 'soft' spending on social services or poverty reduction. Japan has favored projects connected to creating a 'sound investment climate' and to promoting industrial development, particularly in the Asian region.

Since the 1960s, the Japanese government has consistently argued that Japan itself was obliged to repay loans from the World Bank that had financed reconstruction following the Second World War. Japanese officials believe that this forced Japan to become frugal and to develop competitive industries. As with Kojima's argument regarding Japanese FDI, the Japanese view sees Japan playing the tutor to developing countries.

According to the official argument, the advantage of this mix of ODA funding is that it fosters a 'credit culture' in the recipient countries, builds a basis for private-sector-led economic growth, and constructs long-term stable relationships between development partners. Poverty reduction, in turn, will result eventually as the recipient economies grow, develop, and 'graduate' from their need for further loans.[84]

Japan's position has been criticized, not least in reviews of its aid policies conducted by the Development Assistance Committee of the OECD.[85] Japan continues to protect its agricultural sector, and has done relatively little for poverty reduction and social services. Despite being granted for long terms at low rates of interest, the loans must be repaid, and the eventual burdens are substantial. Korea received large amounts of ODA in the form of loans from Japan in the 1960s and 1970s, and has been repaying them ever since. In 2003, Korea repaid a total of US$553 million on its past ODA loans, and 499 million went to Japan.[86] Observers have also noted that some of Japan's ODA directly supports Japanese firms overseas. The Dalian economic zone in northern China was intended for Japanese small and medium-sized firms, who would also benefit from the nearby electric power-generating plant built with Japanese government credits.[87]

Other scholars have concentrated on the negative impact of Japan's demand for natural products, particularly timber. In the Philippines, then in Sabah and Sarawak in Malaysia, then in Indonesia, and more recently in Cambodia, excessive logging has led to deforestation and erosion. Consistent with their longstanding policy, Japanese government agencies have made grants to restore deforested areas, but these are relatively small compared to the extent of the damage, and they are usually in the form of loans. The need to repay the loans leads to pressure on local budgets, which then paves the way for a repetition of environmentally unsustainable logging.[88]

However, as with its FDI, Japan's disbursement of ODA is one of the major factors shaping the environment for other Asian firms. In the past, Japan has made loans to allow the development of strategically important firms, such as steelmaker Posco in Korea, as we will see in Chapter 3. More generally, infrastructure developments funded by Japanese ODA can stimulate the initial phases of growth in local regions. The Dalian electrical plant, for instance, provides power to the entire district, not only to the Japanese industrial park. Further, on the positive side, Japanese aid is far less likely to be 'tied' to requirements to purchase from suppliers in the donor countries, than for instance ODA from Europe or the United States. Despite the criticisms, one of the fears of both private and public sector observers is that political pressure in Japan will result in a lowering of ODA disbursements, with negative consequences for the opportunities available to firms elsewhere in Asia.

FURTHER READING

Elise K. Tipton, *Modern Japan: A Social and Political History* (London and New York: Routledge, 2002), is an excellent general history. In the 1970s, large numbers of works ranging from scholarly to popular attempted to identify the characteristics of Japanese firms that had led to their success. Almost all placed Japanese firms in the context of broader institutional structures and state policy, notably Hugh Patrick and Henry Rosovsky (eds), *Asia's New Giant: How the Japanese Economy Works* (Washington, D.C.: The Brookings Institution, 1976) and Ezra F. Vogel, *Japan as Number One: Lessons for America* (Cambridge: Harvard University Press, 1979). In the 1980s and into the 1990s, attention turned to the firms themselves. See Masahiko Aoki (ed.), *The Economic Analysis of the Japanese Firm* (Amsterdam: North Holland, 1984); James C. Abegglen and George Stalk Jr., *Kaisha: The Japanese Corporation* (New York: Basic Books, 1985); Mark Fruin, *The Japanese Enterprise System: Competitive Strategies and Cooperative Structures* (Oxford: Oxford University Press, 1992); Masahiko Aoki and Ronald Dore (eds), *The Japanese Firm: The Sources of Competitive Strength* (Oxford: Oxford University Press, 1994).

Masahiko Aoki has been a leading exponent of the idea that Japanese firms differ significantly from Western firms, especially in the way they process information. See his *Information, Corporate Governance, and Institutional Diversity: Competitiveness in Japan, the USA, and the Transitional Economies* (Tokyo, 1995; translated by Stacey Jehlik, Oxford and New York: Oxford University Press, 2000). Ikujiro Nonaka and Hirotaka Takeuchi, *The Knowledge-Creating Company: How Japanese Companies Create the Dynamics of Innovation* (New York: Oxford University Press, 1995) took this another step, and their book has been influential in the field of knowledge management generally. Michael L. Gerlach, *Alliance Capitalism: The Social Organization of Japanese Business* (Berkeley: University of California Press, 1992) is a good introduction to the operations of *keiretsu* groups.

An excellent introduction to the semi-popular *nihonjinron* literature that attempts to identify the unique characteristics of the Japanese is Kosaku Yoshino, *Cultural Nationalism in Contemporary Japan: A Sociological Inquiry* (London: Routledge, 1992). Japan has its own version of Sun Tzu, the legendary seventeenth-century swordsman Musashi Miyamoto, and his *Book of Five Rings* (*Go Rin no Sho*) has been recycled in the West in the same way as *The Art of War*; for instance, Donald G. Krause, *The Book of Five Rings for Executives: Musashi's Classic Book of Competitive Tactics* (London: Nicholas Brealey Publishing, 1999).

A good introduction to Japan's economic relations with other Asian countries is Mark Beeson, 'Japan and South-East Asia: the lineaments of quasi-hegemony', in Garry Rodan, Kevin Hewison and Richard Robison (eds), *The Political Economy of South-East Asia: Conflicts, Crises, and Change* (2nd edn, Melbourne: Oxford University Press, 2001). Kiyoshi Kojima, *Direct Foreign Investment: A Japanese Model of Multinational Business Operations* (London: Croom Helm Ltd. and New York: Praeger, 1978) argued that Japanese foreign investment was essentially altruistic, while Walter Hatch and Kozo Yamamura, *Asia in Japan's Embrace: Building a Regional Production Alliance* (Cambridge: Cambridge University Press, 1996) presented a more sinister picture. In addition to the direct role of Japanese foreign investment, firms in other Asian countries have sometimes attempted to adopt Japanese management techniques. See Raphael Kaplinsky and Anne Posthuma, *Easternization: The Spread of Japanese Management Techniques in Developing Countries* (Essex: Frank Cass, 1994).

The idea that Japanese firms would dominate the future world economy took fictional form in William Gibson's famous trilogy, *Neuromancer* (London: Grafton, 1986), *Count Zero* (London: Grafton, 1987) and *Mona Lisa Overdrive* (London: Grafton, 1989). In the early 1990s, Japan was frequently presented as a model for the West, for example by Robert Ozaki, *Human Capitalism: The Japanese Enterprise System as a World Model* (New York: Penguin Books, 1991) and Eisuke Sakakibara, *Beyond Capitalism: The Japanese Model of Market Economics* (Lanham: University Press of America, 1993). Others took a negative view, and many of them drew on Karel van Wolferen, *The Enigma of Japanese Power: People and Politics in a Stateless Nation* (New York: Alfred A. Knopf, 1989). 'Japan bashers' insisted that the Japanese did not play by the accepted international rules; for instance, Eamonn Fingleton, *Blindside: Why Japan is Still On Track to Overtake the U.S. by the Year 2000* (Boston: Houghton Mifflin, 1995). As the period of slow growth lengthened, works that emphasized the weaknesses of the Japanese system multiplied; for instance, John Woronoff, *Japan as Anything but Number One* (New York: Macmillan, 1991) and Richard Katz, *Japan: The System that Soured* (Armonk: M.E. Sharpe, Inc., 1998).

The process of reform and deregulation has been widely discussed. See Craig Freedman (ed.), *Economic Reform in Japan: Can the Japanese Change?* (Cheltenham and Northampton: Edward Elgar, in association with the Centre for Japanese Economic Studies, Macquarie University, Australia, 2001); Magnus Bloomstrom, Byron Gangnes and Sumner LaCroix (eds), *Japan's New Economy: Continuity and Change in the Twenty-First Century* (London: Oxford University Press, 2001); Kozo Yamamura and Wolfgang Streeck (eds), *The End of Diversity? Prospects for German and Japanese Capitalism* (Ithaca and London: Cornell University Press, 2003).

NOTES

1. Yoshino (1992).
2. Arnason (1997).
3. Denoon et al. (1997).
4. E.K. Tipton (2002), ch. 4; F.B. Tipton (2002), pp. 146–62.
5. Morris-Suzuki (1994), pp. 98–104.
6. Tsurumi (1990).
7. Yonekura (1994).
8. Morris-Suzuki (1994).
9. Ogura (2002).
10. Ibid., pp. 21–8.
11. Chandler (1966), p. 10.
12. Gordon (1985).
13. Tsurumi (1990).
14. Nestor (1991), p. 103.
15. Johnson (1982); Johnson (1987), pp. 134–64.
16. Wallich and Wallich (1976), pp. 249–316.
17. 'Xerox and Fuji Xerox', Harvard Business School Case 391-156 (1991), in Bartlett, Ghoshal and Birkinshaw (2004), p. 572.
18. Nestor (1991), pp. 103–7.
19. Weiss (1998), pp. 73–5.
20. Hein, in Gordon (1993), pp. 99–122.
21. Morita, with Reingold and Shimomura (1986).
22. Kahn (1971); Patrick and Rosovsky (1976); Vogel (1979).
23. Noguchi (1994), 291–330.
24. Australia, Department of Foreign Affairs and Trade, East Asia Analytical Unit (1999), pp. 29–33.
25. Stockwin (1999).
26. Leibfritz and Roseveare (1995), pp. 33–7.
27. Shimada (1994).
28. Mitchell (1996); McCormack (1996).
29. Mulgan (2002).
30. Porter, Takeuchi and Sakakibara (2000).
31. Dore (2001), p. 46. See Dore (1986).
32. Nakata (2004).
33. Gerlach (1992b), 79–118.
34. Ogura (2002).
35. Aoki (1994).
36. Gerlach (1992b), pp. 85–6.
37. Wallich and Wallich (1976).
38. Ogura (2002), p. 120.
39. Noguchi (1994).
40. Campbell and Hamao (1994), pp. 325–49.
41. Vitols (2003), pp. 257–8.
42. Gerlach (1992a), ch. 4.
43. Lincoln, Gerlach and Ahmadijian (1996), pp. 67–88.
44. Schrade (1994), 313–14. As Schrade points out, the customary six-year limit on a president's length of service interferes with quantitative attempts to measure Japanese firms' response to poor results, such as those by Kaplan (1994), 510–46; Kaplan and Minton (1994), 225–58.
45. Galenson and Odaka (1976), pp. 648–51.
46. Hofstede and Hofstede (2005), Table 4.1. In the subsequent replication studies, Japan's score was second only to Slovakia, and still much higher than any other Asian country.
47. Galenson and Odaka (1976), pp. 615–16; Tipton (2000), p. 216.

48. Nonaka and Takeuchi (1995).
49. See Spear and Bowen (1999), pp. 97–106.
50. Ishikawa (1990).
51. Lillrank (1995), 971–89.
52. Nonaka and Takeuchi (1995).
53. Cole (1994), p. 75.
54. Spear and Bowen (1999). See Kaplinsky (1997), 681–94.
55. Interview, 2003. The American informant continued, 'It didn't operate like a bank at all. It was more like a government agency.'
56. Chalmers (1989); Roberts (1994); Tipton (2000), pp. 216–17.
57. Coleman (1999).
58. Fama (1980), 288–307.
59. Kaplan (1994).
60. 'Mitsubishi runs out of gas', and 'Chronology of Mitsubishi complaints cover-up', *The Economist*, 25 March 2000.
61. Thelen and Kume (2003), pp. 193–4.
62. Tellzen (2005).
63. Okabe (2002), pp. 25, 70.
64. Miwa, Nishimura and Ramseyer (2002), pp. 197–9.
65. Ibison (2005).
66. Porter, Takeuchi and Sakakibara (2000).
67. Freedman and Blair (2003).
68. Pesek Jr. (2004), Bloomberg report.
69. Jackson (2003), pp. 261–305.
70. Isobe, Makino and Goerzen (2006).
71. Australia, Department of Foreign Affairs and Trade, Economic Analytical Unit (2002), vol. 2, pp. 1–20.
72. Pesek (2004).
73. Tsuchiya and Konomi (1997).
74. Kojima (1978), pp. 146, 148; Kojima (1985), 1–35.
75. Mason (1980), 42–52.
76. Hill (1990), 21–58; Hill (1994), 832–66.
77. Pasuk (1990).
78. Hatch and Yamamura (1996), p. 23.
79. Akamatsu (1962), 7–13.
80. Hatch and Yamamura (1996).
81. See Jomo (1994).
82. Taylor (2001), 601–620. This appears to be a general problem. In the United States, a class action suit by female workers cost Mitsubishi a reported US$34 million. 'Sex harassment case costs car maker $58m', *The Sydney Morning Herald*, 3 June 1998 (Bloomberg, Associated Press reports).
83. Hatch and Yamamura (1996).
84. Kawai and Takaji (2004), 255–80.
85. Organization for Economic Cooperation and Development, Development Assistance Committee (2004).
86. Tipton and Hundt (2006).
87. Hatch and Yamamura (1996).
88. Dauvergne (1997).

3. Managing with charismatic leadership in Korea

> Therefore measure in terms of five things . . . the Way, the weather, the terrain, the leadership, and discipline. . . . Leadership is a matter of intelligence, trustworthiness, humaneness, and sternness. (Sun Tzu, *The Art of War*)

> Ability to initiate and lead by example: comradeship and trust will emerge naturally when discipline and high standards are enforced. (Tao Zhu-gong, the Eleventh Business Principle)

If the key feature of Japanese management is the search for the Way, 'inducing the people to have the same aim as the leadership', then Korean governance leans toward leadership. As 'a matter of intelligence, trustworthiness, humaneness, and sternness', Korean leadership tends to be from the top down. Although they can be benevolent, Korean leaders have typically been autocratic, with a tendency towards sternness. The founders of most of South Korea's *chaebol* groups remained in control for three decades or longer, only passing on control to their successors in the 1980s or 1990s. They were initiators, and they led by example through the remarkable period of expansion.

The Korean 'system' grew out of the position of Korea in the Chinese world system in the nineteenth century, the opening of Korea and imperialist competition, and especially Korea's experience as a Japanese colony from 1910 to 1945. Following independence came the Korean War and the division of the country into North and South. President Park Chung Hee reoriented policy from import substitution to export orientation. Following Park, the centralized military regime yielded power to democratic popular movements, but the state also lost control over the economy. The resulting fluctuations, an inflationary boom, the crisis and collapse of 1997, the recovery and an opening to foreign investment, and the new tensions with North Korea leave South Korean managers facing an uncertain future.

Korea's institutional grid is marked by the close connections between *chaebol* executives and government officials. Government traditionally has exercised influence over business through the banking system, and this remains true even with the reforms and deregulation since 1997. The management grid in turn reflects the internal organization of *chaebol* groups. Their flexible, synergistic structures have produced remarkable successes, but Korean executives continue to grapple with problems of finance, planning, control, and succession. Charismatic leadership can work wonders in some situations, but it leaves a problematic legacy. Korea remains well down the product cycle compared to Japan. In most areas Korean firm competencies remain dependent on imported technologies, and Korean products typically must fit into value chains controlled by others. Indeed Korea has been called a case of 'development by invitation'.[1] Nevertheless, we also need to remember that, like Japan, South Korea is a large foreign investor, and these capital flows again are an important factor in Southeast Asia and China.

BOX 3.1 POINT AND COUNTERPOINT: THE KOREAN SYSTEM AS A SUCCESS STORY – PRESIDENT PARK AND 'KOREA, INC.'

The leader must be steady and calm; recklessness and rashness will lead to many errors and mistakes. (Tao Zhu-gong, the Sixteenth Business Lesson)

Park Chung Hee became President after leading a military coup in 1961. The army leaders purged potential opponents but also introduced reforms in government recruitment and examination systems. Their primary goal was to remain in power, but economic growth quickly became an important element in legitimating their position. Park said, in 1962, that 'the key factor in the May 16 Military Revolution was to effect an industrial revolution in Korea'. He told interviewers that he had consciously attempted to imitate the successful reforms of Japan in the Meiji period.

The new government adopted the proposal of a group of 'technocratic' or 'reform' bureaucrats to create a new 'super ministry' modeled on the Indian Planning Commission, which would combine centralized planning functions with control over the budget and inflows of foreign capital. The plan fitted with the desires of the army leaders to reinforce their control, and the proposal became the basis of the Economic Planning Board. With continued high-level support, the EPB developed a characteristic approach to problem areas, standardized weekly briefings, 'planning and control offices', and monthly and quarterly reports on the implementation and status of projects. These patterns spread from the EPB to other agencies.

From 1965 onward, President Park himself chaired monthly Export Promotion Meetings. Each meeting 'targeted' a sector or an industry. The meetings brought together relevant ministers, trade association leaders, and chief executives of major firms. With data provided by the EPB, plans and targets were assessed, and obstacles to export development identified and dealt with on the spot. Target areas received special treatment such as simplified regulations, preferential laws, or allocations of credit. The meetings kept bureaucrats 'on their toes' as well, because they were required to respond to criticisms from private firms, and to questions from Park. Favored firms received subsidies and indirect support, including cheap credit, tariff-free imports of raw materials and intermediate products, and tariff protection for their output. They also received access to foreign technology, and the capital to develop it. The government publicized export success, through citations, medals, and public ranking of firms according to their performance. South Korea celebrated an Annual Export Day from 1964.

President Park demanded results. Continued subsidies and protection in domestic markets were linked to export performance. Export targets were set for each sector and each firm, and they were monitored monthly by the EPB. Firms usually responded positively. Hyundai, for example, at first refused to enter the shipbuilding industry, but changed its mind after pressure by Park. The firm created a new shipbuilding subsidiary and launched two world-class tankers only 30 months after breaking ground in its new shipyard in 1973. From 1962 to 1986, Korean exports increased from US$55 million to US$35 billion.

Politically, Park could both continually reconstitute his alliances with business interests and extract resources from them. Economically, the system provided the basis for 'discipline' of the private sector in that productive investment was rewarded and poor performance was penalized. The collaboration between government and business had become so close that it seemed to some observers that the border between the public and private spheres had ceased to exist, and public and private actors had been 'rolled into one, into what one might term "Korea, Inc."'

Sources: Leroy Jones and Il Sakong, *Government, Business, and Entrepreneurship in Economic Development: The Korean Case* (Cambridge: Harvard University Press, 1980); Whee Yung Rhee, Bruce Ross-Larson and Garry

Pursell, *Korea's Competitive Edge: Managing Entry Into World Markets* (Baltimore and London: Johns Hopkins University Press for the World Bank, 1984); Alice H. Amsden, *Asia's Next Giant: South Korea and Late Industrialization* (Oxford: Oxford University Press, 1989); Stephan Haggard, Byung-Kook Kim and Chung-in Moon, 'The transition to export-led growth in Korea: 1954–1966', *Journal of Asian Studies* **50**(4) (1991), 850–73; Jung-en Woo, *Race to the Swift: State and Finance in Korean Industrialization* (New York: Columbia University Press, 1991). The phrase 'Korea, Inc.' – in reference to 'Japan, Inc.' – had been circulating since the late 1970s, for instance in 'Korea Inc. – volcano with a lid on', *Business Week*, 1 August 1977.

BOX 3.2 POINT AND COUNTERPOINT: THE KOREAN SYSTEM AS A FAILURE – DAEWOO, 1998

Do not be greedy for credit. (Tao Zhu-gong, the Eighth Business Pitfall)

The 1997 crisis transformed international opinion of the Korean system. Overwhelmingly external observers emphasized the need for reform. The *chaebol* groups were accused of 'inefficient investment' and of excessively close relations to government and to the banking system. New reporting, accounting, and auditing standards mandated by the government were applauded, but the groups' capacity to resist change was seen as a major hindrance to the transition to a more rules and market-based system.

The Daewoo group was founded in 1967 by Kim Woo-Choong, then in his late twenties, and 30 years later he was still its leader. The group had grown to be Korea's second largest *chaebol*. The Daewoo group ranked twenty-fourth on *Fortune* magazine's annual list of the world's 500 largest corporations in 1996. Its member firms had over 250000 employees and sales of over US$65 billion. Kim had become famous as 'the hardest working man in Korea'. Very demanding, he was also reputed to pay well. The group had a structure similar to other *chaebol*. Kim and his wife were involved in management, but the Kim family owned less than 2 per cent of the group companies' total equity. The Kims controlled their subsidiaries and affiliated firms through a pyramid of shareholdings and debt centered on Daewoo Corporation, a trading company that functioned as a holding company.

Kim's father had been one of President Park's schoolteachers. In 1976, Park placed Kim in charge of a state-owned machinery company that had lost money for decades. Kim, whose previous experience was limited to the clothing industry, worked around the clock, slept in his office in the plant, and within a year had produced a profit. With Park's support, Kim similarly acquired and then turned around a shipyard and an automobile firm. Daewoo continued to expand and to profit from its connections with the government, and especially from capital provided on preferential terms for its projects.

The group was highly diversified. Daewoo Motor and related automotive companies made up the core of the group. Daewoo Heavy Industry Co. included a variety of heavy machinery firms, and its shipbuilding unit was the world's second largest. Daewoo Electronics produced televisions, refrigerators, videocassette recorders, other home appliances, and flat panel computer monitors, in factories in the United States, France, Mexico, Spain, India, Vietnam, Malaysia, and other countries.

Kim pushed for growth. Aiming to become a world-class automobile producer, he opened plants well in advance of demand, but where there were also few competitors, in Vietnam, India, Iran, Poland, and the Ukraine. The joint venture in Uzbekistan in central Asia attracted worldwide attention, and was the subject of an admiring case presented at Harvard Business School. During the 1980s, Daewoo also established its own financial arms. By the late 1990s, the group owned Daewoo Securities, Korea Capital Corp., and Orient Investment, and indirectly influenced a number of other financial institutions through share ownership and personal relations with their management, such as its 9 per cent holding in KorAmBank, Korea's first joint venture commercial bank, which had opened in 1983. The group's total debt rose further, from already high levels, to nearly five times reported equity in 1997. 'To call it "related party lending" is putting it politely,' said one of the later investigators. 'Daewoo Securities was a piggy bank for the other companies.'

In retrospect Daewoo's strategy of expanding market share regardless of short-term profit had certainly led to growth, but it had also resulted in a complex and incoherent structure. Not everything succeeded as hoped. Some of the automobile plants could only sell at a loss. The group's weaknesses surfaced in the 1997 financial crisis. Daewoo Securities and other related financial institutions provided large amounts of additional credit, but interest on the group's debt began to spiral upwards out of control. Daewoo's outside creditors extended deadlines for payment, averting bankruptcy, but the core firms reported a loss of US$458 million on their

1998 revenues of US$51 billion, and the situation in fact was far worse, since a number of them had booked inflated values of sales of assets to other group members as income.

In August 1999, President Kim Dae Jung delivered a tough speech outlining the need for restructuring of the *chaebol*. He mentioned Hyundai, Samsung, LG, and SK, as well as Daewoo. President Kim vowed 'to become the first president in South Korean history to reform *chaebol*' and allow the economy to 'grow on the basis of the middle class'. Daewoo became a test case. The South Korean government needed to convince international creditors and potential investors that it was willing to disband Daewoo to prevent the debts becoming a burden on the economy. But Daewoo had already bid for troubled Ssangyong Motors and had also announced a 'big deal' to transfer its electronics division to Samsung. In addition Daewoo had already laid off large numbers of workers, and the government did not want a complete collapse of Daewoo that would increase unemployment and put further pressure on the banking system.

The government allocated further funds to the financial firms threatened by the collapse of Daewoo. Most of Daewoo's creditors by this point had themselves fallen under the control of the government. They were required to trade part of Daewoo's debt for equity in the group's member firms. The government also pressed Daewoo to sell assets to reduce its debt. Daewoo was to spin off its profitable affiliates so foreign investors could buy into them more easily, and the government made further funds available to prepare for the sales. Kim resisted, and his previously cordial and possibly even privileged relations with government officials deteriorated into shouting matches. Kim hoped to sell half of Daewoo Motors to United States automaker General Motors for US$7 to 10 billion. Negotiations had begun before the crisis in early 1997, and the two groups signed a preliminary agreement in February 1998, but they disagreed on the final price, and GM did not want the truck and bus plants. The deal collapsed. Fearing further layoffs, Daewoo workers went on strike.

In August 1999, the government took control of Daewoo's debts, a preliminary step to breaking up the group. In October, Kim failed to return from a trip to China, and disappeared. The government subsequently prosecuted a number of Daewoo's executives for fraud, but was not, apparently, especially eager to pursue the former chairman, who divided his time between Europe and Asia.

Sources: 'Daewoo's globalization: Uz-Daewoo Auto Project', Harvard Business School (1997); 'Daewoo hints of more to come', *Sydney Morning Herald*, 18 August 1999, *Los Angeles Times* Report; 'Loans ease Daewoo jitters', *The Sydney Morning Herald*, 27 July 1999, Blomberg Report; Mark Magnier, 'The octopus emperor who watched his house of cards collapse', *The Sydney Morning Herald*, 8 May 2001, *Los Angeles Times* report; Louis Kraar, 'Wanted', *Fortune* (Europe), **147**(2) (3 February 2003); Australia, Department of Foreign Affairs and Trade, Economic Analytical Unit, *Changing Corporate Asia: What Business Needs to Know* (2 vols; Canberra: EAU, 2002), vol. 2, pp. 43–4; Dong Gull Lee, 'The restructuring of Daewoo', in Stephan Haggard, Wonhyuk Lim and Euysung Kim (eds), *Economic Crisis and Corporate Restructuring in Korea: Reforming the Chaebol* (Cambridge and New York: Cambridge University Press, 2003), pp. 158–63.

THE HISTORICAL GRID

Korea in the Chinese World System

Until the middle of the nineteenth century China was the center of the Asian universe. International relations were hierarchical and depended on China's favor. Korea enjoyed substantial prestige because of its position as a power close to China's periphery. Japan in contrast was inferior because it was further away. The Western barbarians were not part of the system.

But from the perspective of the West and of Meiji Japan, Korea had become backward. In a world of competitive nation states, Korea had serious governmental and social weaknesses. The so-called era of 'in-law' government saw power alternate between factions allied with the ruling queen's family. The *yangban* aristocracy was generally intensely conservative. Korea was overwhelmingly agricultural, with no 'modern' industry and only limited protoindustrial handcraft development.

Korea repulsed foreigners in the late 1860s and early 1870s. Then the Japanese manufactured an incident and forced Korea to accept a trade treaty 'opening' the country in 1876. The Russians also expanded through Manchuria and into Korea. By the 1890s, the competition between Japan and Russia had led to outright hostility, and Japan attacked and defeated Russia in 1904–5. With the agreement of the Western powers, Japan then established a protectorate in 1905, and annexed Korea as a colony in 1910.

Some members of the Korean elite demonstrated an interest in banking. In 1896, the royal family founded the Chon-il Bank with the Crown Prince as president, in 1897, a group including a cousin of the king and senior government officials founded the Hansong Bank; and in 1905, a group of businessmen founded the Han'il Bank, with backing from the Queen's family. There were already extensive Japanese interests in Korea before formal annexation, with mining and manufacturing companies, an electric power company founded in 1898, and the Seoul–Pusan railroad, which opened in 1900. The Korean branch office of the Daiichi Bank served as a de facto central bank.[2] Outside the Japanese firms, there were only ten 'modern' industrial enterprises in Korea in 1903, six owned by Koreans and four owned by Chinese. Together they employed a total of 134 workers.[3]

Korea as a Japanese Colony, 1910–1945

The impact of Japanese imperialism in Korea is a sensitive topic. Korean scholars are often reluctant to see anything positive in the period of Japanese rule. There is obvious evidence of Japanese exploitation, but South Korea today is a developed economy. Even in the crisis of 1997–8, no one expected Korea to de-industrialize. At the very least, therefore, the Japanese did not destroy the potential for development, and there is evidence that Japanese policies laid the foundations for later growth.[4]

Once established, the Japanese colonial administration made efforts to win the support of the Korean elite. The Japanese pictured Koreans as Confucian younger brothers within the 'single body of Japan and Korea'. Some Koreans certainly profited.[5] Members of the Korean aristocracy used 'imperial gift bond' money granted to them by the Japanese to purchase shares in the Hansong Bank, and both the Hansong and Chon-il banks enjoyed substantial government subsidies.[6] Korean landlords retained their land, and wealthy Koreans used the new laws to gain more land. The Japanese land survey confirmed all landlords in their possession of land, restricted the rights of tenants to dispute ownership claims, and protected landlords against claims by tenants.[7] Specialists have shown the important role of native Koreans in industrial development during the period of Japanese rule. Japanese economic and social reforms 'actually enjoyed a wide base of Korean cooperation and support . . . even from the numerous groups bitterly opposed to the Japanese invasion'.[8]

What might have been the effects of Japanese colonialism on Korean entrepreneurship and business leadership? In his widely read survey, Byung-Nak Song, economist and senior advisor to the Korean government, says,

> The Japanese used Koreans mainly in lower positions in organizations. As a result, Koreans had few opportunities to accumulate experience as leaders, managers, or negotiators. Forced into a 'sergeant's' role, they developed a disgruntled sergeant's mentality. This legacy persists, and modern Korea needs badly the mentality of committed 'officers' or 'generals', self-sacrificing leaders, and risk-taking entrepreneurs and innovators.[9]

As seen below, this is not entirely the case. Some Korean entrepreneurs managed to develop large-scale commercial and industrial enterprises under the Japanese, and the most typical style of Korean manager has in fact been called the 'battlefield commander'. However, there were continuities. Some of Korea's leaders descended directly from traditional aristocratic classes. The entire bureaucracy and all of the army officers in South Korea had begun their careers under the Japanese. They were patriotic Koreans, but their solutions to problems had to be based on their experience and therefore tended to 'look' Japanese. In addition, all business leaders in the 1950s began their careers under the Japanese in the 1920s and 1930s, and most continued through the 1960s. Their children continued to lead Korean development in the next generation.

Colonial Korea grew. By the mid-1930s, output was twice as high as it had been a generation before. The share of industry in employment increased significantly, especially in the 1930s. That is, there was substantial growth and development, 'a break from the traditional pattern'.[10] The majority of large modern enterprises were Japanese, and the government discriminated against Korean enterprise. The Japanese thought Korean business should be confined to traditional economic activities, such as lacquerwares and foodstuffs. In 1921, the 1276 private Japanese industrial firms in Korea produced gross output worth 138 million yen, while 1088 Korean firms produced a total of only 24 million yen. In 1937, there were 2307 Korean-owned industrial plants that employed fewer than 50 workers, but only 14 with over 200 workers (nine in chemicals, four in textiles, and one in food processing). In 1944, among incorporated establishments, the 17 Korean firms had a total paid-up capital of 38 million yen, but the 195 Japanese firms a total of 1.3 billion yen.[11]

The Japanese of course managed their colonies for their own benefit, just as European powers and the United States did. Japanese perceptions of their needs changed as the structure of the Japanese economy changed, and colonial policies reflected these changes. In the early 1900s, Japanese leaders saw colonies as a way to improve Japan's balance of payments, as protected markets and sources of raw materials. Then rising food prices in Japan, culminating in the rice riots in 1918, caused Japanese leaders to see the colonies as sources of food. Programs to increase rice production were launched in the 1920s in both Taiwan and Korea. In Japan, farmers demanded tariffs on colonial agricultural products, but they were opposed by industrialists, who argued that tariffs would increase food prices and wages. The government compromised by abandoning agricultural investment programs in the colonies in 1934, which did not affect Taiwan, where the improvements were already in place, but which did hurt Korea.

The further growth of Japanese industry led to concern for sources of raw materials and for secure export markets, and finally, in the 1930s, the colonies played an important role in preparations for war. The Japanese attempted to develop basic strategic industries in each of the colonies. Industrial employment rose, beginning with large textile factories, but moving to machinery and engineering, and including aircraft. Employment in manufacturing industry in Korea increased from 586 000 in 1938 to 1.3 million in 1943.

Korea therefore avoided the dualistic or enclave development of other colonized areas. There was no plantation agriculture, and the Japanese invested heavily in transportation and communications, especially compared to the European and American colonial powers. Public health improved dramatically. Infant and child mortality declined substantially. Education expanded. There were 20 000 schoolchildren in Korea in 1910, 90 000 in 1920, and 901 000 in 1937. This was still only 17 per cent of school-age children and, since most of the increase came in the 1930s, the benefits would only be seen in the next generation, after independence; but it was a very substantial number.[12]

Despite the positive aspects of Japanese rule, Korean historians and economists insist that the incomes and living standards of Koreans actually declined: 'the well-being of the ordinary Koreans worsened in absolute terms. In other words, gross *domestic* product per capita increased remarkably, but gross *national* product per capita for Koreans actually decreased'. The export of rice to Japan is often cited as evidence of Japanese exploitation. The aggregate statistics show that, as rice production increased, exports increased even more rapidly, and Korean consumption actually fell.[13] Korean scholars also blame the Japanese for the large increase in tenancy. Taking over the property of the royal family and state, the Japanese colonial government emerged as the largest landowner, and held nearly 40 per cent of Korea's land area in 1930. Large tracts of land were sold to Japanese investors, who then often sold to Japanese farmers moving from Japan. However, as noted above, the vast majority of landlords continued to be Korean, and population growth and the depression of the 1930s were probably the most significant causes of the increase in tenancy.[14]

THE INSTITUTIONAL GRID

Independence, War and Division

There was continual Korean nationalist resistance to the Japanese. Though widespread, it was ineffective, partly because the leaders were regularly arrested or fled the country. But, as in Southeast Asia, the war meant the end of colonialism. On 15 August 1945, the Japanese asked the Korean nationalist leader Yo Un-hyong to establish an interim administration that would preserve order and protect the lives and property of Japanese citizens. Rather than acting as a figurehead as the Japanese hoped, he established an independent Committee for the Preparation of Korean Independence. Provincial branches of the Committee were formed within days, in two weeks there were already 145 branches covering most cities and towns, and within months 'people's committees' had taken control of local government throughout the country. On 6 September, a representative assembly met in Seoul and formed the Korean People's Republic.

The new government announced a land reform, under which the land of Japanese and the Korean 'national traitors' who had collaborated with them would be confiscated and redistributed to the tenants who worked it. In addition, the government proposed to nationalize mines, large-scale factories, railways, shipping, communications, and banks. Most of these were already owned or controlled by the Japanese colonial state or the *zaibatsu* groups. Small-scale industry and commerce would remain private, though subject to state supervision. The government also announced new minimum wages, an eight-hour day, and a prohibition of child labor.

The new government and its reformist policies enjoyed wide popular support,[15] but Korea became caught up in the new Cold War. In return for Soviet intervention in the war against Japan, the United States had agreed to Soviet occupation of Manchuria and Korea. However, the atomic bomb and Japan's surrender made an invasion of the Japanese home islands unnecessary, and the Americans now wanted to limit Soviet influence. They proposed a division of Korea along the 38th parallel, a line drawn on a small-scale map of Asia by an American army officer in Washington, because it divided the country more or less equally and placed Seoul in the proposed American zone of occupation in the south. The Soviets could have occupied the entire peninsula easily, but they accepted the American proposal.

The Soviets supported Kim Il Sung, a young man famous for his activities with communist guerillas in Manchuria in the 1930s, as leader of a national provisional government. The United States established a formal military occupation government in the South, refused to recognize the People's Republic or the local people's committees, and outlawed the labor union movement. At first they actually attempted to rule through Japanese colonial officials, but then appointed Koreans who had served in the Japanese colonial administration, often the very men who had been removed by the people's committees. As leader of a national provisional government the Americans favored Syngman Rhee (Yi Sung-man), who had lived in the United States and was known for his strongly anti-communist opinions.

By 1948, there were two separate Korean governments, the Republic of Korea in the south and the Democratic People's Republic of Korea in the north. The new South Korean government represented the interests of the property-owning classes, particularly the landlords. The land reform finally announced in March 1948 was confined to rental lands formerly owned by Japanese, about 20 per cent of the total. In the meantime, strikes led to mass demonstrations protesting the policies of the occupation government. United States troops and the new Korean National Police (many of whom were former Japanese police officials) repressed the protests and then moved against the people's committees. The brutal assault on the last committees on Cheju Island in 1949 killed tens of thousands and destroyed three-quarters of the villages on the island.[16]

In 1950, North Korea attacked the South. Veterans who had served in the Chinese civil war, and equipment obtained from the Soviet Union, gave the north the advantage. They pushed far to the south, but the United States, acting on the basis of a United Nations resolution, intervened and drove the northern forces back to the Yalu River. Chinese forces then attacked and they and the North Koreans advanced to the south again, only to be pushed back in turn, to a stalemate along the 38th parallel. A truce was finally signed in 1953. Military and civilian deaths in the south totaled 1.3 million, and have been estimated in the north at 1.5 million out of a population only one-half that of the south. Seoul changed hands four times. American air raids destroyed Pyongyang and other northern cities.

In the aftermath both countries moved in authoritarian directions. Kim established a personal dictatorship that resembled the cult surrounding Mao Zedong in China. He remained in power to his death in 1995, and was succeeded by his son Kim Jong-il. In the south, Rhee organized a new Liberal Party in 1951 and won elections through police surveillance and harassment of opponents, fraud, and violence. Following the war it became more difficult to manipulate elections and, in 1956, despite the death of his major opponent, Rhee received only 55 per cent of the vote, and his vice-presidential candidate was defeated.

This was the period of the 'import-substitution' strategy in South Korea, but the policy was neither coherent nor consistent. The government controlled foreign exchange, bank credit, import licenses, many former Japanese industrial enterprises, and extensive Japanese landholdings, and the constitution gave the state the right to transfer ownership of private corporations to public ownership or to place their management under public supervision, 'when it is deemed urgently necessary'. In fact, Rhee simply distributed favors to his supporters, and they then recycled a share of their gains to government officials, the Liberal Party, and individual politicians. United States aid was a special plum, and the Liberal Party was estimated to have a direct interest in half of all projects receiving aid in 1960.[17] The results were not promising: 'even in 1960, after the damage

inflicted during the war had been repaired . . . few, if any, observers held
out much hope of improvement for Korea's poverty-stricken economy'.[18]

Emergence of the *Chaebol*

The origins of the *chaebol* are disputed. Some observers emphasize the
postwar period, and the distribution of former Japanese firms to friends of
President Rhee. Others argue that prewar Korean enterprise showed many
of the same features as postwar *chaebol*, and that there were direct continuities from the colonial era.[19] There are three well-known examples, the
Min family in the financial sector, Pak Hung-sik's commercial empire, and
the Kim family in the textile industry.

Min Yong-hwi (1852–1935) was a viscount. Appointed to the board of
Hanil Bank in 1912, he became its president in 1915, and turned it over to
his son Min Tae-sik (1882–1951) in 1920. The Mins continued their large
shareholdings in Hanil and its successor Tongil Bank through the 1930s
and into the war years. But the Japanese colonial administration wanted to
control banking, so Hanil and other Korean banks remained small and
highly regulated. A merger in 1931 and a final takeover in 1943 were forced
through by the colonial government.

The Mins' interests show a pattern that was standard for Korean businesses in the colonial period:

1. Firstly, an inner core of family-owned companies. The Mins were
    active in agriculture, real estate, and textile manufacturing.
2. Secondly, major investments with executive responsibility in joint-
    stock enterprises. In addition to their interest in Tongil Bank, the Mins
    were involved in a silk-weaving firm.
3. Thirdly, smaller investments in a number of medium-sized Korean
    firms, but without executive commitments.
4. And, finally, participation in major Japanese investments in Korea. In
    the Mins' case this was helped by their credibility as aristocrats and
    leaders in banking.[20]

Following the war and independence, both Min Tae-sik and his eldest
son Min Pyong-do were among the circle of business leaders around
President Rhee in the late 1940s and early 1950s.

Pak Hung-sik, born in 1903, was an outsider from the north, but not
poor. Family landholdings formed the base for local printing and cotton
investments. Pak moved to Seoul in 1926, where he established Sonil Paper
Goods. Success in this venture was followed by investment in Hwasin
Department Store. The expansion of consumer markets across Korea

provided new opportunities. Hwasin made use of the extensive railway and postal systems to deliver goods to affiliated stores throughout Korea. In 1936, Hwasin Chain Stores had 350 stores throughout Korea. The firm's speed, efficiency, and good financial controls allowed it to compete successfully with both Korean and Japanese department stores.

Pak was a salesman and promoter. In an advertisement for Hwasin he claimed to have established 'commercial Korea'. His interests expanded to wholesaling, retailing, and trading ventures in China and Southeast Asia. He opened a purchasing office in Osaka in 1932 that gave him access to suppliers in Japan. Pak enjoyed close connections with government officials. The Governor-General recommended him for a paper company board, and he was appointed to a Japanese Commission on the Japanese Industrial Economy and attended their meeting in Tokyo in 1942. In business it helps to be a bit lucky as well. Hwasin's ability to extend credit to retail stores without interest was attributed to Pak's purchase of gold and silver just before the embargo on precious metals imposed in December 1931. Pak's portfolio resembled the Mins, though with distinctive features:

1. At the center were closely held and managed interlocking companies. Pak's core enterprises were Sonil Paper, Hwasin Department Store, a construction company, and a real estate firm. The capital came from a small circle of 'friendly' investors, including the Min family. Pak's nephew Pak Pyong-gyo held shares and served on the boards of Hwasin enterprises, and became head of Hwasin in 1946. There were no other immediate male relatives in management, but all of the related companies were run by the same close group of associates.
2. Pak had no second level of joint ventures with management responsibilities. This may have reflected his lack of contracts in Seoul, or the time commitments of his core firms.
3. Like the Mins, Pak had extensive investments in Korean firms without executive involvement. In Pak's case this included especially participation in Korean banks, an attempt to develop independent sources of capital.
4. Pak also participated in large Japanese investments, in real estate and wholesale trade, complementary to his core firms. He was also named to directorships in large Japanese firms, and became president of Chosen Aircraft in 1944.

Pak was prosecuted for 'antinationalist crimes' and jailed in 1948, but he was then acquitted, and like the Mins he belonged to Rhee's circle of business leaders. Hwasin was one of South Korea's leading trading companies in the 1950s. Pak skillfully reoriented its business away from China and towards Hong Kong. He remained unrepentant about his past. When questioned about his 1942 visit to Tokyo, he said it had been an invitation from the Emperor, and it was a chance to meet 'three thousand members of the Tokyo Chamber of Commerce'. Hwasin was again prosecuted for 'illicit accumulation' in 1961.

The story of Kim Yon-su (1896–1979) is probably the best-known example of Korean entrepreneurship.[21] The Kim family's Kyongsong Spinning and Weaving Company was the largest Korean manufacturing firm of the colonial period. The Kims were a wealthy landowning family in 1900, though not aristocrats like the Mins. Kim Yon-su was educated in Japan. He became managing director and then president of Kyongsong Spinning. Samyang Investment Company, based on the family landholdings, became the largest Korean agricultural development company, with land in Manchuria as well as Korea. The firm received subsidies from the government for land reclamation projects. The model of the state supplying capital for development was a pattern that persisted, but in this case it was the Japanese colonial state supplying capital to a Korean-owned firm.

Because it spread across both land and industrial development, the Kims' portfolio was quite diversified:

1. The inner core included a range of manufacturing enterprises.
2. The second level of joint ventures with executive responsibility included firms in both Korea and Manchuria, especially Kyongsong Spinning. The Kims' attempt to establish an independent bank failed, prefiguring the later failure of the *chaebol* to free themselves from dependence on the state for finance.
3. Investments in Korean firms without executive responsibility included silk, engineering, and a gold mining company.
4. The Kims also participated in Japanese firms, including the government printing company, petroleum, hydroelectric power, and railway firms.

Kim Yon-su resigned as president of Kyongsang in December 1945, and leadership was taken over by Kim Yong-wan, his brother-in-law. Kim Yon-su was prosecuted for 'antinationalist crimes' and jailed in 1948, but he too was acquitted and also appeared among Rhee's circle of business leaders. Kyongsang prospered under the republic, with strong support from Samyang Investment, which also continued. Land reform meant the firm had to redirect its capital into trade and light industrial production, for instance sugar and salt. Yon-su's son Kim Sang-hung was prosecuted and convicted of 'illicit accumulation' in 1961.

Other younger men also rose during war and then survived and prospered in the postwar period. Best known is probably Lee Byung-chull, who founded Samsung in 1937, and he was another among the circle of business leaders around President Rhee.

Government and Business

The *chaebol* expanded under Rhee.[22] In the case of the textile industry, important as the first modern industry in all industrializing countries, laws passed in 1954 and 1955 closed the Korean market to foreign cotton textiles. American firms complained of 'harassment' of foreign businesses. State controls over foreign trade ensured that domestic producers had access to raw materials, but foreign firms could not obtain them. Japanese firms were first taken over by the state, and then sold to private interests, who also received government grants to restore plants and upgrade technology. The government sold state-owned banks to insiders such as Lee Byung-chull, but directed their lending to preferred customers, and also controlled the distribution of foreign aid from the United States.

The Rhee government fell in 1959, following student protests and riots. The succeeding unstable government was ousted by a coup, the 'military revolution' of 16 May 1961. Park Chung Hee emerged as the leader, won a narrow victory in a referendum, and reestablished nominal civilian rule with himself as President in 1964. As President he had the power to select the cabinet and Prime Minister, and controlled the judiciary, the press, and public meetings. A Political Party Law restricted political organizations and weakened all parties, including the ruling party.

The new government accused business leaders of 'illicit' acquisition of wealth. Over 120 businessmen were investigated following the coup. A few, including Samsung's Lee Byung-chull, spent time in prison. However, despite the widespread hostility to big business, some military leaders argued that the government needed the support of business leaders to keep the economy functioning. The result was a compromise. About 30 major industrialists were forced to 'refund' their 'illicit' wealth, but were found officially to have gained much smaller amounts 'illicitly' than initially thought.

Most of the businessmen who had profited under Rhee escaped punishment and indeed continued their privileged connection with the government. However, Park told the leaders of the large corporations that their property was not their own, but really belonged to the nation. He admonished them to be frugal in their lifestyle, and to reinvest their profits. Lee, released from prison, pledged his skills to Korea's future development. He was instrumental in founding the Federation of Korean Industries in 1961.[23] Korea's business leaders began to cultivate reputations for dedication and hard work. A generation later, in the mid-1990s, they had become 'battlefield commanders', living legends who slept in their factories, solved problems personally at the work site, and embodied the Korean 'can-do' attitude.[24] A public dispute erupted over the question of whether any Korean business executives should be seen playing golf.

One way for a country to avoid dependence on foreign capital and move toward autonomous development is for the government to sponsor the introduction of advanced technologies.[25] Korea is a frequently cited example. Government planners attempted to guide investment through sequential stages, from textiles and food processing to petrochemicals, ship-building, and electrical machinery (the 'heavy and chemical industries' or 'HCI' drive) in the 1970s, and to consumer electronics, automobiles, personal computers, and microelectronics in the 1980s. There were some spectacular failures, but the government made good the losses. A number of large firms were bailed out of difficulties, and from the early 1970s onward bankruptcy was virtually unheard of among the *chaebol*.[26]

The government attempted to ensure that Korean firms would have access to basic semi-manufactured intermediate produces on favorable terms. This was the logic of the HCI drive. It had also motivated the government's determination to establish a major steel-producing facility. Ignoring the explicit recommendation of the World Bank, which argued that it was 'premature' for Korea to build a large steel plant, in 1968 the government pushed ahead with the foundation of what became Posco, arguably the world's most successful steel company. The funds came from loans granted by the Japanese government, and the technology came from Shin Nippon Steel, also the mentor of China Steel in Taiwan and Bao Steel Company in China. For four decades the firm has ensured that Korea's shipbuilding, automobile, construction, and electronics industries will have the steel products they need on favorable terms. Owned by the government (30 per cent directly, 40 per cent by the government-owned Korea Development Bank, and the remaining 30 per cent by private commercial banks controlled by the government), Posco had a near monopoly on the Korean domestic market until 1996, when Hyundai was granted permission to build a steel plant, reportedly as a reward to Chung Moon-joon, one of the founder's sons, head of Hyundai's shipbuilding division, and president of the Korea Football Foundation and FIFA vice-president, for his success in securing the 2002 World Cup for Korea.[27]

The government also encouraged acquisition of new technologies by Korean firms rather than encouraging direct investment by foreigners. Of all the Korean firms that adopted foreign technologies, only 6.5 per cent did so through investment by foreigners. The others, with government support, paid foreign firms to license technology, hired foreign technicians, trained their own staff, or reverse-engineered imported machinery.[28] Except for designated export processing zones, which were isolated from the Korean market, foreign investors were forced into joint ventures with Korean partners. Foreigners could not purchase land for business purposes, and zoning laws were used to reduce their options even further. Those foreigners that did attempt to enter Korean markets found the regulatory regime arbitrary and opaque.[29] A number of sectors were completely closed to foreigners, in particular the financial sector, where foreigners were not permitted even to offer consulting services. Corporate governance rules favored major shareholders, as did the rules on cross-shareholdings and loan guarantees among subsidiary firms. The government in effect blocked hostile takeovers of any sort, and again the impact was to exclude foreigners.[30]

Park's 'Korea, Inc.' rested on the supply of capital. The military government at first nationalized the banks, and through the 1970s government agencies controlled about two-thirds of all investment funds. Although the banks returned to private ownership, the government controlled the appointment of their chief executive officers, and directed them to lend in preferred areas. Direct allocations, credit rationing, and differential interest rates channeled investment in the direction selected by the government. The government permitted, and in effect guaranteed, the loan guarantees made by members of *chaebol* groups to other members, which allowed the groups to leverage equity in one subsidiary to support another. The government also controlled foreign exchange and therefore controlled access to foreign raw materials, components, and technology. Beginning in 1963, the government guaranteed loans by Korean companies from foreign banks, and the amount of foreign capital borrowed by the *chaebol* rose from 2.2 billion won in 1962 to nearly 70 billion won in 1966.[31]

The interest rates paid by the companies favored by the government were below the rate of inflation in most years from the 1950s through the 1970s. Not surprisingly these firms exploited their position, and borrowed. In the mid-1980s, the average debt to equity ratio for all *chaebol* was over 5 to 1. Hanjin, the seventh largest group, had a debt to equity ratio of 14 to 1. The additional profits gained by the 50 largest groups from the distorted capital market were estimated to equal over US$5 billion in 1980, more than half their total net value.[32]

As seen above, Park demanded and received high levels of performance. Korean executives later said that it was simply unthinkable not to comply with his wishes, and they said that one of the most important traits of successful business leaders was 'a sense of calling for development of the nation'.[33] Park forced the pace of technological change, particularly in export industries. Business leaders had to prove themselves to Park, and they were forced to compete with each other for government favor. From the perspective of the early 1990s it seemed to many observers that, although it might appear to be a contradiction, 'state power and political insulation proved important for achieving a more market-conforming strategy'.[34]

In the late 1980s, the government pressed the *chaebol* to reduce their debt, but without success. Partial deregulation of the financial sector allowed the *chaebol* to own shares in banks and other financial institutions. As seen above, in Box 3.2, Daewoo created its own financial subsidiaries and invested in banks to gain preferential access to credit, and the other groups did so as well. It appears that *chaebol* leaders believed themselves to be 'too big to fail', and continued to borrow on the assumption that the government would save them should they ever encounter difficulties. In such a situation analysts worry about moral hazard, because, if capital is always available, firms can discount the danger of losses, and bad decisions can be covered by more borrowing.

The *chaebol* earned very low returns on their assets, well below West Germany and the United States, and lowest among nine leading Asian economies. During the boom before the collapse of 1997 and 1998 their return on equity actually declined. External observers attributed this to their easy access to credit. Easy money, it was said, had allowed the *chaebol* to expand and diversify beyond their core competencies. The 30 largest groups owned an average of 20 subsidiaries spread across a broad range of sectors, with few complementarities. Although the aggregate size of the top *chaebol* was very large indeed, many of the subsidiary firms were quite small by international standards. Even among the larger groups, in the mid-1990s, Samsung Electronics' sales were 11.6 per cent of those of IBM, and Samsung Chemicals' sales only 3.7 per cent of those of Dupont. Many of the smaller *chaebol* firms would not have been competitive without the support of their group, especially capital provided on very easy terms.[35]

But the *chaebol* leaders get some credit too. In aggregate terms, Korea's productivity rose relatively rapidly, and there are numerous examples of successful innovation and competence building.[36] *Chaebol* needed rapid growth and continual diversification to maintain their relative position. They sought new opportunities and seized them. They attempted to move into each successive stage as an industry's technology evolved. They used the profits generated by low-end manufacturing to develop their own technological capabilities and reduce their dependence on foreign technology. Their diversified structure and centralized decision-making processes made it easier to undertake risky new projects.[37] As a result Korea did move up the product cycle. The domestic content of Korean videocassette recorders, for instance, rose from 55 per cent in 1982 to 80 per cent in 1988.[38] In one of Korea's most famous success stories, in 1983, Lee Byung-chull in effect bet the future of his Samsung group on his decision to manufacture computer memory chips. When world prices collapsed in 1985, Samsung faced devastating losses. Lee and Samsung were saved, not by their own efforts or even by the efforts of their government, but by an agreement between the United States and Japan that placed a floor under the price of chips while restricting Japanese exports to United States markets. This left Samsung ideally placed to satisfy a new upsurge in demand from American computer makers.[39]

Democratization

South Korea has been a very repressive state. Park justified authoritarian rule by an appeal to 'Asian' values. In 1971, he said, 'Asian peoples want to obtain economic equality first and build a more equitable political machinery afterward.'[40] In fact, however, there was widespread discontent. When Park was assassinated in 1979, protests broke out across the country. Then, in 1980, another military coup placed Chun Doo Hwan in the presidency. The government imposed martial law and arrested opposition leaders. In the southwestern city of Kwangju, paratroopers fired on the crowds of protesters, killing at least 240 and injuring over 1600.

Chun said that 'order' could only be based on 'Korean values'. He identified the 'good aspects' of Confucianism as the basis of Korean culture, especially 'discipline' and 'public interest', and argued that Koreans needed to maintain discipline in the name of economic development and national security in order to uphold their 'traditional' values. The bad things were 'foreign':

> The prevalence of toadyism, a blind admiration for all things foreign, a pervasive notion that money is everything, unbridled egoism and the like is indicative that for some, at least, spiritual and cultural interests have taken a back seat to monetary ones. We must rectify perversion and confusion in values . . . only then can a new era be forged.[41]

Chun ruled until 1988. Growth continued, but without Park, Korea, Inc. did not seem to work as efficiently.[42] Under pressure from political dissidents and economic reformers, in June 1987 the government conceded the major demands of the opposition including direct presidential elections, amnesty for dissident leader Kim Dae Jung and others, local autonomy, free speech, and freedom for political parties.

One of Chun's supporters, Roh Tae Woo, won the ensuing elections and became president of the new 'sixth republic'. Roh's regime has received credit for transforming Korea from an authoritarian military system into a constitutional democracy.[43] However, public criticism intensified. A slowdown in economic growth caused dissatisfaction, labor unrest and public protests spread, and dissidents complained of pervasive corruption in the relations between government and business.

In 1993, Kim Young Sam, 'Mr. Clean', a former dissident and reformer, became the first non-military president in 30 years. In late 1995, Chun and Roh were arrested for their role in the 1980 coup and subsequent corruption. The indictment also accused several business leaders of paying bribes, including Choi Won Sok of the Dong Ah group and Kim Woo-Choong of Daewoo. Chung Tae-soo admitted that his Hanbo group, which had risen from obscurity in 1988 to become one of the top 20 *chaebol* on the basis of major public works contracts, had paid huge bribes to President Roh, and Hyundai patriarch Chung Ju Yung said he too had made regular 'gifts' to Roh. Kim Dae Jung, now a contender for the presidency, also admitted accepting large sums from Roh. President Kim Young Sam was accused of taking money from Roh as well, and when the Hanbo group went bankrupt in January 1997 13 of his aides were charged with having continued to accept bribes from the firm. Kim Dae Jung won the presidential elections in 1997, but by the time he took office Korea had been overtaken by the Asian crisis, and Kim found himself forced to implement an austerity program dictated by the International Monetary Fund and other international agencies.

Structural Problems

As noted above, from 1962 to 1986, Korean exports increased from US$55 million to US$35 billion. However, imports also rose, from US$442 million to US$35 billion. Until 1980, imports consistently exceeded exports, and the deficit was financed by an accumulating international debt, which had reached US$40 billion in the mid-1980s. The subsequent trade surpluses of the late 1980s resulted from lucky circumstances, the 'three lows' of low interest rates, low oil prices, and a low exchange rate of the won to the yen and dollar. In the early 1990s, although some industries had reduced their dependence on foreign technologies, others remained confined to the low end of their markets. As the democratization process enabled workers to agitate and strike for higher wages, these firms found themselves struggling against competitors in other countries with lower labor costs.[44]

State intervention favored firms that satisfied the government's demand for increased exports. Even under Park some of the most successful had done so, not by improving technology, but by importing components for assembly. The government rewarded firms with the highest volume of exports, not necessarily those with the highest value added. Therefore exporters did not have any particular incentive to invest in plants that manufactured parts and intermediate products, which would have required large and long-term investment in capital, technical resources, and training. Rather, they collected the bonuses available from the government by importing parts and assembling products for export. In some cases large firms bought up the orders and sales of smaller companies at a premium simply to ensure that they were ranked number one in their industry.[45]

The government attempted to take advantage of international markets while at the same time pursuing policies that would minimize dependence on those markets. Domestic markets for successful exporters and for consumer goods were always protected. There were tariffs and a range of non-tariff barriers ranging from quotas to health and safety regulations. An 'import source diversification policy' blocked imports from Japan in particular.[46] Hoping to reduce food imports, the government virtually forced the adoption of new rice varieties despite scientific doubts and the opposition of Korean farmers.[47] The 'heavy and chemical industries' (HCI) drive of the 1970s, an attempt to 'skip stages' of technological development, required huge investments in the target industries. It led to closer links between government and *chaebol* groups, and a higher level of direct intervention in the economy. Critics at the time and since have insisted that the program led to serious misallocations of investment resources, and the tendency to favor a few of the largest groups created a situation where those groups became 'too large to fail'.[48] In addition, borrowing to finance HCI projects contributed to the financial weakness of some of the *chaebol* in the 1980s.

Korea became a dual economy. Large private enterprises and certain regions benefited. In the early 1990s, five of the six largest *chaebol* groups, which together produced some 50 per cent of South Korea's national product, were located in the southeast. Many government leaders came from the southeastern districts of North and South Kyongsong and Taegu. In the 1980s, over 40 per cent of high-level government officials had been born here, far more than would be expected on the basis of population, and they fostered the growth of their home region.[49]

In addition, under the Park regime, small- and medium-sized enterprises did not receive preferential loans or other forms of government support. In the early 1960s, these smaller firms accounted for nearly 80 per cent of employment in mining and manufacturing, and 65 per cent of value added. Their share declined to 40 per cent of employment and 25 per cent of value added in 1973. This changed with the regime change in 1979–80. In 1982, revisions to the Banking Act imposed limits on the share of any individual bank's lending to *chaebol* groups, measures intended to re-direct bank lending to SMEs, but also to agriculture and fisheries. The share of bank loans to SMEs and their share of industrial output both rose through the mid-1990s. Small firms may have become relatively more profitable during this period. A comparative study reported higher rates of profitability for *chaebol* firms than for non-*chaebol* firms in the years 1975 to 1984, but data for the 1985–96 period show *chaebol* firms to have been less profitable than independent firms.[50] However, because of their dependence on bank loans, in 1997 and 1998 many small firms found themselves in even worse difficulties than *chaebol* members.[51]

THE MANAGEMENT GRID[52]

Planning and Decision making, Organizing, Leading and Controlling in the *Chaebol*

The 'Korean style' or 'K-type management' includes the notion of business leaders as 'battlefield commanders' but also as patriots with 'a sense of calling for development of the nation'. In addition successful Korean managers show superior 'network-building ability' and a commitment to 'an endless development of technology'. Above all, however, they show 'respect for employees' and especially the 'spiritual care of employees' and 'achievement of a community oriented concept'.[53] Many argue that the distinctive traits of Korean managers derive from Confucian tradition. It is said that Korean society is particularly Confucian in its conservatism, emphasis on hierarchy, and group orientation. Korean firms are held to embody these Confucian values, with father-like authority figures at the top, and self-sacrificing workers who labor for the good of the firm.[54]

The expressed values of Korean business executives are not always consistent. At the same time, many Korean managers have studied in the United States, most Korean firms have formal mission statements, most recruit on an open competitive basis, most have quite precise formal job classifications and descriptions, and many employ some form of quantified measurement of employee performance, commonly a variation on management by objectives. That is, many and possibly most Korean firms 'look' very Western. But, it is said, looks can be deceiving. 'We talk the talk, Western-style', said one executive, 'but we walk the walk, Confucian-style.'[55]

In their structure the *chaebol* can be compared with the prewar Japanese *zaibatsu*, but there are important differences. Like the *zaibatsu*, *chaebol* are family-controlled, pyramid-shaped groups. The owner family's direct equity shares in group firms can be quite low, less than 10 per cent for the largest groups in 1994, for instance. The 1987 Fair Trade Law restricted cross-shareholdings, but these indirect shareholdings still amounted to 38 per cent, so the owner families in fact controlled nearly half of the equity of all member firms.[56] There has frequently been a flagship firm that acts as a holding company, but legal restrictions mean that its role is typically obscured. Samsung Everland, for instance, is an unlisted company that operates an amusement park. Almost wholly owned by the Lee family, in 1999 Samsung Everland owned over 20 per cent of Samsung Life Insurance, which in turn owned stakes in at least nine other major firms. Among them was Samsung Electronics, which in its turn had controlling interests in a range of companies, including specialized electronics firms, but also Samsung Card (59 per cent) and Samsung Finance (73 per cent).[57]

In contrast to Japan, as seen above in Korea, finance has usually been directly controlled by the government, both under Japanese rule before 1945 and under the republic through the 1980s. Whereas the *zaibatsu* each owned their own bank, Korean groups struggled to found banks under the colonial regime. The Rhee government allowed favored *chaebol* groups to purchase shares in privatized banks in the 1950s. Samsung gained control of Hanil Bank in 1957, Commercial Bank of Korea in 1958, and Chohung Bank of Korea in 1959. Following the 1961 coup, the government nationalized the banks again. Samsung lost its three banks as Lee Byung-chull was charged with corruption, but in 1963 Samsung took over Tongbang Life Insurance Company 'for its continuous financial purposes'.[58] The changes in the law in the 1980s restricted bank lending to the *chaebol*, but also allowed *chaebol* to develop their own financial arms, as with Daewoo or the cases of Samsung Card and Samsung Finance. With the effective renationalization of the banks, as seen below, the government has once again regained control over the financial system.

In addition the notion of a 'family' firm differs from that of Japan. In Korea, inheritance has been guided very strictly by blood. Pre-colonial *yangban* aristocrats might have several wives or concubines, but only the eldest son of the senior wife, who had to be of equal aristocratic status to her husband, could inherit. Even younger sons of the senior wife could be shut out, and sons of junior wives could not inherit. These inheritance practices were reinstituted following independence. In further contrast to Japan, Korea has no widespread tradition of adoption. The narrow notion of family based strictly on blood ties and inheritance based strictly on primogeniture carries over into the *chaebol*.[59] Although there are cases of in-laws who have become active in senior management, in general managers who are not family members cannot be 'adopted' and do not achieve ownership positions. Yoo Keun Shin says bluntly that 'CEO in Korea means owner–manager who founded the company or the founder's descendants.'[60]

In a further contrast to the prewar *zaibatsu*, in the *chaebol* family members tend to take active managerial roles. Chung Ju Yung's three brothers and seven sons (the 'seven princes') managed a total of 32 of the operating companies in the Hyundai group in the early 1980s. Samsung was one of first *chaebol* to adopt open competitive recruiting in 1957, and only a few of its senior executives are members of the owner family. But in the 1980s the group included companies headed by two sons, two daughters, a daughter-in-law, and a father-in-law of founder Lee Byung-chull. His third son, Lee Kun Hee, succeeded him when he died, and in the mid-1990s his second son and two sons-in-law continued to hold top executive positions as well.[61]

Rapid growth created a need for additional managers. By the late 1980s, 30 to 40 per cent of Korean *chaebol* executives came from outside the firm, compared to 10 per cent or less for large Japanese firms. Nevertheless, 31 per cent of the senior executives in the top 20 *chaebol* groups belonged to the owner families.[62] Further, in general as the size of the *chaebol* increased, the share of the owner family in senior executive positions declined, but the percentage of ownership by the family rose. That is, smaller *chaebol* owned a smaller fraction of their subordinate firms, but exercised more direct managerial control.[63] Therefore the *chaebol* are 'entrepreneurial' or 'family' firms in the literal sense, and moreover they have been firms that show a preference for very direct control.

Again in comparison to Japan, almost by definition, this sort of firm does not use group decision making. Authority in the *chaebol* derives from family ownership, and this carries with it the right to overrule subordinates. Decisions do not emerge from the lower levels of the company, but are imposed from the top. This means the *chaebol* avoid the possible disadvantages of group decision making, and can react swiftly and decisively to opportunities or threats as they arise. Synergies result from sharing of technology and human resources across the groups, from the creation of an internal pool of capital, and from the creation of a common brand.[64]

However, the *chaebol* lose the advantages of group decision making and the potential benefits of horizontal sharing of information. 'Bottom-up and lateral communications are consistently promoted only to fail.'[65] 'The boss does not want to hear alternate views,' said one executive. Lee Byung-chull moved into the semiconductor industry despite opposition from government officials and his own executives, and, as seen above, was saved only by a lucky shift in world markets. In 1994, he decided to take Samsung into the automobile industry. A collector of automobiles, he wanted to build them as well. In a period of intense competition and consolidation in the world automobile industry, the likelihood of success was small, and Lee again was warned of the risks, but pressed ahead with technology acquired from the Japanese firm Nissan. Samsung member firms, and many individual Samsung executives and employees, purchased shares in Samsung Motors, but Lee himself did not, apparently because he was reluctant to invest in a company that would lose money for several years. In 1999, Samsung Motors went into receivership, and although Lee himself was not held responsible, the investors all lost their money. The operating efficiencies of the group in effect had been cancelled by a failure of strategic decision making. As Sea-Jin Chang concludes, 'Samsung failed not because its individual affiliates failed to create synergies but because the decision to enter the automobile industry was wrong.'[66]

The process of planning involves identification of the firm's mission, setting of goals, formulation of plans, attainment of goals, and feedback into the next cycle. A mission statement identifies the firm's purpose or its fundamental reason for existence. However, although an entrepreneurial or family-owned firm may have a mission statement, it will not in fact identify the fundamental reason for the firm's existence. For example, Samsung's statement of the group's 'vision and philosophy' reads,

What makes SAMSUNG one of the world's leading companies?
How we got here
Ever since it was founded in 1938, SAMSUNG has continually refined its mission statement to respond both to change in itself and in the world: 'Economic contribution to the nation,' 'Priority to human resources,' 'Pursuit of rationalism.' Each slogan represents significant moments in SAMSUNG's history, reflecting different stages of the company's growth from a domestic industrial leader into a global consumer electronics powerhouse.
In the 1990s, we once again acknowledged the need to transform our mission statement to keep pace with our growing global operations, rapid changes in the world economy, and escalating competition from well-established rivals.
Our Management Philosophy
'We will devote our human resources and technology to create superior products and services, thereby contributing to a better global society.'[67]

This motherhood statement conceals as much as it reveals, both about the firm's history and about its direction. The firm's purpose has reflected rather the idiosyncratic motives of the founder, and the ongoing desire to maintain family control.

As with a mission statement, an entrepreneurial, family firm may have formal planning processes and formal management objectives. In fact many of the *chaebol* have adopted some form of management by objectives (MBO); see Table 3.1. It is widely recognized that, in general, setting explicit goals is a superior way to improve employee performance. Typically, the process involves a division into strategic goals (5+ years), tactical goals (1–5 years), and organizational goals (1 year). Each level of goals has its appropriate level of plan, and the articulation of plans is the arena in which commitment to goals is achieved. Plans in turn are translated into concrete, specific objectives, and studies show performance is enhanced by

Table 3.1   Management by objectives (MBO)

Strengths	Weaknesses
Aids coordination of goals and plans	Tends to falter without strong, continual commitment from top management
Helps clarify priorities and expectations	Necessitates considerable training of managers
Facilitates vertical and horizontal communication	Can be misused as a punitive device
Fosters employee motivation	May cause over-emphasis on quantitative goals

Source: adapted from Kathryn Bartol, Margaret Tein, Graham Matthews and David Martin, *Management: a Pacific Rim Focus* (enhanced edition; Boston: McGraw-Hill, 2003), p. 194.

setting challenging targets rather than by encouraging everyone to do their 'best'.[68]

As with group decision making, management by objectives has both advantages and possible pitfalls. As with the mission statement, moreover, there are particular problems in the case of an entrepreneurial or family-owned firm where authority is derived from ownership and decisions may simply be imposed from the top. The successors of entrepreneurial 'founders' may inherit their ability, but this is unusual. 'Unlike wealth, the management prowess of chaebols' founders does not seem to be inherited.'[69] Even if they possess genius, decision makers may be rational, or they may not. If they are not rational, but they belong to the owner family, they can change the direction of the firm at will. If they are rational, they may have their ability to be rational constrained or 'bounded' by time, search costs, or lack of expertise, but as owners they have no obligation to consult widely.

For an entrepreneurial or family firm, formal processes such as management by objectives may function better when search costs are low and quick responses are required, in the early phases of growth in a new industry, or when a succession of new opportunities appears. That is, this style of management may suit a country in the position of Korea in the 1960s and 1970s. The conflict between authority structures based on ownership and the requirements of formal planning become worse when complex analysis is required, or when there are several competing alternatives, in maturing industries, or when the competitive environment changes. That is, this style of management may be less suitable for a country in the position of Korea in the late 1980s and 1990s.

Entrepreneurial or family control becomes increasingly difficult as a firm expands and subsidiaries are added. No one has the time or the expertise to manage two dozen large firms in two dozen different industries. Over time the obsession with control may lead to the use of fairly primitive quantitative measures of performance, especially when the active managers are not members of the owner family. Further down the hierarchy, the insistence on control and performance from the owner family may lead subordinate managers to 'drive' their employees in a harsh and punitive manner.

An entrepreneurial leader or a single family may attempt to maintain control over an expanding business empire by imposing a strict hierarchical order for decisions. Although the founder or his successor can intervene at any level, most Korean firms have become quite 'tall' structures with several levels of management. Each level executes the orders received from the next higher level. In the case of Samsung, this eventually resulted in a structure with 21 layers, each requiring a personal seal of approval, a process that could delay a new project for months.

As seen above, *chaebol* groups expanded by adding new subsidiary firms, frequently in response to government encouragement or pressure. As a result the groups have not always gained the potential benefits of synergy, and instead have suffered from the disadvantages of an 'M'-form structure of relatively independent divisions: there can be a duplication of resources in each subsidiary firm, and consequently a reduction of in-depth expertise. Competition among subsidiary firms may restrict potentially beneficial sharing of knowledge. Coordination and control become problematic. Samsung and other groups created a staff serving the founder to organize information and deliver orders to subsidiary firms. The numbers employed in Lee Byung-chull's 'secretarial office' rose from between 60 and 70 in the 1970s, to 150 in 1985, and peaked at 250 in 1990. There followed a reduction to 100 in 1993. In 1994, Samsung's 50 subsidiary firms were consolidated into 24, organized in four core groups. Routine management was decentralized to member firms, and the layers of approval were reduced to three wherever possible.[70]

The president of an individual firm within the group has little power and no control over the firm's strategic direction. There are regular meetings of presidents, but unlike the *keiretsu* president's clubs, these are meetings where the presidents listen to the group chairman and receive praise or blame, 'a council in the king's presence, where the participants are in a high state of tension'.[71] Before 1997, although the group chairman held office as the dominant shareholder and exercised absolute control over member firms, the office did not carry legal responsibility for wrongdoing by member firms, and the pyramid of shareholdings and debt guarantees by member firms insulated the owner family against losses. In the aftermath of the 1997 crisis, it became obvious that minority shareholders could be and in many cases had been systematically expropriated,[72] and the changes in corporate governance rules outlined below have been intended to shift the balance of power away from the owner families.

The *chaebol* did expand, of course, and they also moved into new areas. As seen above, they were 'innovative' in that sense. But their motives were as much defensive as strategic, to grow and to maintain their relative position relative to other groups. Under Park the government forced them to compete with each other, and they were often forced into new areas by government policy. They typically responded by establishing a new firm, with controlling interest remaining with the core company. There was very little expansion by merger and there were very few strategic alliances. No *chaebol* was willing to compromise its independence or to be absorbed by another. All studies of the *chaebol* report very high levels of intragroup transactions. They have frequently refused to do business with each other even when it was in their interests, and have commonly refused to deal with firms that do business with a rival group.[73]

Many *chaebol* firms remained by choice assemblers of components purchased from outside the country, until they were able to manufacture themselves. They were also not as close or supportive in their relations with subcontracting firms as major Japanese firms. Small suppliers producing essential components have been bought up, or on occasion had their technology appropriated without return. The others, those producing unimportant, low value-added components, have been squeezed 'mercilessly' in good times and driven into bankruptcy in bad times. This has forced small firms to cut costs at the expense of technical improvements and training for their workers. In Japan, small and medium enterprises have provided invaluable support to large firms. In Taiwan they have formed an important pool of innovation and technological improvement. In the aftermath of the 1997 crisis many pointed to the failure of government officials and *chaebol* leaders to foster smaller firms as a key weakness in the Korean system.[74]

Korea's 'battlefield commanders' prided themselves on promoting innovation through their own personal connection with the production process. General theoretical and empirical studies give mixed results regarding leadership style. Sometimes autocratic leadership leads to better outcomes, and sometimes democratic leadership is better. Styles can be arranged along a continuum from 'boss-centered' to 'employee centered',[75] but this does not tell us which of the styles of behavior might be 'best'. Each situation will determine what will work, and very often you will not know until afterwards that it did not. But note that 'boss-centered' relationships place a very heavy burden on the boss, in terms of gaining information and developing plans. As technologies and the competitive environment become more complex, the advantages of group decision making may increase, relative to the strengths of entrepreneurial insight.

Korean firms often have problems with motivation. The founders of the *chaebol* were often genuinely charismatic figures, and as such they did generate enthusiasm and commitment. Charismatic leadership inspires subordinates to achieve more than they believe they can. As these groups grew, founders brought in their relatives, and some of these new leaders demonstrated exceptional competence as well. But, despite extensive technical training programs, there has been little effort to encourage strategic leadership from outside the family. Senior executives from varying backgrounds do not have the corporate identity and sense of belonging that Japanese executives are supposed to have. And Korean executives particularly resent younger members of the owner family being placed over them. As a result it has been common for *chaebol* to poach executives from other groups, and the disgruntled turncoat often takes a group of subordinates to the new firm.

Eventually firms must move from charismatic leadership to bureaucratic leadership, that is recruitment on the basis of certified qualifications and promotion on the basis of demonstrated ability. Further, over time a successful firm must develop leadership that helps subordinates to recognize and accept responsibilities, increases their confidence, and helps them to grow into new roles. That is, all firms must become 'managerial' firms if they are to continue to succeed.

This shift poses problems. After a firm has achieved substantial size, strategic organizational decisions can be difficult. If the original structures remain unchanged, they will respond well to those situations that 'fit' their strengths, but badly to those that do not. If there is a new technology or product that is either already within the capabilities of the group, or can be relatively easily purchased off the shelf, then a new company can be established to apply it. Lee purchased technology and recruited engineers and key executives from the United States to push forward Samsung's semiconductor project, for example. Likewise, under Park and his successors, if the new technology or product would lead to increased exports, then financing was available at subsidized rates. But, although a number of the larger groups maintained elaborate research facilities, it was not a system that encouraged pure research, development of genuinely new processes or products, or improvements in efficiency for goods and services for the domestic market.[76]

With regard to organizational control, again, it was never likely that these entrepreneurial and family firms would choose the 'best' form of control, because of their desire to maintain control in the family. Effective control is future-oriented, multidimensional, cost-effective, accurate, realistic, timely, monitorable, acceptable to organization members, and flexible. These goals are not always consistent, and effective control is therefore flexible. The personal, family-centered style of organization may achieve an effective style of control, but this is likely to be an accident. At lower levels, authoritarian habits may lead to overcontrol, to 'driving' workers, possibly actually inhibiting effective job performance. In manufacturing production, Korean managers through the 1980s knew they could rely on the state to suppress any resistance by workers. At higher levels, family members in senior positions were not constrained in their decision making, and through the 1990s they knew that they would have access to borrowed money to implement their decisions. When the situation changed in the 1990s, the *chaebol* proved to be vulnerable.

Labor Relations

As in Japan, in Korea the ideal for large firms is 'lifetime employment' – to hire young graduates who will remain with the company for their entire career. Recruitment of young executives and technicians became much more competitive in the early 1990s. Previously, Korean businesses had recruited on the basis of '*yon-go*' (special relationship) connections based on family, school, or birthplace. However, the limited supply of management and engineering graduates from the top universities had caused more and more of the *chaebol* to adopt the '*gong-chae*' (open employment) system first implemented by Samsung in 1957. Firms used batteries of written examinations followed by interviews (sometimes in groups, and sometimes conducted 'blind' or without biographical information to eliminate the 'halo' effects of background factors) and plant visits to rank potential employees. Some offered internships to promising candidates before graduation in the hope of gaining an advantage.[77]

In contrast to Japan, however, even a very positive evaluation of the new 'open employment' system notes that the average interview lasted less than ten minutes, and concluded that Korean firms 'have made few attempts to validate selection procedures'.[78] Korean executives dismiss the formal processes and report that family, school, and regional connections remain the key determinants of who gets hired. Even more important, they report that these connections form the basis for cliques among employees in all firms, and that these cliques in turn can lead to debilitating divisions within the firm.

Below the executive level, Korean employers prefer to present their labor relations as harmonious and familial, another aspect of 'Asian', 'Confucian', or 'traditional' values.[79] In addition to showing 'respect for employees' and creating a 'community-oriented concept', successful business leaders must be concerned with the 'spiritual care of employees'.[80] Of the five Confucian relationships, there must in particular be 'justice' (*eui*) in relations between superiors and subordinates, and 'trust' (*shin*) between friends or equals:

> Confucian values permeate every aspect of a Korean's behavior . . . In the work organization, the traditional values are reflected in the subordinate's loyalty to the superior (or to the company) and the latter's benevolence and paternalism toward the former . . . Centralized authority, vertical hierarchical order, harmony among employees, diligence and hard work, and a seniority-based reward system are all closely related to the traditional Confucian values.[81]

An additional cliché among managers is that 'harmony' (*inwha*) means sharing pain in times of adversity, so that those who are negatively affected by their superiors' decisions accept their sacrifice as a necessary contribution to the continued existence of the firm.[82]

At the lower levels Korean firms vary their industrial relations according to the particular industry. In effect they have been monopsonists in the labor market. The power of firms over their workers was backed by government force.[83] As elsewhere in Asia, independent unions were illegal and labor protests were suppressed by the police and military.[84] Workers labored under the 'three prohibitions' (*samkeum*) codified under President Chun in 1980. They were prohibited from having more than one union, so they were in effect forced into the single company unions organized under the official Federation of Korean Trade Unions. All 'third parties' – including the officially recognized unions – were prohibited from intervening in disputes between employers and workers. Finally, unions were prohibited from political activity, including election campaigning and political fundraising.

In the case of Hyundai, for example, the firm's mission statement describes its labor relations in glowing terms:

> Hyundai is adopting a systematic global approach to the management of its human resources in order to raise the quality of its employees' lives so that they feel well rewarded and proud to be members of the Hyundai family.
>
> The employees enjoy an extensive number of fringe benefits such as company-funded travel to their hometowns on national holidays plus financial assistance for child education, household moves, automobile purchases and maintenance, to name just a few. By putting the needs of our people first, the company is motivating the employees to attain even greater heights of productivity and efficiency.[85]

In fact, Hyundai has adjusted its policies to extract maximum profit from its workers. Its construction arm, Hyundai Engineering and Construction Company, has exploited a pool of relatively uneducated young men, who have been given minimal training and then forced to work long hours on dispersed sites at home and overseas. The shipbuilding company, Hyundai Heavy Industries, marketed its ships on the basis of speed of delivery rather than technical sophistication. It drew from the same pool of workers as the construction division, but the combination of long hours and low wages here led to friction on the single centralized site in the Ulsan industrial estate. In contrast, Hyundai Motor Company, which began as a knock-down assembler under contract to Ford, but then moved to produce its own automobiles with technology licensed from Mitsubishi, relied on relatively skilled workers with technical high school and college qualifications, who then required further additional training to meet the standards of Hyundai's foreign partners. They received much more lenient treatment in order to reduce turnover.[86]

Lower-level employees perceive management as oppressive. Despite the rhetoric of 'Confucian' values, workers see their firms not as 'extended families' but as companies operated for the benefit of the owner family.[87] Korean labor relations have been confrontational and violent, despite repression, and labor unrest played an important political role in the regime changes in 1959, 1979, and 1987. Following 1987, independent unions emerged in the Hyundai plants, and the strikes and protests often led to violence.[88] Another firm that maintains an official culture of paternalism ended open competitive recruitment in the late 1980s and returned to 'connection hiring' in order to ensure the exclusion of potential agitators. One worker said, 'it is worse than the army'. Echoing other studies, the authors conclude, 'Korean workers are not particularly docile. Their apparent docility has been the result of governmental control, not the cultural tradition.'[89]

This did not improve much under Kim Young Sam or Kim Dae Jung. Both argued that Korea could not afford to allow labor costs to rise because export markets would be lost. In fact real wages had risen substantially following political liberalization in 1987, and Korea was losing markets. A proposed 'grand compromise' would have seen the 'three prohibitions' lifted in return for workers agreeing to grant employers 'three systems', the right to lay off workers, to hire on a temporary basis, and to allocate hours flexibly. Then, in late December 1996, in a secretive pre-dawn session of parliament attended only by members of Kim Young-sam's party, the government rushed through new laws that granted employers their three systems, but without the promised laws that would have legalized union activities. Widespread strikes followed, and in early 1997 the government delayed implementation of the new laws and recognized the outlawed union confederation that had organized the strikes.

Following the 1997 crisis, the strikes called in response to layoffs were also suppressed by the new administration of Kim Dae Jung. The government established a Tripartite Committee in 1999 to work towards a compromise in labor relations, but hard-line labor unions refused to participate. The ongoing restructuring and sale of *chaebol* firms to foreign companies continued to cause unrest. In February 2001, Daewoo Motors workers struck to protest the firing of 1700 workers, and the government broke up the strike and issued arrest warrants for the leaders. In April, riot police brutally attacked union members demanding access to their office in a Daewoo Motors factory.

Again, as in Japan, there remains the question of gender. At the executive level many *chaebol* groups in the mid-1990s did not accept female applicants. Those that did frequently eliminated them in the early stages of the selection process. In 1995, although 40.5 per cent of the 170 000 college graduates on the job market were women, the 50 largest *chaebol* hired only 2000 female college graduates, less than 8 per cent of the total hired. Despite lip service to 'open employment', the vast majority of female applicants were screened out before the interview stage. This was attributed to 'the impact of Confucianism'.[90] However, Confucian values did not preclude widespread employment of women in manufacturing firms and particularly in the export processing zones. Here they were subjected to harsh and sometimes brutal conditions, and it is notable that protests by women workers have frequently spearheaded labor activism.[91]

THE CRISIS AND RESTRUCTURING

The 1997 crisis, and the collapse of the value of the won against the United States dollar and other currencies, exposed the weaknesses of the *chaebol* and of the system that had supported them. A rescue operation mounted by the International Monetary Fund and other international agencies provided a record US$57 billion in credits. In return the Korean government obligated itself to introduce a long list of reforms. President Kim Young-sam had already agreed, in response to direct pressure from United States President Bill Clinton, and incoming President Kim Dae-jung was forced to implement a program that he had opposed during the election campaign. The reform program in effect assumed that the collapse had been caused by policy weaknesses and institutional inefficiencies in Korea. It also reflected the interests of foreign investors. Along with restrictive monetary policies and wage restraints intended to reduce costs and improve the balance of payments, rules on foreign investment were to be liberalized, and changes in corporate governance were to be implemented that would protect the rights of minority shareholders, including foreigners.

After a decline of 7 per cent in 1998, the Korean economy rebounded and expanded by 10 per cent in 1999 and by another 9 per cent in 2000. By 2003, observers were speaking not merely of recovery, but of a 'second miracle'. However, the role of the government and what it could mean for Korean firms was not clear. There were substantial discrepancies between policy and performance, and between the ideal of market liberalization and the practice of state intervention. President Kim Dae-jung was accused by some of being a 'fervent neoliberal' who dogmatically believed that 'What we need now, more than anything else, are foreign investors,' as he said in an address to the United States Congress.[92] To others his economic successes appear due to 'old-style interventionist practices'[93] and 'the most intriguing aspect of the Kim administration is the increasing use of *informal executive guidance*'.[94] A former dissident, hounded, hunted, and imprisoned by the government, he was unlikely to be particularly sympathetic to business leaders who had enjoyed close relations with previous presidents. Nevertheless, he was still willing and able to use the powers of the presidency.

The crisis was first and foremost a financial crisis, and the government's response was directly interventionist. By late 1999, the government had liquidated nearly 200 financial institutions, and suspended the licenses of another 68. A number of banks were forced to merge, including three of the major commercial banks. The surviving institutions all received government grants to provision them against the non-performing loans remaining on their books. Standard and Poor estimated the total cost at US$125 billion, or some 30 per cent of Korea's gross domestic product in 1999. As a result, by 2002, the government owned approximately one-third of the entire financial sector. In addition the various rescue operations mounted to allow major firms to survive, including parts of Daewoo and several of the other *chaebol* groups, contained provisions for the banks to trade debt for equity in the firms. The limit on the share of any corporation a bank was permitted to own was consequently raised from 10 to 15 per cent.

The financial sector was restructured under a new Financial Supervisory Commission. The new system mandated transparent rules for decision making and specified that banks' boards have a majority of outside directors and committees responsible for governance, compensation, audit, and risk management. The proportion of outside directors had reached 60 to 80 per cent by 2003. Market-oriented analysts have argued that the banks' improved returns and the resulting increase in confidence led, and by inference, caused improvements elsewhere in the economy.[95] At the same time, however, the government could nominate the chief executive officers of banks it controlled. All banks were forced to adjust their loan portfolios in accord with government policy. And the banks became the vehicle for the government's plans to restructure the entire corporate sector, not through market forces, but through directed lending and credit rationing in return for compliance.

The top five *chaebol* were to reduce the number of their subsidiaries by half, and to merge firms or swap firms in different areas. The intent was to eliminate overcapacity and concentrate their expertise around core areas. The announcement of the 'big deal' in December 1998 created great enthusiasm. However, it was criticized internationally as a regression to the old policy of sectoral targeting that the government had foresworn as part of the price of admission to the OECD in 1996. It was also not clear which deals were directed by the government, or merely encouraged, and which had been initiated by *chaebol* leaders independently. Finance and Economy Minister Kang Bong-Kyun said in July 1999 that 'the reform initiatives were first made by *chaebol* themselves', but others said *chaebol* leaders were simply presented with demands by government officials. Some of the deals were not actually transfers of businesses from one group to another, but new companies with joint ownership. Several were not concluded, the trade of Samsung Motors for Daewoo Electronics failed, and the proposed merger of Hyundai and Samsung's petrochemical arms collapsed. Ultimately, only two deals succeeded, as Hyundai Electronics acquired LG Semiconductors, and Hyundai Oil Refining acquired the oil refining division of Hanwha Energy.

For the sixth through sixty-fourth *chaebol* (and 12 of Daewoo's member firms), there was a program of 'workouts' enforced through the banks, with the threat of bankruptcy and receivership if they did not cooperate. Whereas the largest groups were held to be too big to be restructured by the commercial banks, these 'medium sized' firms would not cause too much of a shock to the economy even if they collapsed. In return for debt forgiveness, debt-for-equity exchanges, and new credits, the firms agreed to sales of assets and subsidiaries, sale of part of the firm to foreign investors, and changes in management. Dominant shareholders were invited to contribute their private wealth as compensation for previous mismanagement. Asset sales and new capital raisings (about half from foreign investors) generally succeeded, but sales of subsidiaries generally did not. Again the government was criticized, this time for delaying the exit of failing firms. And, again the overall impact is disputed. In many cases the creditor banks themselves were suffering, or did not possess the expertise to oversee the workout programs. Because incumbent managers, the owner families or their associates, usually remained in control, they often found ways to sidetrack or subvert the process.[96]

It may be that the most important legacy of the crisis period will not be any specific measure taken, but the general effect of changes in rules of corporate governance. There is no term for corporate governance in Korean, the nearest equivalent being 'ownership structure'. The old rules discriminated against minority shareholders, and made it relatively easy for the owner families to control their subsidiary firms with quite low ownership stakes. Ownership of listed firms is widely dispersed in Korea, with individual small shareholders making up 97 per cent of the total, and owning some 60 per cent of outstanding shares in the 1980s and 40 per cent in 1997. However, the law required a shareholder to own at least 5 per cent of a firm in order to demand a company meeting, inspect the firm's accounts, or file a derivative suit. The more substantial holdings of institutional investors were also disfranchised, because they were required to 'shadow' the voting of other shareholders in voting their shares, rather than voting their shares as a block.

The need to reduce opportunities for owner families to expropriate minority shareholders has been widely recognized.[97] Stock exchange listing requirements now specify that at least 25 per cent of board seats must be held by independent outside directors, and the proportion was estimated to be 30 per cent in 2001, compared to only 11 per cent in 1998. Financial reporting requirements have been tightened, especially in regard to transactions in financial derivatives or loan guarantees to other firms. Shareholders with 3 per cent of an unlisted company's stock, or 1 per cent of a listed company, may now insist on a shareholders' meeting, which may for instance remove directors for unsatisfactory performance.[98] Cumulative voting allows a new and more powerful role for institutional shareholders, both domestic and foreign.[99]

Korea has become far more open to foreign ownership generally, and both portfolio and direct investment by foreigners have risen dramatically. A number of Korean banks now have foreign equity partners, and foreigners have acquired large shareholdings in semiconductors and telecommunications. Korea's automobile industry has been rationalized and three of the remaining four firms are controlled by DaimlerChrysler, General Motors, and Renault. China's Shanghai Automotive Industry Corporation (SAIC) has acquired a large minority interest in Ssangyong Motors. Foreign investment can be viewed positively, as a source of capital and technology, and as a source of discipline over owner families. But it can also be viewed negatively, as a loss of national independence, and as a potential source of instability as the winds of investor fashion shift overseas.[100] There has been a nationalistic reaction to the increased foreign presence, and in late 2004 the government was reported to be considering imposing a residence requirement on foreign directors of Korean banks.[101]

For the rest of Asia, South Korea, like Japan, is a major foreign investor. South Korea rapidly became an important investor in China following the normalization of diplomatic relations between the two countries in 1991. By 1994, South Korea had surpassed Germany, Canada, Thailand and Australia and become the seventh largest investor in China.[102] Korean manufacturing firms have primarily sought lower labor costs. In late 2003, Samsung, facing a sharp fall in profits due to declining prices, announced that it would move production of personal computers and liquid crystal flat screens to China, which would become Samsung's 'main production base' by 2005.[103] In addition, the Korean government has been promoting Korea as the 'hub' of Northeast Asia and as a platform for other countries to export to China. According to the journal of the Korea Trade-Investment Promotion Agency, Korea offered geographical proximity to the China market and world-class logistical and infrastructure support. Tariffs would fall as a result of China's membership in the WTO, particularly on automobiles, petrochemicals, and electronic products. In comparison to China, Korea had improved protection of intellectual property following the implementation of the WTO's Agreement on Trade-Related Aspects of Intellectual Property Rights (TRIPs Agreement). And, with only 12 per cent of the labor force unionized (lowest among OECD members), and greatly reduced labor unrest since 'the struggle for democratic rights' in the 1980s, foreign investors rated Korean labor relations overwhelmingly as either 'relatively good' or 'very good'.[104]

FURTHER READING

Carter J. Eckert, Ki-baik Lee, Young Ick Lew, Michael Robinson and Edward W. Wagner, *Korea Old and New: A History* (Cambridge: Harvard University Press, 1990) is an excellent general history. Byung-Nak Song, *The Rise of the Korean Economy* (updated edition, Hong Kong: Oxford University Press, 1994), surveys economic development from the perspective of a senior economic advisor to the government. The classic study by Alice H. Amsden, *Asia's Next Giant: South Korea and Late Industrialization* (Oxford: Oxford University Press, 1989) focuses on the role of government. Heather Smith, 'Korea', in Ross H. McLeod and Ross Garnaut (eds), *East Asia in Crisis: From Being a Miracle to Needing One?* (London and New York: Routledge, 1998), pp. 66–84, is a neoclassical account that emphasizes the structural problems that predated the 1997 crisis. In contrast, Bruce Cumings, 'The Korean crisis and the end of "Late" development', *New Left Review*, September/October 1998, pp. 43–72, emphasizes the role of foreign powers and especially the United States. For developments following 1997, see Brian Bridges, *Korea after the Crash: The Politics of Economic Recovery* (London and New York: Routledge, 2001).

The rise of the South Korean economy led in the 1980s to an interest in the *chaebol* groups, for instance Richard M. Steers, Yoo Keun Shin and

Gerardo R. Ungson, *The Chaebol: Korea's New Industrial Might* (New York: Harper & Row, Ballinger Division, 1989), and in the distinctive patterns of Korean management, for instance Sang M. Lee and Sangjin Yoo, 'The K-type management: a driving force of Korean prosperity', *Management International Review*, **27**(4) (1987), 68–77; T. Morden and D. Bowles, 'Management in South Korea: a review', *Management Decision*, **36**(5) (1998), 316–30. There also have been studies of individual *chaebol* and their leaders, such as Donald Kirk, *Korean Dynasty: Hyundai and Chung Ju Yung* (Armonk: M.E. Sharpe, 1994; Hong Kong: Asia, 2000) and Richard M. Steers, *Made in Korea: Chung Ju Yung and the Rise of Hyundai* (New York: Routledge, 1999).

Interest in the lessons to be learned from Korean managers continued through the 1990s, for instance Kae H. Chung, Hak Chong Lee and Ku Hyun Jung, *Korean Management: Global Strategy and Cultural Transformation* (Berlin and New York: W. de Gruyter, 1997) and Youngil Lim, *Technology and Productivity: The Korean Way of Learning and Catching Up* (Cambridge: MIT Press, 1999). Since the 1997 crisis, the main concern has been with the weaknesses of the *chaebol* and possible remedies. See Sea-Jin Chang, *Financial Crisis and Transformation of Korean Business Groups: The Rise and Fall of Chaebols* (Cambridge and New York: Cambridge University Press, 2003), and Stephan Haggard, Wonhyuk Lim and Euysung Kim (eds), *Economic Crisis and Corporate Restructuring in Korea: Reforming the Chaebol* (Cambridge and New York: Cambridge University Press, 2003). Chris Rowley, Tae Won Sohn and Johngseok Bae (eds), *Managing Korean Business: Organization, Culture, Human Resources and Change* (London: Cass, 2002) attempts to move away from either praise or condemnation and concentrates generally on the cases of successful adaptation by the *chaebol* to changed circumstances.

NOTES

1. Cumings (1987), p. 68.
2. Song (1994), p. 38.
3. Juhn (1973), p. 115.
4. See Ho (1984), pp. 347–98.
5. Robinson (1991), pp. 216–17.
6. Juhn (1973), p. 115.
7. Gragert (1994).
8. Moskowitz (1982), 76, 84–5.
9. Song (1994), p. 41.
10. Ho (1984).
11. Juhn (1973).
12. Ho (1984).
13. Song (1994), p. 40.

14. Eckert, Lee, Lew, Robinson and Wagner (1990), p. 307.
15. Ibid., pp. 331–3.
16. Ibid., pp. 337–9.
17. Haggard, Kim and Moon (1991), 850–73.
18. Song (1994), p. 57.
19. McNamara (1990).
20. McNamara ranks these as a hierarchy, despite the large size of the investments in the final 'outer' fourth level of large Japanese enterprises.
21. McNamara's presentation closely follows that of Eckert (1991).
22. McNamara (1992), 701–18.
23. Mathews and Cho (2000), p. 106.
24. Yoo (1998–99), 40–48.
25. Amsden (2001).
26. Castells (1992), pp. 38–9; Kwon (2000), p. 47, note 5.
27. Amsden (1989), ch. 12; Hogan (1994), p. 40; *Financial Times*, 4 July 1996.
28. Bishop (1997), p. 132.
29. Hynson (1990).
30. Kwon (2000), pp. 28–9.
31. Park (1991), p. 48.
32. Jung (1989), p. 20.
33. Yoo (1998–99), p. 47.
34. Haggard et al., (1991) p. 851. See Wade (1993), 147–68.
35. Asian Development Bank (2001).
36. Lim (1999).
37. Chang (2003), pp. 99–103, 118–21.
38. Lim (1994), pp. 193–4.
39. Hobday (1995), ch. 4; Mathews and Cho (2000), ch. 3.
40. Haggard et al. (1991), p. 858.
41. Chun Doo Hwan, 'The 1980s meeting a new challenge' (1981), cited in Robinson (1991), p. 219.
42. Moskowitz (1982), pp. 72–3.
43. Bedeski (1994).
44. Chon (1992), pp. 150–75; Song (1994), p. 213.
45. Rhee et al. (1984), p. 27.
46. Sohn (1997), pp. 211–38.
47. Burmeister (1988).
48. Il (1993).
49. Chon (1992).
50. Chang and Choi (1988), 141–58; Chang (2003), pp. 249–63; Sung and Kim (2003), pp. 111–14, report even more negative results for the *chaebol* in the early 1990s and believe that Chang and Choi's 1988 study exaggerated *chaebol* profitability for the earlier period.
51. Park (2003), pp. 199–201.
52. This section draws in part on a series of very frank interviews with a group of a dozen executives from three Korean business groups, who have asked that they and their firms remain anonymous.
53. Yoo (1998–99), p. 41–3; Lee and Yoo (1987), 68–77.
54. See, for instance, Song (1994).
55. See Morden and Bowles (1998), 316–30; Rowley (2002), pp. 178–92.
56. Kang (1997), p. 46.
57. Lim, Haggard and Kim (2003), pp. 4, 6.
58. Kang (1997), p. 41.
59. Biggert (1990), 113–33. Hamilton and Feenstra (1995), 79–80, believe inheritance laws to be the prime cause of Korea's distinctive corporate structure.
60. Yoo (1998–99), p. 40.
61. Biggert (1998), p. 316.

62. Lee and Yoo (1987), p. 71.
63. Hattori (1989), p. 89.
64. Chang (2003), pp. 87–98.
65. Cho and Yoon (2002), p. 79.
66. Ibid., pp. 107, 176–7.
67. http://www.samsung.com/AboutSAMSUNG/ValuesPhilosophy/index.htm.
68. Richards (1986).
69. Chang (2003), p. 178.
70. Kang (1997), pp. 43–4, 52.
71. Ibid., p. 53.
72. Chang (2003), pp. 176–85 details some examples.
73. Biggert (1998), p. 316.
74. Ibid.
75. Tannenbaum and Schmidt (1973), pp. 162–80.
76. Aubert (1996), pp. 35–9.
77. Lee (1998–99), 26–39.
78. Ibid., pp. 35–6.
79. See Song (1994), ch. 11.
80. Yoo (1998–99), pp. 41–2.
81. Lee (1998–99), pp. 27–8.
82. Tu, Kim and Sullivan (2002), pp. 39–46.
83. Kwon and O'Donnell (1999), 272–94.
84. Deyo (1989).
85. http://worldwide.hyundai-motor.com/intro/corporation/corporate_index.html.
86. Kwon and O'Donnell (2001).
87. Robinson (1991), pp. 223–4.
88. Kwon and O'Donnell (2001).
89. Kim (1992), p. 198; see Janelli and Yim (1995).
90. Lee (1998–99), p. 35.
91. Hampson (2000), pp. 170–87.
92. Crotty and Lee (2001), pp. 28–31, 37.
93. Bridges (2001), p. 88.
94. Mo and Moon (2003), p. 138, emphasis in original.
95. Choe and Lee (2003), 483–508.
96. Park (2003).
97. Chang (2003), pp. 208–12.
98. Australia, Department of Foreign Affairs and Trade, Economic Analytical Unit (2002), vol. 2, p. 58.
99. Solomon, Solomon and Park (2002), 211–24.
100. Crotty and Lee (2001).
101. Fifield (2004).
102. Mock (1989), 421–39; Sun and Tipton (1998), 159–86.
103. 'Samsung makes China shift', *The Australian*, 15 October 2003, (www.australianIT.com.au).
104. Duerden (2003), pp. 22–6; Lee (2003), pp. 8–12.

4. Managing the boundaries of the firm in Qing and Nationalist China

> So there are three ways in which a civil leadership causes the military trouble. When a civil leadership unaware of the facts tells its armies to advance when it should not, or tells its armies to retreat when it should not, this is called tying up the armies. When the civil leadership is ignorant of military affairs but shares equally in the government of the armies, the soldiers get confused. When the civil leadership is ignorant of military affairs but shares equally in the command of the armies, the soldiers hesitate. Once the armies are confused and hesitant, trouble comes from competitors. This is called taking away victory by deranging the military. (Sun Tzu, *The Art of War*)

If we substitute 'business' for 'military' and look at the role of the Chinese state in the economy in the nineteenth century, it seems a clear case of the 'civil leadership' interfering in areas where it was ignorant. In the face of Western imperialist expansion, China's response was therefore 'confused and hesitant'. Following the Revolution of 1911 and the disasters of the warlord period the Nationalist state also failed to direct the economy successfully. The struggle against Japanese invaders and Communist rebels was hampered by government intervention 'deranging' business enterprise.

The Chinese institutional grid determined the relations between government and business. Enduring traditions grew out of the legal system and these in turn were reflected in the formal provisions for corporate governance. Whether these inherited traditions actually caused the observed patterns of Chinese business remains a topic of dispute. Both historians and management theorists have been struck in particular by the absence of large firms. Many have followed the arguments of Mao Zedong and emphasized the role of Western imperialism in the nineteenth century and Japanese imperialism in the twentieth century. Others such as Ramon Myers have looked further back into China's Confucian past and cultural traditions passed down from previous generations.

The predominance of small firms marks the management grid of the Chinese 'Confucian' firm. As will be seen in Chapters 5 and 7, this has ongoing implications for firms in Hong Kong, in Taiwan, and among the 'overseas Chinese' of Southeast Asia. Here we look at the Chinese historical and institutional contexts, because they shaped the background of today's Chinese managers. In China, success could certainly come from adapting to these constraints, but the conditions of success could also lead to problems of strategic planning and to problems of succession. The Confucian firm may have developed its characteristic features in response to transaction costs and problems of expansion. As such it is a particularly good example of the ways in which all firms must decide between hierarchies and markets, and the variety of ways in which firms draw the boundary between themselves and the external environment.

BOX 4.1   POINT AND COUNTERPOINT: MAO
                 ZEDONG – CHINA AS A COLONIAL,
                 SEMI-COLONIAL AND SEMI-FEUDAL
                 SOCIETY: FOREIGN INVASION AND
                 COMPRADOR CAPITALISM

Mao Zedong, leader of the Communist Party against both the Nationalist government and the Japanese, victor in the civil war, and ruler of China from 1949 until his death in 1976, wrote a textbook in 1939 that presented a view of Chinese history and the Chinese economy that has deeply influenced the thinking of three generations of Chinese leaders. Many Western scholars looking at Chinese history, the Chinese economy, and Chinese business structures have also been influenced by Mao's approach. Even where they disagree, their arguments have reflected his interpretive framework.

Mao saw China as unique in the length and richness of its national history. However, he also insisted that the Chinese economy operated according to the same rules that had determined the development of capitalism in the West. 'For 3,000 years Chinese society remained a feudal society', in which the landlords, nobility, and emperor owned most of the land and extracted rent from the peasantry. Nevertheless, 'As China's feudal society developed its commodity economy and so carried within itself the embryo of capitalism, China would of herself have developed slowly into a capitalist society even if there had been no influence of foreign capitalism.'

Where China differed from the West was in having to contend with external forces. 'The penetration of foreign capital,' argued Mao, accelerated the development of capitalism in China, but it did so in a particular way:

Foreign capital played an important role in disintegrating China's social economy, because on the one hand it destroyed the foundation of her

> self-sufficing natural economy and disrupted her handicraft industries
> in both the cities and peasant homes, and on the other hand it acceler-
> ated the development of commodity economy in town and country . . .
> this situation also created certain objective conditions and possibilities
> for the development of China's capitalist production. For the destruction
> of the natural economy created a commodity market for capitalism, and
> the bankruptcy of large numbers of peasants and handicraftsmen
> created a labor market for it.

The 'stimulus of foreign capitalism' in the middle decades of the
nineteenth century led some Chinese merchants, landlords, and
bureaucrats to invest in modern industries, a development that
accelerated during the First World War when the European and
American imperialist powers 'temporarily relaxed their oppression
of China'.

The imperial powers, however, 'certainly do not invade China
with the purpose of transforming a feudal China into a capitalist
China'. Rather, 'Their aim is just the opposite – to turn China step
by step into a semi-colony or colony.' Crucially, the Western powers
were aided in this by an alliance with certain elements of the
Chinese elite. Firstly, they created a 'comprador class' of Chinese
merchants to assist them in penetrating Chinese markets.
Secondly, 'imperialism makes the Chinese feudal landlord class
the mainstay of its rule over China'. Thirdly, the imperialist powers
'have never slackened their efforts to poison the minds of the
Chinese people, that is, to carry out a policy of cultural aggression'.
Missionary activities, hospitals, schools, newspapers, and encouragement of Chinese students to study abroad, all are intended 'to
train intellectuals to serve their interests and to fool the great
masses of the Chinese people'. More directly, the Japanese invasion had reduced large areas of China from semi-colonial to
directly colonial status.

Therefore, concluded Mao, 'national capitalism has played a
considerable part in China's political and cultural life, but it has not
become the principal social-economic form in China'. It is 'feeble'
because it remains tied both to foreign imperialism and to China's
own domestic feudal structures. The Western powers, much less
the Japanese, will not allow China to develop independently, and
in addition Chinese capitalists are opposed by China's feudal
classes, who maintain themselves precisely by allying themselves
with China's enemies, the Western and Japanese imperialists.

In 1939, Mao saw the crucial task of the Chinese revolution to
be the expulsion of the Japanese, but he believed that it would be

impossible to overthrow imperialism unless at the same time the peasantry could overthrow the landlord class, or, as he put it, 'As the main task of China's national revolution today is to oppose Japanese imperialism . . . the task of her democratic revolution must be fulfilled in order to win the war.' However, the situation was not promising. Among the key elites in China, Mao said, the land-lord class 'obstructs the political, economic and cultural develop-ment of Chinese society'. Among those involved in commerce and industry, the 'big bourgeoisie of a comprador character' is unreli-able because it 'serves the capitalists of the imperialist countries'. The 'national bourgeoisie' is both 'oppressed by imperialism' and 'fettered by feudalism', and therefore has fought both against impe-rialism and against governments dominated by bureaucrats and warlords. However, it is 'economically and politically flabby' and likely to 'follow the big comprador bourgeoisie as its accomplice in counter-revolution'.

For Mao, therefore, China was a case of normal but arrested development. Landlords continued to dominate rural society, extracting rents by force. In the modern sector, large firms were linked to the government or to foreign interests. The much greater numbers of small firms were prevented from reaching their poten-tial by political factors, the most important being the alliance of Chinese landlords, bureaucrats, and comprador capitalists with foreign imperialists.

Source: Mao Tse-tung [Mao Zedong], 'The Chinese Revolution and the Chinese Communist Party' (1939), in Mao Tse-tung, *Selected Works* (New York: International Publishers, 1954), vol. 3, pp. 72–101.

BOX 4.2   POINT AND COUNTERPOINT: RAMON MYERS – CHINA AS A CONFUCIAN SOCIETY

As seen in Box 4.1, Mao Zedong argued that Chinese capitalism moved according to the same rules as Western capitalism. However, the values of Chinese capitalists are disputed. Ramon Myers, for decades a leading expert on Chinese economic and social history, wrote a paper in 1989 that spoke for many Western scholars in seeing the structures of the Chinese economy not as the result of foreign invasion, but rather as the outgrowth of Confucian values and family structures. Myers argued that Confucian traditions were clearly evident in the structure and behavior of Chinese firms in the nineteenth and twentieth centuries, as most preferred to remain small, simple in organizational form, family owned and managed, centered around a family authority figure, with customs based on highly personal relations. Even in successful areas such as tea, silk, and rural-based handicraft manufactures, the management and organization of firms did not change. Instead of internalizing costs by developing more complex multidivisional structures, Chinese businesses continued to rely on intermediary firms or agents to handle their relations with suppliers and customers. As a result they lost market share to new competitors with lower transaction costs, firstly to Western firms and then especially to the Japanese.

From the perspective of the late 1980s of course, it was obvious to Myers that some of the values commonly attributed to Confucian societies could and did support economic development, notably in Hong Kong and Taiwan. The high value placed on learning, hard work, diligence, thrift, and respect for superiors could all contribute to economic success. However, Myers said, for centuries they had not, and he believed there were two reasons for this. First was the importance of the family lineage and the reverence paid to ancestors. Every family traced its ancestry to a common founder. The heads of the current branches of the family were supposed to serve as the source of moral authority and as role models for other members of the family, and if they did so their moral authority would be transferred to their eldest sons in turn. As Confucius put it, 'When parents are alive, serve them according to ritual; when dead bury them according to ritual and sacrifice to them according to ritual.' This caused enormous psychological pressure to expand the family estate to glorify the ancestors. However, the achievement of wealth brought with it the need to celebrate the family's status publicly through elaborate and costly ceremonies. In the intensely competitive business environment of China, this resulted in family cycles of ascent and decline, a phase of intense labor to achieve wealth, followed by a phase of conspicuous consumption that dissipated the wealth.

Second was the Confucian emphasis on proper behavior and the need to maintain self esteem or 'face'. The distribution of esteem had been institutionalized in the way in which individuals were held to embody accepted virtues. For each individual, 'face' depended on the opinion of others. As a result, said Myers, Chinese society had become a 'judgmental community' in which each individual continually evaluated the behavior of others, and in which each individual believed others were continually evaluating them as well. As a result, said Myers, Chinese today continue to experience deep anxiety over what others think of them, and therefore they behave very cautiously in their relationships with others, trying in particular not to offend them. Already strong in dealings with family members and friends, this anxiety is heightened further when dealing with strangers. The inherited fear of what others will think, concluded Myers, leads Chinese to prefer personal relationships, because family members or people within a small circle of close acquaintances have opinions that are already known. People who are not close acquaintances may have negative opinions, and dealing with them leads to heightened anxiety. As a result Chinese are uncomfortable with large, impersonal organizations. They prefer to keep their firms small, so that all those in the firm will be close acquaintances. And, rather than establishing new branches, they prefer to act in distant markets through intermediaries who are also close acquaintances.

In sum, said Myers, although Chinese might accumulate substantial wealth, they would tend to spend it again on conspicuous consumption to please their ancestors. And, in the present, Chinese firms in general would not grow beyond a size that corresponded to the circle of family and close friends of the owner. That is, for Myers and others who emphasize the role of tradition, China's firms reflected the unique values imparted by Confucian training passed down from generation to generation. Capital accumulation was restricted, Chinese firms fell behind, and China's economy failed to modernize. China was indeed a case of arrested development, but the fault lay not in the foreigners but in the Chinese themselves.

Source: Ramon H. Myers, 'Confucianism and economic development: Mainland China, Hong Kong and Taiwan', in Chung-Hua Institution for Economic Research, *Conference on Confucianism and Economic Development in East Asia, May 29–31 1989* (Chung-Hua Institution for Economic Research, Conference Series No. 13. Taipei: Chung-Hua Institution for Economic Research, 1989), pp. 282–304.

THE HISTORICAL AND INSTITUTIONAL GRIDS: LATE QING AND NATIONALIST CHINA

China's Market Economy

Whether we agree with Mao Zedong that China was 'feudal' or not, it is not true that China was backward compared to the West. China had a well-developed system of markets and commerce before the period of Western imperialism in the nineteenth century. Adam Smith, the father of Western economics, wrote in *The Wealth of Nations* in 1776 not only that China was an advanced economy, but also that it had been so for a very long time:

> The improvements in agriculture and manufactures seem likewise to have been of very great antiquity . . . in some of the eastern provinces of China . . . several great rivers form, by their different branches, a multitude of canals, and by communicating with one another afford an inland navigation much more extensive than that either of the Nile or the Ganges, or perhaps than both of them put together. It is remarkable that neither the antient Egyptians, nor the Indians, nor the Chinese, encouraged foreign commerce, but seem all to have derived their great opulence from this inland navigation.[1]

Inland trade rested on a market economy in which labor, raw materials, and finished goods were exchanged for money. Adam Smith posited that economic advance resulted from specialization, and that specialization depended on the extent of the market. In the second quarter of the nineteenth century, a Magistrate of Jining, in Shandong province, reported on one of the districts under his supervision: 'In Gaotang there is more land sown under cotton than under foodgrains. The rich do not store grain, and the poor rely entirely on hiring out and the board that comes with wage labor.'[2]

Further, China's economy was growing. The population more than doubled between the late seventeenth century and the mid-nineteenth century, from around 250 million to nearly half a billion people. If we ask how, the answer cannot be a high birth rate, because Chinese birth rates were no higher than those recorded in Europe at the time. Rather, the answer must lie in the general development of the economy. Farmers and artisans bought and sold goods in local markets, and these in turn were linked to district markets and integrated into a complex structure of regional economies. William Skinner argued that the world of the Chinese peasant farmer was bounded, not by the village, but rather by the 'standard marketing area' including about 1500 households in about 18 villages, covering a hexagonal area of about 50 square kilometers.[3] Connections among these local marketing areas depended on transport costs, with the most intense relations among marketing areas located along navigable waterways. Skinner extended his scheme to a tiered hierarchy of central places culminating in eight 'macroregions' with relatively densely populated lowland core areas surrounded by peripheral areas or hinterlands.[4]

China's macroregions were economic units, in the sense that commerce within them was more intensive than commerce among them. Most trade remained local. Until the early twentieth century, on average 30 to 40 per cent of all farm output was marketed, but only 7 to 8 per cent entered long-distance trade.[5] However, as Smith was arguing in the passage cited above, water transport was the cheapest means of shipping bulky goods, and where water transport existed or could be created, long-distance trade was extensive. In the eighteenth century the southern provinces shipped food grains along the Grand Canal to northern provincial capitals and especially the capital city of Beijing.[6] In the late eighteenth and early nineteenth centuries a fleet of 3500 ships traded between the northeastern ports and Shanghai. Interregional trade led to high levels of commercialization and specialization of individual peasant families and of districts. The North China plain, for instance, exported large amounts of soybean cake to the Lower Yangzi region, where it was used as fertilizer.[7]

Urban growth accompanied economic development through the early decades of the nineteenth century. In 1660, Beijing contained one million residents, three cities had over 300 000 and a further 42 provincial or district centers had populations ranging from 30 000 to 300 000. These 45 cities contained a total of 3.6 million persons. In 1830, the population of Beijing was still around one million, but there were now nine cities with populations over 300 000, and another 100 with populations over 30 000, and these 109 cities possessed a total population of 13 million.

Government and Business in Qing China

Because China was a market economy, there have always been entrepreneurs in China. But Chinese society did not allow scope for all possible entrepreneurial activity. As seen in our two case studies, Mao Zedong blamed Western and Japanese imperialists, while Western scholars have blamed inherited traditions and cultural values. But, as Ramon Myers also emphasizes, there is no logical reason why inherited Chinese values – respect for authority, hard work, frugality, and the emphasis on formal education – should not support economic growth. We need as well to look at the role of the state and those aspects of Confucian tradition emphasized by China's traditional elites. Following the paraphrase of Sun Tzu suggested above, China's civil leadership may very well have tied up and deranged the economy.

Mencius is the most famous Chinese philosopher after Confucius himself. He outlined the role of government:

> Po Kuei said, 'I should like to fix the rate of taxation at one in twenty. What do you think of it?'
> 'Your way,' said Mencius, 'is that of the Northern barbarians. In a city of ten thousand households, would it be enough to have a single potter?'
> 'No. There will be a shortage of earthenware.'

'In the land of the Northern barbarians, the five grains do not grow. Millet is the only crop that grows. They are without city walls, houses, ancestral temples or the sacrificial rites. They do not have diplomacy with its attendant gifts and banquets, nor have they the numerous offices and officials. That is why they can manage on a tax of one in twenty. Now in the Central Kingdoms, how can human relationships and men in authority be abolished? The affairs of a city cannot be conducted when there is a shortage even of potters. How much more so if the shortage is of men in authority?' (Mencius, VI, B, 10)

This passage reminds us that there was one obvious difference between China and Europe, the existence of the single Chinese state. A more subtle difference, however, was the coordinated interdependence of government and markets. In China, farmers, artisans, and merchants operated under the supervision of representatives of a single, centralized government. Until the end of the nineteenth century, their transactions took place under the eye of the local district magistrate, whose responsibility for maintaining public order included supervision of markets, the frequency of market days, quality guarantees, price regulations, regulation of merchant guilds, and resolution of disputes. Local officials also collected taxes, and the taxes paid for public works.[8]

Officials were very few in number, and they exercised control indirectly. The accepted interpretations of Confucian precepts prescribed the behavior appropriate to every individual in every situation. Over centuries these rules permeated all institutions, not only schools, but also families, village communities, guilds, and other economic organizations. A merchant might not be a Confucian scholar, but he would be a dutiful son, husband, father, guild member, and so on. When the rules were violated, punishments were horrible, intended to become legends in their own right that would exemplify the frightening consequences of any deviation. Gary Hamilton cites a case that occurred in 1865, of a family in which the wife had attacked and beaten her mother-in-law. Both the wife and her husband were skinned alive in front of the mother and the skins displayed in a number of towns. The greatuncle of the husband, the eldest of his close male relatives, was beheaded, his uncle and two brothers hanged, and the heads of his collateral families beaten and banished. The wife's mother had her face tattooed with the words 'neglecting the daughter's education' and was paraded through seven provinces, and her father was beaten and banished. The couple's nine-month-old son was given a new name and taken into the care of the county magistrate. The educational officer of the town was beaten and banished as well, and the family's land was laid to waste 'forever'. Finally, all the punishments were recorded on a carved stone pillar, and rubbings of the inscription were taken and distributed throughout the empire.[9]

In the 1850s and 1860s, the temporary loss of the central provinces to the Taiping Rebellion very nearly destroyed the dynasty. The Qing dynasty survived, but the suppression of the rebellions required armies and money. The armies were raised by provincial authorities, and the provincial authorities were also responsible for new taxes intended to support the armies. The most important of the new taxes was known as the *likin*. Introduced in 1853, it was a tax on trade, levied on goods in transit or in stock. However, the central government had no idea how much was collected by the new taxation system, because the collection, accounting, and disbursement of *likin* revenues remained under regional control. That is, this major source of tax revenues, and the regional armies, although they were nominally part of the central administrative apparatus, in fact created a new balance between central and regional governments that shifted steadily in favor of the regions.[10]

By the late nineteenth century, the Qing state could no longer generate sufficient resources to support the economy. In the late eighteenth century, the central government may have had an annual surplus of 8 or 9 million taels from a revenue of 43 to 44 million, and the surplus had paid for canals, river dykes, roads, and famine relief. By 1862–74, the budget showed annual deficits of 10 million taels, with 60 million income against 70 million expenditures, reflecting the cost of suppressing the rebellions. Deficits were covered by foreign loans, but the immense size of the indemnities levied by the Japanese in 1895 after the Sino-Japanese War and by the coalition of Europeans, Americans, and Japanese in 1901 following the invasion and suppression of the Boxer Rebellion, took the deficits and foreign borrowing to new heights.

Confucian Values and the Gentry

Even had the government wished to support modern development, it would have faced great difficulties. There were modernizers, the leaders of the 'self-strengthening' movement. Most were provincial governors such as Li Hongzhang, who as governor of Shandong was given the task of dealing with the Japanese in 1894. But they were a minority. Li and others like him confronted an intransigent conservatism, the values of the educated elite. As Li wrote,

> The gentry class forbids the local people to use Western methods and machines, so that eventually the people will not be able to do anything . . . Scholars and men of letters always criticize me for honoring strange knowledge and for being queer and unusual. It is really difficult to understand the minds of some Chinese.

The Chinese elite typically were landowners. As Myers noted, successful merchants and industrialists did not expand their operations into other regions, but invested their profits in land. In addition, those who made money from holding government office could and did purchase land. The elite of wealthy landowners, however, were not active farmers. Most land was rented, particularly in the South. If you passed over the threshold and became wealthy, renting land did not require supervision. Most rich farmers who became landlords also withdrew from their home villages. Living in the sophisticated urban centers, they devoted themselves to the pursuit of culture and the education of their sons, though they might also invest in real estate or lend money to fund commercial enterprises.

There were risks. The traditional practice of dividing the inheritance among all sons could and frequently did transform a wealthy family into several poor families, another reason for family cycles in addition to the wasteful consumption on ancestor worship emphasized by Myers. China differed in this compared with Korea, where the eldest son inherited the estate. And further, in comparison with Japan and England, some have argued that the division of inheritance in China prevented younger sons from seeking their fortune elsewhere and therefore reduced social mobility.[11]

As Mao emphasized, the state protected the rights of landlords to extract rents. And most importantly the state offered the opportunity of joining the elite through the examination system, with the chance of income and wealth far beyond the possibilities open to an ordinary landlord. The annual income of a district magistrate was 30 000 taels, and a provincial governor 180 000, in the nineteenth century, compared to possibly 100 taels for a moderately successful landlord. 'The truly successful landlord was one who became a member of the gentry, and the truly successful degree-holder was one who became an official.'[12] 'Become an official and become rich' was the common proverb. Successful landlords could support their sons in study for official degrees, but if he succeeded in obtaining a degree, the fortunate young man was drawn to the cities.

There was therefore no reason for wealthy landlords to remain in the village. Nor was there any reason for an official to concern himself with village affairs, unless some problem should bring the village to his attention. The role of the state was pervasive, far greater than that of European states before the late nineteenth century, but contact between the village and the elite and government was indirect. Villagers paid their rents to distant landlords, and district officials exercised their authority through hired assistants.

The values of this distant Confucian scholar gentry were unbendingly conservative, as seen above in the despairing outburst by the modernizing official Li Hongzhang. Despite being continually involved in market economy, the gentry absorbed an anti-profit, anti-merchant bias. The framework of their inherited tradition equipped Confucian scholars with a mechanism for considering new challenges by a process of analogy with what had gone before. Officials could search their libraries for precedents, and they believed that, if a problem arose, someone somewhere would have encountered the same problem previously and devised a solution. It was not a framework which encouraged innovation, nor was it one which endorsed Adam Smith's propensity to truck, barter and exchange.

As noted in Chapter 1, the work of Max Weber has deeply influenced studies of the connection between religion and economic development. Weber argued that Confucian values were inherently anti-capitalist, and he came to this conclusion on the basis of his study of European development.[13] Weber argued that the basic features of capitalism corresponded closely to the basic features of Protestantism. For capitalists, instrumental rationality leads to future orientation and systematic planning. Profits are saved and added to the capital of the firm. For Protestants, in turn, the division between the elect and the damned is fore-ordained. God is all powerful and all knowing, so what will be, must already be determined. But in this world, individuals still can choose to do right or wrong. No one knows for certain whether they belong to the elect. So Protestants have a powerful motive to achieve, to prove to themselves that they belong to the elect. Weber called this a 'secular asceticism' that led Protestants to struggle for success in the world, not to withdraw from it.

Weber believed that these characteristics of Protestantism led Protestants to save rather than wasting their money on display, food, drink, or charity. It was better to give someone a job, or encourage them to succeed on their own. Savings should be invested in productive undertakings. Protestants worked diligently in whatever business they engaged in, because diligence in their 'calling' demonstrated their virtuousness. They also planned their business systematically, because their future success would be evidence of their virtue. And they supported each other, so their savings were available for worthwhile undertakings to people of good character.

In the case of Europe, Weber argued that the characteristics of Catholicism did not fit so well with capitalism. The Church told Catholics what was right or wrong, so the role of the individual conscience was reduced. As long as they are genuinely contrite, Catholics could gain absolution for their sins through confession and penance. For Catholics there was no preordained group of elect souls. Catholics gained merit through their good works, and especially by supporting the Church or by charity. And, traditionally for European Catholics, the ideal was the religious ascetic life, to withdraw from the world entirely and become a monk, nun, or priest. Therefore, said Weber, Catholics had less motive to save, and a strong motive to spend money on the Church or on charity. Catholic countries therefore had low savings ratios, lower investment, and less initiative by individuals, and therefore remained relatively poor.

In the case of China, in analogy with Catholicism in Europe, Weber argued that there was the lack of correspondence between the fundamental characteristics of capitalism and Confucianism. Like Catholicism, Confucianism was hierarchical, authoritarian, and left little role for individual activity. It was not future-oriented, and ancestor worship led to burdensome expenses for funerals, memorial services, and monuments. Confucian values and the social dominance of the educated gentry class explained the failure of China to develop a capitalistic economic system:

> Completely absent in Confucian ethics was any tension between nature and deity, between ethical demand and human shortcoming, consciousness of sin and need for salvation, conduct on earth and compensation in the beyond, religious duty and socio-political reality. Hence, there was no leverage for influencing conduct through inner forces freed of tradition and convention.[14]

Weber's claims were strongly disputed in the discussion that followed the translations of his works into English in the 1950s.[15] As we will see in Chapter 5, advocates of contemporary 'Neo-Confucianism' reject Weber's conclusions and insist that Confucian values can indeed provide the basis for modernization and industrialization. Further, as we will see in Chapter 9, there is no particular reason why for instance Muslim or Buddhist values cannot support economic development. Nevertheless, if we look at the texts that successive generations of Chinese students committed to memory, we find a consistent bias against economic activity. There is not a single reference to merchants in *The Analects*. There are only a very few explicit references to the acquisition of wealth, to profits, or to markets, and those references are uniformly negative:

> The gentleman seeks neither a full belly nor a comfortable home (Confucius, *The Analects*, I.14).
>
> The gentleman understands what is moral. The small man understands what is profitable (Confucius, *The Analects*, IV.16).
>
> If wealth were a permissible pursuit, I would be willing even to act as a guard holding a whip outside the market place. If it is not, I shall follow my own preferences (Confucius, *The Analects*, VII.12).

Further, as Li also complained, Confucian tradition did not value technical expertise and did not encourage the search for new inventions:

> Even minor arts are sure to have their worthwhile aspects, but the gentleman does not take them up because the fear of a man who would go a long way is

that he should be bogged down. . . . The artisan, in any of the hundred crafts, masters his trade by staying in his workshop; the gentleman perfects his way through learning (Confucius, *The Analects*, XIX.4, XIX.7).

As argued below, despite their pervasive influence, these Confucian precepts did not interfere with the commercial, profit-seeking actions of the vast majority of Chinese. Further, even at the elite level, some scholars did attempt to cope with the challenge posed by the West. However, the self-strengthening movement remained confined to particular provinces and individuals. As with Li, the leaders of the self-strengthening movement were provincial governors. In the absence of firm central leadership, they were rivals with each other, rather than collaborators in a coordinated program. Li failed to support one of his colleagues against the French in Vietnam in the 1880s, and in turn that colleague declined to lend his navy in support of Li against the Japanese in 1894.

The self-strengtheners also suffered some of the traditional weaknesses of the governing elite. Their programs were organized from the top down. They displayed the gentry's contempt for merchants, and they discouraged private enterprise in favor of their own projects. They did not trust anyone outside their own families and small circle of friends. The emphasis on connections led to corruption, for instance in the supply of ammunition to Li's navy by his son-in-law when it fought the Japanese. Some of the Chinese gunners found their shells filled with sand.

Leadership and individuals do matter, and the long period of power enjoyed by the Dowager Empress deprived China of the opportunity to respond to the threat posed by the West, and by Japan. In the aftermath of the defeat by the Japanese, China experienced a brief '100 Days' of reform in 1898, but the Emperor lost power in a coup supported by the Dowager Empress, and the reform program failed. Corruption began at the highest levels with the notoriously venal Palace officials. Nepotism, favoritism, embezzlement, and bribery penetrated from the center through the provinces and districts, down to the local level. Local and regional authorities not only retained control over collections and disbursement of taxes, but also sold exemptions as well as accepting bribes in individual cases. Inconsistent and opaque administration interfered with the flow of business.

Following the Boxer Rebellion, the foreign intervention and the capture and sacking of Beijing, and the imposition of yet another huge indemnity, pressure for reform mounted again. In the public sector the old examination system was ended in 1905 and henceforth officials in theory were to be selected on the basis of the mastery of a modern Western-style curriculum. The British government had stated that it would consider an end to the humiliating conditions of extraterritoriality, under which cases involving foreign citizens could only be heard in courts administered by the foreigners themselves, if China modernized its legal system. As part of the program to satisfy the foreigners, in 1904 the new Ministry of Commerce issued China's first Company Law. The expressed intent of the new law was to 'facilitate commerce and promote industries'. However, as William Kirby concludes, this 'did not mean that the Manchu court was now "pro-business" '. The government intended the law to help make the case for the ending of extraterritoriality, and, even more important, it intended the law to increase the power of the central government, by defining and controlling the new modern firms. Commercial disputes, for instance, were heard not by the courts but by the Ministry of Commerce. The law was widely ignored, and by 1908 only 227 companies had registered, most of them small shops, pawnbrokers, and native banks.[16]

Government and Business under the Nationalists

Since Adam Smith economists have agreed that economic development proceeds best in normal times. The Republican period that followed the revolution of 1911 was not normal. The new state inherited many of the problems that the Qing had failed to surmount. The government failed to increase its revenues. In the early 1930s, the total taxes collected by all levels of government may have amounted to only 5 to 7 per cent of total output.[17] The Republican government also inherited the foreign debt of the Qing. To pay the interest and amortization charges, China's tariffs were set and administered by an international consortium led by the British. Little was left for positive economic initiatives. For instance, the Chinese government did not support the silk industry in the 1920s and 1930s, while the Japanese government did, and Chinese silk lost international market share to Japanese producers.

These serious financial problems, however, seem minor compared to the near collapse of central power from 1916 to 1927 and the emergence of some 50 regional 'warlords'. Large areas suffered from civil war, first among the warlords, and then between the emerging leader of the Nationalist Party, Chiang Kaishek, and his former Communist allies. Chiang overcame the most dangerous of the warlords and destroyed the Communist Party in the urban centers, and a new Nationalist government was established in Nanjing in 1928. However, the government faced further challenges from powerful regional commanders, internal factional divisions, and a new rural Communist movement under the leadership of Mao Zedong. And, from 1931 onwards, the government had to contend with open aggression and then full-scale invasion by the Japanese.

Clearly the conditions for normal business operations were lacking. But even if political conditions had been more stable, it is not clear that the Nationalist government would have supported the emergence of private business enterprise or general economic development. Either explicitly or implicitly following Mao's argument, many scholars have concluded that the Nationalist government was dominated by rent-seeking coalitions with roots in China's past. The growth of 'bureaucrat-capitalism', private firms controlled by top government officials, says Parks Coble, was 'not an aberration but the reemergence of a traditional pattern of official domination'.[18] Through its legislation and a host of administrative edicts, the Nationalist state proclaimed its right to control private enterprise. However, within the new and more powerful state structures, senior government officials exploited their personal and family connections to create personal economic empires. Possibly three-quarters of the shareholders, directors, and chief managers of Chinese coal mines between 1912 and 1927 came from the civilian and military bureaucracies.[19] In 1935, the government nationalized most of the banking industry and launched plans for a large state industrial sector, and by 1943, in the regions still controlled by the Nationalists, state firms accounted for 70 per cent of the paid-up capital of all incorporated enterprises.[20]

As before, business proceeded and the economy continued to grow, despite the malfeasance of these corrupt government officials. Relations between the Nationalist government and business were not always one-sided. The government depended on and in some cases deferred to private capitalist interests. Richard Bush, for instance, emphasizes the weakness of the Nationalist government in its dealings with industrialists in the expanding textile industry.[21] That is, although government officials may have inherited traditional Confucian attitudes, the majority of Chinese may have continued to operate in the market as they had done for centuries. As seen below, however, their operations were constrained by the supply of credit and by the need to minimize transaction costs, which reflected back on the structure of the firm.

THE MANAGEMENT GRID IN CONFUCIAN CHINA

Capitalism and Credit

China's economy grew particularly rapidly in the later decades of the nineteenth century. The rebellions and natural disasters of mid-century may have reduced the total population from 410 million in 1850 to 350 million in 1873, but the population then rose again, to 500 million in 1900. Farm families combined subsistence farming, cash crop production, and hand-craft production, shifting from one to another in response to market oppor-tunities. Cash crops and handicraft products were bought and sold by local merchants in district markets. Local merchants exchanged some of their goods with other wealthier merchants who passed them on to yet other Chinese merchants for sale in other regions, or to foreign merchants for sale overseas.

As the economy grew, the share of total output being marketed rose steadily, and so too did the share being produced by true industrial tech-nologies. As in other industrializing countries, the textile industry was the first to expand and develop. In 1860, 45 per cent of China's peasant house-holds wove cloth. Four-fifths of these textile-producing families grew their own cotton and spun their own yarn before weaving it into cloth. The cloth they produced was often for their own use, and only a little over half of all cloth produced was sold through the markets. Factory production had only begun. Less than 1 per cent of yarn used by village weavers was machine spun and only 3 per cent of cotton cloth was machine woven. Two genera-tions later, in 1936, 30 per cent of peasant households still wove cloth. However, very few of these families still grew cotton or spun yarn, for 87 per cent of all cotton grown was marketed, and over 75 per cent of all yarn used in village hand-woven cloth was machine spun. Factory production domi-nated weaving as well. Hand-woven cloth was less than 40 per cent of total consumption.[22]

Production and trade were both financed by sophisticated credit arrange-ments. By the late 1890s, over 10 000 'native banks' (*qianzhuang*) served local markets. Local bankers took deposits from relatives and friends, extended credit to select customers, and issued notes that were accepted as means of payment in their home districts. Local financial markets were connected by a network of 27 'remittance banks' (*piaohao*). Remittance banks took deposits mainly from state agencies and officials, and they issued notes as well. They provided credit to local native banks and to large merchants. And, most important, they provided the means for the transfer of both private and public funds over long distances. In doing so they dealt in and guaranteed payment in the currencies created by the multitude of native banks.[23]

The individuals, families, and firms, and the further firms that provided them with credit and supplies, and the others that marketed their output, used techniques of calculation that demonstrate systematic and rational approaches to their enterprise. Weber was incorrect in a number of specific assertions he made about China. He believed that the Chinese numerical system interfered with rational calculation, but this is clearly not the case. He also thought the use of the abacus would hinder tabular reckoning, but the evidence of company records shows it did not. Chinese textbooks from the nineteenth century show solutions to problems such as calculation of exchange rates or distribution of profits very similar to European methods. In fact Chinese businessmen also developed an indigenous double entry system, but, as in the case of Western businesses, it was not always necessary and therefore was not always employed.[24]

However, growth and development may not yet have led to a capitalist transformation. As Myers might put it, the traditional family-centered 'Confucian' firm – authoritarian, cautiously conservative, and both inward and backward looking – may have retarded China's development. The native banks were perceived as obsolete, and as noted above banks were prominent among the few firms that made use of the new Company Law. By 1911, there were 17 joint-stock banks and, between 1912 and 1927, 266 new banks were founded. However, caught between inherited ways of doing business and the difficulties of the unstable environment, over half of them failed. There were large Chinese firms, such as the Nanyang Tobacco Company or the Rong industrial conglomerate in Shanghai, but these firms and others like them did not evolve into bureaucratized or managerial firms on the Western model.[25]

On the other hand, as Mao might put it, China was not allowed to develop on its own. Foreigners were exempt from internal tariffs and taxes. The nine foreign banks operating in China in 1900 had ruthlessly exploited their extraterritorial status to gain control over foreign remittances and state loans. Linsun Cheng estimates that their paid-up capital, deposits, and note issue approximately equaled that of the 10 000 native banks, or that of the 27 remittance banks.[26] Further, as Mao was well aware, foreigners played a large role in the modern industrial sector of the economy. In the 1930s, a substantial fraction of the machine-spun yarn and the machine-woven cloth was being produced in factories owned and managed by British and Japanese firms located in the protected foreign sections of Shanghai and other coastal cities.

Transaction Costs and Firm Structure

In standard economic theory, every firm maximizes its profit by equalizing the ratio of marginal output to price for all its factors of production. However, standard theory is silent on the way in which this is accomplished. In the two previous chapters we have looked at the internal structure of Japanese and Korean firms and the ways they deploy their resources. In addition to this internal view, however, we also need to consider the way the firm relates to its external environment. Standard theory assumes that the managers of each firm possess perfect knowledge, of prices in distant markets, and of the reliability of other firms, for instance. This is clearly false. The costs of obtaining information and of enforcing contracts are substantial, and minimizing such 'transaction costs' is one of the critical functions of every manager. Every manager has the option of performing these functions within the firm, or hiring some other firm to perform them, and the resulting balance of internal hierarchies and external markets determines the boundaries of the firm.

In general it is assumed in Western management theory that, over time, firms will expand and develop their internal hierarchies to fulfill an increasing number of specialized functions. New regional branches allow the firm to expand into distant markets, new product divisions allow the firm to produce and deliver goods and services more efficiently, and new functional offices provide services such as accounting, personnel support, and marketing to the branches and divisions. By re-drawing the borders of the firm as it expands, managers lessen their reliance on markets and reduce the costs of acquiring information and enforcing contracts. Employees in such a firm are 'bureaucratic' in that they are hired on the basis of their formal qualifications and evaluated on the basis of their objective performance.

In contrast, however, Chinese family firms relied on the marketplace to handle their transaction costs. They did not develop the capability to handle these costs within the firm. They hired brokers to provide market information, paid middlemen to arrange contracts and underwrite them, and joined and paid fees to guilds to control quality. The reliability of the brokers, the honesty of the middlemen, and the efficiency of the guilds, were all assured by the fact that they belonged to the circle of personal acquaintances of each firm's owner. Firms regularly drew on funds provided by other members of the circle. The circle might be drawn in different ways. It could be limited to the immediate family, or it might extend to the entire lineage. It might rely on networks of friendship in a single village, local marketing area, or province. Circles overlapped, and the connections among circles allowed for dealings across all of China.[27] These were, as Gary Hamilton emphasizes, horizontal networks based on a sharing of information, risk, and profit, differing both from Japanese *keiretsu* and from Korean *chaebol*. Trust and ongoing relationships (*guanxi*) were crucial. In a sense Chinese firms had 'two types of owners', those (usually an individual or family) who controlled the firm's assets directly, and in addition those ('*guanxi* owners') who contributed money or credit and who expected a return on their investment, but who had little or no direct involvement in the firm's operations.[28]

Because the number of individuals that any one person knows is limited, limiting the firm's dimensions to the personal acquaintances of the owner will restrict its size. Typically, Chinese firms did not expand into other markets by establishing separate divisions with impersonal, bureaucratic teams of managers. Instead, successful families diversified their investments in their own home city or region by purchasing farms, urban property, shares in other companies, and government bonds, or by investing as silent partners (Hamilton's '*guanxi* owners') in other businesses. They were certainly able to concentrate on the business, as Tao Zhu-gong would have recommended, but they perhaps were less able to diagnose and seize opportunities and combat threats than he would have liked.

Restricting the firm to the circle of acquaintances must at some point become counterproductive. Concentrating on the inherited ways and avoiding innovation at some point passed into stubbornness, Tao Zhu-gong's Fifth Pitfall. There were large Chinese firms, but they were rare. Even the largest firms, such as manufacturing firms or banks in the treaty ports, were still individually or family-owned. They might take the form of joint-stock corporations under the new Company Law, but they remained essentially family holding companies. The head of the Rong family served as chief executive officer of all of the 12 flour mills and six cotton mills controlled by the group in Shanghai.[29] Nanyang Brothers Tobacco Company, facing intense competition from the British–American Tobacco Company and desperately needing new capital, finally registered as a joint-stock company. The proposed by-laws named family members to all the positions on the governing board, stipulated that new shareholders would have no voice in board appointments, and installed the largest family shareholder as the firm's 'permanent president'. The government rejected the by-laws, and the firm revised them, but then made the appointments and continued to operate as they had originally proposed.[30]

Through the 1920s and 1930s Chinese business leaders knew about Western forms of management and corporate governance and, as in the case of Nanyang Brothers, sometimes adopted them. However, a secure system of governance requires an environment of stability, certainty, and trust. This was evidently lacking. Chinese business leaders avoided government regulation when they could, notably by not registering their firms as joint stock corporations. In addition to political upheaval, William Kirby notes that the 'blizzard of codification' imposed by the Nationalist government also subjected business to a broad range of new taxes, export duties, and import tariffs. In addition, the provisions of the 1929 revision of the Company Law re-defined the corporation in a manner that exempted government enterprises from its provisions. It also contained a new article that limited the voting power of any shareholder to one-fifth of the votes of all outstanding shares, regardless of the actual number of shares owned. Ostensibly a measure to protect the interests of minority shareholders, it also provided a lever for a rapacious minority interest to block and possibly expropriate majority shareholders. As Kirby concludes, 'The private sector's response to the new law was predictably tepid.' Less than a quarter of Chinese-owned factories were incorporated in the 1930s, and almost none in the key textile industry.[31]

The development of Chinese firms therefore was driven by a range of forces, some of them conflicting, but all with longer-term consequences. Inherited traditions influenced both private firms and their relations with the government. The Japanese invasion and the division between Nationalists and Communists set the scene for the civil war following Japan's defeat. The Nationalist government, having lost the civil war, moved to Taiwan, and many of their supporters fled to Hong Kong, and we will look at their development in Chapter 5. Others joined the 'overseas Chinese' in Southeast Asia, as we will see in Chapter 8. And of course, in China itself, the Communist victory eliminated private firms for a generation, with further long-term effects, but they have reemerged as one of the drivers of growth since the late 1970s, and we will consider that very complicated story in Chapter 6.

FURTHER READING

The quotations from Confucius and Mencius are from the excellent translations by D.C. Lau (London: Penguin, 1970 and 1979).

John K. Fairbank, *China: A New History* (Cambridge: Harvard University Press, 1992), is the final magnum opus by the recognized dean of Chinese studies in the United States, completed shortly before his death. Gracefully written, it is sympathetic to Mao and presents a very negative picture of the Nationalists. Immanuel C.Y. Hsu, *The Rise of Modern China* (6th edn; New York and Oxford: Oxford University Press, 2000) is also a very good book, but written from a strongly anti-Communist perspective. Successive revisions have cut sections from earlier chapters and added chapters on recent developments. The additional chapters are based on current news reports and give a good feel for the changes in opinion regarding Chinese development, but the complete chapters of the first edition (1970) are preferable for the period up to the death of Mao.

Two important articles on the behavior of Chinese firms are Gary G. Hamilton, 'Competition and organization: a reexamination of Chinese business practices', *Journal of Asian Business*, **12**(1) (1996), 7–20, and William C. Kirby, 'China unincorporated: company law and business enterprise in twentieth-century China', *Journal of Asian Studies*, **54**(1) (1995), 43–63. Case studies dealing with the late Qing and Nationalist periods include William T. Rowe, *Hankow: Commerce and Society in a Chinese City,*

1796–1889 (Stanford: Stanford University Press, 1984); Marie-Claire Bergère, *The Golden Age of the Chinese Bourgeoisie 1911–1937* (Cambridge: Cambridge University Press, 1989. (French original, Paris: Flammarion, 1986), and Sherman Cochran, *Big Business in China: Sino-Foreign Rivalry in the Cigarette Industry, 1890–1930* (Cambridge: Harvard University Press, 1980). The banking industry has received considerable attention recently. See Linsun Cheng, *Banking in Modern China: Entrepreneurs, Professional Managers, and the Development of Chinese Banks, 1897–1937* (New York: Cambridge University Press, 2003).

NOTES

1. Adam Smith, *Wealth of Nations* (1776), Book I, Chapter 3.
2. Huang (1990).
3. Skinner (1964–5), 3–43, 195–228, 363–99.
4. Skinner (1977), pp. 211–52, 275–351.
5. Perkins (1969), pp. 136–7.
6. Myers (1980), p. 82.
7. See for instance Huang (1985), p. 118; Huang (1990), pp. 88–90.
8. Hsu (1980).
9. Hamilton (1984), p. 417.
10. Mann (1987).
11. Fairbank (1992), p. 21.
12. Huang (1985), p. 247.
13. Weber (1904–5; 1958).
14. Weber (1920–21; 1951), pp. 335–6.
15. See Green (1973).
16. Kirby (1995), 43–63.
17. Rawski (1989).
18. Coble (1980), p. 260. See Fewsmith (1985); Bergère (1989), French original Paris: Flammarion, 1986.
19. Wright (1984), p. 146.
20. Kirby (1995), p. 53.
21. Bush (1982).
22. Huang (1990), p. 98.
23. Cheng (2003).
24. Gardella (1992), 317–39.
25. Cochran (1980); Bergère (1989).
26. Cheng (2003).
27. Rowe (1984); Watson (1985); Faure (1991), 1–3.
28. Hamilton (1996), 16–17.
29. Bergère (1989).
30. Cochran (1980), pp. 98–101.
31. Kirby (1995), p. 52.

5. Managing the Chinese firm in Hong Kong and Taiwan

Assess the advantages in taking advice, then structure your forces accordingly, to supplement extraordinary tactics. Forces are to be structured strategically, based on what is advantageous. (Sun Tzu, *The Art of War*)

Ability to be agile and flexible: hesitation and indecisiveness will end in nothing. (Tao Zhu-gong, the Fifth Business Principle)

The Chinese Confucian firm has two direct offshoots in Hong Kong and in Taiwan. As we have seen in Chapter 4, China enjoyed the benefits of an advanced market economy for centuries, but neither the Qing nor the Nationalist state supported the development of private enterprises. As we have also seen, scholars such as Ramon Myers have argued that Confucian values can support very rapid pursuit of new opportunities and therefore very rapid growth. However, this can only happen if government policy is oriented toward 'instrumental rationality', a phrase Myers borrows from Max Weber, implying the purposeful organization of resources to achieve future goals. Confucian values could and would support economic growth and development, but only if and when the political structures changed.[1]

Two places where government did – eventually – come to support Chinese firms are Hong Kong and Taiwan, but they supported them in different ways, with different results. Both Hong Kong and Taiwan are remarkably successful export-oriented economies. Both are also characterized by the very large numbers of relatively small enterprises. Both have the ability to be agile and flexible. But Hong Kong and Taiwan firms differ, and the differences arise from their historical experience. It could be said that governments in both Hong Kong and Taiwan structured their forces strategically, 'based on what is advantageous', and their actions had important long-term consequences for the firms they guided.

In Hong Kong, the historical and institutional grids reflect the British colonial state's role in the economy, the subordinate position of Chinese firms, war and the establishment of the People's Republic, immigration and new firms, and the more active role of the colonial state in the post-war period. Here the role of government, though limited, appears more

positive than in Qing and Nationalist China. The return to China of course
marks the immediate past. Hong Kong's managers have adjusted in turn to
life under the colonial state and under the People's Republic. In addition,
the flow of capital and the expansion of Hong Kong firms into southern
China make Hong Kong an important background factor for development
there.

Taiwan's historical grid reflects the heritage of Japanese colonialism, the
imposition of Nationalist rule and the split between mainlanders and
Taiwanese, and more recently democratization and sharing of power. The
institutional grid in turn reflects the changing role of the Nationalist state
in the economy, the impact of pilot agencies and government targeting, and
export orientation and imported technology. The management grid parallels these developments. Managers in Taiwan have benefited from direct
and indirect government support, and they can draw not only on their
Chinese heritage but also on a state-sponsored Neo-Confucian ideology.
And, as with Hong Kong, investment flows and the expansion of Taiwan
firms into China helps shape development across the straits.

BOX 5.1   POINT AND COUNTERPOINT: HONG KONG GARMENT AND THE STRENGTHS AND WEAKNESSES OF THE HONG KONG SYSTEM

Do not expose oneself readily. (Tao Zhu-gong, the Seventh Business Pitfall)

Hong Kong Garment was founded in 1985. It produced clothing primarily for retailers in the United States. Headquartered in Hong Kong, the firm located its manufacturing facilities in China to take advantage of the low wages. Growth was rapid, and profits remarkable. In 1995, the firm earned a gross margin of 37 per cent on sales of some US$146 million. In 1992, the firm had listed on the Hong Kong Stock Exchange, with the founder, who also served as CEO, holding 65 per cent of the outstanding shares. The stock exchange listing raised new equity for the firm and lowered its borrowing costs, promising further growth and continued profitability.

However, the founder/CEO had decided to use a substantial fraction of the new equity, plus a large amount of borrowed capital, to establish a freight distribution network in China. A partnership with a United States freight distribution company envisaged Hong Kong Garment buying property and taking responsibility for construction of infrastructure in China, while the United States partner would provide advice, computers, and ongoing management expertise. The partners planned to expand the business into a national distribution network.

Hong Kong Garment's founder/CEO had no previous experience in the freight distribution industry. 'The selection of this industry was based simply on the fact that an opportunity had suddenly presented itself to the owner and he decided to pursue it.' His lack of experience led to a series of poor decisions in the freight business, and then, in mid-1995, the firm was also hit by a drop in orders from its clothing customers in the United States. In early 1996, the firm suddenly asked its creditors (one international and 15 local banks) for a moratorium on interest and principal payments. The founder/CEO promised improved collateral, sales of non-core assets, and increased equity. Past due accounts had blown out to US$23 million, and these were in fact reduced to US$5 million. The assets of the freight distribution system were sold, along with several pieces of property in Hong Kong. The founder/CEO sold part of his shareholdings but refused to reduce his holdings below 55 per cent of the total. He also continued to see the way out of his problems as further expansion and diversification: 'The outside investors and lenders found it difficult to change that focus.'

In late 1996, turnaround advisers discovered that Hong Kong Garment was burdened by additional previously undisclosed liabilities. At the end of the year the creditors demanded either that new capital be found or that the firm be liquidated. An investor was in fact found, who provided new capital and assumed part of the firm's debt. A full 18 months after the initial failure to meet interest payments, the founder/CEO was finally removed. The banks wrote off some of their loans and converted another portion into equity. The new investor ended with a 43 per cent stake in the firm, the banks now owned 38 per cent, and the original founder/CEO's shareholding had been reduced to 8 per cent. Sales declined to US$94 million in 1997, but they still brought a healthy 25 per cent gross profit margin, and under its new leadership the restructured firm appeared on the way to recovery.

Source: Garry D. Bruton, David Ahlstrom, and Johnny C.C. Wan, 'Turnaround Success of Large and Midsize Chinese Owned Firms: Evidence from Hong Kong and Thailand,' *Journal of World Business* **36**(2) (2001): 146–165. Hong Kong Garment is a pseudonym.

BOX 5.2   POINT AND COUNTERPOINT: THE
           ACER GROUP AND THE STRENGTHS
           AND WEAKNESSES OF THE TAIWAN
           SYSTEM

Sales must be conducted at any time; procrastination and delay lead to
lost opportunities. (Tao Zhu-gong, the Tenth Business Lesson)

Acer was established in Taiwan in 1976, and over the next 25 years
grew to become one of the world's ten largest producers of personal
computers. Operating through 120 offices in 41 countries and
employing over 35 000 people, in 2002 it had total revenues of nearly
US$13 billion. Acer's founder, Stan Shih, has modeled some of his
business strategies on the Chinese strategy game of Go, in which
success often depends on establishing a firm base at the edges of
the board before attacking the center. Shih is also famous for his four-
character phrase 'circle of dragons with no head'. He uses the phrase
to describe Acer's distinctive structure of autonomous business
cells, in which none of the group's member firms exercises direct
supervisory authority over the others. Each member firm supplies
products and services to other members of the group as well as to
external customers, but no member is bound to source its needs
exclusively from other group members. Ongoing collaboration, a
developing history of quality products and services, and ultimately
the trust that this creates, are the basis for the group's coherence.
Member firms have varying structures, and some are involved in joint
venture partnerships with non-member firms. Shih says the less he
owns the richer he gets, because the flexibility and responsiveness
of the group have led to such rapid growth.

   Acer in fact has passed through several distinct phases of development, not always smoothly. It began as a small firm acting as an
agent for United States microprocessor firms and providing services to Taiwan manufacturers of electronic games. The company
saw an opportunity to become a low-cost producer of IBM-
compatible computers, working primarily under contract for other
larger firms that would sell the machines under their own brand
names. Acer benefited from expertise provided by the Industrial
Technology Research Institute, a government research and development laboratory. In 1981, manufacturing operations began in the
government-funded Hsinchu Science-Based Industrial Park. Five
years later, Acer earned US$400 million, but Shih announced a

ten-year plan to expand globally and generate US$5 billion annually. The previous 'relaxed' approach to managerial initiative was dropped, a new chief executive was recruited from IBM, and a tighter, more centralized, 'serious management' style was adopted. Acer grew, but the costs of borrowing to fund expansion outran revenues, and by 1991 Acer faced a major financial crisis.

Acer remained one of Taiwan's most successful firms, but Shih refused to retreat from his global ambitions. Instead he and a small group of senior managers restructured the group. In response to complaints from some divisions that their profits were supporting losses made by other divisions, Shih and his colleagues 'bit the bullet and "broke" Acer up into a series of autonomous operating entities, allocating market responsibilities to some (called the RBUs or regional business units) and production and technology responsibilities to others (called the SBUs or strategic business units)'. The business units were to contract directly with each other, a process Shih dubbed the 'client-server' model, based on three broad principles, 'no excess baggage', meaning cost control, 'if it doesn't hurt, help', meaning giving the best possible deal to other units in the group, and 'each man the lord of his castle', meaning autonomy for units in dealing with outside suppliers and clients. A 'fast food' model of delivery placed assembly as close to customers as possible rather than shipping fully assembled machines from Taiwan, and this led to further autonomy for the regional units.

Shih aimed for '21 in 21', that is, at least 21 independently listed companies in as many countries by the beginning of the twenty-first century. Sales grew through the mid-1990s and neared US$6 billion annually, but then stagnated. Cyclical factors, the Asian financial crisis, and intense competition in retail sales all hurt. Competitors replicated the fast food model. More important, though, was the intensive and time-consuming negotiations required to maintain effective relations among the units and particularly between the global strategic units and the regional units. Following another conference, in early 1998, Shih and his senior colleagues introduced a global matrix structure, with 'lines of business' in major areas connecting the strategic and regional business units, supported by a new Corporate Executive Committee (CEC) and an enhanced corporate headquarters providing services such as information technology infrastructure and brand management.

The matrix model failed to gain support from managers across the group, and was discarded after only a few months. Instead Shih and the CEC dissolved the existing business units and recombined them into a cluster of global units with worldwide responsibility for designated products and services. End-to-end responsibility would, they hoped, lead both to greater customer focus and to enhancement of the Acer brand. Under the leadership of the CEC, the units can and did expand, shrink, and divide with conditions changing and new opportunities arising. Separate and independent ownership of these units is encouraged. This allows for Acer's 'local touch' relationships with partners in different countries. It also allows for new units to be formed that can focus on new products or services. And finally it allows younger managers to be given responsibility as heads of new units, and avoids the conflict that might arise if 'Chinese norms of seniority' were violated and junior managers promoted over the heads of their seniors.

Growth resumed, and Acer's 'fuzzy' structure seemed to serve it well. Shih now described the group as an 'Internet organization'. Nevertheless, although regional components of the group were listed in Taiwan, Singapore, and Mexico City, and Depository Receipts could be traded on the London Stock Exchange, Acer had not achieved listing on any major exchange. A 'cluster of global businesses' rather than a 'global corporation', Acer still faced problems of coordination among its units. Attempts to expand into new markets through joint ventures with local firms were also not always successful. Acer's 'Mega e-infrastructure' initiative aimed explicitly at small and medium enterprises, and according to Acer's president J.T. Wang would be launched 'in Taiwan first' before expanding to other regions.

In the major markets in the United States, Europe, and Japan, Acer remained a maker of commodified products rather than a major brand in its own right. A premium line of laptops featured the Porsche automobile logo as a marketing tactic, but customers were buying the Porsche brand, not Acer. BenQ was spun off as a separate brand in 2001, and acquired Siemens' mobile handset business in 2005, but faced difficulties due to heavy marketing expenses, possible cultural conflicts with its new European workforce, and retaliation from Motorola, its major customer, which slashed orders for handsets when BenQ began competing directly with its own branded phones.

Sources: John A. Mathews, *Dragon Multinational: A New Model for Global Growth* (New York: Oxford University Press, 2002), pp. 55–80, 132–57 (the reference to 'Chinese norms of seniority' is on p. 151); 'Twin daggers to cut a brand in Taiwan', *The Australian*, 30 August 2005 (*The Economist* report). See http://global.acer.com for statements by Shih and Wang, and descriptions of Acer's products and services.

GOVERNMENT AND THE INSTITUTIONAL GRID IN HONG KONG

Hong Kong was created as a trading outpost of the British Empire. To force open a market for the only product it possessed that the Chinese wanted to buy, Britain launched the Opium War in 1839. The possession of a small steam vessel allowed the British to blockade the Grand Canal where it intersected the Yangtze River, cutting off food supplies to Beijing. China capitulated and ceded Hong Kong to Britain in 1841. The British later annexed Kowloon, and in 1898 forced China to lease the New Territories for 99 years. The end of the lease was the occasion for reversion of all of Hong Kong to China. Until then, Hong Kong was a British Crown colony, ruled directly by the Colonial Office. An appointed governor wielded wide powers, limited only by a tradition of consultation with an advisory council that included a few Chinese representatives.

Through the 1930s, Hong Kong served as an entrepôt for the surrounding regions. Chinese firms, the comprador capitalists that Mao Zedong despised, provided access to China for British firms. After the Second World War, Britain retained Hong Kong. Despite the fact that Hong Kong was not profitable, Britain, like other imperial powers, wanted to keep everything. In addition, for the newly founded People's Republic of China it may have appeared too much trouble to invade and re-conquer Hong Kong. China was involved in the Korean War, and would probably regain Hong Kong at the expiration of the lease on the New Territories in any case. In addition, supplying food to Hong Kong and using the city as an opening for the re-export of other goods provided China with some useful foreign exchange.

Despite the continued contacts with China, Hong Kong was for the most part cut off from its natural hinterlands and forced to find other means of survival. That is, Hong Kong was more or less forced to produce goods for export. In addition, the defeat of the Nationalists by the Communists resulted in a large migration of Nationalist supporters to Hong Kong. From around 600 000 in 1945, the population grew to over 2 million in 1950 and 2.6 million in 1956. Many Chinese-owned banks relocated to Hong Kong.[2] In addition many of the migrants were industrialists and workers, and in some cases they were complete firms. Shanghai migrants dominated the early development of textile production in Hong Kong. In the 1980s, possibly 80 per cent of the cotton spinning mills in Hong Kong were majority-owned Shanghai enterprises.[3]

The colonial state played a continuous and active role in the economy.[4] Centralized and authoritarian, its first concern was public order. Hostility between Communists and Nationalists led to strikes and serious riots in

1956, and then again in 1966 and 1967. The provision of social services and expanding employment became a means of reducing unrest. In the 1970s and into the 1980s, the government used its control of housing development, rents, education and training, as well as its influence over investment, to promote growth and external trade. The government defined all land as 'crown land'. It profited from sales and leasing of land, but it also subsidized housing projects and guided industrial development through the creation of industrial estates and 'flatted' factories. Eventually nearly half of the population was accommodated in housing blocks constructed with government support that provided homes at far lower cost than would have been possible through private construction. Estimates for data from the early 1970s indicated that the effect of government subsidies could add from 50 to 70 per cent to the incomes of working-class households.

However, the colonial government was not notably effective in encouraging improvements in productivity. Tax policies encouraged savings and investment, which rose to a high share of total income, but after deducting for these increases in capital, some estimates show no improvement in productivity at all from the mid-1960s to the early 1990s.[5] Manufacturing did not shift significantly toward more high-tech and high value-added areas, and even in the electronics industry, for instance, Hong Kong firms remained largely at the relatively labor-intensive end of production.[6] The Hong Kong Productivity Council attempted to promote quality enhancement and improved technological capabilities, but its efforts suffered from lack of funds and from the official policy of laissez faire and non-intervention of British government officials. The British were happy to manipulate the property market and food prices and to control infrastructure development, but resisted the notion of investing in new technology or subsidizing its adoption by private firms. 'With Thatcher demolishing British industry at home, they certainly were not going to push it in the colonies,' recalled a Hong Kong Chinese businesswoman.

As the date for the return to China approached, many worried about how the Chinese government would treat Hong Kong. The Hong Kong and Shanghai Banking Corporation (HSBC), the largest local bank, relocated its headquarters to London in the early 1990s, but surely they would not kill a goose that laid golden eggs? 'Our history is littered with dead geese,' said the same businesswoman before the handover. In theory the phrase 'one country, two systems' defined the new situation. A Basic Law established Hong Kong's status as a Special Administrative Region, and a complex series of agreements governed for instance the treatment of Hong Kong's massive foreign exchange reserves and migration from other provinces of China into Hong Kong. Hong Kong was to retain its existing, largely British, economic and commercial legislation almost entirely intact, along with its generally open markets and receptiveness to foreign investment.

The formal reversion to China in July 1997 was followed immediately by the Asian financial crisis. Following a policy dating from the early 1980s, the Hong Kong Monetary Authority decided to maintain the 'peg' of the Hong Kong dollar to the United States dollar. Banks were warned not to facilitate speculation against the Hong Kong dollar. An announcement that 'repeated borrowers' of Hong Kong dollars would be charged penalty rates of interest caused interest rates to rise, and the overnight rate reached an astonishing 280 per cent on 23 October 1997.[7] In consequence, asset prices dropped. A one-third decline in real estate prices hurt not only home-owners in Hong Kong, but also the Japanese banks that had lent money to Hong Kong developers. The share market also dropped by a third. However, in this case the authorities did not want prices to collapse completely. In August 1998, the Monetary Authority purchased large blocks of shares in the major listed firms and company groups, including 12.3 per cent of Swire Pacific, 10.3 per cent of Cheung Kong, and 9 per cent of HSBC. In all, these purchases amounted to US$25 billion, over one-quarter of Hong Kong's entire share market capitalization.

The arrival of new political officials, and new requirements such as Mandarin instruction in the schools, caused initial friction, but Chinese leaders did indeed seem conscious that the goose was better alive than dead. As the businesswoman put it, 'we waited for the other shoe to drop, and either they didn't drop it, or they put it down very, very gently'. In response to concerns about political interference in the companies whose shares had been acquired by the Monetary Authority, these shareholdings were transferred to an independent Exchange Investment Fund. A mutual fund was also established through which individual investors could purchase units at a substantial discount. The Monetary Authority continued its conservative financial policies. Foreign investors continued to be welcome. The Productivity Council continued its efforts to facilitate improvements along the 'value chain' of Hong Kong firms, but as before its programs were largely confined to informational briefings and industry trade fairs.[8]

GOVERNMENT AND THE INSTITUTIONAL GRID IN TAIWAN

Taiwan as a Japanese Colony, 1895–1945

Taiwan was annexed by Japan following the war with China in 1895. Isolated from the mainland, it had been a full province only since 1885.

The last governor had begun a modernization program on the model of other leaders of the self-strengthening movement, and following the Japanese victory the Taiwanese declared a republic and elected him president. The independence movement was repressed by the Chinese, who then handed Taiwan over to the Japanese. Following a two-year struggle to 'pacify' the island, the Japanese colonial administrations made efforts to win the support of local elites. Taiwanese landlords kept their land, and the curriculum of the schools reflected conservative Confucian values.

As in Korea, the Japanese period saw substantial growth. The population rose rapidly, but per capital product increased on average by 2 per cent per year. The Japanese worked to improve agricultural output and productivity, first of sugar and later of rice. The government extended irrigation, established credit and cooperative associations, introduced the use of chemical fertilizers, and sponsored research and development of new sugarcane and rice varieties. The railway system expanded, and the Japanese continued railway construction during the depression. Public health improved dramatically. The death rate in Taiwan declined from 33 to 19 per 1000 from 1906 to 1940. Education expanded. One-third of all children were in school in 1930–31, and 71 per cent in 1943–44.[9]

Zaibatsu interests worked in cooperation with military authorities. Semi-government corporations were established and grew into large conglomerates, notably the Taiwan Electric Power Company and the Taiwan Development Company. In the 1930s, Japan's leaders came to view the colonies as military and naval centers. This led to an additional push to develop strategic industries in addition to supplies of food and raw materials. As in Korea, in Taiwan the share of industry in employment increased significantly. These factories were mostly in food processing. There were possibly only two cotton mills in 1945, but some advanced manufacturing related to war production had begun, for instance Taiwan Aluminum and Taiwan Machinery. Most modern enterprises were Japanese, but certain individuals and groups benefited enormously from colonial development, and again as in Korea a small but significant number of Taiwanese established extensive commercial and industrial enterprises.[10]

The Nationalist Government and the Institutional Grid

In 1945, the Nationalist Chinese government seized control of Taiwan from the defeated Japanese. Treating Taiwanese as enemy collaborators, Nationalist politicians and senior military officers confiscated goods, land, and industrial firms for their personal profit. In early 1947, protest demonstrations were repressed. The massacres on 28 February 1947 killed 8000 to 10 000 persons, including many educated leaders of the Taiwanese community.[11]

Following the victory of the Communists and the establishment of the People's Republic, the Nationalist government shifted to Taiwan. Formally, Taiwan remained under the 1948 Temporary Provisions for the Period of Mobilization of the Suppression of the Communist Rebellion until 1991. Martial law, imposed in 1949, remained in place until 1987. The government considered itself the legitimate government of all of China, and the surviving representatives of all Chinese provinces continued to sit in the legislature until 1991. The Nationalist Party, the Kuomintang or KMT, was the only political party allowed until 1989. Taiwan also remained effectively under the rule of one man. After changing the constitution that had prohibited the President from serving more than two terms, Chiang Kaishek continued as President until his death in 1975. In 1978 his son, Premier Chiang Ching-kuo, became President, and remained in office until his own death in 1988.

Beginning in the 1970s, the government gradually relaxed restrictions on political activity and began to bridge the gap between mainlanders and indigenous Taiwanese. As Premier, Chiang Ching-kuo sponsored the appointment of Taiwanese to senior government positions and the expansion of the legislature to allow the election of more Taiwanese representatives. As President he continued along this line. In 1980, the first competitive national elections were held. Though the KMT remained the only recognized party, organized opposition groups emerged. Liberalization of the KMT itself included election of officers for fixed terms and inclusion of more Taiwanese. In 1986, Chiang appointed a commission that recommended the lifting of martial law, legalization of political parties, greater power to the legislature, and greater local autonomy. Six of the previously illegal opposition parties filed for official status, and in 1986 Taiwan had its first multi-party election.

Following Chiang's death in 1988, Vice-President Lee Teng-hui became Taiwan's first native-born President. In 1988, restrictions on publishing newspapers were lifted, and in 1989 a new Civic Organizations Law allowed the formation of new professional, social, and political organizations. Lee continued the movement towards a Taiwanese majority in the leadership of the KMT and in the government, and he also continued the development of the KMT from a 'revolutionary party' to a 'regular party', willing to surrender power if defeated at the polls. This did not please all members of the KMT, and the party split, with the breakaway New Party retaining something like the old commitment to 'saving' China. From 1989 to 1991, a reduction in the size of the legislature and phased retirement of the remaining mainland-elected members culminated in the general elections of 1991, which the KMT won with 71 per cent of the vote. As the capstone of democratization, the presidency was made an elective office, and Lee himself was elected with a 54 per cent majority in 1996.

Taiwan is a functioning democracy, but the split between indigenous Taiwanese and mainlanders remains. In fact democratization may have reinforced the division by making competition for political power possible.[12] Looming in the background is the question of reunification with China. China regards Taiwan as a province. Any demonstration of independence by Taiwan's leaders brings violent denunciations in the Chinese press, and there have been threatening military demonstrations. Within Taiwan itself, public opinion polls suggest that most voters, whether they identify themselves as Taiwanese or as Chinese, may in theory favor reunification with China, but in practice would like to postpone it to some future date. Most Taiwanese leaders have attempted to appeal to this majority by avoiding confrontation with China while implicitly relying on the power of the United States to maintain the status quo.

Neo-Confucianism

During the period of one-party rule the KMT described itself as a 'revolutionary party'. In addition, however, because it considered itself the legitimate government of all of China, the Taiwan government also believed itself to be the custodian of traditional Chinese culture. It therefore defended Confucian values, in contrast to the anti-Confucian Communist values of the People's Republic. The government subsidized museums and research centers to support its claims. As economic growth accelerated it became increasingly plausible to link modern economic success with inherited social norms. The Taiwan government drew support from eminent overseas Chinese academics, notably Tu Wei-ming, Professor of Chinese History and Philosophy at Harvard University. Tu insisted that Confucian 'habits of the heart' were 'pervasive' in the East Asian 'Sinitic sphere'. In addition to China itself, Hong Kong, and Taiwan, Tu believed the Sinitic sphere included Korea, Japan, Vietnam, and Singapore. He also thought that 'overseas' Chinese everywhere continued to share these inherited Confucian tendencies.[13]

Tu argued that the Confucian concept of the individual differs fundamentally from that of the West. East Asians belonging to the Sinitic sphere, he said, learn the five relationships (parent to child, husband to wife, older brother to younger brother, ruler to subject, and friend to friend) within their extended family. The extension of these patterns of thought outside the extended family setting gives them a much more sophisticated ability to relate to others than Westerners. As he put it, the Confucian ethic 'seems to have centered in an efficacious location much more generative and dynamic than the lonely self: the self that is not an island but an ever-expanding stream of interconnectedness'.[14]

This is important, said Tu, because 'the values people cherish or unconsciously uphold provide guidance for their actions', particularly in the economic sphere. In the contemporary world, 'Neo-Confucian' values had become 'an amalgam of the family or collectively-oriented values of the East and the pragmatic, economic-goal oriented values of the West'.[15] Tu saw a direct link between Confucian values and business success:

> The Confucian conception that the self is a center of relationships and that, as a dynamic center, it constantly evolves around an ever-expanding network of human-relatedness seems to have helped East Asians to develop a form of modernization significantly different from that achieved by Western individualism . . . The ability of East Asian entrepreneurs to take full advantage of the human capital, be it family loyalty, a disciplined work force, or supportive staff is not an accident. They are the beneficiaries of the Confucian way of life.[16]

Others drew slightly different boundaries, but the conclusions remained the same. In Korea, Taiwan, Hong Kong, and Singapore, said Chung-ying Cheng, 'Confucian ethics forms a component of the total forces toward transformation and development and has thus become absorbed as an organic part of the driving forces behind the successful launching and sustaining of economic development in East Asia.'[17] It was true that 'modern Chinese have to understand modern life and the modern world', but Confucian ethics could achieve this through series of stages linked with the principle of 'learning'. First, intellectuals' consciousness of 'misgivings' or 'profound care' intersect with the masses' virtues of patience and stamina. Second comes appreciation of creativity and flexibility. Third are efforts to absorb Western knowledge and values, a stress on learning, and emphasis on education. This leads, fourth, to a new valuation of all Confucian virtues according to their potential contribution to 'maintaining individual integrity and social harmony or national coherence'. Thus even 'feudalistic' precepts such as 'loyalty' or 'filial piety' can support nationalism or act as motivating forces in economic development. Values such as 'thriftiness', 'hard-working,' and 'arduousness,' said Cheng, 'are actually powerful virtues of the Chinese people as a whole and they may actually derive from past agricultural social experience'. They lead directly to willingness to work hard and to save a high proportion of income, crucial for the early stages of economic development. Fifth, 'benevolence' and 'righteousness' can serve as the basis for supportive government policy. Sixth, 'wisdom' can receive a 'cognitive' orientation.

Seventh, and finally, said Cheng, 'popular pragmatism of profit-seeking' is 'highly significant' in development. Cheng admitted that Confucius says it is only the 'small man' that seeks profit, but he insisted that Confucius does not denounce profit making itself as base, and 'the fact remains that the general public will have profit-seeking as their goal'. But profit must be sought through 'right means', and one should always have the public good in mind. So 'the productiveness of common people motivated by self-interest and the policy-making of superior men motivated by interest for the public good' in combination 'constitute the spiritual resources and abilities to make the right decisions and coordinate the right actions for modernization'.[18]

In the specific case of Taiwan, Cheng developed an interpretation of Taiwanese economic development using analogies drawn from Confucian rhetoric. Confucius' injunction to populate the people, make them rich, and educate them (Analects 13.9) leads to an identification of periods in Taiwanese development: (1) 1952–63, enforcing the land-to-the-tiller policy and reaping the results of this policy so that agricultural development could be used as a basis for industrial development; (2) 1964–76, development of international trade and buildup of infrastructure for industrial develop-ment; (3) 1977–81, accelerated development of industry, especially manu-facturing; (4) 1982–87, enhancement of commerce and service industries, consolidation of the economic system, and continued investment in heavy industry; (5) 1988 to the present (that is, 1989), upgrading of industry, pre-cision industries, and the beginning of liberalization and internationaliza-tion of financial laws and policies.

The five stages of Taiwanese development thus reflect the traditional five powers. First, 'earth' stands for the 'policy of development in totality and mutuality', the first ten years when government planning was important, and 'benevolent policies' combined with cheap labor, willingness to work hard, diligence, and frugality. Second, 'metal' stands for 'conscious and consistent use of timely development strategies'. Third, 'water' stands for 'opening up to the international economic system', the export-oriented policy. Fourth, 'wood' stands for the 'wide and wise use of manpower and the synergic coordination and harmonization of labor and management', the increased use of educated and skilled workers reflecting the virtues of learning and education. And fifth, 'fire' stands for 'recruitment and explor-ation of skilled and expert manpower' and 'cultivation of the information and knowledge industry'.[19]

Since the 1980s, many observers in East and Southeast Asia have identified Confucian or Neo-Confucian values as the basis for the region's rapid growth. It is difficult to measure the 'unconscious' impact of Confucian concepts, but we can trace the direct flow of ideas in some cases. With input from Neo-Confucian academics, the Taiwan government attempted to bolster its authority by fostering conservative values in the school curriculum and in neighborhood development programs. Further, as will be seen in Chapter 7, some of these same academics acted as advisers to the government of Singapore when it introduced a course in Confucianism into the secondary schools. And in addition, as also seen in Chapter 7, overseas Chinese living in Southeast Asia have been extremely successful, and this might be attributed to their inherited Confucian values.

However, when the precepts of Confucian thought are examined, they prove to be quite broad, broad enough indeed to justify very different forms of behavior. Further, attitudes in East Asian countries vary substantially, and they have changed significantly over time. In particular, in the case of Taiwan, an autonomous civil society has emerged in parallel both to the process of economic growth and to the process of democratization outlined above. According to Ambrose King and Thomas Gold, this means firstly that Confucianism is 'no longer the state ideology', and secondly that, although Taiwan's leaders may continue to draw on the 'Confucian repertoire', nevertheless 'the dominant influences will come from elsewhere', that is from the West and especially from the United States.[20]

The formulations of Neo-Confucian scholars obviously served to justify the continued rule of the KMT and the domination of mainlanders over indigenous Taiwanese. In addition, two ways in which all Taiwanese employers benefited during the period of one party rule were the absence of labor unions and the subordinate position of women. The government justified both the repression of independent worker's movements and the exploitation of female workers with Confucian arguments. Workers should be subordinate to their employers in the same way that subjects should be subordinate to their rulers, and of course, in the large state sector examined below, employer and ruler were the same.

Women were to be dutiful wives and mothers, in the family home. However, economic development also required that women be available as workers. Responding to surveys that showed there were many 'idle women' in local communities, the government proposed a scheme of 'living-room factories' (*keting gongchang*). Special loans were made to families to purchase machinery to set up in their homes, allowing female family members to undertake contract work for manufacturing firms. In consequence 'many "living rooms" were converted into "factories", housewives became workers, and work became "housewifeized"'. The government program of weekend 'mother's workshops' (*mama jiaoshi*) included training in the establishment and operation of such living room factories. Families did indeed earn additional income, but employers were spared the minimum wages and health insurance to which factory workers were entitled, as well as saving on the costs of buildings and machinery.[21]

The State and Economic Development

Taiwan's economic potential in the 1950s appeared unpromising. It was relatively small, but had a very high population density, and the 2 million migrants from the mainland included the remnants of the corrupt Nationalist regime. It needed to import both raw materials and technology. This could have meant a limited domestic market combined with chronic food shortages, and stagnation. But over time the gulf between Taiwanese and mainlanders was overcome and a high degree of cultural homogeneity achieved – Acer's Stan Shih was born in Taiwan in 1944, for instance. The economy began to grow. As in Hong Kong, the mainland migrants included a large number of professionals, skilled workers, and former managers of commercial and manufacturing enterprises. The infrastructure laid down under Japanese rule increased productivity in agriculture, and Japanese enterprises provided a base for a modern industrial sector. The United States continued to insist that the Nationalist government was the government of 'China' until 1979, and to bolster it against the People's Republic, Taiwan received large amounts of American military and economic aid.[22]

The Taiwan government actively guided economic development from the beginning, possibly because KMT leaders had taken to heart Chiang Kai-shek's 1949 statement that, 'We must frankly admit that our party has done more for the political phases of our National Revolution than for the economic and social phases. Many of our members speak for social reform in theory, while in practice they rarely go into the heart of society and work for social improvement.'[23] Taiwan invested heavily in education at all levels – among many other examples, Stan Shih graduated from National Chiao Tung University in 1968. A comprehensive land reform reduced tenancy from 40 to 15 per cent of farmland. The government's first two four-year plans (1953–56 and 1957–60) aimed for import substitution and the development of Taiwan's own industrial sector. The following three plans (1961–64, 1965–68, and 1968–72) aimed to increase exports and targeted industries and firms with tax incentives and financial credits.

Foreign-trained technocrats played a key role. K.Y. Yin, who had earned his degree in electrical engineering in the United States, 'was given a free hand to design and implement Taiwan's economic strategies'.[24] K.T. Li, a Cambridge-educated physicist, served as Minister of Economic Affairs and then as Minister of Finance in the late 1960s and early 1970s, 'from where he directed the flow of capital into Taiwan's industrialization programs'.[25] He established the first export processing zones as well as playing a key role in the semiconductor industry. A Statute for Encouragement of Investment (SEI) targeted specific industries, and was repeatedly revised from the 1970s onwards as the government's emphasis shifted from labor-intensive exports, first to more capital-intensive industries, and then to technology-intensive areas.[26]

Taiwan also developed an institutional equivalent of Japan's MITI and Korea's EPB. At the center, the Council for Economic Planning and Development (CEPAD) grew out of the Economic Stabilization Board of the 1950s. Other agencies such as the Taiwan Textile Federation and the Taiwan Electrical Appliances Manufacturer Association supported specific industries. Government agencies developed very efficient sources of information, notably statistics on imports and exports. During the decades of one-party rule, officials were insulated from pressure from the legislature or interest groups, and many, such as Yin and Li, had technical training. In addition, reportedly the press was fairly free to criticize the government in the economic sphere. Assistance offered to firms was conditional on their success, while officials knew that their actions would be evaluated and criticized, and this has been given credit for both the continuity and the generally high quality of decisions.[27]

Exports rose rapidly through the 1970s and 1980s, and accelerated again in the early 1990s. In the background the popular and successful land reform helped the rural and urban sectors to merge socially and economically. The growth of the economy kept unemployment low, government policy held inflation low, and wages rose from the 1980s onwards. Therefore, despite repression, there was relatively little labor unrest. The government's taxation policy contributed to Taiwan's relatively equal distribution of income and the high rate of domestic savings. Through the early 1980s strict controls over foreign exchange and the banking sector allowed the government to channel investment into target areas. Although, as in the case of Korea, these initiatives were not always successful, Taiwan became one of the textbook examples of state-led economic development.[28]

In the 1980s massive trade surpluses threatened a runaway inflation. At the same time Taiwan's export industries faced new competition from emerging countries with lower wages. In 1984, the government announced a policy of liberalization, internationalization, and 'institutionalization' to upgrade industry and transform Taiwan into a 'science-and-technology-island' as well as a 'regional operations center' for the Asia-Pacific. New areas were opened to foreign investors. The previous ceilings on foreign exchange purchases were raised and tariffs substantially reduced. Beginning in 1991, the government licensed new private banks and began to privatize government-owned banks. From 1981 to 1996, the share of 'technology intensive' industries (electrical and electronic equipment, machinery and precision machinery, and vehicles) in manufacturing output rose from 20.2 to 37.5 per cent, and from 1989 to 1996 their share of exports increased from 24.3

to 38.0 per cent.[29] When the financial crisis struck in 1997, insulated by the trade surplus and large reserves, the government decided to allow the exchange rate to float. The rate did decline by 24 per cent, but interest rates increased only slightly, and the economy grew nearly 7 per cent while the stock market rose 4 per cent. Taiwan was one of 'the ones that got away'.[30]

As output shifted toward technology-intensive industries, the share of the state sector in total production declined from almost 50 per cent in the 1960s to less than 20 per cent in the 1980s.[31] However, this did not mean an end to direct state investment, nor did it mean that the government had withdrawn from the economy. Rather government leaders shifted their approach to indirect management and encouragement of high-technology initiatives. The most spectacular case was the government's sponsorship of Taiwan's semiconductor industry. Y.S. Sun, who became Premier in 1979, had followed Li as Minister for Economic Affairs in the early 1970s. He sponsored the establishment of the Industrial Technology Research Institute (ITRI) near Hsinchu in 1973. In 1974, he met Wen-Yuan Pan, a colleague and friend employed by the research arm of the United States firm RCA. With Pan's assistance Sun identified and recruited Chinese engineers and scientists working in the United States, set up the Electronics Research Service Organization (ERSO) under the ITRI, and persuaded RCA to license semiconductor technology to a pilot plant staffed by Pan's recruits. 'It is out of this group that virtually the entire senior echelons of the subsequent semiconductor industry in Taiwan was formed.'[32]

Having retired as Finance Minister, Li worked with a committee under Premier Sun to establish the Hsinchu Science-Based Industry Park, opened in 1980, and to stock it with both government-funded enterprises spun out of the ERSO such as United Microelectronics Corporation (UMC) and with private firms including Stan Shih's fledgling Acer.[33] In the early 1980s, a debate erupted over whether to rest content with a second-tier position, or to take the risk of attempting to create cutting-edge technological capabilities. ERSO's advisors wanted to close the gap between Taiwan's semiconductor firms and the world leaders. CEPAD officials, more concerned with macroeconomic stability and not wanting to over-emphasize any one industry, took the more cautious line. Premier Sun favored ERSO, and President Chiang himself appears to have intervened in favor of the more ambitious approach. NT$2.9 billion (about US$72 million) was allocated, a fourfold increase in funding, and a five-year deadline set to overtake the world's leaders. Several attempts were made, not all of them successful, but seed money in the universities created the design capabilities, and in 1986 a joint venture with Philips, involving both Taiwan government funding and 'arm twisting' of private firms for further capital, created Taiwan

Semiconductor Manufacturing Company (TSMC), a world-class fabrication plant that could serve Taiwan's microchip firms.

Through the 1990s, continued government support for the semiconductor industry included a NT$5.5 billion (US$222 million) five-year program to develop a plant capable of sub-micron chip fabrication. The relatively large firms, wholly or partly funded by the government, formed a core, around which smaller private firms clustered and from which they drew support. A number of these, notably Acer, are no longer small. And, as will be noted below, these firms in turn continued to seek new technological capabilities through links with overseas partners in strategic alliances, joint ventures, or acquisitions.[34]

THE MANAGEMENT GRID

Chinese Firms in Hong Kong

Within the framework established by the British colonial government's infrastructure investment and consumption subsidies, Hong Kong's economy came to be dominated by private firms, overwhelmingly small, and overwhelmingly Chinese. Over 90 per cent of manufacturing firms in the 1980s employed fewer than 50 workers, and as the manufacturing sector had grown the average size of firms had declined substantially, from 55 in 1950 to 17 in 1988. Less than 1 per cent of all firms had over 500 employees, and they employed less than 10 per cent of all employees. These large firms were primarily public or semi-public corporations, branches of foreign firms, or long-established local firms such as HSBC. There were exceptions, but most of the senior executives of these large firms were European.

Among the Chinese firms it was common for workers to leave their jobs to establish their own independent businesses. In addition to their savings, many of them also received assistance from their circle of connections. The circle might include their previous employers or senior partners, immediate family, or traditional lineage relationships, and in some cases the lineage organization might itself act as a firm.[35] Small firms had a predictably high mortality rate, but the subsidy system 'created a safety net for low-risk entrepreneurialism'. Aspiring entrepreneurs might 'bet their small savings' to launch their new businesses, but if they failed they could fall back on public housing and other benefits.[36]

Not surprisingly, foreign trade contributed most to overall growth in Hong Kong, and success in export markets led to positive trade balances and the substantial cushion of foreign exchange reserves that protected

Hong Kong in 1997 and 1998.[37] Through the 1970s Hong Kong's key competitive advantage remained its low labor costs. Migration of course had
substantially increased the labor force. In addition the labor force increased
further thanks to a rising female participation rate. The wide range of government subsidies reduced pressure for wage increases. Following the riots
in 1967, Hong Kong enjoyed a long period of industrial peace. Therefore
'small business could concentrate on competitive pricing, shrinking and
expanding their labor force according to variations in demand'.[38]

Hong Kong firms continued to externalize their transactions costs as the
Confucian firms of Qing and Nationalist China had done. Rather than
expanding or diversifying into upstream production or downstream distribution, they tended to make use of their networks of connections. At their
own level, many firms were linked by subcontracting relationships. For
instance, a firm might call on the firms of former employees if orders
outran its capacity. Alternatively, new capital for expansion might be raised
by involving members of the owner's circle, and these '*guangxi* owners'
would share the profits.[39] In turn, the many small manufacturing firms were
connected to world markets by a further large number of equally small
firms. Some of these specialized in the import of raw materials or components, especially important in higher-level technologies. Others specialized in
the export of finished goods. Far from being a disadvantage, this dense
network of small firms has been cited as another reason for Hong Kong's
continuing ability to respond rapidly to shifting opportunities in global
markets.[40]

Hong Kong firms remained largely family-controlled. Of a sample of
330 companies surveyed in the late 1990s, 72 per cent were controlled by
individual families. This is not surprising for small firms founded by individuals, but, even among the companies listed on the Hong Kong Stock
Exchange, one family owned more than half the shares of 53 per cent of
the firms. As in the case of Hong Kong Garment, typically the majority
shareholder was serving as CEO, and members of the controlling families
dominated the boards of directors. Measured by market capitalization,
only 7 per cent of corporate control rights were widely held, and these were
generally smaller companies. This suggests that smaller firms were forced
to rely relatively heavily on share issues to raise funds.

To avoid diluting control, family-controlled firms preferred to raise funds
through bank loans. Debt-to-equity ratios of Hong Kong's listed firms averaged 160 per cent in 1996. In addition the listed companies frequently
belonged to large and diverse business groups, connected to other group
members by cross-shareholdings and pyramid structures. Within a group
some firms might be publicly listed, but others could be unlisted private
firms. Li Kai-shing's Cheung Kong group, for instance, shared ownership of

Hong Kong Chinese Bank through its subsidiary companies. Additionally, firms showed a preference for diversifying across a broad range of sectors, 'reflecting the owners' preference for maximizing market share over profit'. Return on assets remained low, although the high gearing and pyramid structures may have allowed higher returns on the controlling families' equity.[41]

Despite the widely admired transparency and completeness of Hong Kong's corporate governance and reporting standards, such structures create risks for minority shareholders. The problems emerge in crisis situations. As we saw in Box 5.1, Hong Kong Garment's founder/CEO was less than candid with his creditors. The collapse of Akai Holdings in 1999, with total losses of over US$1.7 billion, revealed the weaknesses in provisions for the investigation of company collapses. The proceedings in bankruptcy cases are largely secret, and culpable directors can conceal or destroy records with little risk of severe punishment. Directors and insiders are protected by cultural norms that make formal bankruptcy uncommon, and the Hong Kong Association of Banks' *Guidelines on Corporate Difficulties* supports informal workouts. A shareholder can petition to wind up a company, but the law specifies that the court must feel it is 'just and equitable' before it can grant the petition.[42]

In Geert Hofstede's study of national cultural values, Hong Kong ranked quite high on the 'power distance' scale, and quite low on 'uncertainty avoidance' and 'individualism'. High power distance scores are associated with greater centralization of decision making, more autocratic managerial styles, a reluctance of employees to trust one another, and also a reluctance of employees to disagree with their boss. A low score for uncertainty avoidance is associated with low employee loyalty to the current employer, lower job satisfaction, and higher labor turnover. Low scores for individualism are usually associated in Asian countries with a high value placed on family connections.[43] Many CEOs of Hong Kong firms, who typically are the dominant shareholders as well, have quite autocratic and paternalistic management styles.[44] At the next level down, supervisory personnel tend to be quite rigid and hierarchical, deeply concerned to maintain 'face' in dealings with subordinates.[45] Flexibility means in practice that lower-level employees are dispensable, taken on and thrown off as the firm needs them. To protect themselves, employees may form patron–client relations with their superiors, at the cost of loyalty to the firm as a whole.[46] Finally, gendered perceptions mean that many firms fail to create commitment among their female employees.[47]

Demand fluctuates and fashions change rapidly in the fields where Hong Kong has excelled, such as textiles, clothing, toys, and consumer electronics. Quick decision making and flexibility make Hong Kong firms competitive, but this comes at a cost. At the strategic level, as the case of Hong Kong Garment shows, even experienced CEOs can make poor decisions, and without sufficient oversight from board directors this can damage the firm severely. At the operating level, labor turnover in Hong Kong has been high, from 21 to 28 per cent annually from the late 1980s through the early 1990s. As noted above, Hong Kong's record of productivity improvement is poor, and there was little initiative from the government pushing firms to improve quality or raise their technological capabilities. Rising wages in Hong Kong therefore could have presented a problem, but the opening of the People's Republic to outside investors allowed firms such as Hong Kong Garment to expand into adjacent areas of China where they could take advantage of new supplies of cheap labor. And, again as seen in the Hong Kong Garment case, low wages could lead to very impressive profit levels.

Like many others around the world, Hong Kong's business leaders were aware of Japan's rapid growth through the 1970s, and like many others they made attempts to introduce 'Japanese' management techniques. In 1981, the Hong Kong Productivity Council sent a group to attend the International Convention on Quality Circles in Tokyo. Over the next decade a Hong Kong Quality Circle Association held annual meetings, published case studies, and surveyed Hong Kong firms on the progress of Quality Circle (QC) programs. A large survey at the end of the 1980s found that many of the larger Hong Kong firms had attempted to introduce QCs, but also that there had been a high failure rate. Only one-sixth of the programs had survived for five years or longer, and most involved only a small share of the firm's employees. The two main reasons cited for failure were high labor turnover and excessive work pressures. In the background was 'the unwillingness of Chinese organizations to spend money on this activity'. Short time horizons of both workers and managers, lack of top management support, and lack of commitment from middle managers reinforced the top-down management style in undermining and sapping what had often been a high degree of initial enthusiasm.

One of the few successful QC programs was the Mass Transit Railway Corporation, a statutory but semi-autonomous corporation. Significantly, it was not a typical Hong Kong firm at all, being large and having historically a very low labor turnover rate. Highly skilled and relatively well paid, its workers were led by a largely European expatriate management team. Even here an attempt to introduce QCs failed in 1982, but the program launched in 1987 was accompanied by a conscious attempt to change the organizational culture away from an autocratic task-centered style and towards a more open and participative approach. 'Respect for the individual' was announced as a core value, and senior managers backed their commitment with substantial resources for training and their own personal participation. Over 100 projects were submitted and completed by 37 teams over the next four years. That is, already benefiting from major organizational prerequisites, including some of the interlocking attributes of a 'Japanese' firm, management also introduced a shift in cultural values that increased the chances of the program's success.[48]

Chinese Firms in Taiwan

Like Hong Kong, the Taiwan economy is characterized by a very large number of small firms.[49] Depending on definition and time period, small and medium enterprises may make up as many as 98 per cent of all firms and employ 80 per cent of the labor force. Overwhelmingly these are family-controlled firms, with the owner families filling most board positions and senior executive posts. However, in contrast to Korea or Hong Kong, there is relatively little cross-shareholding among firms, and relatively little tendency to pyramid holdings. Further, many small and medium firms have listed in the stock market. Among listed firms, nearly half are controlled by an individual or family, but over a quarter are widely held, and another quarter are controlled either by a widely held parent firm or by a widely held financial institution. In 2001, of Taiwan's 22 million people, around four million held broker accounts, individuals held nearly half of the market's total capitalization, and individuals accounted for 85 per cent of stock market transactions, one of the highest proportions in the world.[50]

Explanations for the continued domination of small firms in Taiwan's economy vary. Anthropologists looking at Taiwan's villages in the 1970s emphasized the importance of small, face-to-face relationship (*guanxi*) networks, and at the time it appeared that these patterns persisted in business relationships as well.[51] Observers in the 1980s emphasized the networks of independent firms built upon local connections.[52] Gary Hamilton and Robert Feenstra believe the influence of inheritance laws to be the prime cause. In contrast to the primogeniture embedded in Korean legislation, which they believe has contributed to Korea's distinctive corporate structure, the principle of division of inheritance of late imperial China passed on to Taiwan. Rather than the lineage, the separate household became the key unit of action. The land reform of the 1950s, which distributed land in small plots to individual families, reinforced this tendency. Government attempts to stimulate the private sector of the economy also took the form of encouraging traditional Chinese family economic practices. The resulting household-based economy carried over into the expanding industrial sector, and Taiwan developed a system of relatively small, independent firms that might work together but that did not merge into single corporate entities.[53]

William Kirby takes a different approach. Extending his analysis of the suspicion with which business regarded government in Qing and Nationalist China, he notes the distrust of indigenous Taiwanese of the new government, dominated as it was by mainlanders. The Nationalist government imposed its existing legal system on Taiwan. The Company Law of 1929 and 1946 remained in force and, although amended in 1966 and 1980, it retained its emphasis on regulatory control of private firms. Therefore it was important for state-owned corporations and for large foreign investors, but was largely irrelevant to the small firms that led development in the 1960s and 1970s.

The Company Law required firms above a certain size to offer shares to the public – in the 1980s this meant that a firm with a capitalization of more than US$5.6 million was required to list. To avoid doing so, most firms that had grown to that size had simply formed another firm alongside the original one. The law also prohibited a company from carrying on any business not explicitly granted in its original articles of incorporation, and again as they expanded into new areas growing firms found it easier to establish new companies rather than re-draft the articles of the existing company. Not surprisingly, these groups of firms shared senior managers and board members, and again not surprisingly many of these were related. Y.C. Wang served as chairman of the board of nine of the ten companies in the Formosa Plastics Group. W.C. Tsai chaired seven of the ten firms of the Cathay Group, and his son chaired another two. Such groups were closely held family businesses. Among the 97 largest business groups in Taiwan in 1983, 84 could be 'strictly classified as family-owned business groups'. As Kirby concludes, the Company Law 'unwittingly reinforced preexisting organizational tendencies'.[54]

Further, the Company Law and the Banking Law, which also dated from the Nationalist period, may have contributed to the very large proportion of the Taiwanese economy that remained entirely unregulated. In addition to the large number of unincorporated enterprises, there were many completely unregistered family factories, unmonitored savings associations and credit clubs, and other informal economic activities. Whether literally setting up factories in their living rooms or not, families could raise capital from circles of acquaintances, or from informally organized groups of savers, buy their machinery and raw materials, and go to work as subcontractors for other firms. They could avoid the cost of registration, the intrusiveness of regulation, and the irksomeness of control by government agencies, and they possibly could evade fees and taxes as well. Estimates are of course speculative, but the 'underground' economy may have accounted for as much as 40 per cent of economic activity in Taiwan in the 1980s.[55]

As we have seen in the case of Qing and Nationalist China, and again in the case of Hong Kong, small family firms can develop substantial competitive advantages, and these can be leveraged and multiplied through their networks of contacts. Joseph Bosco argued in the early 1990s that Chinese family firms were entrepreneurial units that in fact were particularly well suited to operate Taiwan's small factories. The credit clubs could provide finance by mobilizing a circle of contacts larger than the single family, another variation on the theme of '*guanxi* owners' noted in Chapter 4 and above.[56]

In addition to the small family firms, there were two other significant models of management. Firstly, as noted above, state-owned enterprises produced something like half of industrial output in the 1960s. The shift from import substitution to export orientation did not mean a reduction in the size of the state-owned sector. The 'ten major projects' launched in 1973 included infrastructure such as roads, railways, harbors, a nuclear power plant, and an airport, but also a steel mill and a shipbuilding facility. The following 'twelve new projects' begun in 1979 and the 'fourteen key projects' begun in 1985 continued infrastructure development, but also expanded government manufacturing enterprises, for instance the China Steel Corporation and the China Ship Building Corporation.[57] A large refining complex in the 1970s and new petrochemical plants in the 1980s played a role analogous to the semiconductor plants described above, providing a conduit for new technologies as well as supplying intermediate products to firms in the chemical and synthetic fiber industries.[58]

At first, state enterprises were dominated by mainlanders, and for a longer time they were dominated by those with good connections to the KMT. However, because of their size and because they were government-owned, they were not family companies, and over time their growing need for trained personnel intersected with the greater willingness to recruit and promote Taiwan-born leaders. There were exceptions, but in large measure they came to hire on the basis of formal qualifications and to promote on the basis of demonstrated achievement. As they did so, they influenced the practices of the smaller firms in their industries. Privatizations in the 1990s worked in the same direction. In addition, over time both CEPAD and government-sponsored trade organizations overcame the suspicion of indigenous Taiwanese and developed effective working relationships with private firms, and these successful interactions also affected private firm practice.

Secondly, the Taiwan government also used foreign direct investment as a lever to promote growth. FDI rose from US$15 million in 1960 to US$139 million in 1970, US$400 million in 1980, US$2.4 billion in 1989, and US$7.6 billion in 2000. The Statute for Encouragement of Investment (SEI), the Statute for Investment by Foreign Nationals (SIFN), and the

Statute for Investment by Overseas Chinese (SIOC) guided investment flows. Consistently overseas Chinese were permitted to invest in areas where 'foreign nationals' were restricted or prohibited. Through the 1980s, overseas Chinese accounted for 31 per cent of total foreign investment, followed by the United States with 30 per cent, and Japan with 17 per cent.

Initially foreign investment was sought to increase exports. Three Export Processing Zones were opened in the 1960s, two in the south near Kaohsiung and one near the central city of Taichung, and by 1980 FDI-funded enterprises produced 22 per cent of total exports. Over time targets shifted and successive areas were opened. The short lists of industries where foreign investment was permitted were broadened and then replaced by 'negative lists' posted from 1988 onwards, which assumed that foreigners would be permitted and encouraged to invest in any area not forbidden. Having been extensively liberalized, the SEI was replaced in 1991 by a new Statute for Upgrading Industries (SUI), intended to encourage both domestic and foreign investment.[59]

This meant that in one industry after another Taiwan firms were exposed to foreign competition. The government also wanted FDI to contribute to improving and upgrading Taiwan's own industry. Foreign partners were sought to facilitate the spread of new technologies. During the 1960s and early 1970s, some three-quarters of the projects approved under the Statute on Technical Cooperation were agreements between Taiwanese and Japanese firms.[60] As with their collaboration with state enterprises, alliances and joint ventures with foreign firms also pressured Taiwan firms to alter their practices.

When asked about the differences between Hong Kong and Taiwan, the Hong Kong Chinese businesswoman already quoted above said, 'Look, if you do business in Hong Kong you go to a lot of dinners. Same in Taiwan. But, in Hong Kong your hosts are always trying to impress you with how much the dinner cost, while in Taiwan they are trying to explain to you how the food is prepared and why it tastes the way it does. Taiwanese are keen on the technical details.'

This may not be universally true as yet, but those that are not keen on the technical details may be feeling the heat. According to the head of sales of a small telecommunications company:

Interviewee: He [the boss] is a business management major [from a University in Taiwan]. His wife is also a business major. She interferes a lot. We will not confront him or her, but we try to make him see how these things would not work. They still have the old-style idea that they are reluctant to release any power to us . . . Many Taiwanese small businesses are like that. The boss has the full power. *Interviewer*: But you said your competitors are not like that. *Interviewee*: [That's] because they are all technical people, not business people.[61]

The available surveys indicate that the majority of small enterprises in Taiwan continue to show the characteristics of typical Chinese firms. Planning and decision making are centralized, often opportunistic, and frequently based on information gathered from the boss's personal networks. Organizational structures are simple, often not formally defined, and flexible. Leadership is paternalistic and authoritarian, with little initiative allowed to subordinates. Control is achieved through family or family-like relationships of managers to subordinates. However, Paul Hempel and Daphne Chang also found two additional factors. Firstly, the firms in their sample that were located in high-technology areas were much less likely to show the entire range of Chinese features. Secondly, even in the firms that appeared the most traditionally Chinese, the managers they interviewed showed a high level of awareness of management theory, and a possibly surprisingly critical attitude towards their own companies' practices. Hempel and Chang conclude that Taiwan firms in areas where traditional management forms are inappropriate have altered their structures, in particular by allowing subordinates greater room for individual initiative.[62]

Hempel and Chang concentrate on small and medium-sized firms, but their conclusions appear to fit what is known about Acer and other leading Taiwan firms.[63] These companies are by no means 'small' by international standards, especially if we consider them in comparison to others in their specific niches. Alice Amsden lists, as of 1998, Lite-On Technology (the world's fourth largest maker of computer monitors), Winbond (the world's tenth largest maker of memory integrated circuits), Delta Electronics (the world's leading maker of switching power supplies), Macronix (the world's seventh largest maker of nonvolatile memory products), Primax Electronics (the world's leading producer of hand-held scanners), and Siliconware Precision Industries (the world's third largest independent integrated circuits packager, after Anam Industrial of South Korea).[64] Many of these have been connected to the government–university–science park network and, as noted below, many have connections overseas, particularly in the United States. The expectations of the highly trained professional employees who constitute in themselves the firms' competitive strength may be driving organizational change in the direction of a new model, or a new hybrid mix of old and new.

GLOBALIZATION AND THE FUTURE

The Expansion of Hong Kong

Among the most significant of the Chinese government's economic reforms was the opening of China to foreign investment. In 1978, the State Council issued a series of directives permitting the establishment of joint ventures by foreign companies and establishing the first of the Special Economic Zones (SEZs). The first SEZs opened in 1980, and Hong Kong firms immediately began to exploit the new opportunities. Through the early 1990s Hong Kong provided over two-thirds of the total pledged foreign direct investment in China, far ahead of the United States (6.7 per cent), Japan (3.9 per cent), Singapore (2.2 per cent), and Britain (1.3 per cent). In the late 1990s, the flow of investment from Hong Kong into China made up approximately one-quarter of *all* private foreign capital flowing into developing countries worldwide.

In the initial stages of the open door policy, Hong Kong investment was dominated by assembly and processing projects. They tended to be relatively small in size. They concentrated in Hong Kong's traditional areas, the labor-intensive manufacturing sectors including electronic and electrical appliances, plastic and rubber products, bicycles, food processing and beverages, footwear, textiles and clothing, and toys. They produced mostly for export markets. The increasing openness of China's domestic market provided further opportunity. In particular, Hong Kong investment partially shifted to infrastructure projects, and over time the average size of investments increased.

Hong Kong firms found investment in China desirable especially because of the rapid growth of labor costs in Hong Kong. As Hong Kong's labor-intensive manufacturing industries lost their traditional advantage and declined in competitiveness, they transferred their operations into southern China, particularly Guangdong province. Geographic proximity and cultural closeness, especially the shared Cantonese language, facilitated location decisions. By 1991, it was estimated that over a third of Hong Kong's manufacturing industry had been moved across the border to the Pearl River Delta. Hong Kong firms tended to use wholly owned subsidiaries as their entry mode. They appeared to prefer direct control over these relatively small operations, and did not need joint venture partners to help with access to local facilities and labor.[65]

From one perspective the expansion of Hong Kong firms into southern China has been fabulously successful. There have been problems, however. Hong Kong managers have found it difficult to vary their management style to suit their mainland employees, who in consequence perceive them as arrogant, insolent, and contemptuous.[66] In addition, observers worry that Hong Kong investment in China has not been accompanied by widespread structural transformation from labor-intensive to technology-intensive industries. Many Hong Kong firms operate as subcontractors for Western or Japanese firms, with the Hong Kong firm seeking out low-wage locations to manufacture goods for global designer brands or giant retailers. Henry

Wai-Chung Yeung has studied the resulting pattern of 'globalization' of Hong Kong firms. He finds that the successful firms have leveraged their existing strengths and have tended to retain their inherited ways of doing business. According to Yeung, Hong Kong's 'transnational entrepreneurs' use the intangible and tacit knowledge gained from their circle of business and personal contacts to gain and hold competitive advantage. However, in both China and Southeast Asia, they have continued to concentrate on low-cost, labor-intensive production, a 'defensive strategy to regain cost competitiveness', rather than seeking to improve their technological capabilities by absorbing new techniques from the United States, Europe, and Japan.[67]

The Expansion of Taiwan

The first Special Economic Zones opened by the Chinese government in 1980 included Shantou and Xiamen, in Fujian province directly across the straits from Taiwan. However, Taiwanese investment in China was forbidden by the Taiwan government until 1988, when the Chinese government's new Regulations on Encouragement of Investment by Compatriots from Taiwan intersected with the ongoing political changes in Taiwan. The response was immediate and lasting. Among foreign investors in China, Taiwan rose quickly to rank second to Hong Kong, with nearly 9 per cent of total pledged investment. Like Hong Kong firms, Taiwanese firms have also expanded not only into China but elsewhere as well, especially into Southeast Asia.

Taiwanese projects in China resembled Hong Kong investment. Through the early 1990s, two-thirds were wholly owned subsidiaries. They were in the same areas of consumer goods manufacturing and assembly, they were largely for export markets, they were quite small, and they also served as subcontractors for Western or Japanese firms. The motives of Taiwanese investors were also similar, especially the desire to reduce labor costs, which could be as little as one-third of those in Taiwan. Also, as with Hong Kong, geographical proximity, cultural closeness and shared language have played a role. Taiwan's investment is largely located in Fujian, many of whose people speak the Minnan dialect common among Taiwanese.[68] It is also true that Taiwan firms have not always succeeded in China, and 60 per cent experienced 'crises' in the late 1990s. Their problems arose variously from lack of managerial talent, failure to anticipate invisible costs, or 'stagnant' marketing systems.[69]

However, there is an additional aspect of Taiwanese foreign investment that has attracted attention. Taiwan's leading firms have emerged from their dependent status and have sought out both production platforms and sales opportunities in the expanding Southeast Asian economies, Latin America, the United States, and Europe. There are surveys and case studies that show that many Taiwan firms expand abroad to gain access to assets only available in advanced foreign countries, particularly emerging technologies. As in the case of Acer, as they do so, they link strategically with networks of firms in the foreign countries, through acquisitions, mergers, joint ventures, formal alliances, or informal relationships. And, like Acer, they also attempt to deploy the resources gained across their other divisions.[70]

In addition, in comparison to Hong Kong, Henry Wai-Chung Yeung believes Taiwan firms have benefited from an 'institutional fix'. Along with its role in the domestic economy the Taiwan government has fostered strategic overseas expansion with subsidized loans, tax incentives, and negotiated intergovernmental agreements.[71] As seen above, in the case of semiconductors the initial developments came through government funded organizations, especially ERSO. From the mid-1990s onward, however, 'the private sector has itself become involved in a series of technology import measures'. Winbond, for instance, has licensed or purchased designs from large United States firms and joined in partnerships with others. It also has taken equity stakes in smaller emerging United States firms, a risky approach but one that ensures that, if the target technology succeeds, then Winbond will share the benefits.[72]

The Future

There is an edgy energy to business in Hong Kong, and what some observers perceive as an almost excessive competitiveness. The future is cloudy, as is the viability of the Hong Kong model of networks of small enterprises.[73] While the supply of cheap labor in the neighboring regions lasts, Hong Kong's manufacturing firms will continue to prosper. As a major financial center and as one of China's main windows to the global economy, Hong Kong will also remain a key provider of services to firms doing business in southern China. An expanding educational sector adds another dimension to the provision of services in the region, and may also form the basis for a higher level of technological innovation. Hong Kong's administrative status is secure, but over the longer term integration into China will mean coordination with national needs and policy goals, and this will alter the institutional grid within which Hong Kong's firms will need to frame their actions.

In contrast, the sense in Taiwan is that the future is bright for those with energy and expertise, for people who are keen on the technical details. Despite periodic crises, the cloud of reunification remains well below the horizon. Rather than becoming a regional center within a very large national economy, Taiwan will continue to have an independent government that will continue to support development regardless of which party gains power. The more immediate danger appears to be China as a competitor. The decline in foreign direct investment in Taiwan to US$3.2 billion in 2002 resulted partly from the global recession, but also from the emergence of China as a competing destination for FDI seeking abundant labor, access to markets, and target incentives. Taiwan joined the WTO in 2002, and in 2003 announced further liberalization of foreign investment while still wooing high-end technologies with special tax exemptions and credits for investment in research and development. Within this institutional grid, Taiwan firms, large enough to compete, small enough to be flexible, able to recognize and exploit new technologies as they emerge, believe themselves well placed to succeed.

FURTHER READING

On Hong Kong, Alvin Rabushka, *Hong Kong: A Study in Economic Freedom* (Chicago: University of Chicago Graduate School of Business, 1979) is a classic statement on the benefits of the free market, but A.J. Youngson, *Hong Kong: Economic Growth and Policy* (Hong Kong: Oxford University Press, 1982) emphasizes the role of government. Robert Ash (ed.), *Hong Kong in Transition: The Handover Years* (Basingstoke: Macmillan, 2000) surveys developments before and after the return to China.

On Taiwan see Samuel P.S. Ho, *Economic Development of Taiwan, 1860–1970* (New Haven: Yale University Press, 1978); Y.D. Hwang, *The Rise of a New World Economic Power: Postwar Taiwan* (Westport: Greenwood Press, 1991); Gustav Ranis (ed.), *Taiwan: From a Developing to a Mature Economy* (Boulder: Westview Press, 1992); Y.W. Ku, *Welfare Capitalism in Taiwan – State, Economy, and Social Policy* (New York: St Martin's Press, 1997).

Taiwan's successful high-tech firms have excited considerable international attention. Cases on Acer have been prepared at the INSEAD, Ivey, and Harvard business schools. See John A. Mathews, *Dragon Multinational: A New Model for Global Growth* (New York: Oxford University Press, 2002), p. 82, note 19 for references. Acer's founder Stan Shih has written several books, including Stan Shih, *Growing Global: A Corporate Vision Masterclass* (John Wiley & Sons, 2001). The story of government support for Taiwan's semiconductor industry is told brilliantly in John A. Mathews and Dong-Sung Cho, *Tiger Technology: The Creation of a Semiconductor Industry in East Asia* (Cambridge: Cambridge University Press, 2000), ch. 4.

The best introduction to Neo-Confucianism is Tu Wei-ming (ed.), *Confucian Traditions and East Asian Modernity: Moral Education and Economic Culture in Japan and the Four Mini-Dragons* (Cambridge: Harvard University Press, 1996). The very influential work of S. Gordon Redding, *The Spirit of Chinese Capitalism* (Berlin and New York: Walter deGruyter, 1990), based primarily on interviews with managers in Hong Kong and Taiwan, gives equal weight to inherited cultural values and the institutional structures of Imperial China, considered in Chapter 4.

Taiwan and Hong Kong have both been cited as models for others, but interpretations have varied. See for instance L. Xue, 'Promoting industrial R&D and high-tech development through science parks: the Taiwan experience and its implications for developing countries', *International Journal of Technology Management*, Special issue on R&D management, **13**(7–8) (1997), 744–61. John Mathews argues in *Dragon Multinational* that the example of the Acer group's cellular organization can be generalized to other firms from peripheral countries, notably the Hong Kong industrial supply and logistics firm of Li & Fung and the Singapore conglomerate Hong Leong Group.

On foreign investment by Hong Kong and Taiwan, see Haishun Sun and Frank B. Tipton, 'A comparative analysis of the characteristics of foreign investment in China, 1979–1995', *Journal of Developing Areas*, **32**(2) (1998), 159–86. Henry Wai-Chung Yeung, *Entrepreneurship and the Internationalisation of Asian Firms* (Cheltenham and Northampton: Edward Elgar, 2002) considers the impact of foreign expansion on the internal structures of Hong Kong and Singapore firms.

NOTES

1. Myers (1989), pp. 282–304.
2. Schenk (2001).
3. Wong (1988).
4. Youngson (1982).
5. Lau (1999), pp. 45–76. Other estimates do show positive values for technical progress. See Krueger (1995), pp. 9–36.
6. Lui and Chiu (1996), pp. 221–46.
7. See Cheng, Wong and Findlay (1998), pp. 162–78.
8. See Hong Kong Productivity Council, http://www.hkpc.org.
9. See Ho (1984), pp. 347–98.
10. Gold (1988), pp. 101–17.
11. Lai, Myers and Wou (1991).
12. Wachman (1994).
13. Tu (1989), pp. 70–71.
14. Tu (1989), pp. 74–5.
15. Tu (1984), p. 110.
16. Tu (1989), pp. 74–5.

17. Cheng (1989), p. 24.
18. Ibid., pp. 38–43.
19. Ibid., pp. 48–50.
20. These conclusions appeared in a volume edited by Tu himself; King (1996), p. 242; Gold in ibid., p. 258.
21. Cheng and Hsiung (1992), pp. 233–66.
22. For a contemporary positive evaluation see Jacoby (1966); So and Chiu (1995) emphasize Taiwan's status as a client state, and its 'semiperipheral' position in the world capitalist system.
23. King (1996), p. 235.
24. Ibid.
25. Mathews and Cho (2000), p. 159.
26. Li (1988).
27. Wade (1993), 147–68; Weiss (1995), 589–616.
28. Amsden (1985); Johnson (1987), pp. 136–164; Wade (1990).
29. Kuo and Liu (1998), p. 182.
30. See Kuo and Liu, 'Taiwan'. The phrase is from Haggard (2000), pp. 126–38.
31. King (1996); Cheng (1989), p. 252.
32. Mathews and Cho (2000), p. 158.
33. Xue (1997), 744–61.
34. Mathews and Cho (2000), ch. 4.
35. Watson (1982), 589–622.
36. Castells (1992), pp. 47–9.
37. Gapinski and Western (1999), pp. 149–70, which also shows positive overall productivity growth.
38. Castells (1992), p. 49.
39. Hamilton (1996), p. 18.
40. Castells (1992), pp. 47–9.
41. Claessens and Djankov (1999); Claessens and Lang (1999).
42. Australia, Department of Foreign Affairs and Trade, Economic Analytical Unit (2002), vol. 2, pp. 88–9.
43. Hofstede and Hofstede (2005), Tables 2.1, 3.1 and 5.1. Taiwan ranked substantially lower than Hong Kong on power distance, lower on individualism, and higher on uncertainty avoidance.
44. See Vertinsky, Tse, Wehrung and Lee (1990), 853–67.
45. Redding and Ng (1982), 201–19.
46. Chen, Tsui and Farh (2002), 339–56.
47. Chiu and Ng (1999), 485–502.
48. Kirkbride and Yang (1993), 100–111.
49. Abe and Kawakami (1997), 382–400.
50. Australia, Department of Foreign Affairs and Trade, Economic Analytical Unit (2002), vol. 2, pp. 64–6.
51. Jacobs (1976), 79–97.
52. Numazaki (1986), 487–534; Numazaki (1997), 485–508.
53. Hamilton and Feenstra (1995), 79–80.
54. Kirby (1995), p. 57.
55. Kirby (1995), p. 58; Winn (1992), 1–8. Note that, as the share of the underground economy declines, the proportion of recorded 'private' economic activity will also rise, as will recorded national product. Some of the high rates of growth reported in the 1980s and 1990s may have reflected existing firms beginning to report their activities officially.
56. Bosco (1992), 1–4.
57. Wade (1990), pp. 305–6.
58. Chu (1994), 781–94; Chu and Tsai (1992).
59. Chan (1998).
60. Chuang and Lin (1999), 117–37.
61. Hemple and Chang (2002), p. 77.

62. Ibid., p. 92.
63. See Chang (1992), pp. 193–214.
64. Amsden (2001), p. 195.
65. Sun and Tipton (1998), 159–86.
66. Selmer (2002), pp. 23–4.
67. Yeung (1998).
68. Sun and Tipton (1998).
69. Wu (2001), p. 163.
70. Chen and Chen (1998), 13–30; Chen and Chen (1998), 445–68.
71. Yeung (2002), pp. 15–16, 136–9.
72. Mathews and Cho (2000), pp. 181–3.
73. Carney (1998), 137–62.

6. Managing relations with state agencies in the People's Republic

So a military force has no constant formation, water has no constant shape: the ability to gain victory by changing and adapting according to the opponent is called genius. (Sun Tzu, *The Art of War*)

Ability to diagnose and seize opportunities and combat threats: shrewd business practices require the ability to sell and store at the right time. (Tao Zhu-gong, the Tenth Business Principle)

Let a hundred flowers bloom, let a hundred schools of thought contend. (Chairman Mao Zedong)

The heritage of Mao Zedong dominates China's historical grid. Under Mao the economy was from one perspective a rigid centrally planned unity, but from another a multifarious structure marked by the deep divisions between central and provincial authorities, between the urban and rural regions, and between the coastal and inland provinces. From yet another perspective the economy as such came a distant second in Mao's thinking, and his preoccupation with creating socialist men and women left a heritage of continuous disruption. The death of Mao and the rise of Deng Xiaoping accelerated initial attempts to bring the economy up to date. The de-collectivization of agriculture, the creation of the special economic zones, and the subsequent designation of open cities and open economic regions appear in retrospect to have a logic about them, but in fact the speed of development overwhelmed government attempts to control and guide it. Continued growth at an average of 8 to 10 per cent annually since 1978 makes China the most spectacular case of national economic growth in world history, but social dislocation, regional disparities, inflation, and widespread environmental degradation pose ongoing problems.

Water may have no constant shape, but its flow is constrained by the form of the land. China's institutional grid is dominated by one political factor, the continued leading position of the Chinese Communist Party. Management must conform to the parameters established by government agencies and the Party. State agencies still control the banking system, the large state-owned enterprise (SOE) sector, and the even larger township and village enterprise (TVE) sector, and the state continues to be deeply involved in the rest of the economy despite privatization and deregulation. Policy is not always consistent, in part because China's leaders are still learning to manage a market economy, but also because of divisions within the Party and conflicts between levels of government, central, provincial, and local. There are also two overriding social factors, the mass migration from rural areas into urban centers, and the emergence of the new affluent middle class. Specialists dispute whether the Party has discovered a new balance, a 'socialism with Chinese characteristics' combined with a 'capitalism with Chinese characteristics', or whether older Confucian patterns of thought and behavior are reappearing.

But, like water, Chinese management has no constant formation. China's managers have discovered many ways to seize opportunities and combat threats. Distinct forms of enterprise have emerged, and planning and decision making, organizing, leading and controlling vary in the separate sectors. Ironically, despite Mao's intentions, a hundred flowers have bloomed. Firms in the SOE sector, though with common management features, vary widely in structure and performance. The TVE sector, connected to local governments, shows further distinctive features. 'Private' firms take on a variety of forms, and have been possibly the most dynamic sources of growth over the past decade. The 'foreign invested enterprise' (FIE) sector has been the vehicle for massive foreign direct investment. Strategic options, notably whether to aim for export or for the domestic market, present complex choices for all of these firms, and Chinese managers themselves wonder if they are discovering a 'management with Chinese characteristics'.

THE HISTORICAL GRID: ECONOMIC ORGANIZATION UNDER MAO ZEDONG

When Mao Zedong and the Chinese Communist Party defeated Chiang Kaishek and the Nationalists and established the People's Republic of China, some provinces had not been at peace for 40 years. More than half a century later, the legitimacy of the government continues to rest on the simple fact of bringing an end to the wars. Important features of the new People's Republic have continued to the present. The Chinese Communist Party remains in power. National organizations for workers, youth, women and other groups remain a fixture of life. Under Mao mass campaigns periodically sent tens of thousands of chanting demonstrators through streets across the country. The government is still capable of mobilizing very large resources to support specific projects, for example the 2008 Olympics. Despite the rejection of 'Maoism', Mao remains the legitimating figure for the Party and the government, and the style of the campaigns remains pervasive, in the gold characters on huge red banners, and in the didactic tones and slogans adopted by officials and business executives on public occasions.[1]

Nationalization and the state-owned enterprises in the industrial sector are considered below. For most Chinese, rural land reform was the most significant change. The government sent teams of Party cadres into villages, where they organized the 'peasants' to attack the 'landlords'. The complexity of rural China's market economy meant that it was not easy to differentiate exploiters from exploited in any objective sense, and in effect anyone with an enemy in the village could be singled out as a 'landlord', 'rich peasant' or member of the 'bad gentry', denounced, publicly humiliated, and then tried, dispossessed, and quite possibly killed. The brutal logic of the situation was that, the more families named as 'class enemies', the more land there would be to redistribute among the rest. Confused by parallel campaigns against Nationalist supporters and suspected unreliable elements in the army and Party, the destruction of the landlord class cost at least a million persons their lives.

The age-old dream of land to the tiller seemed to have been realized. However, as in Russia, the new socialist government came to believe that, if peasant families owned land, they would inevitably retain capitalist attitudes. Private property therefore must be abolished. The government forced collectivization in stages. Local officials first moved peasants into mutual-aid teams, then organized them into agricultural producers' cooperatives, and then between 1954 and 1956 pressed them into 'higher level' collective farms where they would all work for wages. In 1958, collectivization culminated in the establishment of the communes, which typically combined a number of villages into a single unit, and also functioned as the basic unit of local government.

Under the regime of collectives and communes, peasants were supposed to produce only agricultural products. The state defined a fraction of the year's output as 'surplus' and purchased it at a fixed price. Manufactured goods were supplied to the communes by state enterprises. The state used the difference between the prices it paid for agricultural products and the prices it charged for industrial products to provide food for the urban centers and capital for industrial expansion. This Soviet model of 'primitive socialist accumulation' would in theory result in higher standards of living for all, sometime in the future. What remained of each village's output went to the 'three retained funds', for seed, for animal feed, and finally for the individual villagers' rations. Members of production teams received a basic ration, but this was set well below subsistence. Villagers also received additional amounts of food based on 'work points' earned for their labor. Competition among the teams determined the number of work points. Work points could also be earned for Party service, administrative duties, or serving in local government. Within the villages the activist cadres of Party members quickly entrenched themselves as a new elite.[2]

Agricultural output barely kept even with the rising population.[3] In 1956, planning agencies discussing the upcoming second five-year plan proposed fewer large industrial plants and more incentives to farmers. At the same time, the 'hundred flowers' campaign aimed to integrate intellectuals into the new socialist state: the campaign took its name from Mao's proclamation, 'Let a hundred flowers bloom together, let a hundred schools of thought contend.' However, the campaign brought an outburst of criticism of the government and of the Party. The government closed down the campaign and replaced it with the 'anti-rightist' campaign of 1957–8. Some 300 000 to 700 000 writers, publishers, teachers, administrators, and skilled workers lost their jobs. Deng, at the time General Secretary of the Party, played an active role in this purge.

Mao had decided, he said, to dispense with the services of intellectuals and 'experts' entirely, to abandon the 'fetish' of technology, and to rely on the energy and enthusiasm of the people. In the spring of 1958 he launched the 'great leap forward'. The results were disastrous. The farm villages had not yet recovered from the dislocation caused by collectivization. Millions of workers were mobilized for the projects of road and dam building, and thousands of villages melted down iron farm implements and cooking utensils in backyard ovens to make steel. The weather in 1958 was good, but the weather in 1959 was poor. The cities were fed, but, in the countryside, between 20 million and 30 million people starved to death.[4]

Many senior officials such as Deng concluded that economic planning should be placed on a more rational basis, and that greater incentives would have to be introduced to motivate farmers to produce more. Mao, however, concluded, not that he had been wrong, but that an even greater effort of will was necessary to create a classless socialist society. In 1966, he launched another campaign, the 'great proletarian cultural revolution'. Mao, his wife Jiang Qing, and a few other close associates encouraged groups of young 'red guards' to take direct action to oust anyone who opposed the 'thought of Chairman Mao'. Deng and others were denounced as 'capitalist roaders'. He escaped execution, but along with hundreds of thousands of officials at all levels, he lost his official positions. Schools and universities closed, because the only learning needed was contained in the *Quotations from Chairman Mao Tse-tung*, the 'little red book'. A number of provinces descended into civil war as factions within the Red Guards began to fight each other. Economically and intellectually China stagnated for a decade. The 1982 census reported only 6.3 million 'science and technology' personnel. Of the

2.4 million engineers, only 50 per cent had tertiary qualifications, and of the 370 000 persons listed as scientific researchers only 75 per cent had tertiary qualifications.

THE INSTITUTIONAL GRID

The Beginnings of Reform

Mao died in 1976. He had named Hua Guofeng as Premier, hoping that this would pave the way to power for Jiang Qing and her allies, who would then continue the Cultural Revolution. Party, army, and government officials, however, all had reason to oppose them. Following Mao's death, Hua gained the support of army leaders and Deng and his allies. Jiang Qing and her supporters (the 'Gang of Four') were arrested. Hua was confirmed as Mao's successor, and Deng, whom Mao had already partly rehabilitated, was restored to his former offices. In 1980, the Gang of Four and their main supporters were brought to trial, convicted, and imprisoned. The trial undermined Hua's position as well, though, because it highlighted his own previous support of the excesses of the Cultural Revolution. Hua's supporters were ousted, Deng's supporters replaced them, and Deng emerged as China's new leader.

It is tempting to attribute the economic reforms and the rapid growth of the Chinese economy since 1978 to a preconceived plan, forced through by Deng over the opposition of conservatives.[5] The repression of the student demonstrations in Beijing's Tiananmen Square in 1989 could be interpreted as a triumph of these anti-reform forces. It seemed to some observers that reform did in fact stall for a time, but then was revived by Deng's famous 'southern tour' in 1992.[6] Deng himself said in an interview in 1979 that China possessed the same number of lathes as Japan had in 1960, and therefore should be able to attempt a similar economic takeoff. In fact, however, 'there was no "plan" of reform in the sense of a clear idea of some ultimate end-state and a series of steps or phases to reach it'.[7] Deng also said that the process of reform had been like crossing the river, feeling for stones one step at a time, and this is closer to the mark.[8]

The new orientation did not begin with Deng alone. Zhou Enlai, one of Mao's oldest colleagues and the guiding force in China's foreign relations, had advocated both an opening of China to the outside world and economic restructuring. In 1975, he outlined a program of 'four modernizations' of agriculture, industry, defense, and science and technology. Zhou said this would require China to import advanced technologies, paid for by earnings from trade. To this end he had pursued better relations with both the United States and Japan. Zhou at one time during the Cultural Revolution had denounced Deng, but Deng later said that, if he had not, Zhou himself would have fallen, and the ultimate result would have been even worse. As a sort of protégé of Zhou's, it is not surprising that he followed Zhou's line.

Regional leaders also experimented with reforms. In Sichuan in 1977, the provincial government led by Zhao Ziyang began to allow farmers to work on their own account after fulfilling their obligations to their communes. This led to a rise in agricultural output, particularly specialized crops that could be marketed under the new 'dual track' system of prices, but it also led to the establishment of non-agricultural enterprises in rural districts.[9] Zhao rose to become Premier and General Secretary of the Party, but he was accused of being too lenient with the Tiananmen protesters. He was replaced by Jiang Zemin, who went on to become President after Deng died in 1997.

In 1978, Premier Hua announced a ten-year plan, dated as having begun in 1976 with Mao's death, that aimed to raise agricultural output by increasing capital intensity, especially increased use of electrical power. In the industrial sector, the plan called for 120 major industrial projects, many of them complete 'turnkey' factories imported from the West. However, the target for increased electrical power-generating capacity would not have covered the hoped-for increases in industrial production, and left nothing for agricultural electrification. The imported factories were expensive, and many used inappropriate technologies.[10] Exports increased, but imports rose as well.[11] Increases in wages and procurement prices for farm products and other raw materials drove up the general price level. Government budgets showed heavy deficits and, in June 1979, Hua announced a three-year commitment to 'readjustment, reform, streamlining, and upgrading'. The government slashed investments in heavy industry and construction, including joint ventures with foreign firms. Japanese losses were estimated at US$1.5 billion.

Agriculture

To overcome the crisis, the government attempted to draw on the reserves of the agricultural sector, but without the promised increases in capital. In 1979, the government offered farm families in some areas the opportunity to work independently as contractors for their communes. In these districts, land would remain public property, but the communes would allocate plots to families in return for a promise to deliver a specified quantity of crops at the end of the season. These families received 'full responsibility' for production, and permission to sell their surplus production in private markets.

The government intended the scheme to be strictly limited, 'a concessionary measure appropriate only to poorer communes'. Nevertheless, once introduced, the new system spread irresistibly. Across the entire country, farm families abandoned the communes, and by 1984 virtually all farm households were operating under the 'household responsibility' system.[12]

Having failed to predict or control the expansion of private enterprise in rural areas, the central government now left agriculture to muddle through on its own. For several years all went well. Output increased substantially and rural incomes rose.[13] Local officials interviewed in the late 1980s said market forces had motivated farmers to increase output.[14] On the other hand, the increases in output often merely reflected higher levels of intensity of labor. The slowdown came in 1985 and agricultural output stagnated in the late 1980s.[15] This could have led to another crisis, but output began to rise in the early 1990s and has continued to do so. New technologies improved productivity. Machines such as those that transplanted large numbers of rice seedlings at once substantially reduced the number of workers required. Workers freed from farming took jobs in local manufacturing enterprises, or moved to jobs in other regions, as will be seen below.

The Special Economic Zones and Foreign Investment

The government's hopes turned to the manufacturing sector and foreign trade. Following Zhou Enlai's logic, exports of manufactured goods would pay for imports of advanced technology. However, following both the more recent logic of Mao and an older logic from China's past and the history of Western imperialism, foreigners would provide both the technology and the exports, but those dangerous foreigners would be kept under strict control. As Mao put it in 1956, 'Use the past to serve the present, make the foreign serve China.' As we have already seen in Chapter 5, in 1978 the State Council issued regulations that allowed foreign companies to establish joint ventures in China. In 1980, the government allowed foreign investors to locate in 'certain areas' in the cities of Shenzhen, close to Hong Kong, Zhuhai, close to Portuguese-controlled Macau, and Shantou and Xiamen, in Fujian Province across the straits from Taiwan. The zones initially were surrounded by barbed wire fences and guard posts, and were strictly off limits to unauthorized Chinese citizens. In the early 2000s, entry through the Customer Gate of the Shenzhen SEZ still required special permission from the local police.

In 1984, the government approved a further 14 SEZs in cities along the entire coastline. The cities included suggest that that the central government in fact was responding to pressure from provincial and local governments. Not all of the new zones were in large cities, but now every coastal province had one, and large cities that had been left out (particularly Shanghai and Guangzhou, inland from Hong Kong) were now included. In 1986, some of the previous restrictions on foreign direct investment were removed, and the number of 'open' areas where such ventures enjoyed autonomy and preferential treatment was increased. In 1988, Premier Zhao Ziyang announced that provincial and local authorities would be encouraged to foster the development of township enterprises and agriculture. To do so they were permitted to establish contact with foreign companies who could help to build up processing plants for export. Local studies suggest that by now local officials were rushing to set up 'their' zones whether they had the central government's approval or not.

Circumstances forced the government's pragmatism and flexibility. Population growth meant that China would need 19 million new jobs every year through the year 2010. Despite rising agricultural output, China needed food imports, as urban incomes rose and consumers shifted from grains to meat. This could have posed problems, but the flood of foreign investment softened the impact of the government's financial difficulties by creating jobs and stimulating growth. By the end of 1994 over 220 000 foreign invested enterprises (FIEs) had been approved, and the FIEs directly employed 3.2 million persons, nearly 4 per cent of the entire labor force.[16]

Problems

Rapid growth brought mass migration. Millions moved towards the coastal regions and the cities. Factory dormitories filled with *dagongmei*, a new and derogatory word combining *da-gong* meaning 'working for the boss' or 'selling labor', a hired hand of lower status than the Marxist proletarian or *gongren*, and *mei*, literally 'younger sister', a single, unmarried, young female, again of low status.[17] Migrant men tended to work on the construction sites that transformed China's urban landscape. These 'floating people' did not fit into the legal categories used by urban officials, and were denied the services provided to properly registered inhabitants.[18] Urban growth also led to widely reported environmental problems. China possesses huge coal reserves, but coal mining has been poorly regulated, and burning coal for energy and heat has created permanent haze in many cities.[19] Hydroelectric power poses its own environmental problems, as with the massive Three Gorges dam. Overall, China is short of supplies of clean water, so expensive waste treatment plants will need to be extended.

Rapid growth also brought rising prices. To combat inflation, the budgets of government departments and state-owned enterprises were cut repeatedly in the late 1980s and early 1990s. In 1993, the government announced an austerity program including budget cuts, compulsory bond purchases, increased interest rates, cancelled loans for 'speculative' projects, and a 20 per cent reduction in government employment.[20] As they imposed the credit squeeze, senior government officials said they would 'take away the firewood from under the pot'.[21] The phrase is from *The 36 Stratagems* and means do not attack an enemy directly at his strongest point, but find ways to sap his strength. But prices continued to spiral upward, although inflation dropped in the aftermath of the Asian financial crisis. The 1993 reforms failed to reduce government employment, and in 1998 further cuts of 4 million jobs were announced, again without obvious success.

Rather than taking away the firewood, the government in the early 2000s appeared more often merely to threaten to take away the firewood. China, newly admitted to the World Trade Organization, needed to portray itself as a responsible economic manager to international observers. However, provincial and local authorities generally continued to spend on their own projects in disregard of central government policy. Further, the government relied on continued growth to solve a number of intractable problems, to narrow the income gap between urban and rural areas, to compensate for the absence of a social security safety net, to help weak state-owned enterprises, and to pay for imports of raw materials, food, and technology. Rapid growth also increased China's power and prestige, and therefore the geography across which Chinese business had to flow seemed likely to continue to incline towards expansion.

The Banking System

One of the factors impeding government attempts to manage the economy has been the unresponsiveness of the banking system. On the surface this appears odd, since the four major commercial banks are state enterprises and they account for over 60 per cent of loans, and other state financial institutions provide another 30 per cent. However, the banks remain prisoners of their past. Under the old system of central planning, they did not actually function as banks. The planning system used money only as a unit of account, because like the rent from land, according to the labor theory of value, capital itself could not earn a return because it was not a direct payment for labor. Plants and equipment represented only the physical residue of past labor, and money as such had no intrinsic value at all.

The government established financial institutions to serve specific industries or regions. They did collect deposits from enterprises and from individuals, and they did pay interest. However, their main function was to provide credits to government departments and enterprises when ordered to do so. Enterprises with deficits ran up negative balances. These appeared formally in the banks' accounts as loans, and they might have interest charged against them, but they were actually the means used by government agencies to channel resources to achieve their targets. With no consideration of repayment or profit, each branch could operate independently, allocating credit as directed by the various central, provincial, or local authorities. The banks' internal culture reflected their status as government departments, with Party appointees at the national level, branch managers appointed by provincial governments, and lower-level employees working in lifetime tenured jobs.

The banks remain connected to the state owned enterprise (SOE) sector. There were no equity markets until the establishment of regional stock exchanges in the 1990s. An estimated 85 per cent of the working capital of SOEs comes from the banks. SOEs account for over 60 per cent of the banks' total loans. In theory the amounts owed are now loans in a commercial sense, but, as seen in the case of Sunve Pharmaceutical, SOEs have enjoyed preferential rates of interest. Sunve is a strong SOE, but further estimates suggest that a large fraction of state enterprises will never be able to repay their debts. The estimates of the proportion of insolvent SOEs range from 25 to 45 per cent, and Standard and Poor estimated in 2004 that the banks' impaired assets and non-performing loans equaled 43 per cent of China's yearly gross domestic product. Many believe that, if the banks accounted for these outstanding loans according to international standards, they themselves would be insolvent.[22]

China escaped the Asian financial crisis, because of its trade surplus, controls over capital flows, and large foreign exchange reserves. However, the banks' situation worsened, because many SOEs (in the coal industry, for instance) did suffer as international demand declined, and therefore the number of non-performing loans increased.[23] Since the crisis, reforms in the banking sector have paralleled reforms in the SOE sector. The new commercial bank law of 1995 had already made the banks responsible for their own profits and losses. In 1998, they were required to conduct regular audits of their branches' accounts. In 1998 and 1999, they moved to vertical authority chains, with provincial and local branch managers appointed by the banks' own headquarters rather than by provincial governments. Reportedly, some banks began to appoint their own boards and senior managers, not necessarily Party members. In 1998, the previous credit allocation system was ended. Regulations now require banks to make new loans based on risk and return assessments, and managers are responsible for non-performing loans. Legislation has progressively raised reserve requirements. From 2007, banks must have a tier one capital ratio of 8 per cent (the international standard), or face sanctions, including the threatened removal of senior staff.

The four major banks have asset management corporations that have assumed ownership positions in SOEs, by exchanging debt for equity. Nevertheless, even if the state were to exit completely from the SOE sector, through privatization, sales to investors, or allowing SOEs to fail, something would still need to be done about the loans that remain on the banks' balance sheets. In the meantime the government continues to direct lending to areas and to enterprises that it regards as strategically significant. For their part the banks have been reluctant to lend to the private sector. They do not have sufficient capacity to assess risk, nor is there a strong bankruptcy regime in place. Therefore the banks attempt to minimize risk by lending to the stronger SOEs, or to enterprises connected to provincial or local governments, in the hope that the central government will be more likely to compensate them for losses than to punish them for increasing their non-performing loans.

The banks suffer from an overhang of poorly trained older staff, and relatively low salaries make recruitment difficult. In addition to the governance problems in the banks themselves, their relationship with the central bank remains unclear. A new China Banking Regulatory Commission was established in 2003, but incomplete formal legislation and limited skills and resources restrict the central authorities' ability to regulate the commercial banks. International experience suggests that it takes time to create the equally important informal conditions for effective regulation, a shared set of expectations of central bank officials and managers of commercial banks. The problem of moral hazard also remains. If the banks believe the government will prop them up, then they will continue to lend, and the firewood will remain in the fire.[24]

Because the major banks are themselves state enterprises, in the short run there is no danger of a banking crisis. Nevertheless, Yiping Huang and others believe that the fragility and vulnerability of China's banking system make it even more crucial for China to implement further reforms as quickly as possible. China's official estimates may seriously understate the size of its total debt. As the current account payments system is liberalized, debt repayment could suddenly become difficult, leading to a credit shortage. This in turn would slow or even halt domestic growth, reducing government revenues and further increasing the difficulty of meeting payments on the debt. But reform poses a knife-edge problem. If the reforms are inadequate or hesitant, the financial system will remain fragile or weaken further, increasing the risk of a collapse triggered by a balance of payments crisis. If the reforms are too radical, however, they could themselves trigger a crisis and collapse by disrupting the domestic economy.[25]

Like all nations China has been very reluctant to open its financial markets to foreigners, although it is obligated to do so under the terms of its accession to the WTO. The government announced plans to list the four largest banks in 2004, and the initial public offering, for China Construction Bank, took place in 2005. Bank of America and Singapore's Temasek Holdings had already purchased stakes of 9 and 5.1 per cent, respectively, ahead of the listing. However, as with other corporatizations, it remained unclear what role the new shareholders would play in the banks' governance. The maximum foreign ownership remained at 25 per cent, and it was unlikely that the government would surrender control of a major bank.[26] It has also been suggested that foreign competition could provide the impetus to strengthen the banking system. However, the incumbents' huge branch networks, and their continuing connection with the government, remained significant competitive advantages, and even firms with longstanding connections in China, such as HSBC, seemed likely to inhabit niche markets.[27]

THE MANAGEMENT GRID: STATE-OWNED ENTERPRISES

BOX 6.1 POINT AND COUNTERPOINT: THE REFORM OF STATE-OWNED ENTERPRISES – SUNVE AND VITAMIN C

Financial matters must be handled judiciously; carelessness will lead to problems and woes. (Tao Zhu-gong, the Fifteenth Business Lesson)

The Shanghai Second Pharmaceutical Factory was established by the Shanghai Metropolitan Medical Administration Bureau in 1958. Like most state-owned enterprises, it was a single large factory dedicated to making a single product, Vitamin C. Its relatively advanced production process made it the technological leader in China, and it won numerous awards both for the quality of its product and for the quality of its management. Government agencies and the general public viewed it as a 'model SOE'. However, again like most SOEs, it remained confined to its own home region, supplying 80 per cent of Shanghai's needs, but with less than 10 per cent of the national market.

In 1992, Shanghai Second Pharmaceutical Factory was granted the status of a 'quasi-foreign-capital entity', which gave it the taxation and administrative privileges enjoyed by companies under the rules designed to encourage investment by foreigners. The firm introduced programs to improve marketing, to extend research and development, and to move towards an incentive compensation system for employees. In 1993, the firm was selected to be among the first 100 SOEs to undergo financial restructuring and economic reform, a high and hotly contested honor. The name was changed, and Shanghai Sunve Pharmaceutical Corporation registered as a corporation and introduced responsibility accounting in a number of newly defined business units.

Sunve launched a diversification program as well as updating the technology in its core Vitamin C business. While increasing its domestic sales, Sunve also became a leading exporter of pharmaceutical products. Sunve's main competitors in its home region market are foreign manufacturers, and observers attributed Sunve's responsiveness to the highly competitive environment. From 1993 to 1995, the firm's formal management structure changed. Under the old system the Communist Party Secretary, the representative of the Shanghai municipal government, had been the ultimate authority in the firm, the 'real boss'. Now, as 'Vice President (Political Affairs)', the Party Secretary became one of four vice presidents, in charge of public relations, auditing, and relations with the labor union. Sunve remained a state-owned enterprise, but the function of the Party in the business had changed significantly. The planned diversification of product lines also had led to a more decentralized structure with greater latitude for the managers of over a dozen subsidiary companies.

In 1994, the State Council selected Sunve as a candidate for stock exchange listing and an initial public offering. Following 'endless meetings and consultations', it was decided to combine the major SOEs in Shanghai into a conglomerate, the Shanghai Industrial Group. The group was listed publicly on the Hong Kong stock exchange in 1996, and rapidly became one of the major firms traded on the exchange. The success of the group's listing led to suggestions that member firms such as Sunve might be spun off and floated independently.

Sunve's strong reputation and its ability to export some of its output clearly impressed government authorities, and Sunve benefited from a range of explicit and implicit subsidies. The most important figure for the manager of any state-owned enterprise is 'retained earnings', the amount of income the firm is allowed to keep after the state has decided how much of the profits it will take for itself. Sunve's retained earnings declined in the early 1990s, but then increased by 20 times from 1993 to 1994, from less than 7 to over 57 per cent of total profits.

As a quasi-foreign capital entity, Sunve paid only 15 per cent in taxes on net income, and was allowed to deduct costs of repair and maintenance, interest, infrastructure investment, and employee compensation and benefits 'above the allowance to SOEs'. Had the firm been a normal SOE, it would have paid 33 per cent in taxes, and not been allowed the deductions and, instead of RMB$159 544, its 1992 tax bill would have been RMB$3.5 million. However, at the same time, because it was an SOE, it paid just under 11 per cent on its borrowings from state banks, rather than the market rate of 18 per cent. As with other SOEs, Sunve also benefited from subsidized rent. Unusually for an SOE, however, Sunve had virtually no 'social overhead'. It relied on the Shanghai municipal government to deliver services to its workers, rather than providing housing, medical care, child-care, education, and other services itself. A restructuring process had eliminated older workers and the large numbers of unpro-ductive workers that burdened many other SOEs. In 1994, the firm supported 1100 pensioners, but there were no active workers over 60.

Jevons Lee, who served as consultant to the United Nations Development Program, believes Sunve to be 'one of the best-run SOEs in China'. Nevertheless, he also concludes that, without the subsidies, Sunve would have lost money. Dependent on a single product in a mature market with very low margins, it was not clear whether Sunve had either the scale or the scope to compete in the absence of the special treatment it received from the government. Despite its size and importance, it was also not clear how the Shanghai Industrial Group functioned, except as a holding company, and therefore it was not clear how the separation of the more successful firms from the group would affect the results of the remaining members. Sunve certainly handled its financial matters judiciously, but Lee concludes that what he terms 'political prowess', the ability to anticipate and exploit changes in economic policy, were 'key for SOEs' economic success'.

Source: Chi-Wen Jevons Lee, 'Financial restructuring of state owned enterprises in China: the case of Shanghai Sunve Pharmaceutical Corporation', *Accounting, Organizations and Society*, **26** (2001), 673–89.

The Origins of the State-owned Enterprise Sector

Although they are almost always studied as a single category, state-owned enterprises (SOEs) have varied widely in size and structure. Under the system of central planning, existing enterprises came under the control of central government ministries responsible for particular sectors, but they could also be established or acquired by other organizations such as the army or the Party, or by provincial or local government authorities. Whatever their form, however, they were first and foremost government agencies. Managers were political appointees who took orders from their ministry, controlling agency, provincial or local government, or local Party organization, and sometimes from all at once. 'I remember in the old days the missionaries saying a man could not serve two masters,' joked the retired head of a textile plant, 'but I had to juggle a half dozen at least. There were weeks when I did nothing but go to meetings.'[28]

The Nationalist government already owned or controlled most large industrial firms. Following their victory, the Communist government proclaimed the socialization of the means of production, and these existing enterprises passed directly to the new ministries. The government set high targets for industrial production. Planning agencies, partly following the precedent of the Nationalist government and strongly influenced by the example of the Soviet Union, favored large, capital-intensive plants. About half of the new investment during the early 1950s was concentrated in large projects supported by the Soviet Union with technical assistance and loans. Another major wave of formations of SOEs came as part of the Cultural Revolution. Mao wanted to decentralize China's industry, to create a 'third front' that would be safe from foreign attack. Local authorities were given control over planning, and they channeled resources into comparatively small manufacturing plants and power stations. Although total investment and industrial output rose rapidly, Third Front projects produced at relatively high cost, and the lack of control over regional authorities led to wasteful duplication.[29]

The system operated from the top down. National totals emerged from complex negotiations among central ministries and between national and provincial authorities, but, once the plan was set, planning agencies assigned output targets to each enterprise and allocated resources to achieve the target output, using credits provided by banks or other financial agencies, as noted above. The Soviet-style material balance system of allocation meant, on the one hand, that managers had no control over their inputs. On the other hand, they also did not need to concern themselves with marketing. They relied on branches of central agencies to supply them with raw materials, and on commercial departments at provincial and municipal levels to transfer their output to other state agencies. Managers also did not control their labor force or their wages. The local labor bureau assigned workers to enterprises. Wages were set nationally, an eight-class scale for blue-collar workers and a 21-class scale for white-collar employees, based on their education and experience.

In addition each enterprise or 'work unit' provided its workers with a broad range of social services. SOEs have been described as 'urban villages' and 'mini welfare states'. Appointed by the controlling agency, managers occupied an 'iron chair' so long as they did not offend the leader of the local Party organization, who, as in the case of Sunve, was often known as the 'real boss'. At the same time, 'fixed workers' (96.8 per cent of SOE employees in 1983) could remain with the enterprise for life. Their 'iron rice bowl' granted them a privileged position. Labor bureaus assigned young people to jobs on completion of their schooling. Workers lived in housing provided by their work unit, often physically within the industrial complex. They married and had children, sent their children to schools, and went to medical clinics and hospitals provided by their work unit. Throughout, their interests were represented by work committees, formal labor unions in the larger enterprises, and the Party. Retirement brought a pension, also provided by the work unit. The children then might almost literally inherit their parents' jobs.[30]

The system did not encourage SOEs to introduce new technologies. The labor theory of value defined physical capital as the congealed form of past labor. As such its value lay in its ability to assist current workers to transform raw materials. As long as it did so it remained useful, and therefore no provision was made for depreciation. As a result plants and equipment continued in use long after the end of their economic life. Enterprises were not upgraded over time. Jevons Lee, the UNDP consultant for Sunve, observed SOEs in the 1990s that still used machinery installed in the 1930s and 1940s under the Nationalists.[31]

Despite the security of their iron chairs ('whoever heard of a comfortable iron chair?' asked the textile manager), managers did not press for increased efficiency. As in the Soviet Union and East Europe, direct funding and quantitative output targets created a risk-averse environment. Each plant was supposed to produce according to plan. Therefore managers attempted to hoard stockpiles of raw materials and inventory to ensure they could meet their assigned targets. They did not risk scarce resources to attempt to do things differently. They did not have much personal motive to innovate, since their own wages were determined according to the national scale. Within the enterprise, workers' committees and unions could resist change. In contrast to East Europe, where labor unions functioned to repress workers' dissent, in China the anti-elitism of the Party and the worker's organizations meant that managers were severely constrained in their ability to organize and control their workers. Nor was there much pressure from above. Concentrating on their output targets, central ministries did not seek out new technologies, and new plants repeated the tried and true methods of old plants.[32]

Reforming the SOEs

Reformers saw the SOEs as the home of the 'three olds' of old factories, old equipment, and old ideas. 'I was the fourth "old",' laughed the textile manager, but then added, 'seriously, old workers were a problem, particularly if they had never learned to do their job properly'.[33] SOEs suffered from chronic overstaffing, but they had no motive to save labor, because they did not have the right to hire and fire, and each work unit was required to provide for its assigned labor force.

Reform of the SOEs paralleled the opening to foreign investment, but, as with other aspects of economic reform, it was a gradual process of trial and error. The complete turnkey factories imported from the West in the 1970s came to be regarded as very wasteful, an inappropriate 'Western leap' that had failed.[34] Policy shifted to selective acquisition of technical know-how, aimed especially at existing small and medium-sized plants in the machine building and electronics industries, but the large number of projects (8000 in 1983–7), made control difficult and led to overlapping and duplication of plans at regional and local levels. Some municipal governments such as Tianjin and Shanghai received authority to negotiate technology imports within this framework, but, as with the creation of special economic zones, other cities began authorizing their own programs as well.

The government wanted to improve labor productivity, and therefore gradually undermined the iron rice bowl of SOE employees. Foreign investors were allowed to attract workers by offering them higher wages, and these individual labor contracts became the model for conditions in the SOEs. In 1978, pay bonuses, which had been abolished during the Cultural Revolution, were reintroduced, and state enterprises were allowed to use piece rate payments more widely. Both changes gave SOE managers more discretion over wages. In 1983, the government stipulated that new workers in SOEs would be employed on individual contracts. Widespread opposition delayed extensive implementation until 1986, but the proportion of SOE workers on labor contracts rose from less than 1 per cent in 1983 to 22 per cent in 1993. In 1994, a new national labor law required all employees in the state sector to enter into labor contracts covering term, job description, labor protection, compensation, and termination conditions. 'It was easier for me to do this, since I had been the Party Secretary,' said the textile manager.

The government also decentralized management control. In the early 1980s, a contract system for SOEs was introduced that resembled the household responsibility system that had spread through the agricultural sector. SOEs were permitted to acquire inputs through the market and to sell a fraction of their output.[35] However, the managers of many SOEs responded by bargaining for higher levels of retained earnings, that is, for a larger share of profits, leaving less for the state. To protect its revenues, in 1983 the government imposed a 55 per cent tax on enterprise profits. This proved highly unpopular, and reported profits declined; the tax was with-drawn in 1985 and then reintroduced, but with a sliding scale. In 1987, a revised contract responsibility system allowed enterprises to negotiate terms over a three-to-five year period. The relatively short periods encour-aged a short-term outlook, and the system placed a premium on each manager's circle of contacts and negotiating skills, so the program was gen-erally held to have failed to stimulate improvements in productivity.[36]

In 1987, a more radical change introduced the selection of managers by bidding. Private entrepreneurs and some officials emerged as bidders. The process was halted for ideological reasons, but was resumed in 1992. In 1992, the government also introduced 'corporatization' of SOEs. Corporatized firms became legal entities responsible for their own profits and losses. They could decide independently on their levels of output, hiring, wages, and asset management. The corporatized firms issued shares, but this was not yet 'privatization', because government agencies held most of the shares issued. Even when non-state ownership was permitted, the shares were frequently held by public collective entities, 'legal persons' such as banks, investment companies, pension funds, or labor unions, rather than individuals. However, as Keun Lee reports in one case, workers in a firm could become its collective owners through their labor union, the legal person that held the shares, and as such they participated in management decisions and received dividends.[37]

In 1993, the State Council announced a three-stage program to restruc-ture SOEs, a 'hundred, thousand, ten thousand' approach which would see the experiences of the first 100 used to guide reform for the next 1000 and then the next 10 000 enterprises. Competition to be included in the first 100 was intense, as it brought recognition of the achievements of the managers as well as tangible benefits in terms of taxation, regulation, and consulting services provided by the United Nations. In the mid-1990s, policy shifted again, and government leaders said that, rather than reforming the entire SOE sector, they would 'grasp the large, let go of the small'. In 1996, a new goal called for 70 per cent of the SOEs in 'pioneering provinces' to be privatized. The remaining 30 per cent, the largest, would become 'national champions', a phrase possibly taken from Japan in the 1960s. A 'national team' of the largest 120 enterprises was designated. Most the enterprises selected as members of the national team were from the strategic 'commanding heights' of the economy, a phrase that comes from Lenin and the Soviet Union's New Economic Policy in the 1920s. They included coal, petroleum, electricity generation, steel, transportation, and heavy construction, areas that would continue to give the government leverage over the rapidly growing private sector.[38]

At the Fifteenth Party Congress in 1997, President Jiang Zemin announced that more than 10000 of the 13000 large and medium SOEs would be sold and organized under the corporate system. In 1997, the government reportedly did sell 10000 small and medium SOEs, and another 20000 were reported sold in 1998. Asset management companies took control of some larger enterprises, as noted above the banks traded debt for equity in others, and a few entities such as the Shanghai Industrial Group was listed publicly. In 2003, a new State Assets Supervision and Administration Commission assumed ownership of 196 large SOEs from a variety of government and Party organizations. The new body was to act as a unified source of policymaking, and to pave the way for a transfer of ownership to local branches of the commission, which in turn might sell stakes in their portfolios to private investors. Some thought local governments would take on something close to ownership rights, but others objected that this might in fact impose new and onerous responsibilities on poorer regional governments in the interior provinces.[39]

Managing a Reformed SOE

As this brief account makes clear, managers of SOEs have been under continual pressure. Along with other government departments, their budgets were cut through the early 1990s. Their debit accounts with state banks became commercial loans. The definition of their 'profit' shifted, and the proportion of their earnings they were allowed to retain was altered repeatedly. Accounting procedures changed, and they were required to absorb new charges against income such as depreciation of plant and equipment. Under the 'dual price' system, some of their inputs were purchased and some of their output sold in competitive markets, but with an arbitrary fraction of their operations still subject to central directives. The government imposed new taxes and administrative charges, which could vary capriciously. Entry barriers were lowered, subjecting them to new competition, for instance from foreign firms that enjoyed lower tax rates and that were not obligated to provide social services to their workers.

The share of the state sector in China's gross domestic product declined from around 80 per cent in the late 1970s to possibly 25 per cent in the late 1990s. Profits of SOEs also declined continuously. Corporatization, particularly where the employees owned shares, appeared to create incentives to increase profits.[40] Compared to the remaining SOEs, corporatized firms improved productivity, and the evidence of an intensively studied sample suggests they did so by offering direct incentives. They lowered both their welfare expenses and their basic wages, but they did not lower piece rates or overtime payments. Further, those that paid the most to their managers also tended to pay the most to their production workers. This and other evidence led many observers to call for rapid corporatization, and preferably full privatization, of the remaining SOEs, subject only to the qualification that excessively rapid reform might destabilize labor markets.[41] Those who favor complete privatization also usually argue that the developing share markets will impose discipline on managers.[42]

However, this is not the whole story. The SOE sector did not decline in absolute terms. Through the 1980s and into the 1990s, output in the state sector increased by an impressive average of 8 per cent annually. In 2000, SOEs produced 28 per cent of China's industrial output. Despite the burdens imposed on them, on average their financial performance through the mid-1990s was at least as good as corporatized or private firms.[43] The reported averages also conceal the tendency for successful SOEs to be corporatized or privatized, thereby moving to the non-SOE sector, and joint ventures between SOEs and foreign firms are counted as 'foreign invested enterprises', not as SOEs. Most observers agree that the 'problem' SOEs tend to be small. A substantial majority of large SOEs reported net profits, and those that reported losses tended to be concentrated in sectors such as coal, petroleum, and natural gas, where the central government retained control over output, distribution, and prices.[44]

SOEs have remained on average less profitable than non-SOEs, but Carsten Holz argues that the gap in profitability results from two factors, the higher capital intensity of SOEs, and the fact that they are required to pay higher taxes. SOEs predominate in the sectors where the maximum value added tax rate is charged. Most of them are 'large' firms and pay the full rate of 17 or 13 per cent, whereas small firms (mostly private) with less than one million yuan annual sales revenue pay only 6 per cent, and foreign firms and joint ventures that produce for export pay no value added tax at all. The rate of sales taxes and surcharges paid by firms is highly correlated with market concentration, which Holz believes to be a political decision, because it is easier for the government to collect tax from a monopoly, for instance the tobacco industry, or from a few large state firms, than from many small firms.[45]

Not only are they taxed more heavily, but SOEs also continue to provide a large fraction of China's social services. Housing, childcare, education, medical care, and pensions made up over half of labor costs, according to a World Bank study in the mid-1990s.[46] Another way of putting this is to say that social overhead expenses effectively double SOE labor costs. Pensions can be a particularly serious burden, as they were not funded under the old system, but now constitute a charge against current income. There have been high levels of disguised unemployment, and SOEs have absorbed large amounts of labor. The inefficiency of the SOE sector could be considered the price that has to be paid for their role in providing a social security safety net.[47] When they suffer losses, as in the energy sector, this reflects the government's decision to set prices at a low level to subsidize the rest of the economy to promote growth.[48]

These structural problems are particularly severe in interior regions. Chongqing, the largest and most heavily industrialized city in the Southwest, for instance, contains a large number of plants constructed as part of the Third Front program in the 1960s and early 1970s. Many of Chongqing's SOEs are located in remote mountainous areas, and many are statutory towns where the enterprise functioned as a city and provided all infrastructure and social services for the residents. Many also were in defense industries. The national plans of the 1980s emphasized development in the coastal provinces, and priorities shifted away from military production. Chongqing's SOEs 'were left to find their own way,' and predictably, 'some have succeeded in the transition, but many have been struggling'.[49]

Successful SOEs improved productivity; that is, they produced more output per worker. 'It's not rocket science,' said the textile manager. 'This is a mature industry, so we knew how to upgrade our equipment, and we had loans for that, organized by the city government. The keys are cost control, especially labor costs, and knowing the market, and even that was no problem at first, because of the huge demand for consumer goods.' Following the changes in the laws governing employment conditions, 'restructured' SOEs attempted to reduce their social overhead. They sometimes created subsidiaries to provide the services, as well as to absorb unwanted workers. Many of China's hospitals are former SOE facilities, for instance. Many of them cut labor costs by shifting workers to part-time or laying them off entirely. SOEs laid off nearly a million workers every year through the 1990s. Less successful enterprises also paid lower wages and gave less generous bonuses. For truly unlucky enterprises 'reform' meant being shut down. In 1999, the government reportedly closed 7900 large and medium SOEs and 4 million workers lost their jobs.[50]

'Our labor force doubled through the 1990s,' continued the textile manager, 'but we also doubled productivity. Our new workers were almost all girls from the interior provinces. We provided housing and they got the same wages, but they were more disciplined and flexible.' On average, estimates show static or declining wages for SOE workers with only primary or secondary education, and rapidly rising wages of employees with tertiary education. In the early 1980s, tertiary-educated employees earned about 50 per cent more than workers with a high school education or less, but ten years later they earned six and one-half times as much. Workers with rare skills, such as engineers, could demand more.[51] 'As our people upgraded their skills we had to pay them more,' said the textile manager.

Another of the changes in the SOEs appears to have been that managers began to pay themselves more. Through the 1980s, managerial wages rose less rapidly than those of production workers.[52] In the 1990s, they increased in line with tertiary-educated employees generally. Official rates of compensation for SOE managers remain low by international standards, but they can supplement their salaries, for example by sponsoring new investments by the firm to increase the assets they control. Some also withdraw illegal 'hidden' income from the firm, possibly in collusion with other employees. If they cannot find ways to raise their income, they are tempted to leave for township enterprises or private firms.[53] In the late 1990s, Chongqing municipal officials reported that they found newly-appointed factory directors were frequently able to turn loss-making enterprises around, but that after about two years would begin to take part in graft, embezzlement, bribery, and 'most frequently' the appropriation or 'pirating' of state assets. They attributed this to a combination of lax law enforcement and the lack of effective incentive mechanisms.[54]

Reforms have addressed governance and agency issues. The new corporate system in theory separates enterprise management from government agencies.[55] Transfer of equity to asset management corporations is also intended in part to remove political influences from the firms' decision making. Public listing is a further step in the same direction.[56] Corporatized firms have boards of directors intended to represent shareholder interests, and firms in which employees' own shares appear to enjoy particularly good results.[57]

However, problems remain. The shares of corporatized firms are held by 'legal persons', not by individuals directly, and the individual or institutional investors in listed firms have little influence on management. As shown in Figure 6.1, when SOEs list, the publicly listed company is typically a subsidiary of the corporatized 'group' which usually contains other subsidiary companies as well. Therefore the listed vehicle often does not correspond either to the legal or the operating entity. In addition, the corporatized group often remains under the administrative control of an economic commission or central ministry.[58] Some two-thirds of the shares of listed firms are non-tradeable, and most of these are held by government

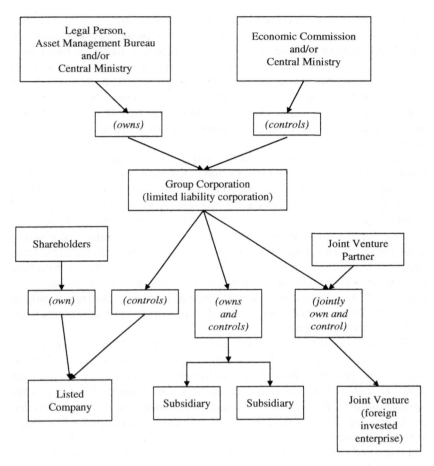

Source: adapted, with additions, from Marshall W. Meyer and Xiaohui Lu, 'Managing indefinite boundaries: the strategy and structure of a Chinese business firm', Department of Management, The Wharton School, July 2003, Figure 4.

Figure 6.1   China: group corporation structure

agencies. Regulators and outside observers worry that this means many controlling shareholders are unconcerned about share prices and therefore markets will not operate to enforce performance. Further reform poses problems, though. Dumping the non-tradeable shares onto the market would almost certainly deflate the price of the current tradeable shares, but compensating existing shareholders with additional shares or warrants, as in the case of Baosteel, simply transfers public assets to them for nothing.[59]

Managers of SOEs and their listed subsidiaries are appointed by the controlling government agencies, not by boards representing shareholders,
and therefore remain 'bureaucrats' to some extent. Further, as many have
pointed out, loosening of central control also gives managers and workers
the opportunity to maximize their own benefits at the expense of the
owners, whether government or private.[60] In consequence, as with the share
holdings of state agencies, there is no guarantee that share markets will
monitor and impose discipline on managers as they are supposed to do in
Western theory.

Despite these problems, the SOEs will not disappear. Large SOEs are
China's largest firms nationally. In 2002, *Fortune* estimated that the government owned 98 of China's top 100 firms, although, as in the example of
the Haier group outlined in Box 6.5, the 'government' may be a provincial
or municipal body, not necessarily the central administration. Many SOEs
have monopolies in their home regions, because of their inherited position
as incumbents, and frequently because they enjoy favored treatment from
their 'home' provincial government. As such they will continue to dominate
their industries for the foreseeable future. They also have proved quite
resilient. As seen below, their senior managers are well aware, not only of
new technologies in their fields, but also of world standard management
and accounting techniques.

Whether large SOEs will be able to compete globally in the longer term
remains an open question. As noted in Chapter 1, Peter Nolan and his colleagues are generally pessimistic, although their judgment varies from
sector to sector. Thus there may be no hope for China to develop its own
aircraft industry, for instance. 'Not one "latecomer" country has succeeded
in challenging the aerospace giants of the developed countries.'[61] China's
automobile and electric machinery firms might be better off if they consolidated and merged with foreign partners.[62] Sanjiu, China's largest pharmaceutical company, specializes in traditional Chinese medicines, but
again, since international markets are controlled by global conglomerates,
if the demand for traditional medicines continues to increase, Sanjiu may
find itself squeezed out by these large firms.[63] On the other hand, in the oil
and petrochemical industry, the size of emerging state holding companies
such as China National Pretroleum Corporation (CNPC) and China
National Petrochemical Corporation (Sinopec) makes them at least potentially competitive in world markets.[64]

Bureaucrats in Business: the Expansion of the SOE Sector

The thrust of corporatization and privatization of course has worked to
reduce the size of the SOE sector. However, there is another side to this story

as well. During the 1990s, many government agencies established new businesses, profit-seeking enterprises intended to earn income and to provide employment for their officials. Although analogous in some respects to the township and village enterprises examined in the next section, they differed from them in that they were neither planned as part of the market reform program nor welcomed and supported by the central government authorities. A widespread and spontaneous response to a variety of opportunities, as Jane Duckett emphasizes, they are unique among cases of liberalization policies worldwide, and they are not predicted by the literature on the political economy of market reform.[65]

The early 1990s presented officials with both problems and opportunities. As noted above, central authorities cut their budgets and ordered them to reduce their staff, but also demanded that they provide new or expanded services. However, at the same time there were relatively loose controls over their finances, especially 'extra-budgetary' funds outside the formal state budget, and they could also still borrow from local branches of state banks. Government departments were work units in the same sense as SOEs, and therefore had an inherited obligation to their workers. The new businesses were established using capital drawn from their extra-budgetary funds, loans, and sometimes money from joint venture partners. They were staffed by bureaucrats, technicians, and clerical staff from the parent department, and the senior officials sometimes became the business managers as well. The profits went into slush funds or 'small treasuries' controlled by the senior officials and were shared with the parent department to supplement salaries eroded by inflation, to refurbish staff offices, and to upgrade technology.

The extent of these new enterprises is unknown. One of Duckett's informants said, 'Everyone was doing this,' and there are reports of army, industrial, commercial, and agricultural departments, at national, provincial, and local levels, that established such businesses. Duckett's research was confined to the city of Tianjin, but one account estimated that in some regions up to 70 per cent of government departments had set up 'economic entities' and another that in Hunan province there were 10 000 of them, employing over 40 000 people. The officials who established them became increasingly reluctant to reveal their existence or details of their profitability in the late 1990s, as higher levels of government increased their efforts to regulate them and in particular to gain control over their income.

The enterprises vary in size and scope, from small trading companies or restaurants to large department stores and real estate development companies. Departments whose functions had been eroded by the expansion of the market seemed particularly likely to have established new enterprises. Commerce departments, for instance, found their functions reduced as

consumer goods were now supplied by markets, and responded by establishing new businesses to provide alternative employment for their officials
or, as in Tianjin's case, in effect transforming themselves into enterprises.
Public property departments, although less directly threatened by marketization, were under pressure to provide improved public housing, and frequently established enterprises to assist in redevelopment projects.

Throughout, the officials responsible for the creation of these enterprises
have relied on their position as officials, not only for funding and personnel,
but also for access to information about new opportunities opened up by
rapid economic growth. Their position is ambiguous. The central government is committed to reducing state involvement in direct economic activity and naturally is also concerned about the possibilities for corruption and
'pirating' of state assets. But at the same time central authorities know that
these enterprises permit reductions in government employment and relieve
pressure on government budgets at all levels. Controls over departmental
budgets were tightened, beginning in 1996. In Tianjin, numbers of enterprises now pay their profits to the parent department via the local government finance bureau, but others have retained their original informal links
to their departments.

THE MANAGEMENT GRID: THE TOWNSHIP AND VILLAGE ENTERPRISE SECTOR

BOX 6.2   POINT AND COUNTERPOINT: KELON, A LARGE TOWNSHIP AND VILLAGE ENTERPRISE

Diligence is needed in managing the business; laziness will destroy
everything. (Tao Zhu-gong, the First Business Lesson)

Kelon is the one of the largest refrigerator manufacturers in China,
with a capacity of 8 million units per year, under the Kelon and
Rongsheng brands, and something over 20 per cent of the domestic market. It is also one of the largest township and village enterprises (TVEs) in China, with over 6000 employees. Expanding
from its base in refrigerators, it has become one of the largest air
conditioning manufacturers in China, with a capacity of 4 million
units per year. In the late 1990s, it also began producing freezers,
and now has a capacity of a million units per year. It exports about
10 per cent of its output, mainly to Southeast Asian markets.

Kelon began in 1983, when local officials in Shunde Township in Guangdong Province decided to establish a manufacturing firm to take advantage of the opportunities they believed would result from the process of economic reform. They sent a team of workers around China to investigate what products were most desired by consumers. The team reported that refrigerators were in high demand and, despite having no previous experience, the township's leaders decided to manufacture refrigerators. Kelon began with a loan equivalent to US$10 000 from the township, and a vice-mayor became CEO. Most of the firm's equipment was handmade, because it could not afford to purchase machinery. Compressors, which were not manufactured in China, had to be imported.

The firm produced its first refrigerators in October 1984. They proved popular, because of an innovative design feature, separate doors for the freezer and refrigerator sections. This was the result of a further marketing insight, the realization that, for most customers, the refrigerator would be a major purchase, likely to sit in the living room rather than the kitchen and therefore likely to be regarded as a piece of decorative furniture as well as a functional appliance. Kelon's range now includes small children's refrigerators or 'I-box' with shapes such as polar bears, penguins, or dogs, and incorporating 'English voice/words guidance' and other appealing features.

The firm also maintained the national approach of its original market research by developing a sales network that eventually included over 400 offices and provided coverage to all provinces and major cities. This was a very unusual decision at the time, and Kelon remains one of the few firms, whether domestic or foreign, to allocate the resources necessary to support such an extensive network. Having sales representatives in each area helps avoid distribution problems, such as the widespread tendency for provincial authorities to interfere with companies that compete with local firms.

Kelon succeeded in gaining access to capital and technology for further growth, but without losing its core focus. The township government arranged for a large loan from a bank. A joint venture in 1987 allowed upgrading and expansion, and Kelon emerged with one of the most modern production facilities in China. In the early 1990s, Kelon took over two 'troubled' refrigerator manufacturers, one in the north and one in central China, allowing geographical diversification. In 1995, Kelon became the first TVE to list on the Hong Kong stock exchange, providing access to additional capital to fund the move into air conditioners and freezers. In 1996, Kelon opened a research unit in Japan, one of the first Chinese firms to establish a research center outside the country, and struck deals with Sharp and with Sanyo.

Of Kelon's first 300 employees, only three had any form of higher education. The firm has committed itself to continual upgrading of employee educational levels. In the late 1990s, it employed the most individuals with MBA degrees of all the mainland firms listed on the Hong Kong Stock Exchange and had plans for an additional 75 persons annually to study part-time for an MBA. From the beginning Kelon has based recruitment and promotion of executives on ability, not Communist Party membership. However, a small group has remained in control of the firm. The original CEO served until 1999. His successor was relatively young, at 42 years of age, but had spent his entire working life with Kelon. Five of the seven members of the board of directors had been with the firm since its foundation. Most of the senior executives are from the same region, and 'their careers depend on being successful in that region'.

Kelon's spectacular success means that it is widely regarded as 'a model of how a Chinese firm can be a successful world competitor'. For the future, continuity of senior personnel implied that the 'extensive network of support' built up over the years by the original CEO would also be retained. The refrigerator market was still far from saturated, but consolidation of the dozen major producers was widely predicted, because observers believed that larger firms would be better able to cope with China's complex distribution channels. The air conditioner industry was far more fragmented, with possibly 100 firms. Again, consolidation was predicted, although with the additional near certainty of very intense competition and reduced margins.

Source: Garry D. Bruton, Heilin Lan and Yuan Lu, 'China's township and village enterprises: Kelon's competitive edge', *Academy of Management Executive*, **14**(1) (2000), 19–29; http://www.kelon.com.cn.

Origins and Growth of Township and Village Enterprises

Township and village enterprises (TVEs) appear as 'collectively owned enterprises' in China's classification of types of ownership. They produced between 10 and 20 per cent of industrial output in 1978. This rose to a peak of 55 per cent in 1995. In 2000, they produced 38 per cent of China's vastly increased industrial output, more than the SOEs (28 per cent), private enterprises (19 per cent), or foreign invested enterprises (15 per cent).

Under the central planning regime, the TVEs should not have existed at all. Nevertheless, officials in the agricultural communes began to establish non-agricultural enterprises. As noted above, mechanization made agricultural workers more productive. The new enterprises absorbed the surplus agricultural workers, often men who found they earned more in their TVE jobs than on their farms. Initial capital came from the communes' accumulated earnings. The new enterprises frequently used raw materials that had been allocated to existing state enterprises. The suppliers might be well-connected middlemen, or managers of SOEs willing to sell their hoarded excess materials. These transactions were illegal, but the practice spread. Faced with widespread evasion of the regulations, the government tried to confine communal enterprises to the 'three locals' – getting inputs locally, processing them locally, and selling their products locally. These restrictions were also widely ignored, but the risk of prosecution by zealous officials remained a real threat.

With the reforms, it became much easier for local governments to establish new enterprises, as in the case of Kelon. As the dual price system spread, it also became easier for TVEs to compete openly for raw materials. TVEs had an advantage when raw materials were produced in dispersed centers, as with wool or tobacco. There were price 'wars' over tobacco, and the Shanghai Cigarette Factory, one of the largest SOEs in the industry, ran out of tobacco for part of the year in 1990. SOEs had an advantage in procuring supplies of raw materials produced in central factories, such as steel, and in getting access to electric power. They frequently re-sold these supplies, or on-sold access to power, to rural enterprises. Because of the large difference between the plan and market prices, they were able to earn more re-selling than they could have made producing their planned output. Repeated decrees against this illegal trade were ignored.

Rural industrial output rose dramatically, and rural enterprises increased their productivity impressively, particularly compared to SOEs.[66] They paid lower taxes than SOEs, and they were not responsible for social services. However, they did pay high market prices for their raw materials, and most used outdated technologies and second-hand equipment. The sense of involvement, and the knowledge that the benefits would remain in the local community, played a role. The young director of a TVE, asked why there was no supervision of workers, replied, 'We have all grown up together and I knew who worked hard and who didn't in my village before I chose workers from among them. Therefore I trust my workers and know they will not let me down.'[67] However, there is a darker side. Local workers are flexible in part because they are considered 'farmers' and as such presumed to have farms to which they can return if laid off. And, although some have good records, as they have expanded many TVE firms have severely exploited migrants from other areas, particularly young women from inland provinces.[68] This means that high productivity has depended on low wages and poor conditions for their workers.

Rural enterprises also began to borrow money to finance their growth, especially from the Agricultural Bank of China (ABC), and from rural credit cooperatives, which were controlled by the ABC until 1996. Outstanding loans of TVEs doubled from 1985 to 1990, and doubled again from 1991 to 1996. These loans frequently were made without collateral, a risky situation that has restricted lending to small and medium enterprises in other developing countries. In China's case, however, as we saw above, local bank branches were relatively independent, and branch managers had close connections with local government officials. Therefore, when they lent to enterprises sponsored by commune authorities, they could rely on an implicit joint liability of borrowers and the ability of local officials to monitor the behavior of the managers of the enterprises.[69]

Deng Xiaoping said, 'What took us completely by surprise was the development of township and village industries . . . This is not the achievement of our central government.' It was rather the achievement of a varying alliance of local government officials, Party cadres, and prominent members of local communities, that is, of the groups that gained benefits under the old system of communes, and who profited when the commune system collapsed.[70] Many observers have described local governments themselves as analogous to business corporations, 'with officials acting as the equivalent of a board of directors'.[71] Some lucky villages have become rich, and the original families have retired to a quasi-rentier existence as increasingly professionalized managers supervise the labor of migrant workers from less fortunate districts. In late 2003, a rather shabbily dressed farmer shocked a snobbish young saleswoman in a Shanghai department store by ordering 1000 plasma screen televisions for the families of his village, which owns three substantial factories.

Not all villages are lucky. Township and village governments operate under a 'hard budget constraint', that is, they must rely on their own ability to raise revenue. They are allowed to retain tax revenues and profits from their enterprises above an amount negotiated with country or provincial authorities, and it is this surplus that they have used for development.[72] In interior regions, there may be no surplus, and government authorities in 'paralyzed villages' have no funds to invest.[73] In another pattern, in districts close to Hong Kong and other points of entry for foreign invested enterprises, well-financed and well-connected foreigners have overwhelmed local communities. Although local governments can profit from renting land to foreign firms, no indigenous industry has developed.[74] Central and provincial governments have never allocated inputs to rural enterprises, and state marketing organizations have never helped them sell their output, so unlucky villages will remain unlucky, and even lucky villages will be left behind if their enterprises lose out in the increasingly competitive environment.

Problems of the TVE Sector

Although the output of TVEs has continued to increase, their share of total industrial output has declined continuously since 1995. As they become larger and more complex, higher-level technical and managerial skills become essential. But overall the TVE sector suffers from very low levels of educational attainments of its employees. Only 1.2 per cent are graduates of higher educational institutions, the lowest percentage of any class of business. Kelon is an exception in encouraging employees to acquire higher qualifications.[75] TVEs are also generally small, with Kelon again an outstanding exception. This gives them flexibility, for 'only small boats can easily change direction', but it also makes them vulnerable.

Connections with local government have included access to funding, but the reforms in the banking sector may make finance a problem as well. Legal changes in the mid-1990s made suits for recovery easier, which made collateral a more efficient way to secure loans. Real interest rates also rose substantially, and profitability declined across many sectors. This increased the risk of default, and therefore raised the risk of lending to unsecured borrowers. Competition in the banking sector also increased. The agricultural cooperatives became independent of the ABC in 1996, and other banks were also allowed to enter the rural market. At the same time the reforms in the banking sector itself put pressure on all financial institutions to improve their asset quality. These factors together caused a change in the attitudes of banks. In a survey in 1994, 'nearly all' local bank managers said that, other things equal, they would prefer to lend to TVEs, but only three years later, 58 per cent preferred private firms, and only 14 per cent preferred to lend to TVEs.[76]

Governance and ownership rights pose problems for even the most successful TVEs. Formal ownership varies. Some county governments simply instructed all villages to create a 'cooperative shareholding system' that would include all collective property, but without specifying the actual distribution of shares. In one village each infant whose parents are native to the village receives one share at birth. They receive a second share at age 17, a third at age 35, and a fourth at age 55. Shares cannot be sold or given away. A person's shares disappear when he or she dies, or if the family moves away from the village. A woman loses her shares if she marries out of the community, though a woman from outside who marries a man in the community acquires shares. Immigrant families and their descendants, and the large numbers of migrant workers, are completely excluded.[77]

However, even where ownership is 'collective', ownership does not give control. The TVEs are government enterprises and, as Barry Naughton insists, 'China is not a democracy, even at the village level.' County officials appoint township and village officials, and their compensation depends among other things on the performance of TVEs under their direction. They appoint the managers of their TVEs, and frequently the managers are themselves government officials.[78] Since the mid-1990s, local officials have sometimes corporatized poorly performing TVEs, with managers and workers holding the shares, or transferred them to private owners.[79] Privatization can also occur by stealth. Profitable TVEs have been sold on favorable terms to insiders. In a sort of grey area, some managers have appropriated the capital invested in manufacturing plants by local governments, as over time they come to regard themselves and their families as the 'owners' of the factories.[80]

THE MANAGEMENT GRID: THE PRIVATE SECTOR

BOX 6.3   POINT AND COUNTERPOINT: A VILLAGE OF PRIVATE TEXTILE FIRMS

Goods must be well organized and displayed; sloppiness will cause obsolescence and waste. (Tao Zhu-gong, the Fifth Business Lesson)

Xiqiao township in Guangdong has benefited from its location. On the edge of Nanhai county in the heart of the Pearl River delta, it is close enough to Guangzhou to share in the region's ongoing industrial and construction boom. However, lying on the far side of Guangzhou from Hong Kong, it has been protected by distance from the competition of foreign enterprise. At the same time, being just outside of the administrative area of Guangzhou, it has been relatively free to follow its own development path. Silkworm cultivation, silk reeling, and silk weaving were long-established cottage industries in the district. Following the establishment of the People's Republic, the small modernized establishments that had developed were amalgamated into four collective factories. In 1984, workers from these factories were the first to establish

---

private textile firms, using small electric looms. Others followed, and by the late 1990s the district of 135 000 people contained over 1600 textile firms, as well as hundreds of other factories, most of them small private enterprises, but including several large tile factories established by government officials.

Xiqiao's niche is the production of cloth from synthetic fibers, a wide variety of inexpensive, low-quality materials aimed at China's domestic clothing market. The need to upgrade machinery as the scale of production has increased presses continually on firms, and the rising expense of each round of upgrading has caused firms to fail. The survivors must keep continually abreast of trends in demand in an industry where margins are low and an incorrect decision can mean months of production unsold. The display of goods is crucial. From the beginning local firms rented small shop-fronts in the streets, alleys, and courtyards of the downtown district, where traveling representatives of clothing firms could come, inspect wares, discuss prices, place orders, and equally import-antly provide insight into market trends. In 1997, there were some 800 of these tiny outlets.

Government authorities in Xiqiao have supported private indus-try from the beginning, even assigning deputy township heads to oversee village communities considered to be lagging in develop-ment. However, top-down control is not appreciated by private businesspeople. One deputy head, who portrayed himself as a modernizer, created hostility because of his enthusiasm for new roads, paid for out of village revenues. Another pursued a grandiose project to create a tourist park on a local mountain, which required among other things that the ancestral graves on the mountain be relocated, again at local expense. A textile research institute failed, as did initiatives to recruit outside scientific experts, because the information they provided was not directly relevant to local firms. Official pressure on firms to purchase a new generation of com-puterized looms has been resisted, because of their high cost and complex operating requirements.

Possibly most irritating of all, the township government decided that the sales precinct was too backward and untidy. The govern-ment borrowed a large amount of money to erect a new wholesal-ing center outside the town, several hundred identical three-storey buildings with sales areas downstairs and offices upstairs. They then issued an 'urban planning' regulation that forced firms to close their existing outlets and purchase or rent space in the new complex. Factory owners complained that the added expense made no difference to their sales, drained local resources, and benefited no one but the officials.

Sources: Jonathan Unger and Anita Chan, 'Inheritors of the boom: private enterprise and the role of government in a rural South China township', Working Paper No. 89, Asia Research Centre, Murdoch University, January 1999; Jonathan Unger, 'The rise of private business in a rural Chinese district: the emerging characteristics of entrepreneurship in the PRC', Working Paper No. 90, Asia Research Centre, Murdoch University, January 1999.

Origins of the Private Sector

The socialization of the means of production by the People's Republic meant that China's private firms disappeared. For a generation employees of state enterprises procured virtually all their needs from their work units. In the rural sector farmers obtained supplies from their collectives or communes. Then, private enterprise reappeared. Something over a fifth of China's industrial output is now produced by private firms, designated as 'individual' enterprises of eight or fewer employees, partnerships, 'private' enterprises employing more than eight persons, or larger corporate shareholding companies or limited liability companies. Many private firms produce consumer goods or deliver services in urban areas, and many are small. However, some are quite large, many are in rural areas, and a surprising number are in 'producer goods' industries such as coal mining.

Some private firms were formerly state-owned enterprises or township and village enterprises. In some cases a profitable 'core' of an SOE was carved out and acquired by private owners, leaving the loss-making remnants either to struggle on, or to be closed down. Some of the former TVEs, as noted above, were the less profitable enterprises that local officials preferred to drop from their portfolios, and some are successful enterprises that have been sold or acquired by private owners. Some former TVEs may never have been collective enterprises at all. Many 'collective' enterprises in rural districts were 'red caps' that took the legal form of TVEs but in fact were privately owned. This was particularly the case in the Wenzhou district of Zhejiang province, where private businesses developed with the consent and encouragement of local officials.[81]

Nevertheless, many thousands of private firms are genuinely private, created by individuals to take advantage of opportunities in the market. Husband and wife teams founded many of the early textile firms in Xiqiao, and frequently it was the wife who possessed the technical expertise, based on her experience working in the former state textile factories. There are many other examples. Sun Dawu, a former soldier and bank employee, founded Dawu Agriculture & Animal Husbandry Group in 1985. Located in Xushui county, in a farming district about two hours south of Beijing, the firm produces animal feeds and a range of food products including vacuum packed roast chicken. In 2003, Dawu employed 1500 workers and ranked 350th on a list of China's largest private companies.[82]

Some have seen the emergence of private firms as a return to older patterns. Many of the private firms are small, and many of the larger private firms revolve around a single individual or, even more significantly, around a family group. Gordon Redding reports a conversation with an elderly professor in Guangdong in the late 1980s, in which the professor said, 'The thing you must remember about China is that for the past thirty years we have all been acting.'[83] Ole Bruun argues that the growth of the private sector reflects the 'reappearance' of the family as an economic unit.[84] Kai-Alexander Schlevogt reports a 'proliferating' or 'spawning' of firms as they reach a certain size. 'Instead of trying to grow in size, many Chinese enterprises facilitate close ties with family members, who might otherwise search for employment elsewhere.'[85] For all of the reasons considered in Chapter 4, especially the unsympathetic and possibly hostile attitude of government officials to private business, family support may be a primary means of minimizing transaction costs.

As they expand outside their local districts, private firms have also sometimes adopted older styles of operation. Founder–owners pursue a proactive, entrepreneurial style of decision making, unconstrained by formal organizational structures. Many private firms are embedded in webs of connections with other firms. In contrast to state enterprises, private enterprises, like the township and village enterprises examined above, existed from the beginning in markets. They depended on accurate information. However, being small, they could not afford to establish separate divisions in distant regions to acquire information. Xiqiao has brought clients to the town. Other districts developed networks of traveling purchasing and marketing agents, who could 'endure many hardships, cross many miles, speak many dialects, use many means' to inform them of the availability of raw materials and changes in demand in distant regions. In the early 1990s, firms in Wenzhou's textile industry may have employed as many 100 000 such agents.[86]

Another mode of expansion has occurred through 'competitive networks' of small family firms, especially when the production process involves a number of stages or the manufacture and assembly of components. Localities in Zhejiang, Fujian, and Guangdong Province along the southeastern coast have enjoyed spectacular success in specialized consumer goods. Wenzhou in Zhejiang produces 70 per cent of the world's output of cigarette lighters, and has driven the previously dominant Japanese and Korean firms out of business. Wenzhou, Jinjiang (Fujian), and Dongguan (Guangdong) together produce half the world's shoes. Shenzhen and Chenghai (both in Guangdong) share 26 per cent of the global market for toys. Shengzhou (Zhejiang) supplies 20 per cent of the world's neckties. In each case the district contains hundreds of small firms 'operating as a cohesive, interdependent entity'.

The firms belonging to competitive networks typically began as family operations. Many have remained small, but like other forms of enterprise they have drawn large numbers of migrants from inland provinces. A dozen young women may live in a room above the workshop and eat meals provided by their employer, and in return they are paid very low wages. The networks also enjoy very low administrative expenses. They gain their responsiveness to changes in demand by hiring foreign experts and developing alliances with leading overseas designers. Their problem, predictably, is 'to get a network to coalesce out of a rabble of competing firms', some of which must resign themselves to producing intermediate components rather than assembling the final product, the most prestigious position on the supply chain. The secret, and the reason that the networks can remain virtually invisible to external observers, is the role of local government officials. They encourage competitive small firms to specialize and to integrate themselves into the overall effort, through direct incentives, but also through their control over licenses and approvals. A nondescript hybrid form of organization, competitive networks 'don't conform to the conventional notion of a globally competitive organization'. Their success is undeniable, but whether they will have developed the higher-level competencies needed to survive by the time China's pool of cheap labor dries up remains to be seen.[87]

In at least one case, an ethnic religious identity has formed the basis for 'economic activism', in David Goodman's phrase. The Salar, a Sunni Muslim group of some 100 000 persons, is centered in Xunhau Salar Autonomous County of Qinghai province, located at the point where the Huang He (Yellow River) passes from Qinghai into Gansu Province, and to the southeast of Qinghai Lake. Still relatively poor in comparison with the coastal provinces, Qinghai has nonetheless moved ahead rapidly since the early 1990s, and development has been led by Salar entrepreneurs, particularly in the woolen industry, construction, and transportation. Salar construction and transportation firms provide services across much of northeastern China, and the textile industry has established itself as an international producer of Islamic religious cloth, hats, and embroidery. The Salar are generally fundamentalist in religious and social orientation, but one of the most successful Salar entrepreneurs is a woman, Han Zenaibai, a former prominent basketball player who still answers to her nickname 'Player Number Eight'. She said, 'In the beginning [of reform] men started to set up businesses. I knew there were women starting businesses in foreign countries, and I wanted to try. In 1996, I successfully applied on my own to get 400,000 *yuan* from the Development Bank in Xining [the provincial capital].' She is currently the owner and CEO of an agricultural and live-stock development firm and other enterprises, including a sizeable hotel.[88]

Problems of the Private Sector

Deng Xiaoping blessed economic growth when he said, 'To be rich is glorious.' The owners of successful private firms typically belong to the same circles that benefited under the communes, that profited with the communes dissolved, and that have led local development projects since the reforms. Those with the best connections have frequently gained the most. In rural districts from the early 1980s onward, the household responsibility system allowed families to appropriate the 'implicit rent' of more productive land, which the government had previously siphoned off through the communes. Party cadres and local officials could allocate the best resources on contract to their own families and collateral relatives. In urban areas incomes diverged, as both incentive pay and property income increased dramatically after 1985.[89] The appropriation of public and communal assets by well connected individuals led to the emergence of an entrenched property-owning class who could use government powers in their own interests, in Tim Wright's phrase, 'a million millionaires – with close links to the old bureaucracy'.[90]

   However, relations between private business leaders and government officials are not always smooth. As we have seen, local governments must support themselves. In addition to profits from their own enterprises, they raise income by imposing taxes and fees on private firms, and this is a frequent source of conflict. Firms that belong to the competitive networks of the southeast may appreciate the efforts of local officials, but the owners of Xiqiao's textile firms complain about excessive fees and waste in government. In one autonomous region, Ross Garnaut and his colleagues cite 17 separate types of fees collected for 'collateral appraisal and registration' of private firms.[91]

   The funds that stay with the country or township in theory go to support local development projects, but they may simply be siphoned off to benefit individuals. Every year national, provincial, and local governments prosecute thousands of persons for corruption, for taking bribes, imposing illegal taxes, or appropriating public property. Even where the money is spent properly on development projects, opinions can diverge regarding priorities and perceived benefits. Taxes and fees levied equally on all firms may still be resented. They may also be frankly discriminatory, to favor particular firms or to encourage them to participate in the district network. They may also be corrupt, to give an insider an unfair advantage in return for a kickback. They may lie in a grey area, to favor the government's own enterprises, for instance, or in a possibly lighter shade of grey, for example to encourage a foreign firm to locate in a village.

These complexities make it imperative for managers of private firms to cultivate relations with government officials. A sort of 'commercial clientelism' structures many markets. Private firms may find that the enforcement of contracts depends on the favorable attitude of local officials. They may also find that the views of officials affect the degree of competition permitted in local markets. In urban districts local labor bureaus can intervene in relations between employers and employees.[92] Any form of real estate development requires official approval and cooperation. Public listing, important for any firm wanting to grow and crucial in new areas such as information technology, also needs official approval. For those who refuse to collaborate, the hostility of local officials can have unpleasant consequences. Sun Dawu's success has made him famous. He embarrassed Xushui county officials by accusing them of waste and corruption on his website, as well as at invited speeches at Beijing University and China Agricultural University in Beijing. He and his two brothers were imprisoned for six months while county officials searched his records and eventually prosecuted him for illegally paying interest on deposits taken from local farmers.[93]

Despite the official announcement at the Sixteenth Party Congress in 2002 that the government would support the growth of private business, private sector managers work in an environment that remains unsympathetic in many respects. Some areas remain closed to private investment. In others the government may suddenly restrict activity, as happened in the coal industry in 1998. Some government leaders continue to find individual wealth offensive. *Euromoney China* publishes an annual list of China's richest individuals, and several have been prosecuted for fraud or tax evasion after appearing on the list. Observers recommend further reform in public sector governance to reduce corruption, as well as changes in taxation and revenue systems to reduce the burden on private business. Despite the reports of changing attitudes of local bank managers cited above, for example, independent private entrepreneurs frequently insist that it is very difficult for private firms to obtain bank loans. Sun Dawu complained that he could not obtain a loan from the local agricultural cooperative without paying a kickback. When they are able to gain bank finance, private firms must pay market rates, in contrast to favored SOEs such as Sunve. As a result, especially if they are small, many private firms obtain funding in a variety of regional informal 'curb markets'.[94]

Laws and regulations have proliferated and become increasingly complex. Both the laws themselves and their implementation impede the private sector. In part this reflects the underdevelopment of legislation during the Mao period and the need for more extensive codification as the economy has grown. However irritating it may be to private entrepreneurs, regulation is required to prevent abuses. However, the legal system also reflects an underlying philosophical principle. The Chinese government continues to view law as an instrument to give it control over society, not as a set of rules regulating relations among citizens and between citizens and the state.[95] Government authorities have no desire to allow the law to restrict their own powers. In addition the agencies responsible for policy and enforcement in particular sectors are also responsible for drafting the laws in that sector. The interests of local, regional, and national government agencies also may differ. Courts, although nominally independent, are subject to various forms of political pressure, and some judges may retain the Maoist hostility to private enterprise. Judgments and enforcement are often inconsistent, and officials can and do use the law to pursue their own agendas. The results can be frustrating for all business leaders, but especially perhaps for those in the private sector.

THE MANAGEMENT GRID: THE FOREIGN INVESTED ENTERPRISE SECTOR

BOX 6.4   POINT AND COUNTERPOINT: AUSTRALIANS IN CHINA – VOLUME TABLEWARE

Do not over-rely on current products. (Tao Zhu-gong, the Twelfth Business Pitfall)

Australians Aaron Keating and Adam and Dean Montgomery operated a small catering equipment business in Melbourne. They were dissatisfied with the quality of porcelain they were importing from China, and in 1998 they formed a joint venture with a Chinese partner to manufacture their own. They began with a plant in the pottery manufacturing district of Chauzhou, in the interior of Guangdong province. After a year they bought their partner out, and set up a second plant to produce dish warmers and other restaurant equipment. In 2003, Volume Tableware employed 270 persons, and sold its products in Europe as well as Australia.

Not content with relying on current products, Volume expanded into adjacent product lines. In 2003, the firm began manufacturing a range of souvenir pottery. The client was an Irish distributor that had recently closed down its own plant in Galway where 150 people had been employed. The firm was also extending its range into glassware. Keating and Montgomery had purchased the equipment of a British glassware manufacturer that had gone out of business and shipped it to China. The glassware machinery was to be installed in a new 400-worker factory in a neighboring town. There is irony to be found in the fact that these British jobs 'lost' to China have in fact been lost to a relatively small Australian firm.

Volume's competitive advantage rests on several foundations. The firm has saved 'millions' by purchasing secondhand machinery. In common with other successful firms in China, low labor costs are a crucial support of the firm. However, as Keating and Montgomery emphasize, their advantage in this respect reflects not only relatively low wages but also the supply of experienced workers available in the district. Finally, support from local government has also been important. Volume purchased their new factory site, leveled and ready, from the local government for approximately one-third the market price. 'The big consultants will tell you to go to Shanghai,' says Montgomery. 'That is totally off. You should look for a small town that doesn't have a lot of money and wants to progress.'

Source: Hamish McDonald, 'Made in China', *Sydney Morning Herald*, 18–19 October 2003.

The Problems of Foreign Investors: Managing in China

Since 1978, an astonishing 420 000 foreign invested enterprises have established themselves in China. The inward flow of investment continues to set new records. As we have seen, Hong Kong has been the largest 'foreign' investor, responsible for some two-thirds of all realized foreign investment. Hong Kong Garment, cited as Box 5.1 in Chapter 5, represents the most common form of Hong Kong investor, a 'wholly foreign owned enterprise' in a consumer goods industry using low-cost labor to achieve competitive advantage. Taiwan, the second largest investor, and Korea, the third largest, also have profited from the supply of cheap labor, though typically their projects have been further up the technology ladder: for instance, Samsung's decision in 2003 to shift its personal computer production to China.

Some Westerners have also done well in China, as seen in the case of Volume Tableware. But the plains of China are also littered with the bones of disappointed foreign investors. A 1998 survey of large foreign investors showed 25 per cent were unprofitable and a further 25 per cent only barely broke even. In 2003, a survey by the American Chamber of Commerce in China again showed 25 per cent of United States operations to be unprofitable. The chief factor cited was an overestimation of potential demand. In sectors where China has absorbed foreign technology, competition is intense and in some, such as televisions, supply consistently outruns demand. Prices have dropped, destroying profit calculations. Costs have often been higher than expected, owing to unforeseen taxes and fees, changes to regulations, and especially rising land and labor costs. Whirlpool, Caterpillar, and Pepsi Cola, among United States firms, have withdrawn from China, the latter after 20 years and a US$500 million investment. Motorola's mobile phones continue to sell in increasing numbers, but have been losing market share to Chinese competitors, some of them new firms using foreign technology.

Large capital-intensive investments have been especially problematical. In mid-2004 alone, four high-profile projects came to grief. International petroleum firms Shell, Exxon, and Gazprom had negotiated for three years to construct a US$18 billion gas pipeline in partnership with PetroChina. Reportedly, PetroChina suddenly insisted on cutting the guaranteed return on the investment, because it discovered it would not be able to sell the gas for as much as it had anticipated. The three foreign firms complained that, not only had they lost the contract, but they had left behind their designs, field development plans, and technology as well. Thames Water, a British subsidiary of German utility conglomerate RWE, withdrew from a US$73 million waste water treatment plant it had built and was operating in Shanghai, because the central government ruled that the guaranteed return Thames had negotiated with the Shanghai government was too high. British American Tobacco, a firm with a long history in China, had negotiated for three years to construct a US$1.5 billion cigarette factory, the first such foreign-controlled plant. Then, when BAT announced the agreement, it was contradicted both by China's state tobacco monopoly and by the central government, leaving the deal uncertain. International brewer SABMiller had acquired a share of Harbin Brewery, but was shut out when the firm's management and the Harbin city government, which also owned a share, together decided to sell the firm to United States firm Anheuser-Busch.[96]

These cases demonstrate some of the typical problems faced by foreign, and especially Western, investors. The inexperience and possible bad faith of joint venture partners have caused problems for many. Conflict between levels of government is another area of concern. Opposition from entrenched interests, especially state-owned enterprises such as the tobacco monopoly, has blocked many proposals. The Harbin case shows the difficulties posed by unclear property rights and inadequate protection for minority interests, especially when government bodies are involved.

Foreigners continue to be subject to discreet, and sometimes not so discreet, surveillance. A large bureaucracy attempts to control the foreign presence, and libraries of books instruct Chinese on how to manage relations with foreigners.[97] In cases of conflict, legislation has become much more complete and transparent, and legal enforcement of contracts has improved.[98] Nevertheless, foreigners suffer the same problems as Chinese in dealing with the government and the legal system. Even in the more favorable environment, only about a third of foreign investors' successful arbitration cases actually received the full payout foreseen in their judgment.[99]

The Problems of the Chinese: Managing Foreign Investment to serve China

To 'make the foreign serve China' meant China would tolerate foreigners in return for their trade and technology. The SEZs would become 'China's window on the world', centers of high technology that would spill over onto the rest of the economy, but the window would be carefully screened to keep the foreign mosquitoes contained. The 1978 and 1979 regulations governing the new special economic zones and the new category of 'foreign invested enterprises' clearly specified that 'products of the enterprises in the special economic zones are to be sold on the international market', and 'the technology or equipment contributed by any foreign participant as investment shall be truly advanced and appropriate to China's needs'. Foreign firms required special permission to sell in China, and if they did, they would be required to pay import duties.

Foreign invested enterprises were not intended to supplant domestic firms in the domestic market. Products in theory were approved for the domestic market only if they were not produced in China, or if they were in critical short supply. This mercantilist conception of trade as zero sum game has remained influential. Many officials continue to believe that joint ventures compete with domestic producers, and they therefore work to protect their local firms against outsiders, whether foreign or Chinese from other regions.[100] The government maintains an annual list of priorities for foreign investment, identifying those areas where foreigners will be encouraged and those where they will be discouraged. In some areas, such as automobiles, foreign firms are required to form partnerships with Chinese firms. The government also has a program to develop 'famous Chinese brands' in order to capture the premium between low Chinese production costs and high selling prices for goods in the high-end markets of the United States,

Europe, and Japan. Reports vary, but from 20 to as many as 50 firms may have been singled out by different ministries for preferential treatment. In 1997, the State Economic and Trade Commission publicly named six firms it would support in order that they could become 'World Top 500 Enterprises', that is, among the largest 500 firms in the world.

Foreign investment has certainly contributed to growth, but not as the government hoped. The overwhelming bulk of foreign investment comes from firms looking for cheap labor in low end areas such as textiles, clothing, shoes, toys, and electronics assembly. The SEZs did not become centers of management innovation. As already noted in Chapter 2, for instance, Japanese-invested firms imposed tighter discipline and increased the intensity of work, but without paying higher wages, investing in training beyond the specific requirements of the job, or committing themselves to long-term employment. There have been frequent strikes. The Japanese managers also found that, when they did introduce quality circles, their Chinese employees did not exchange information on improvement horizontally, but instead used the circles as a vertical channel for complaints.[101] The SEZs also did not become centers of high technology. Western and Japanese firms have often hesitated to invest because of inadequate infrastructure and what are frequently called China's 'nightmare' logistics. Foreign firms in high-technology areas complain when Chinese firms appropriate their technologies. To protect themselves, foreign firms in high-tech industries maintain a significantly higher share of equity in joint ventures.[102]

As was seen above, the central government appears to have lost control over the establishment of SEZs. Encouraged and sometimes directly sponsored by local governments, Chinese enterprises moved to the zones, for example Haier in Qingdao. Because both foreign and domestic firms in the SEZs imported their raw materials and intermediate products, the SEZs ran deficits in their foreign trade through the early 1990s. This of course is not what the government intended, but it may merely reflect China's stage of development. Eventually the supply of cheap labor will decline, but, in the meantime, many of these firms, such as Haier, have become successful exporters.

How will foreign firms fare in China? History appears to be against them. As Gary Hamilton points out, the intensely competitive Chinese markets have proved difficult for generations of foreigners. When foreign firms have launched new products, near substitutes have rapidly appeared, delivered at significantly lower prices. And foreigners have usually faced not one but several Chinese competitors.[103] Over the next years the special benefits offered to foreign firms by national, provincial, and local governments will be phased out as part of China's compliance with WTO rules. On the other hand, as Peter Noland and his colleagues insist, major international firms continue to enjoy the advantages of scale and scope. David Eldon, chairman of HSBC, sees two main opportunities for his firm, its ability to facilitate international trade when competing for high-end customers, and the potential for promoting Internet banking. He argues that, if foreign firms treat the complex China market with the respect it deserves and do not simply rely on current products, then there is no reason why they should not succeed in the long run.[104]

LEADERS, WORKERS, AND RELATIONSHIPS: TOWARDS A MANAGEMENT WITH CHINESE CHARACTERISTICS?

BOX 6.5   POINT AND COUNTERPOINT: ZHANG RUIMIN AND THE HAIER GROUP

Do not adore grandeur. (Tao Zhu-gong, the Second Business Pitfall)

In 2004, the website for the Haier Group featured a statement by the Chairman of the group, Zhang Ruimin:

> Haier should be like the sea. Because the sea can accept all the rivers on earth, big and small, far and near, coming all the way to empty into it.
>
> Once in the bosom of the sea, every drop will function as a whole and rush together pertinaciously and dauntlessly, under the command of the sea, to a common goal. They will rather be smashed to pieces than retreat as deserters, hence the overwhelming force of the sea.
>
> The sea offers all of itself to mankind and never demands anything in return. Only through this bounty and unselfishness can the sea become an everlasting existence providing for all living beings.
>
> Haier should be like the sea – accepting all talented people from around the world for an ambitious goal. Every Haier employee should be capable rather than mediocre and redundant, for they are the backbone and guarantee of Haier's future development.
>
> Concerted efforts will generate power of the sea. This will be backed by a spirit – 'Dedication to the Motherland by Pursuing Excellence' which Haier persistently advocates. Therefore, everything deemed unbelievable and impossible can be real and possible, and the Billow of Haier will rush past everything on its way and roll on and on.
>
> Thus, Haier should be like the sea – making contributions to mankind 'sincerely forever'. In so doing, it will exist forever for the good of all. Haier will be part of the whole society.
>
> Haier is the sea.

In 1984, Zhang, then the vice-manager of Qingdao Home Appliance Company, was appointed head of Qingdao Refrigerator General

---

Factory, a heavily indebted state owned enterprise. He lined up 76 defective units out of the 400 on the plant floor, and ordered those responsible to destroy them with a sledgehammer. 'The real problem was that workers had no faith in the company and didn't care,' he said in a 1999 interview. They had to learn that 'there is no A, B, C, or D level of quality. There are only two, acceptable and unacceptable'.

The firm entered into a joint venture with a German firm to improve its technology and was renamed Qingdao Haier Refrigerator Company. Astonishing growth followed. In 2003, the Haier Group had become the fourth largest home appliance firm in the world, with 96 major lines, 15 100 models, and sales in 160 countries, including a 30 per cent share of the market for small refrigerators in the United States. Haier employed some 30 000 workers, and its subcontractors another 200 000. In addition to four 'industrial parks' in Qingdao, there were factories in four other cities in China, and in the United States, Pakistan, and Jordan.

Haier's website continues to celebrate Zhang's leadership. His biography lists his international awards and presents the firm's history in terms of his ideas (1984–91), Zhang's 'famous brand strategy' of improving quality (1991–99), his 'diversification strategy' implemented 'to avoid having all one's eggs in the same basket', and, since 1999, his 'multinational strategy' of one-third of production in China for domestic sales, one-third of production in China for export, and one-third of production overseas for foreign sales.

Zhang, according to the site, has succeeded by 'combining traditional Chinese culture with advanced Western management concepts'. Intriguingly, the two specific management concepts mentioned on the site are typically Japanese. A program of total quality control (TQC) implemented in the 1980s underpinned Zhang's efforts to establish Haier as a recognized brand. Today Haier sells at premium prices in China, and designs products to suit particular markets, such as wine refrigerators for the United States. Through the 1990s a program of just in time (JIT) inventory management led to cost reductions and, like large Japanese firms, Haier has imposed its JIT approach on its subcontractors. Haier's human resource management looks much less Japanese. Employees are encouraged to think in terms of strategic business units and even to consider themselves as SBUs, but Zhang posts a 'hit chart' of the 80 divisional heads outside the headquarters staff canteen, with their latest monthly performance rating and an

arrow pointing up or down. The top 10 per cent can expect promotion, and the bottom 10 per cent demotion or worse. In 2002–3, 13
of the 80 fell and were replaced.

Zhang is one of the great leaders of modern business, but his
success is hard to evaluate. Apart from a figure for total sales, no
financial information is available on the website. Haier's ownership
remains opaque. Officially, Haier is a 'collectively owned' enterprise. In a dispute over Internet domain names in 2001, Haier identified itself as 'a super-large state-owned enterprise'. Ming Zeng
and Peter Williamson report that 'Qingdao municipal government,
local investors, and the company's managers jointly control Haier's
equity,' but this may not include the entire group. Haier listed on the
Shanghai Stock Exchange in 1993, and raised further funds with
three additional rights issues in the 1990s, but the listed firm is a
subsidiary, and these investors evidently play no role in corporate
governance.

The group has enjoyed continual government support. Haier, as
emphasized by Robert Crawford and by Zeng and Williamson,
'grew rapidly by acquiring dozens of unprofitable collective and
state-owned enterprises in the early 1990s'. This can only occur
with the consent of the agencies involved. The stock exchange
listing and rights issues also required government approval. In the
1990s, the website featured a picture of Deng Xiaoping visiting
Haier's main plant. The website currently does not mention the
Party, but, according to a *Business Week* report, Zhang 'leads a
network of Communist Party members who work at Haier', and he
has become a member of the Party's national central committee.
The government facilitated the plants in Pakistan and Jordan.
Haier belongs to the group of firms the government supports as
'famous Chinese brands' and is one of the six selected to become
'World Top 500 Enterprises'.

'Do not adore grandeur' means not to be distracted and lose
focus. Despite the undoubted successes of the growth-by-
acquisition strategy, diversification has led Haier into a number of
highly competitive areas. Financial services and logistics build on
the group's sheer size, but televisions, video-cassette recorders,
and mobile phones are only distantly related to its core competencies, and software development, not to mention pharmaceuticals
and a chain of restaurants, appear speculative at best. The Hong
Kong telecommunications firm acquired during the technology
boom as of the late 1990s has apparently made losses since the
collapse. Haier has also engaged in a fair bit of monument building

and trophy collecting. The Qingdao headquarters, in Haier Park, is on Haier Road, and the park also contains a Haier Technology Museum. Camden, South Carolina, where Haier's United States plant is located, also re-named one of its streets after Haier. The website enthuses that the United States headquarters opened in 2002 is a 'landmark classical building, the former offices of the Greenwich Savings Bank, on Broadway, Manhattan, New York, an indication that Haier had moved into a new phase for globalization'. In 2003, Haier set up an electric billboard among the other gaudy displays in the Ginza shopping district in Tokyo as evidence of its determination to succeed in Japan.

Sources: http://www.haier.com.cn; Zhang's speech was at http://www.haier.com/english/about/ceo.html, in September 2004, but was no longer on the site in early 2006; 'Zhang Ruimin, CEO, Haier Group, China', *Business Week Online*, 14 June 1999; Robert Crawford, 'China's Haier Group: growth through acquisitions', INSEAD, Case 300-129-1 (2000); Russell Flannery, 'China goes global', *Forbes*, 8 June 2001; Hamish McDonald, 'Made in China', *Sydney Morning Herald*, 18–19 October 2003; Ming Zeng and Peter J. Williamson, 'The hidden dragons', *Harvard Business Review*, October 2003; Boston Consulting Group and Knowledge @ Wharton, *China and the New Rules for Global Business* (2004), p. 13, http://knowledge.wharton.upenn.edu.

The Role of the Leader

Successful Chinese firms have followed some identifiable patterns. They have keenly sought foreign technology, usually through partnerships. Haier's English language website says bluntly, 'We can provide OEM and ODM for your company', and Haier clearly sees technology acquisition as a benefit of subcontracting in original equipment and original design manufacturing (OEM and ODM) relationships with foreign firms. Shanghai Automotive Industry Corporation (SAIC), another of China's world top 500 firms, includes technology transfer as part of its joint venture agreements with Volkswagen and General Motors. This contrasts with Japanese firms, which have tended to undertake their own research in-house, and with Korean firms, which began by relying on Western firms' technology but then developed their own capabilities.[105] It also differs from the Taiwanese model of direct government support for a few strategic large firms that could then provide intermediate products, services, and technological expertise to smaller private firms.

Also Chinese firms have not globalized as quickly as, for instance, Korean firms. The size and the rapid growth of China's domestic market have led Chinese firms to emphasize domestic distribution.[106] Haier's ambitious international program is unusual, and it is as yet unfulfilled. More typical is SAIC, which has acquired a stake in Korea's Ssangyong, but produces primarily for the domestic market. In the domestic market Chinese firms have relied on low prices to claim and defend their 'territory' against competitors. Low prices have been achieved, not so much through technological innovation, but through supply chain management, and above all through control over their labor force. As the textile manager cited above said, cost control and especially labor costs are critical. Haier's programs of total quality control and just in time inventory management fit this pattern as well.

In implementing these strategies, successful firms frequently have been driven by a single energetic leader such as Haier's Zhang Ruimin. The pattern extends across sectors as well as enterprise types. The proactive, aggressive strategies of the founder–owners of small private firms were noted above. Among large firms, a typical case is Wang Hai, who was appointed Party secretary of Double Star, a government-owned shoe manufacturing firm in Qingdao, in 1983, and who then led a 21-fold increase in sales over the next 15 years. Double Star employs some 30 000 workers in a number of divisions, and already in the early 1990s was exporting over 250 000 pairs of shoes annually to the United States. A former soldier, Wang recruited over 200 army officers to management positions. He has become famous for his slogans and principles, the 18 pieces of 'Double Star experience' and the 72 'Double Star maxims'. His 'Input–Output One Dragon Management Method' includes 1561 management standards classified under 225 headings, and 233 technical standards under 42 headings. There are also 51 standards for the images of different offices, and 29 standards for the 'spirit' of different offices. Workers assemble in the factory courtyards each morning to sing the company anthem, an expression of what Double Star executives believe is a combination of 'family' and 'military' values.[107]

Chow Hou Wee, the interpreter of Tao Zhu-gong's classic of business principles, believes the Chinese conception of leadership rests on an ancient tradition. The leader must not only be competent in all the usual senses, but in addition must be 'a model to the rest of the organization'. Further, this exemplary quality means 'not only being a role model within the organization, but being a role model to the rest of society as well'. Chinese leaders must serve others, not themselves. Wee quotes a folk saying, 'A person must not work for gains that only benefit himself; rather, he must labour for gains that benefit others and mankind at large.'[108] Some 95 per cent of Double Star's employees regarded the morality of CEO Wang Hai as high, and 40 per cent said that the firm's managers always acted ethically.

Sacrifice is also valued. Aimen Chen says flatly, 'China still relies on the incentive mechanism of spiritual reward.' As already noted, compensation for managers remains comparatively low, for example niggardly annual bonuses in the early 1990s of US$20 to US$50 for managers at Double Star, and annual salaries of US$42 000 in the early 2000s for senior executives at Shanghai Baosteel, China's largest steelmaker and also among China's world top 500 firms. The national media celebrate 'model managers' who take a salary no more than 50 per cent higher than an ordinary worker, who live in an apartment smaller than that of their chief engineer, and who of course work extraordinarily long hours. Best of all, in these stories, is for managers to continue to work at the cost of their own health. The manager of one of the Chongqing SOEs studied by Chen became famous when he not only overcame losses at his own firm, but also at the same time rescued another firm threatened with failure, ignoring his deteriorating health and refusing a bonus offered by the municipal government. He and others are celebrated as 'Lei Feng spirits', after the self-sacrificing soldier popularized by Party propagandists during the Cultural Revolution in the 1960s, who lived and died under the slogan 'it is glorious to be a nameless hero'. The national media contrasts their heroic efforts with the 'crisis' created by the large number of managers who were lazy or corrupt and 'pirating' state assets.[109]

As seen in the cases above, the leaders of successful firms have not always been willing to remain nameless heroes, and the point of these exemplary stories is precisely that most managers fail to meet the standard. Formally, their position is insecure. There are exceptions, for instance in real estate development and listed information technology companies, but in general the CEOs of China's largest firms do not own their companies or control them through holding companies, as do the leaders of Korean *chaebol* or the heads of Southeast Asian Chinese firms to be examined in Chapter 8. Also they do not owe their position to seniority and selection by the previous CEO, as in Japan, and they do not serve a board representing major shareholders, as in Western firms.

Heads of SOEs and TVEs are appointed by their controlling government agencies, and the same remains true of many corporatized firms as well. The controlling agency may want to rescue an ailing enterprise, as with the Chongqing government and its numerous SOEs, or the Qingdao authorities and Haier, but there may be other motives as well. These motives could be political, or they could be social, for instance to maintain employment, or to maximize short-term income in order to support local social services. CEOs in this situation must both satisfy their masters and strive for independence. Security of tenure depends on long and successful incumbency, and on their political skills, as with the ability of Sunve's management to anticipate and exploit changes in policy.

Despite references to traditional Confucian values, if the roots of today's Chinese business leadership style lie in Chinese culture, it is not in *The*

Analects. As we saw in Chapter 4, Confucius' 'gentleman' was a scholar who might serve as a government official, but was unconcerned with money, markets, or technology. As noted in Chapter 1, many Chinese cannot recall all of the five relationships.[110] Among other possibilities, some observers believe Chinese business leaders model their decisions on Sun Tzu's *Art of War*.[111] Mao was a great reader of the military classics, and most Chinese are aware that one of his favorites was *The Thirty-Six Stratagems*. Again, however, the evidence of direct influence is thin. Double Star's CEO Wang Hai compares the market to a battlefield, but he has not borrowed from Sun Tzu. Instead he has consciously adopted an eclectic mix of Confucian ideas such as 'compassion', and 'appropriateness', and Buddhist concepts such as 'doing good' and 'gathering blessings', that he hopes will motivate his employees, many of whom are semi-literate Buddhist migrants from interior provinces. Thus two of his aphorisms are 'Relentless disciplines, Compassionate leadership', and 'Producing good quality goods is the greatest doing-good and gathering of blessings.'[112]

   Even if they are only casually familiar with the classic texts, however, the fact that many CEOs of large firms are Party members, and the fact that many of them have served in the army or as government officials, may have resulted in a tendency to think, if not exactly in military terms, then at least in terms of hierarchical order. In striking contrast to Japanese executives, most senior Chinese managers are aware of current Western management literature. Haier's website, for example, contains a flow chart replete with up-to-date acronyms identifying strategic decision-making processes. Nevertheless, studies of management behavior have repeatedly shown that orders and initiative come from the top down. Power remains in the hands of the CEO directly, or with a small group of senior managers and Party officials. Delegation of power is restricted, and middle managers typically have very little scope for independent initiative. At the same time, despite their centralized and authoritarian style, within the institutional structures outlined above, senior managers are not individually responsible for their decisions.[113]

   Symbolic occasions reinforce the image of the leader. Banquets are punctuated by a speech by the chairman, formal and didactic, delivered in high, ringing tones, recalling the firm's accomplishments and calling for redoubled efforts by all employees. These exhortations frequently resemble Zhang Ruimin's 'Haier is the sea' speech, which in turn recalls an article Mao wrote in 1919 following the May Fourth Movement, in which he said China's progressive forces must 'question the unquestionable. Dare to do the unthinkable', and continued, 'The vast and furious tide of new thought is already rushing, surging along . . . Those who ride with the current will live; those who go against it will die.'[114] Whether he is quoting Mao directly or not, like Wang Hai, Zhang from the beginning has seen his role as instructing and guiding his workers, and he continues to drive his section heads. Another example is Xie Qihua, president of Shanghai Baosteel, who is the highest ranking female corporate executive in China. Asked about her relations with her predominantly male colleagues, she said, 'It doesn't matter that I'm a woman, as long as they listen when I talk.'[115]

Joseph Schumpeter, the original theorist of entrepreneurship, defined the function of the entrepreneur as the ability to see an opportunity and combine resources to exploit it. As we will see in Chapter 9, Schumpeter worried that, as government bureaucracy had expanded and large businesses had become more bureaucratic, the scope for entrepreneurship and the 'creative destruction' that powered economic growth had narrowed. The presumption that bureaucrats cannot function as entrepreneurs influences much work on economic development.[116] The facts that so many of China's leading firms are government enterprises, and that so many of China's business leaders are current or former government officials, therefore appear paradoxical.[117] However, the paradox is more apparent than real. Firstly, as we have seen in previous chapters and will see again, government agencies and government officials can play entrepreneurial roles. Secondly, the discussion above shows that there has been no shortage of entrepreneurial activity across all the diverse sectors of the Chinese economy. Finally, in place of Schumpeter's driving individual ambition there is a pervasive patriotism. Although they may not all be Lei Feng spirits, many of China's business leaders do feel a 'Dedication to the Motherland by Pursuing Excellence' in Zhang Ruimin's phrase, or they subscribe to the simpler 'We have to work hard for the country', which occurs repeatedly in interviews.[118]

Notwithstanding the undoubted successes, as we have seen in the case of Korean *chaebol*, a boss-centered system places a heavy burden on the boss. The obverse of the role of the single entrepreneurial leader is reflected in common problem areas that mark Chinese firms. Some firms have lost their original strong focus and diversified into areas where their expertise may be less relevant. The reliance on the CEO to make all company decisions has led to underinvestment in executive development programs. Chinese firms have also been criticized for their lack of investment in research and development. Finally, linked with the tendency to diversify, is a difficulty in effectively integrating companies.[119] These are problems in any system, but where accountability is blurred and reporting incomplete, the difficulties may be magnified. Competitive advantage for some large firms still depends on preferential treatment by the government, effective monopolies in their home markets, and low labor costs, and as these are eroded new responses will have to be found.

Labor Relations and the Internal Structure of Firms

Although the style of China's CEOs is top-down, it can meet a bottom-up response. As noted above, during the Mao period workers' committees, unions, and especially the Party organization, all played a key role in the management of state-owned enterprises. Workers were free to criticize managers, as long as they did so in the context of political orthodoxy. Managers exercised authority only by virtue of having been selected by the agency that controlled their enterprise, and they retained their positions only so long as they had the support of the Party secretary, the 'real boss' of the enterprise. Managers, and those same Party secretaries in turn, all lived under the suspicion that they might have bourgeois or capitalist tendencies. During the many campaigns to rectify 'incorrect' thought, and particularly during the Cultural Revolution, this suspicion could easily take concrete form. They could be denounced by workers' committees, forced to engage in self-criticism, and possibly beaten or even killed.

Some aspects of the Mao period remain. Workers in state-owned enterprises are widely regarded as being especially difficult for managers to control. When SOEs are involved in joint ventures with foreign firms, 'traditional' attitudes from the Mao period are often blamed if the joint venture experiences difficulties.[120] However, from another perspective, the institutions of grassroots democracy can become very effective tools of mobilization. The ideological purpose of Maoist campaigns was not only to seek out and punish incorrect thought, but to encourage every individual to engage directly with their neighbors to study and understand Mao Zedong thought and its concrete application in their own lives. At Double Star, Wang Hai has attempted to create a sense of ownership by employees, building on the pre-existing structures. A Management Committee for Corporate Democracy with elected worker and management representatives sits atop a pyramid of elected teams at factory, group, and unit management level in all plants and offices. The teams have the power to discuss and review the reports and plans, and to monitor the performance of 'management cadres' at each level. Exceptionally able workers can be recommended for promotion to management, and poorly performing managers can be demoted.[121]

Double Star's bottom-up review system is unusual, and of course the state-owned enterprises no longer dominate the economy. As noted above, the model of individual contracts has become the standard for labor relations. In establishing the Special Economic Zones, the government specified that labor relations would be governed by individual contracts and that wages would be set by the market. Although at first workers in the SEZs were assigned by the local labor bureaus, labor unions and workers' committees were excluded. As with the concepts of strategic management, contemporary approaches to human resource management are widely discussed. However, as with top-down, boss-centered management practice, the reality of HRM is much less inclusive. SOEs and corporatized firms are often divided between a privileged core of workers, especially if they are direct or indirect shareholders, and the rest. Many firms, both domestic and foreign, hire former soldiers as supervisors. They do so, however, not because they hope to combine military discipline with family values, but rather because they want to extract maximum effort from their *dagong-mei*, the young migrant women whose low wages are the source of their competitive advantage.

Conditions for ordinary workers range across a broad spectrum, from good to atrocious. Subcontractors for major foreign firms such as Nike have received unfavorable international publicity, but may be no worse than other purely Chinese firms. In the absence of an independent labor movement or a social security safety net, individual workers have little option except to change jobs. That option is a real one, and TVEs in particular have been reported to treat migrants humanely, for fear that dissatisfied workers will complain to their families and friends at home, making the recruitment of new workers more difficult. Wages in coastal manufacturing districts are of course very low compared to wages internationally, but they are high relative to the available alternatives. Migrants are themselves divided, with those from one province looking down on those from another. Many of them also believe their sojourn as factory workers will be temporary, lasting only until they have saved enough to return to their home village.

Those who experience the most intense pressure may in fact be the middle managers, caught between the demands of a dynamic CEO and the recalcitrance of ordinary workers. The general lack of in-house management training opportunities reflects the insecure status of middle managers. At Double Star they sarcastically refer to themselves as 'blackboard managers' whose names can be easily erased if they receive a poor evaluation. At Haier, Zhang Ruimin imposes rating standards on his division chiefs and expects them to meet or exceed their targets or face demotion.

As we have seen, the legal, operating, and listed entities of large firms frequently differ. Reporting standards are low, and in fact many firms do not yet have the systematic financial controls that would make adequate reporting possible. The piecework payment of individual employees can be noted, and is frequently publicized, and for low-level supervisors the aggregated piecework payments of the workers under them can provide an indication of their performance as well. Above this level it rapidly becomes impossible to evaluate performance objectively without more sophisticated accounting tools. For those at the middle or above, therefore, satisfying the CEO and possibly the external controlling agencies must in some degree involve the cultivation of personal relationships. Their jobs in part consist of, and in part depend upon, the same political skills that the CEO must deploy in dealing with the firm's external environment.

The Firm's External Relations and the Role of Connections

In the Chinese context, successful managers must have 'space' in which to operate. The unpredictability and arbitrariness of state power leads to defensiveness and insecurity, and a corresponding tendency to attempt to gain the support of powerful allies, and to trust only those known personally. This possibly lies behind the results of a study of the effects of the system of auctioning the management of state-owned enterprises which showed that, following the auction, if the winner were an outsider, there was no improvement in performance, but if the winner were the incumbent manager the firm's performance did improve.[122] Double Star carefully describes its separate divisions as 'state-owned, privately run economic units'. Similarly, the success of China International Marine Container (Group) Company, Ltd. (CIMC), a Shenzehen based firm that has risen to dominate the international market for shipping containers, resulted in large part from the ability of its CEO to develop and maintain an independent position with respect both to the government agencies that were the major shareholders, and to the Party committees to which CIMC management was nominally subservient.[123]

Many attribute the success of China's CEOs to their use of networks of connections and 'relationships' or *guanxi*. Gordon Redding argued that paternalistic and personalistic networks constitute the social relations of Chinese business, and others have followed this line.[124] This is often expanded to an assertion that Chinese society itself operates through *guanxi*. Some believe this to result from inherited tradition. Yadong Luo says, 'Guanxi . . . has been pervasive in the Chinese business world for the last few centuries.'[125] Some believe it rests on distinctive modes of thought. As we saw in Chapter 5, neo-Confucian theorists such as Tu Wei-ming have said that, in contrast to the West, the Confucian personality exists not as an isolated individual but as a center of a network of personal connections, as 'the self that is not an island but an ever-expanding stream of interconnectedness'.[126]

Others argue that institutional factors have played a role. Parallel to Redding's argument regarding Qing China, Mayfair Yang argues that, in the People's Republic, the essential failure of the state redistributive apparatus in effect forced the emergence of a 'gift economy'. Individuals were forced to cultivate relations with officials in order to receive goods and services that in the West they could have expected to obtain either through the market or as public services. Rather than a simple bribe to purchase a service, however, gifts in this context are intended to reinforce personal connections such as classmate or native place, and thereby transform them into useable social capital on which the gift-giver can draw in the future.[127]

The problem with analyses based on *guanxi* is that they explain both too much and too little. It is easy to fall into an error of attribution, to attribute a quality to a person or group and then assume that this quality must be the cause of their behavior. *Guanxi* is an exact equivalent of the English word 'relation', as it is for the Japanese and Korean words that use the same characters. However, as Souchou Yao reminds us, 'relations' can be many things, including international, economic, political, social, familial, personal, or sexual. To say a relationship is based on *guanxi*, therefore, does not say anything more than that a relationship exists. The meaning of the relationship, and its effect on behavior, depends on the social context and the expectations of the individuals involved.[128]

As we will see in Chapter 8, ethnic Chinese firms in Southeast Asia often make use of personal connections, but even here, as Yao notes, the relationship can be ambivalent, seen by participants as both advantageous and a burden. In China the evidence is mixed. The work of Ole Bruun and Kai-Alexander Schlevogt noted above emphasizes the ties among family members, but in Xiqiao, the textile village studied by Jonathan Unger and Anita Chan, informants reported a tendency for family partnerships to fail, and most said they would not hire on the basis of *guanxi*. The head (with his wife) of one of Xiqiao's most successful firms said, 'I don't take people because of *guanxi* . . . I have to build up my reputation, but for that it's quality that's most important. I don't even use *guanxi* to obtain business orders. Treating others to meals isn't useful to me.'[129] Double Star's management in fact believes that *guanxi* is pervasive in Chinese society. However, Double Star regards this as a problem, and has consciously constructed a system of 'public and objective' rules, 'from bottom up' through consultations endorsed by the worker representative committees, that apply 'impartially to every member of the Group regardless of rank and office'. Among their other functions, these rules are intended to prevent favoritism, and informants assured Po-keung Ip that all Double Star employees 'revere these rules as "house rules" which they dutifully follow'.[130]

The managers of large firms do not in general rely on family relationships.[131] They do, however, actively maintain a large circle of connections. There may no longer be quite as many masters as the textile manager complained of, but relations with Party organizations and government agencies at all levels are still critical to a firm's success.[132] Harmonious relations with controlling agencies are obviously important. In addition, connections can provide information as to what policy changes may be under discussion and allow the firm to anticipate their impact. Connections with state bank officials give access to funding. Defending regional territory against competitors might also mean, for example, encouraging government authorities' conception of trade as a zero sum game, to reinforce their in-built inclination to look unfavorably on firms that threaten the position of local firms.

Leaders also act as facilitators of networks. In addition to the didactic banquet speech, China's senior executives play another role, that of genial host. Typically at smaller dinners, relative strangers may be brought together to become acquainted, under the smiling patronage of their mutual friend, the host. Not so much to create connections for the host, these functions serve more to create and solidify the interconnections among the host's friends. This is social capital of a slightly different kind, the building of long-term relationships whose mutual benefits may flow well beyond their initial boundaries.

There is if anything an over-supply of foreigners seeking to give advice to China. Recent debate centers on the impact of the WTO,[133] whether Chinese firms will adopt 'Western' forms of management in response to market pressures,[134] and whether privatization of state-owned enterprises should continue. Nicholas Lardy concluded, 'reforms to date have failed in large portions of the state-owned sector'.[135] Some agree, but as seen above there are substantial reasons to question the pessimists' case regarding the SOEs. There is reason for optimism in the high-technology areas of information technology and biotechnologies, where the sheer size of China's rapidly expanding scientific community will place China in a competitive position. Development in these areas may be led by smaller firms in the private sector, but they could be supported by large SOEs, following the example of Taiwan. Further, in many areas it may not be necessary for Chinese firms to compete in global markets. As China continues to grow and develop, China itself will become a world market. Chinese firms may become sufficiently large to protect themselves, simply by supplying goods or services in one or several of China's regional markets. The combination of strong leadership, networking, and interpenetration of the public and private sectors that marks all of the diverse forms of enterprise in China may in fact be moving towards something different, a management with Chinese characteristics.

FURTHER READING

Philip Short, *Mao: A Life* (New York: Henry Holt, 2000) is a well written and generally balanced account. The best way to sample Mao's thought is

Quotations from Chairman Mao Tse-tung (Peking: Foreign Languages Press, 1966), the 'little red book' carried by the Red Guards during the Cultural Revolution. The complete texts of his basic works are in Mao Tse-tung, *Selected Works* (5 vols, New York: International Publishers, 1954). For Deng, see David S.G. Goodman, *Deng Xiaoping and the Chinese Revolution: A Political Biography* (London: Routledge, 1994). For China's evolving political system, see Joseph Fewsmith, *China since Tiananmen: The Politics of Transition* (Cambridge and New York: Cambridge University Press, 2001) and Tony Saich, *Governance and Politics of China* (2nd edn, Houndmills and New York: Palgrave, 2004).

Gordon White, *Riding the Tiger: The Politics of Economic Reform in Post-Mao China* (Houndmills: Macmillan, 1993) and Barry Naughton, *Growing Out of the Plan: Chinese Economic Reform 1978-1993* (Cambridge: Cambridge University Press, 1995), are very good accounts of the reforms through the early 1990s. Ross Garnaut and Yiping Huang, *Growth without Miracles: Readings on the Chinese Economy in the Era of Reform* (Oxford: Oxford University Press, 2001) take the story through the late 1990s.

Nicholas R. Lardy, *China's Unfinished Economic Revolution* (Washington, D.C.: The Brookings Institution, 1998) is very pessimistic about the state-owned enterprise sector. Yiping Huang, *China's Last Steps Across the River: Enterprise and Banking Reforms* (Canberra: Asia Pacific Press, Australian National University, 2001) emphasizes the dangers of continuing weaknesses in firm governance and the banking system. Carsten A. Holz, *China's Industrial State-Owned Enterprises: Between Profitability and Bankruptcy* (Singapore: World Scientific Publishing, 2003), is far more optimistic, while Peter Nolan, Peter Sutherland and Wu Qing, *China and the Global Business Revolution* (London and New York: Palgrave, 2001) lies somewhere between.

On township and village enterprises, see Jean C. Oi, *Rural China Takes Off: Institutional Foundations of Economic Reform* (Berkeley: University of California Press, 1999) and Susan H. Whiting, *Power and Wealth in Rural China: The Political Economy of Institutional Change* (New York: Cambridge University Press, 2001). On private sector firms, see Ole Bruun, *Business and Bureaucracy in a Chinese City: An Ethnography of Private Business Households in Contemporary China* (Berkeley: University of California, Institute of East Asian Studies, 1993); David L. Wank, *Commodifying Communism: Business, Trust and Politics in a Chinese City* (Cambridge: Cambridge University Press, 1999); Ross Garnaut and Ligang Song (eds), *China's Third Economic Transformation: The Rise of the Private Economy* (London and New York: RoutledgeCurzon, 2004). For the emerging high-technology area, see Bhajan Grewal et al. (eds), *China's Future in the Knowledge Economy: Engaging the New World* (Melbourne:

Centre for Strategic Studies, Victoria University, and Tsinghau University Press, 2004).

Most of the works dealing with the foreign invested enterprise sector are aimed at Western audiences. Yadong Luo, *Partnering with Chinese Firms: Lessons for International Managers* (Aldershot: Ashgate, 2000), Carolyn Blackman's books, *Negotiating China: Case Studies and Strategies* (St Leonards: Allen & Unwin, 1997) and *China Business: The Rules of the Game* (St Leonards: Allen & Unwin, 2000), and Joe Studwell, *The China Dream: The Elusive Quest for the Greatest Untapped Market on Earth* (London: Profile Books, 2002) are good in their treatment of the Chinese context.

NOTES

1. White (1993), chs 5 and 6.
2. Oi (1989); Friedman, Pickowicz, Selden and Johnson (1991).
3. Perkins (1983), 345–72; Lardy (1983).
4. Lavely, Lee and Wang (1990), p. 813; Becker (1996).
5. For instance Fairbank (1992), ch. 21; Stevens (1996), pp. 28–32.
6. Brady (2003), ch. 8.
7. White (1993), p. 49. See Garnaut and Song (1999).
8. Herold (2002), pp. 27–8. It may have been Hua Guofeng who first used the phrase 'crossing the river by feeling the stones'. See Brady (2003), p. 187.
9. White (1993), pp. 103, 108–9.
10. Brady (2003), p. 187.
11. Lardy (1991).
12. White (1993), p. 100.
13. See Perkins (1986).
14. Nee and Su (1990), 3–25.
15. White (1993), pp. 107–15.
16. Sun (1996).
17. Ngai (2004), 151–65; Lee (1998).
18. Solinger (1999); Sargeson (1999).
19. Andrews-Speed, Yang, Shen and Cao (2003), 185–96.
20. Murray (1994), p. 55, n. 15, citing *Beijing Review*, 16–22 Aug. 1993.
21. Murray (1994), p. 237.
22. Lardy (1998).
23. Song (1998), pp. 105–19.
24. Australia, Department of Foreign Affairs and Trade, East Asia Analytical Unit (1999), ch. 12.
25. Huang (2001); Nolan, Sutherland and Qing (2001), ch. 12; Australia, Department of Foreign Affairs and Trade, Economic Analytical Unit (2002), vol. 2, pp. 25–7.
26. Chong (2004); Guerrera (2005).
27. Needham (2004), *Sydney Morning Herald* report; Guerrera and McGregor (2004). See Boston Consulting Group and Knowledge @ Wharton, *China and the New Rules for Global Business* (2004), pp. 9–11; http://knowledge.wharton.upenn.edu.
28. Interview (2000). The plant, a large operation producing both cotton and synthetic cloth, opened in the 1950s. The interviewee was appointed as the plant's Party Secretary in 1960, became the Director in 1974, and retired in 1998, but remained as an advisor. 'I'd be on the board of directors, if we had one,' he said.
29. See Joseph, Wong and Zweig (eds), (1991).

30. White (1993), p. 137, note 19.
31. Lee (2001), 673–89.
32. Jefferson and Rawski (1994), 47–70.
33. The reference to the Four Olds was also an intentional pun referring to the campaign launched in 1966 against 'old thought, old culture, old customs, and old practices' as part of the Cultural Revolution.
34. Brady (2003), p. 187.
35. Jefferson and Rawski (1994).
36. Perkins (1996), 414–44.
37. Lee (1996), 105–21.
38. Nolan, Sutherland and Wu (2001), ch. 3.
39. *Far Eastern Economic Review* (20 February 2003).
40. Bersani (1993), 301–28; Jefferson and Rawski (1994).
41. Lee (1999), 702–29; Lardy (1998), p. 22. See Australia, Department of Foreign Affairs and Trade, Economic Analytical Unit (2002), pp. 24–5.
42. Following the argument of Fama (1980), 288–307.
43. Lo (1999), 693–718.
44. Nolan and Wang (1999), p. 185.
45. Holz (2002), 493–529.
46. World Bank (1996), p. 20.
47. Huang (2001), argues that the cost has been higher than necessary, and the economy has lost in aggregate terms.
48. Nolan and Wang (1999), p. 185. Again, because an underpriced asset will be used excessively, the cost, in reduced efficiency, distorted development, and environmental degradation, may be high.
49. Chen (1998), 479–95.
50. Australia, Department of Foreign Affairs and Trade, Economic Analytical Unit (2002), vol. 2, p. 24, citing a report from China Online in 2001.
51. Lee (1999).
52. Groves, Hong, Macmillan and Naughton (1994), 183–209.
53. Zhou and Wang (2000), p. 299. At issue is whether the critical principal–agent relationship is that between the state and enterprise managers, or between managers and workers within the enterprise. See Cauley and Sandler (2001), 293–7.
54. Chen (1998), p. 489 and note 10.
55. Nolan, Sutherland and Wu (2001), ch. 3; Australia, Department of Foreign Affairs and Trade, Economic Analytical Unit (2002), vol. 2, ch. 7.
56. Huang (2001).
57. Bersani (1993), 301–28; Jefferson and Rawski (1994).
58. Meyer and Lu (2003).
59. Dyer (2005).
60. Meng and Perkins (1998), 295–316.
61. Nolan, Sutherland and Wu (2001), p. 239.
62. Ibid., chs 6 and 8.
63. Ibid., ch. 5.
64. Ibid., ch. 7.
65. Duckett (2000), 23–37.
66. Perotti, Sun and Zou (1999), 151–79.
67. Pei (1996), 50.
68. Sargeson (1996).
69. Park and Shen (2003), 498, 499.
70. Unger (1994), pp. 43–63.
71. Oi (1992), 100.
72. Walder (1995), 276–81; Peng (2001), 1343–4.
73. O'Brien (1994), 51–3.
74. Chan, Madsen and Unger (1992).
75. Bruton, Lan and Lu (2000), p. 23.

76. Park and Shen (2003), p. 500.
77. Unger and Chan (1999).
78. Naughton (1994), 267–8.
79. Smyth, Wang and Kang (2000), 30–41.
80. Ho (1994); Walder (1995).
81. Liu (1992), 293–316; Wing (1999), 115–37.
82. McDonald (2004a).
83. Redding (1990), p. 77, note 1.
84. Bruun (1988).
85. Schlevogt (2004), p. 87.
86. See Perris (1993), 242–63; Nolan and Furen (1990).
87. Zeng and Williamson (2003), pp. 97–8. Dongguang in particular suffered from a sudden shortage of migrant workers in mid-2004, threatening production for the Christmas toy season; McDonald (2004b).
88. Goodman (2005), 325–43.
89. Myrdal (1984); Chai and Chai (1994).
90. Wright (1994), 1–2.
91. Garnaut, Song, Yao and Wang (2001), pp. 76–7. .
92. Bruun (1993); Wank (1999).
93. McDonald (2004a).
94. Tsai (2002).
95. Chen (1999).
96. 'Fools rush in', *The Economist*, 7 August 2004.
97. Brady (2003), pp. 235–6.
98. Australia, EAU (2002), pp. 31–7.
99. Needham (2004).
100. See Wedeman (2003).
101. Taylor (2001), 601–20. Taylor also notes Chinese statistics showing that Japanese-invested firms in China experience significantly higher levels of labor unrest, including strikes, than Western-invested firms.
102. Sun and Tipton (1998), 159–86; Child, Yan and Lu, (1997).
103. Hamilton (1996), 7–20; Studwell (2002).
104. Needham (2004).
105. Boston Consulting Group and Knowledge @ Wharton (2004), pp. 12–13 (http//knowledge.wharton.upenn.edu).
106. Taylor (2004).
107. Ip (2003), 64–77.
108. Wee (2001), pp. 262–3.
109. Chen (1998), p. 489 and note 10.
110. See Chapter 1, note 15.
111. Huang, Leonard and Tong (1997), pp. 165–202.
112. Ip (2003), pp. 66, 68–9.
113. See, for instance, Lu and Child (1996); Worm (1997).
114. Short (2000), pp. 93–4.
115. Wang (2004).
116. World Bank (1995).
117. See Duckett (2000), for a discussion of the literature.
118. I have encountered this repeatedly in China, for instance as the reason given by a manager in an international hotel chain in China as to why he would not seek promotion to an overseas posting, and it is the phrase used by numbers of my students to explain why they plan to return to China after receiving their degrees.
119. Silverthorne (2004). These points come from a report on 150 listed Chinese firms by Bain and Company.
120. Jiang (2001), 313–30. In this case, relations were also soured by the fact that the three foreign expatriate managers together earned the equivalent of the combined salaries of 100 workers as well as enjoying the perquisites of chauffeur-driven cars and luxury apartments.

121. Ip (2003), pp. 69–70.
122. Groves, Hong, McMillan and Naughton (1995), 873–92.
123. Meyer and Lu (2003), pp. 25–6.
124. Redding (1990), ch. 6; Chen (2003), ch. 3.
125. Luo (1997), 43–51.
126. Tu (1989), pp. 74–5.
127. Yang (1994).
128. Yao (2004), pp. 233–54.
129. Unger (1999), p. 8.
130. Ip (2003), p. 70. This corresponds to our survey of Chinese Master of Commerce students (Chapter 1, notes 15 and 18), which showed that they generally would not hire on the basis of *guanxi*, but believed that Chinese businesses in general did operate on the basis of *guanxi*.
131. As in other countries, however, having an influential relative can help one's business career. The 'princelings' whose fathers occupy high Party and government posts are obvious examples.
132. See, for instance, Huang, Leonard and Tong (1997), pp. 97–100.
133. Panitchpakdi and Clifford (2002).
134. O'Connor, Chow and Wu (2004), 349–75; Bai, Liu, Lu, Song and Zhang (2003).
135. Lardy (1998), p. 22.

7. Managing under the guidance of a strong state in Southeast Asia

> Therefore use these assessments for comparison, to find out what the conditions are. That is to say, which political leadership has the Way? Which general has the ability? Who has the better climate and terrain? Whose discipline is effective? Whose troops are stronger? Whose officers and soldiers are better trained? Whose system of rewards and punishments is clearer? This is how you can know who will win. (Sun Tzu, *The Art of War*)

> The good and the bad must be clearly distinguished; negligence will lead to confusion and chaos. (Tao Zhu-gong, the Twelfth Business Lesson)

Comparisons reveal the role of history in Southeast Asia, and the complexity of the region. We need to examine four colonial empires and one independent state, the nationalist regimes following independence, and the evolving more open systems of the recent past. One constant theme has been the relatively large role played by central governments, first the colonial regimes and then the new independent states. However, another constant theme has been the inability of these states to achieve their goals. Although 'strong' states in claiming wide competence, the governments of Southeast Asia have typically not possessed the capacity to enforce their will consistently. There have been a number of reasons, sometimes a failure of leadership, sometimes a failure of strength, sometimes a failure of training, and indeed sometimes a failure of the system of rewards and punishments.

This chapter concentrates on the case of Thailand, for both practical and analytical reasons. Focusing on the Thai story allows us to highlight a number of common themes. In the nineteenth century, Thailand's government took Japan as a model. Chulalongkorn's program of centralization, the emphasis on defense and national power, and the role of government in the economy all recall similar aspects of Meiji Japan. So too does the role of the army in the 1930s. However, although Thailand maintained its independence, the claims of the 'strong' state exceeded its capacity. For a century Thailand has been plagued by problems of succession and corruption. The government has also confronted problems of ethnic diversity, and much of the state's potential capacity has been expended on the attempt to persuade or force the very different groups within the population to accept the rule of the central government. Another aspect of ethnic diversity, and further evidence of the lack of state capacity, was the government's use of Chinese immigrants to perform administrative and revenue-gathering functions, which laid the foundations for the ongoing role of the Chinese in the economy examined in Chapter 8.

In the colonial areas, a different pattern emerged, but their historical and institutional grids tended over time to replicate the Thai patterns. Colonial states also claimed to be 'strong' states, but as in Thailand their claims outran their capacity. Although the Dutch, British, French, and American colonial governments maintained themselves, they depended on the cooperation and assistance of native elites, and as in Thailand they frequently relied on Chinese to collect revenue as well as to provide commercial services. They also failed to win ongoing allegiance, and the opposition nationalist movements all drew their leadership from the native elites. Both senior native officials and nationalist leaders frequently came from families already wealthy before the imperialist period, either hereditary aristocrats or landowners, again replicating Thai patterns.

Ethnic divisions remained a feature of the new national states, as did the role of the Chinese in the economy. Within the majority indigenous population, as in Thailand, the imposition of a single definition of the 'national' culture on very diverse groups created conflict. National governments envisaged a large role for the state in the economy. However, as Tao Zhugong might put it, good and bad were not always clearly distinguished as fashion changed. From colonial economic structures, the new governments turned in the 1950s to protectionist programs of import substitution, in the 1960s and 1970s to export promotion, and in the 1980s and 1990s from state ownership and control to privatization and deregulation. The institutional grid reflected the government structures arising from the relatively low levels of state capacity typical of the region. Corruption, the failure of the system of rewards and punishments, remained endemic. As seen in Chapters 8 and 9, this has affected the structures of both ethnic Chinese and indigenous firms.

THE HISTORICAL GRID: SOUTHEAST ASIA IN THE AGE OF IMPERIALISM

Thailand: the Legacy of Chulalongkorn as a Model for the Strong State in Southeast Asia

Alone among the states of Southeast Asia, Siam (Thailand) survived, although it required skilful leadership, a clear focus of central government policy, and good luck. The 'modernizing' regime of Chulalongkorn, who ruled from 1868 to 1910, was almost exactly contemporaneous with Meiji Japan. And, as in Japan, the institutions established in Thailand in the late nineteenth century continue to influence developments. As in Japan, Thailand's leaders adopted the idea that the state can and must be centrally involved in guiding the economy. Later, as will be seen below, similar structures and attitudes emerged in the independent states that emerged after the Second World War.

Thailand was fortunate in being on the upswing of a new dynastic cycle when confronted by the expansion of Western power. Rama I had been proclaimed King by rebels in 1782 and ruled until 1809. He established a monarchical system resting on key sources of support whose importance has echoed down to the present. He won over the aristocracy with offices in return for service. He won over the Buddhist clergy by commissioning a complete revision of the scriptural texts. And, not least, he worked to increase Siamese military power, and the army has remained both a crucial pillar of support for the government and an independent contender for power in the state.

The founder was succeeded by capable successors. The Siamese turned down a British offer to join their war against Burma in 1824. Instead, Rama III negotiated a treaty that exchanged British recognition of Siamese rights over the Malay states for liberalization of trade in Bangkok. Security on the western and southern borders allowed Siam to concentrate on wars against the Lao in the 1830s and the Vietnamese in the 1840s. As a result King Mongkut (1851–68) was well-prepared when John Bowring, the British governor of Hong Kong and minister to China, arrived in Bangkok with new demands for trade and diplomatic relations.

The Bowring Treaty of 1855 extracted the same terms as the treaties Britain had imposed on China, including consular representation, extraterritoriality, low tariffs, and a low limit on taxation of property owned by foreigners. Like the Japanese, the Siamese concluded they had no choice but to concede the treaty and then attempt to reform their finances to increase revenues in order to build up their military strength. However, the government's pressing need for money added a typically Southeast Asian element of support for the monarchy, Chinese business interests. The government created new monopolies in opium, alcohol, and gambling, and a lottery, and these were farmed out to Chinese contractors. Siam also began to export large quantities of rice and teak timber. Dependence on commodity exports became another common feature of Southeast Asian development. The government used the increased revenues to purchase arms and to hire Westerners to drill Siamese troops in their use, again establishing a model for the region, the important role of the military in public life.

Siam remained under threat from the imperialist powers. In 1875, a crisis very nearly led to British and French intervention. The French moved into the area east of the Mekong in the 1880s, and when the Siamese attempted to force them out, the French imposed a naval blockade and annexed the disputed territories in 1893. In 1909, the British seized four of the principalities in the Malay Peninsula that had previously recognized Siamese suzerainty. Siam could have been conquered and divided, but Britain and France did not want either to share a border or to see the other gain too great an influence in the remaining territory of Siam, and therefore they agreed to retain an independent Siam to serve as a buffer between their territories.

During these decades the role of the state was changing and growing in all countries, and the new manner in which the national states of the West were coming to conceive themselves led them to impose that conception on their colonial possessions. The new states were territorial states. Rather than a core area from which power and influence radiated outward in diminishing waves as in France before the revolution of 1789, or federations of kingdoms as in Germany before the wars of unification in the 1860s, the new states defined themselves as uniformly sovereign across the entire area within defined geographical boundaries. So, in the case of Thailand, by laying claim to absolute sovereignty within a territory defined by a map, the Bangkok elite could create the mythic community that validated their power.[1]

In addition, these were secular states which dispensed with the inherited tradition of sacred authority. In Southeast Asia, this was obviously true of the colonial territories, but it was also true of Thailand. When he became king in the 1870s, Chulalongkorn ordered his officials not to prostrate themselves before him. In doing so, however, he was not giving up his power, but was actually demanding a much more comprehensive kind of authority.[2] In Siam, as in most of Europe until the early decades of the nineteenth century, the bureaucracy traditionally had consisted largely of unsalaried officials drawn from the hereditary nobility. Although they abased themselves in the King's presence, in their own territories they could and did behave as independent rulers. Chulalongkorn aimed to transform these potentially rebellious men into disciplined officials whose authority would derive solely from their position in the government hierarchy.

In Japan, as we saw in Chapter 2, the Meiji government launched a broad program of modernization based on the latest Western models. In Siam, as in Japan, the state claimed, and in contemporary Thailand the state continues to claim, that it is modern, and that the rest of society requires its leadership. However, the answer to the question of who and what is 'modern' depends on our standpoint and perspective. Chulalongkorn had 27 brothers, and he relied on them to implement the state's new administrative structures. From the mid-1880s, as older ministers died, he replaced them with his brothers. New functional ministries were established in 1888, each with one of his brothers as minister. A new cabinet government was set up in 1892, and most of the members were his brothers. The provinces were reorganized into new units under commissioners who introduced regular taxation and began to organize local military units based on systematic conscription, and again the new commissioners often were his brothers.

In Thailand, as in Japan, commercial activity had been widespread for a long time, particularly in the textile industry. Silk thread was imported from China and woven into fabrics in specialized towns. Cotton growing, spinning, weaving, and dyeing also took place in specialized districts and towns. Not only commoners but also aristocrats engaged in production and sale of textiles on a large scale. However, members of the aristocracy used their inherited position to exploit economic opportunities. Rather than purchasing their raw materials and labor, they extracted raw cotton, woven cloth, and dyestuffs as tribute. And, rather than purchasing labor in the market as the commoners did, they employed slaves. A British Foreign Office official reported in 1875 that one of the major sources of income of the ruling lord in Chiang Mai was 'the sale of wearing apparel, etc., made by his several hundred slaves'.[3]

That is, there were active entrepreneurs, both aristocrats and commoners, and extensive manufacturing and trade, but the government ignored them and preferred to work through monopolies granted to Chinese or Western agents. Through the 1930s, Thailand's export sector, teak and rice, and then rubber and tin, lay in the hands of Chinese or Western firms, except for the growing of rice. As aliens the Chinese depended on the government. No matter how rich they became, they would never be a threat. Further, since Thailand remained weak compared to the West, it paid to have a number of influential Western firms that benefited from deals with the Thai government. There are close parallels here, for instance, with Indonesia in the 1970s and 1980s.

Education is another area of 'modernization'. Chulalongkorn sent representatives to Japan to study Japanese education. In 1910, they recommended promulgation of a royal decree on education, and Chulalongkorn suggested that it be modeled on Japan's 1890 Imperial Rescript on Education. The project of the royal decree was dropped when Chulalongkorn died, but the system that emerged imposed a uniform syllabus taught from uniform texts, with all instruction conducted in Central Thai (the Bangkok dialect) rather than any of the many local variants. As in Japan, students were told that the 'Thai' people were a uniform ethnic group who had lived under a single line of kings for many, many centuries. This was objectively untrue, for Siam was an 'ethnic muddle' that included Lao, Khmer, Mon, Vietnamese, Malay, and Chinese in addition to the diverse groups calling themselves Thai. The history of the kings was a myth as well, because the dynasty dated only from the rebellious usurper of the 1780s, who was probably Chinese and Mon.[4]

Transportation also contributes to 'modernization' and in the nineteenth and early twentieth centuries this meant railways. The first of the three major lines led west out of Bangkok to counter the French advance through Laos. The second line ran north to Chiang Mai and the third to the south to Penang. Political and strategic motives were paramount throughout. Diplomatic motives are evident as well, particularly the determination of the Thai government to maintain its independence. Chulalongkorn refused to borrow and insisted that the early projects all be paid for out of current revenue, and the Railway Department employed German advisers in preference to British or French.

Chulalongkorn and his successors intended all these measures to defend the kingdom against foreign threats, and to centralize and reinforce power in the hands of the government. The new administration would generate higher tax revenues, and the new school system would create obedient subjects. The railways allowed the government to impose its authority throughout the kingdom by moving troops if necessary. Modernization reflected the interests of the state. Thai development also reflected the exploitation of the mass of the population by well connected members of the elite, and a kind of internal imperialism exercised by Bangkok over the rest of the country, another pattern that has repeated itself, notably in Indonesia and the Philippines.

Imperialism and Development in Colonial Southeast Asia

Westerners remained on the fringes of Southeast Asia until the nineteenth century. Although the Spanish had claimed suzerainty over the entire Philippines archipelago since the sixteenth century, they effectively controlled only Manila and the surrounding districts of Luzon. Similarly, the Dutch had claimed the entire Indonesian archipelago since the seventeenth century, but ruled directly only in Batavia (Jakarta) and the surrounding districts of Java, Madura, and eastern Sumatra. The British expanded in India during the second half of the eighteenth century, and during the Napoleonic wars they seized naval and trading strongpoints on the Malay Peninsula, including Singapore, but without yet extending their control into the hinterlands.

From these small districts the imperial powers expanded to dominate the region.[5] However, several points need to be kept in mind. First, the process was slow, extending into the twentieth century. Second, the process was

violent, and native peoples opposed it at every step. Having purchased the
Philippines from Spain in 1898 after defeating the Spaniards in a short war,
the United States confronted a nationalist movement in the north and an
independence movement in the Muslim southern islands. Possibly a million
Filipinos (one-seventh of the population) died during the subsequent military action that lasted until 1906.[6] The third point to keep in mind,
however, is that the Westerners did in fact win these colonial wars. And,
fourth and equally important, the colonial regimes successfully maintained
themselves against resistance movements in the 1920s and 1930s, until they
were overrun by the Japanese in the Second World War.

One reason the colonial states survived is that, once established, they all
ruled with the assistance of native elites. In the Philippines, says John
Larkin, 'Spaniards wanted labor rather than indigenous commercial
produce, and they enlisted elements of the native ruling class to organize
that work force. This arrangement early on determined the bifurcated
social structure that has predominated to the present.'[7] Carl Trocki continues, saying that, after repressing the nationalist movement, the United
States also 'found it expedient to allow the co-operative elements of the
Filipino elite an increasingly larger role in government and to look the
other way as they enriched themselves at the expense of the peasants and
increased their traditional power within the local communities'.[8]

In Malaya, sultans deferred to their British resident advisors, but the
British in turn relied on the sultans to control the mass of Malay commoners in their villages. In Cambodia and Laos, the French relied on native
kings, and in Vietnam they retained the native Emperor and established two
parallel administrations, one with authority over Europeans, foreign Asians,
and Vietnamese with French citizenship, and the other Vietnamese, to rule
the majority of natives. Traditionally, Vietnamese officials belonged to a
landowning aristocracy who had passed examinations based on the
Confucian classics as in China. The reforming official Nguyen Truong To
had advocated abolition of the system in the 1860s, but after the conquest
the French retained it, and officials in the 'native' administration continued
to be selected by the old Chinese examination system until 1919.[9] In
Indonesia, members of the native *priyayi* aristocracy ruled as regents in each
of the districts, with Dutch officials to guide them. Beginning in the 1870s,
their personal powers were progressively reduced, and by the 1910s they and
their subordinate officials had become paid functionaries of the central
bureaucracy. However, they continued to demand labor services from poor
villagers, and Robert Elson concludes that 'to the end of the colonial period,
there was little real evidence of a transition to a system of free wage labor'.[10]

Westerners claimed to have brought 'modern' economic relations to
Asian societies for the first time, and this became one of the justifications

for imperialism. However, this was not in fact true. As in China and Japan, and as seen above in the case of Thailand, market economies predated the Western intrusion. Southeast Asian producers were well informed and able to exploit the varying opportunities of local, regional, and interregional trade. Rather than expanding opportunities, the actions of colonial governments often interfered with these market relationships. For periods that varied from as few as 30 years to over a century, the regional economies of Southeast Asia were subordinated to the needs of the imperialist powers. As in the case of China, specialist scholars continue to debate the long-term effects of imperialism on economic development. Some, following the lead of Immanuel Wallerstein, argue that Southeast Asia's 'peripheral' position in the capitalist world economy created the conditions for underdevelopment.[11] Others, such as David Landes, argue that economic development depends on the ability of individuals to recognize and seize opportunities, and that this in turn rests on the inherited values of each society.[12]

But, if we think of their effects on social structures, the impact of colonial governments was profound. The role of the state was fundamentally transformed. Part of the change in the conception of the state in Europe, the United States, and Japan during the late nineteenth and early twentieth centuries was an extension of the areas of social life over which the government exercised direct control, from marriage and birth, through education, employment, and old age. The imperial powers attempted to do the same in their colonies. Above all they increased tax revenues. The money went first for military forces to subdue districts where resistance had not yet been crushed, and then for transportation, public health, education, and the infrastructure required by expanding cities.[13]

Colonial regimes were challenged by new nationalist movements, a phenomenon closely linked to economic development. As will be seen below, specialists disagree over the definition of nationalism, and over the precise connection between nationalism and economic development, but there are certain preconditions that seem necessary. The creation of a national community requires an expansion of communications. During the colonial period, steam-powered ships tied port cities together, and on land railways linked commercial urban centers to their hinterlands. Together, the steamship and the railway made it possible to ship much larger amounts of goods, to move greater numbers of people, and to exchange information much faster and much more regularly, than ever before. Japanese colonial officials were better at this than the Dutch, British, French, or Americans, but by the 1930s all the countries of Asia possessed at least the outlines of a modern rail system.

The creation of a national community also requires that large numbers of people be able to read the appeals of would-be nationalist leaders.

Colonial states all expanded education. As we have seen, in the Japanese empire the increase in the numbers and proportion of children attending primary school was impressive. In Southeast Asia, colonial administrators and later apologists pointed with pride to their educational efforts. In the Philippines, the original American teachers had been mostly replaced by Filipinos by 1930, and by 1940 nearly half of the population had achieved basic literacy. However, in the Philippines, primary enrolments were 1.7 million in 1938, only 40 per cent of the five to 14 age group, and the proportions were lower in the other colonial areas. Further, secondary education remained very undeveloped in the colonial era. The imperial powers, Japan included, intended that the overwhelming majority of their subject populations would receive a primary education at most. There were only 140 000 secondary school students in the Philippines in 1938, only 20 000 in Indochina, and 21 000 in all of Indonesia.[14]

Although primary education remained far from universal, the numbers of students were large in absolute terms. For the future, as in Korea and Taiwan, since most of the increase came in the 1930s, the benefits would only be seen in the next generation, after independence. For the prewar generation, success in Western academic subjects proved the native peoples were capable intellectually. This undermined the paternalistic arguments of the colonial powers. At the same time, because the majority of the schoolchildren (and especially the small numbers of secondary school students) came from relatively wealthy families, education reinforced the position of traditional native elites. In addition, as government functions expanded and the number of school graduates rose, the colonial regimes also recruited natives to serve in the lower levels of their bureaucracies, as well as soldiers in their armies. Education and government service therefore became an avenue for indigenous families to improve their social position. As leaders both of 'traditional' native society and of the new 'modern' native society, these educated men and women became the group on which the imperialist powers depended to maintain their rule. However, this same group also provided the leaders of nationalist opposition movements. They were well aware of developments elsewhere in Asia, and looked particularly to the examples of Meiji Japan, of China under Sun Yatsen, and of the Indian independence movement under Gandhi.[15]

Finally, however, would-be nationalist leaders require an audience, and the audience must be concentrated for nationalist texts to have significant impact. Urban centers therefore provide the most promising ground for nationalist agitation. The central urban places of Southeast Asia expanded, and large immigration into these centers followed. Table 7.1 gives population figures for capital cities in Southeast Asia and the percentage of the national population living in those cities. As with education,

Table 7.1 Urbanization in Asia: population of capital cities and shares of total population, 1880–2000

	1880 (000)	(%)	1910 (000)	(%)	1930 (000)	(%)	1960 (000)	(%)	1980 (mill)	(%)	2000 (mill)	(%)
Seoul, Korea	na	na	223	1.7	343	1.8	2445	9.8	8.3	21.9	9.9	20.9
Taipei, Taiwan	na	na	102	3.1	230	4.9	799	7.0	2.2	12.5	2.6	11.7
Manila, Philippines	154	na	234	2.8	325	2.5	1139	4.2	1.6	3.4	9.9	12.4
Bangkok, Thailand	400	5.7	629	7.6	490	4.3	1330	5.1	4.7	10.5	6.3	10.1
Jakarta, Indonesia	97	0.5	139	na	437	0.7	2907	3.0	6.5	4.4	8.4	3.7
Ho Chi Minh City, Vietnam	81	na	182	na	256	1.4	1251	7.9	3.4	6.5	5.2	6.6
Hanoi, Vietnam	na	na	114	na	135	0.8	415	na	2.6	4.9	2.7	3.4
Singapore, Malaya	139	na	303	13.0	558	14.7	1687	na	2.4	na	4.0	na
Kuala Lum-pur, Malaysia	na	na	47	na	114	na	316	3.9	0.9	6.7	1.4	6.4
Phnom Penh, Cambodia	17	na	62	na	96	na	394	7.3	0.5	7.8	1.0	8.1
Yangon, Myanmar	134	1.5	293	2.4	400	2.8	922	4.1	2.5	7.5	5.6	13.4

Notes: Population figures are given in thousands to 1960, then in millions. Years are the closest available; 'na' means 'not available', or, in the case of Singapore, not applicable. The territories included in the city boundaries have frequently changed between censuses, and recently several capital cities have expanded beyond their designated boundaries, so they are in fact larger than their official figures show. Korea includes only South Korea after 1960. Ho Chi Minh City (Saigon) is compared with the total population of South Vietnam in 1960. Phnom Penh, Cambodia had a population of 1 586 000 (22.5 per cent of the national total) in 1970, but suffered a huge decline under the Pol Pot regime.

Sources: Computed from data in B.R. Mitchell, *International Historical Statistics: Africa, Asia & Oceania 1750-1988* (2nd revised edn; Houndmills: Macmillan, and New York: Stockton Press, 1995); United States Census Bureau, International Data Base, Summary Demographic Data; Geohive, http://www.xist.org.

the absolute increases are impressive. In addition, however, the relative size of the capital cities continued to increase after the departure of the imperial powers. The newly independent states all created highly central-ized governing systems, and these political patterns were reflected in the dominance of capital cities. This continues to be important. Thailand's economic development since 1945 has been epitomized as a continual tension between the 'center' in Bangkok and the 'periphery' in the outer provinces.[16] Manila in particular has been criticized for its negative impact on development in the Philippines because of its contribution to over-centralization, the lack of an economically rational hierarchy of urban centers, deterioration of conditions in the metropolis, and the spillover of the city's problems into adjoining areas.[17]

THE MANAGEMENT GRID UNDER THE COLONIAL REGIMES

BOX 7.1   POINT AND COUNTERPOINT: HARRISONS & CROSFIELD – A BRITISH FIRM IN COLONIAL SOUTHEAST ASIA

Accounts must be vigilantly checked and monitored; sloppiness and oversight will lead to stagnated capital. (Tao Zhu-gong, the Fourth Business Lesson)

In Britain in 1844 two brothers, Daniel and Smith Harrison, formed a partnership with Joseph Crosfield to trade in tea in China. They gradually added other commodities and by the twentieth century the group had diversified into plantation agriculture, building sup-plies, engineering, and real estate, as well as shipping, insurance, and financial services. They expanded along the channels of their existing interests. The tea trade, for instance, led backwards to production through acquisition of plantations, and forward to mar-keting and distribution through a long-term relationship with Twinings.

Harrisons & Crosfield (H&C) expanded largely through mergers and takeovers, and was described by opponents as an 'octopus'. In the case of rubber, they acquired a Canadian chemical firm to process raw materials into industrial chemicals and established another to conduct research into production and processing.

Subsidiaries were either wholly owned by H&C or partly owned by H&C and partly by directors of H&C and directors of the subsidiaries. Acquisitions brought talented employees into the firm, and in H&C's view they created a friendly 'negotiated environment' out of the previously competitive one. They also added new capital, gave access to new markets, and replaced contractual relations with equity and managerial control.

H&C developed a strong head office in London to provide information, advice, capital, and logistical support to overseas branches and subsidiaries. Decision making was decentralized, particularly where new technologies were being developed, with support from the center. The specialist departments of the head office controlled functional areas across all branches and subsidiaries, for instance finance, insurance, and an 'export' department that handled equipment purchases, agency contracts and shipping arrangements. The center's control was reinforced by financial and administrative interconnections. Directors and managers were chosen for their abilities, but in addition all had substantial financial stakes in the firm, and they frequently served on more than one company board. Thus, although the subsidiaries were independent, they were controlled through financial connections and interlocking directorates, with directors and senior managers holding shares.

H&C pursued a very conservative financial management policy, with high levels of retained profits and large reserves. Because the directors held major equity shares in the firm and its subsidiaries, they had no particular desire for higher dividends. New capital was raised from existing shareholders, retained earnings, and reserves. H&C also extended their agency business through the establishment of 'sterling companies' as vehicles for British investors. H&C usually owned only a small share of each company, but provided management services. Many similar sterling companies suffered from lack of direction and failed, but H&C's projects enjoyed relatively high rates of success. Although investing only minimal capital itself, H&C exercised the same tight control as over its direct subsidiaries, and applied the same conservative financial approach. Successful sterling companies were sometimes taken over as subsidiaries.

The transition away from the original family firm structure occurred in two stages, both connected with difficult periods for the company. In 1894, the firm was in trouble, and two salaried managers were made partners. H&C became a limited liability

company in 1908, but only one-sixth of the issued capital was held
by investors without a direct link to the company. Beginning in
1911, again in response to problems, family members began to
retire and chairmen were selected from non-family members. The
last family member gave up his active role in H&C when he joined
Twinings in 1916.

Source: Rajeswary Ampalavanar Brown, *Capital and Entrepreneurship in
Southeast Asia* (Houndmills: Macmillan, and New York: St Martin's Press, 1994),
ch. 3.

Western firms dominated the colonial business scene. Among the so-called
'agency houses' in the British possessions, Harrisons & Crosfield enjoyed
consistent success. In fact, the firm did not report a loss in any year for a
full half-century, from 1890 to 1940. As seen in Box 6.5 and as emphasized
by Rajeswary Brown, conservative financial management, sophisticated
head office structures combined with flexibility for local subsidiary managers, and transformation away from a family partnership towards a
'modern' corporate form, all can be cited as reasons for the consistently
positive results. But as Brown also observes, there is another side as well.
Western firms had no desire for a level playing field, and in fact aside from
themselves and their allies no one else was permitted to play. As a British
firm Harrisons & Crosfield enjoyed connections to the London capital
market that were denied to indigenous firms. The mergers and acquisitions
that drove the growth of the 'octopus' were not always friendly. Where competitors could neither be bought nor driven out of business, Harrisons &
Crosfield attempted to create a 'negotiated environment' through cartel
agreements to divide markets and hold prices high.

When the market turned unfavorable, Western firms called on colonial
governments for assistance. Harrisons & Crosfield's directors were active in
influencing public policy. In particular, H. Eric Miller played a key role in
the preparation of the Stevenson Report at the end of the First World War,
which recommended restrictions on rubber production to stabilize prices.
The scheme favored large-scale Western firms and forced small-scale
'native' producers to bear most of the burden of adjustment. As demand
recovered, Miller worked to end the Stevenson scheme in 1928, but then,
with the onset of the depression in 1930, he led in new attempts to impose
restrictions on output.[18]

In their early days colonial governments relied on Chinese firms for
important revenue-raising functions, in particular the sale of opium. As the
states grew they absorbed these functions themselves, and the Chinese were
increasingly confined to small-scale trade and provision of services such as

rice milling. As we will see in Chapter 8, sometimes they could be spec-tacularly successful, building on networks of connections linking their Southeast Asian operations with markets across the region and northward into China. In general, however, most Chinese firms remained confined to highly competitive areas, and most Chinese firms remained small, family operations. However, at the village level these small Chinese firms became dominant because of their connections outside the village. And, because the local Chinese merchants or rice millers were often moneylenders as well, they were frequently regarded with hostility by their customers and clients.

In contrast to the Japanese in Korea and Taiwan, the colonial govern-ments of Southeast Asia actively discouraged so-called 'natives' from entering commerce and industry. In the Philippines, the United States colo-nial government was content to see the majority remain sharecropping farmers under the domination of the landlord class. In Indochina, the French restricted manufacturing to reserve the market for French goods. In Indonesia, the Dutch wanted labor for export crops, and like the French they hoped to preserve the colonial market for Dutch manufacturers. In Malaysia, the British considered that Malays should remain subsistence farmers. Even more than other colonial powers, the British thought in terms of racial hierarchies. Placing themselves at the apex, they assigned certain limited economic roles to each racial group. Chinese were to serve as middlemen and retail traders, Indians were to work as laborers produc-ing goods for export on plantations or in mines owned by British firms, and Malays were to remain in their village communities, looked after by the hereditary native aristocracy who themselves would be under the guidance of their British advisors.

The empires were exclusive. Imperial powers did not invest in each others' empires. As we have seen, the Japanese pushed industrial develop-ment in Korea and Taiwan, but the colonial governments of Southeast Asia did not. They saw the colonies as markets for their own industries, and they imposed tariffs to favor manufactured products from the 'home' country.[19] Within the colonies, governments attempted to reserve the most profitable sectors for 'home' country firms. Because the colonies were conceived as sources of primary products, these included plantation agriculture and mining, the handling of export crops and minerals, shipping, banking, and insurance. Railway systems and urban centers grew, but infrastructure was constructed only when it suited the interests of the colonial powers. Britain explicitly rationed capital in the colonies through the interwar period.[20] Following the financial collapse in 1929, the Dutch government kept the Dutch East Indies on the gold standard while other countries devalued their currencies, worsening the depression in the colonial economy.[21]

These factors together resulted in a long-lasting disjunction between management for expatriate Westerners, and management for natives. For Western managers, the impact of improved transportation and communications on business operations paralleled their effects on colonial governments. Although information flows were not yet instantaneous, complete written reports could be mailed from the colonies and received by senior managers in Europe or the United States in a week, rather than in months or never. And urgent orders in response to those reports could be virtually instantaneous, sent by telegraph. This meant that junior managers in the colonies were now truly junior, rather than being insulated from their superiors by distance. Despite Harrisons & Crosfield's commitment to decentralized decision making, the London head office exercised strict financial control, and the Export Department organized equipment purchases and logistics. The expatriate managers of H&C's plantations, for instance, would find that most of their important decisions were made for them, and further that their day-to-day management was subject to continual surveillance as well.

Improved transportation and communications also had important social consequences, and these had further long term effects. Like their peers in the colonial governments, expatriate managers now could bring their families to live with them. Whereas a Chinese or 'native' firm would have seen immediate and extended family members as potential employees, however, the wives and children of Western managers were purely dependants. Further, broadening the expatriate Western community by including wives and children had the opposite effect of narrowing the range of social contracts between Westerners and natives.

Colonial societies defined social roles along racial and gender lines. Convention and legislation regulated relations to control contact, and most especially sexual contact, between Europeans and natives. In Indonesia, the children of a Dutch man and a native woman fell under Dutch law if the father recognized them, but otherwise they, and the theoretically inconceivable offspring of a native man and a Dutch woman, fell into a legal gray zone between the European and the native communities. Public functions and the routines of daily life reinforced social distance. Natives appeared to Europeans as household servants, subaltern clerks in offices, or overseers on plantations. Otherwise, for Europeans, natives were invisible. For natives, in contrast, Europeans were continually visible, giving orders in the household, giving orders in the office, giving orders on the plantation, or standing beside or behind native rulers when they gave orders or ordered punishments for transgressions.

Colonial governments, and colonial firms, managed through intermediaries. The native administrations, whether Indonesian *priyayi* regents,

Malay sultans, Vietnamese scholar officials, or the clerks in Philippines government offices, acted on orders from their Western superiors in the colonial governments, and stood between the colonial governments and their native subjects. The European managers of plantations and mines gave orders to their native overseers, who organized and directed the work of their gangs of subordinates. Hiring was frequently done through native labor contractors, and almost always when the workers were from other regions, for instance the Indian workers on the Malayan rubber plantations.

Over time the hostility of natives towards the colonial regimes increased. The colonialists showed no commitment to their colonies. As noted above, the 'home' governments saw the colonies as sources of raw materials and as markets for their manufactured goods. Despite their rhetoric about mutual interests, the imperial powers intended their colonies to contribute to the economic well-being of the 'home' country, not the other way around. And in the private sector it was obvious, for instance, that Harrisons & Crosfield's managers in Malaya worked for Harrisons & Crosfield, not for Malaya.

Memories of this humiliation persist to the present. However, the colonial experience also led to the adoption of the attitudes of the colonialists. Those in positions of authority still maintain an exceptional distance between themselves and their subordinates. Both public and private sector governance in Southeast Asia are marked by a pervasive top-down, paternalistic management style. Geert Hofstede's 'power distance' scale measures the degree to which employees are afraid to express disagreement with their boss, and the degree to which they perceive their boss's decision making style as autocratic or paternalistic. However, the scale also reflects the degree to which employees *prefer* their boss to act autocratically or paternalistically. All Southeast Asian countries scored exceptionally high on this scale, and Malaysia tied for the highest score in the world.[22]

Management through intermediaries also continues. Both government agencies and 'indigenous' (that is, non-Chinese) private firms tend to be tall structures with multiple layers of administration or management. In addition, both public sector employees and private sector managers share the notion that a position in government is, and should be, the apex of personal ambition. Government officials believe themselves to be superior. 'We are the nation's elite, and the country depends on us – it is a terrible responsibility,' said a very young official in the Thai finance ministry in 2003. The condescending attitude of government officials towards private citizens is matched by a widespread deference towards those in 'public service'. Even when resented, the need for approval by government agencies is a recognized and generally accepted fact of life. As seen below, and in Chapter 9, this complex of attitudes affects the institutional grid within which business must function, as well as the internal structure of many indigenous firms.

THE SECOND WORLD WAR AND THE POSTWAR ERA IN SOUTHEAST ASIA

Hostility to the rule of the colonial states led to a number of serious revolts, but none succeeded. Not all 'natives' supported the nationalists. As seen above, many collaborated with, and worked for, the colonial states. Nationalist opposition generally remained confined to the urban centers. Unrest in the countryside tended to be episodic and usually traditionalist or millenarian.[23] In addition, colonial governments played on the ethnic divisions in their possessions, for instance the employment of Karens and other minorities by the British in the administration of Myanmar. These divisions, and greed or economic necessity, also made it possible for police agencies to employ native agents, and for colonial armies to recruit native soldiers.

The defeat of the European powers by Japan, and then the defeat of the Japanese, opened the way for nationalist leaders. Southeast Asian elites regarded the war in terms of the opportunities it might provide to advance their own interests. For Southeast Asian nationalists, the war of the United States and the Europeans against Japan was not a crusade, for their enemy was imperialism. Thailand allied itself with Japan, and Indonesians welcomed the Japanese as liberators. Japanese authorities opened new schools, attempted to stimulate economic development, promoted natives to senior positions in the civil administration, and trained large numbers of native soldiers, especially in Indonesia. However, the increasing hardship and the obvious intention of the Japanese to create their own empire then focused anti-imperialist hostility on them. By the end of the war there were widespread guerilla uprisings, particularly in Myanmar, Malaya, and the Philippines, and nationalist parties waiting to seize power, as in Vietnam and Indonesia.

Inter-war Thailand and the Alliance with Japan

Following Chulalongkorn's death in 1910, the royal clan continued to monopolize office. Army and navy officers and commoner officials resented the favoritism shown to members of the royal family. Then, during the depression, Thailand remained on the gold standard rather than allowing its currency to depreciate. Exports declined, and as its revenues dropped the government cut its budget. The salaries of the bureaucrats and army officers were slashed, and many were dismissed. Senior army officers overthrew the government on 24 June 1932. An attempted royalist restoration was defeated, the King abdicated, and as his successor the government selected his ten-year-old son, who was in school in Switzerland.

Control of the government alternated between Pridi Bhanamyong, a professor of law with a leftist reputation, and Phibun Songkhram, an army officer supported by ultranationalist military leaders. Pridi became prime minister following the 1932 coup. He wanted to end royal absolutism and to open a broader participation in political life, and also favored the expropriation of large agricultural holdings, nationalization of major industrial and commercial enterprises, and what he called a complete 'bureaucratization' of the economy. He was denounced as a 'communist' and forced to flee. However, he was recalled from exile by Phibun after the royalists had been suppressed, and subsequently held a number of high offices.

Pridi and Phibun both believed that the state must assume responsibility for both economic and social development. This meant, on the one hand, changing relations with the imperialist powers. Pridi renegotiated the unequal treaties, and renewed British leases on more favorable terms. However, on the other hand, it also meant combating internal 'enemies' and in particular the Chinese. New laws reserved certain occupations for Thais. The government provided grants and other special assistance to Thai businesses. Government funds also provided capital for joint ventures between government agencies and private interests.

Phibun became prime minister in 1938 and, like Chiang Kaishek in China, he began to portray himself as a national 'leader' and adopted much of the rhetoric and symbolism of South American and European-style authoritarianism. The name of the country was changed from Siam to Thailand ('land of the free') in 1939. Religious revivalism, ultranationalism, and militarism went together. Although the government ordered Thais to wear Western clothing as a symbol of modernity, the government also sponsored a new 'national' dance, and non-Buddhists were pressured to convert to the 'national' Buddhist religion.

Thai army leaders admired Japan, and envied Japan's successes in China. When war broke out, Phibun decided that Japan would be the winner, and Thailand declared war on France. Thailand demanded the return of provinces previously ceded to the French. Japan brokered an agreement with the Vichy administration in Indochina, which returned the provinces to Thailand. Thailand granted the Japanese transit rights and supplies, and in return received further gains in Laos, northern Malaya, and the Shan region of Myanmar. As an ally of Japan, Thailand enjoyed relative independence, but discontent increased as prices rose and Japan's imperialist intentions became more obvious. Imports from Europe and the United States were cut off, and by early 1944 the cost of living had risen fourfold and was accelerating.[24]

In the background, Pridi, who had withdrawn from the government when the Japanese arrived and now served as regent for the young king, organized the Seri Thai (Free Thai) movement, an alliance of divergent dissident elements. In mid-1944, Phibun resigned in favor of a civilian government. His wife later said he had resigned because the postwar situation would be easier with a new prime minister, since 'he had declared war on the Allies, and the Allies were going to win'. Pridi negotiated with the Allies, and adapted Thai policy to the new situation. Thailand agreed to surrender its territorial gains, established relations with the Nationalist government in China, and granted most-favored-nation status to the United States, but also legalized the communist party to please the Russians.[25]

Independence and the Postwar Period in Colonial Southeast Asia

Again the Thai example can be generalized. Following the Japanese conquest, native elite groups retained influence, and because the Japanese appointed natives to higher levels in government administration, they in fact could improve their positions. Individuals and families who emerged as leaders in the postwar period were in general already prominent before the war. There was substantial continuity in nationalist leadership. For political leaders, the war provided the opportunity to move toward independence. However, the war had also raised expectations among groups outside the elites, and the new governments all faced insurgent movements that threatened their positions.

In the Philippines, the United States granted independence on 4 July 1946. Much of central Luzon had fallen under the control of the guerilla People's Anti-Japanese Army (known as the Huks). The movement was diverse, and it was directed as much against the Filipino landlord class as against the Japanese.[26] Branded as 'communists' by the landlords, they were deeply suspect to the Americans in the context of the developing conflict with the Soviet Union, civil war in China, and communist-influenced movements elsewhere in Southeast Asia.

Elite families had maintained the lowest possible profile during the war, waiting for the Americans to return. Manuel Roxas, a wealthy landowner who served the Japanese without breaking his connections with the Americans, was pronounced free of any guilt by American General Douglas MacArthur, and became president. The regime which emerged was corrupt, and well-connected individuals appropriated much of the American aid intended for reconstruction. Violence became institutionalized, and politicians maintained private armies to intimidate opponents. There was no social reform, and the Huks, now calling themselves the People's Army of Liberation, continued their insurgency into the early 1950s.

In 1943, the Japanese declared Burma independent. The new Burmese government declared war on the Allies, but was quickly disillusioned by forced labor and requisitions demanded by the Japanese. An Anti-Fascist People's Freedom League (AFPFL) emerged, led by Aung San. At the end of the war the new British governor invited Aung San and other non-communist members of the AFPFL to join his council. The communists, excluded from power, denounced the AFPFL as 'lackeys of imperialism'. In July 1947, Aung San and other leaders were murdered. His successor, the devout Buddhist U Nu, led the country to independence on 4 January 1948, but in addition to the split with the communists, the government faced demands by minority peoples for self-government or independence. A communist uprising in March 1948 was followed by a revolt of the Karen National Defense Organization. Communists and separatists remained in control of some 10 per cent of the country until the late 1980s.[27]

Indonesians at first received the Japanese enthusiastically, and in Aceh and Sulawesi the Indonesians themselves 'liberated' cities and then handed them over to the Japanese. The Japanese quickly reopened the schools.[28] Elite tracks for the brightest students encouraged self-esteem and anti-Western attitudes. Japanese authorities also drafted young men into the army, which numbered more than a million by 1945. In the cultural sphere, the break with the past was sharp and decisive. Although the nationalists had proclaimed in 1928 that a new Bahasa Indonesia would be the national language, Dutch of course remained the official language, and most native writing was in High Malay. The Japanese eliminated Dutch, and Bahasa Indonesia became the official language. The Japanese established an Indonesian Language Committee, which opened new areas where previously only Dutch had been used, sponsored new textbooks, and published a dictionary.

As elsewhere, Japan's imperialist ambitions created opposition. The requirement to bow toward Tokyo and recognize the divinity of the Emperor offended Muslims, and food requisitions and forced labor alienated the countryside. The Japanese split Indonesia into three divisions, and this damaged the economy severely. There were significant policy differences as well. On the outer islands harsh measures by the Japanese created opposition. On Java, General Imamura Hitoshi pursued a pragmatic 'soft' policy, and freed Sukarno and other nationalists imprisoned by the Dutch. The Japanese also established a puppet government with Indonesian leaders and encouraged an anti-Dutch campaign. Under the Japanese, Indonesian leaders were restricted in what they could say, but they had a captive audience, often trucked in from surrounding areas by the Japanese army. In his autobiography, Sukarno recognized that these rallies

organized by the Japanese had the effect of identifying him personally as
'our leader'. The Japanese attempted to grant independence to Indonesia
in the summer of 1945, but Sukarno did not want to accept independence
from them, and declared independence instead.[29]

Meanwhile, in 1941, the Dutch government in exile had promised a conference to discuss Indonesian self-government at the end of the war, but
they returned in 1945 determined to stay. Negotiations led to an agreement
in 1947 for a United States of Indonesia within a larger union of Dutch
colonies, but the Dutch launched a 'police action' against Nationalist territories. Intervention by the United Nations led to a cease-fire resolution by
the Security Council in August 1947 and planned plebiscites, but the
ceasefire broke down. In January 1949, Indian Prime Minister Jawaharlal
Nehru convened an Asian Conference on Indonesia in New Delhi, which
denied the Dutch refueling facilities for their aircraft and shipping. The
Dutch also faced further pressure from the United Nations and from the
United States, and finally yielded to the demand for independence on
27 December 1949.

The Japanese had considered Malays unready for self-government
because of their 'political immaturity' and only ordered preparations for
independence in July 1945. However, because they did not trust the
Chinese, the Japanese recruited Malays into the police, while most Malay
civil servants remained in their jobs and some were promoted. The Japanese
also retained the sultanates, and in effect returned to the British system.[30]
The Japanese treated ethnic Chinese as enemies and forced large numbers
out of the cities into the countryside. Chinese formed the majority of the
guerilla resistance movement, the Malay People's Anti-Japanese Army
(MPAJA). At the end of the war, the MPAJA attacked Malay 'collaborators'. Following a year of violence the British proposed a new Malay Union
with common citizenship, but Malays interpreted this as reduction in their
power, and they established the United Malays National Organization
(UMNO) to campaign for their interests. In 1948, a new Federation of
Malaya restricted citizenship to Malays.

In June 1948, the Malayan Communist Party (MCP) rose in revolt. The
'emergency' delayed formal independence until 1960. The 8000 to 10 000
guerillas were overwhelmingly ethnic Chinese, supported by possibly
500 000 displaced 'squatters'. The MCP did occupy some districts, but
received no support from the Malay population, and no outside help. The
British won Malay support with a commitment to independence, won many
Chinese with the introduction of a new organization to represent Chinese
interests, and laid out 600 fenced 'new villages' to contain the squatters, but
some 2000 guerillas were still fighting on the Thai–Malay border in the late
1980s.

Although the British remained until 1960, power in Malaya passed to a Malay-dominated government under Abdul Rahman in 1957, with a constitution that gave power to the Malay sultans and made Malay the official language. Malay aristocrats who had been civil servants under the British formed the leadership of the UMNO, and the first three prime ministers came from the aristocracy. It became common for influential figures with aristocratic pedigrees to straddle the public and private spheres as company directors, trust managers, and officials of public corporations, earning themselves the ironic title of 'administocracy'.[31] In 1963, a new Federation of Malaysia included Malaya, Sarawak and Sabah (both non-Malay, but Muslim), and Singapore (75 per cent Chinese). The head of the Singapore government, Lee Kuan Yew, aimed to unite all the non-Malay elements in the federation and then secure control of the federation government. To forestall this threat Abdul Rahman expelled Singapore from the federation in 1965.

In Indochina in March 1945, the Japanese deposed the French colonial administration. They encouraged Cambodian King Narodom Sihanouk to proclaim independence, and ordered the Laotian king to declare independence, and then turned to a prince when he refused. In Cambodia and Laos, the native elites were able to contain popular unrest and work out arrangements with foreigners before, during, and after the war. In Vietnam, in contrast, the previous four decades had produced a revolutionary intelligentsia, a land-poor peasantry, a propertyless class of workers, and the eventual leaders of the revolution, members of communist groups who had developed their strategies and tactics in the 1930s. In the countryside, the communists gained support because of their uncompromising demand for independence and support for the needs of rural communities.[32]

The communists established an organization known as the Viet Minh (an abbreviation for Vietnam Independence Brotherhood League) to bring all groups together for immediate independence. Vo Nguyen Giap became the military leader of guerilla forces in mountainous regions. Communist leader Ho Chi Minh was detained by the Chinese Nationalist government for two years, but was released at Chiang Kaishek's orders to lead the resistance against the Japanese and Vichy French. When the Japanese surrendered on 14 August, the Viet Minh formed a National Liberation Committee with Ho as president. They occupied Hanoi, the last Emperor abdicated in favor of a provisional government, and the Democratic Republic of Vietnam (DRV) was proclaimed.[33]

The DRV did not receive international recognition. The Allies had decided to restore French rule, and authorized Nationalist China to occupy Vietnam north of the sixteenth parallel and Britain to occupy the territory to the south of it. The Nationalist Chinese army treated northern Vietnam 'as if it were a conquered country' and 'rampaged through the countryside in a campaign of loot, plunder, and rape'. Ho, arguing that 'it is better to sniff the French dung for a while than to eat China's all our lives', dissolved the communist party and signed an agreement with the French.[34] However, the French, determined to reassert control, created a Republic of Vietnam, which along with Laos and Cambodia was to remain within the French union.[35] In the emerging Cold War world, the United States and Britain recognized the French creation, while the Soviet Union and the newly-established People's Republic of China recognized the DRV. The Viet Minh were supplied from China, and the French from the United States. In 1953, the French attempted to lure the Viet Minh into a decisive battle at Dien Bien Phu, but Giap's forces surrounded them and cut them off. United States Secretary of State John Foster Dulles saw the use of nuclear weapons as the only way to prevent defeat, but would not act without the British, and they refused because of the danger of Soviet retaliation and a new world war.

Dien Bien Phu fell in 1954, just before an international conference in Geneva. The French regime ended, but the Viet Minh, under pressure from the Russians and Chinese, who were then in favor of 'peaceful coexistence' with the West, accepted a division along the seventeenth parallel pending elections to be held in 1956. In the south, a new government under Ngo Dinh Diem emerged with American support and enjoying 'the best possible American political thinking', in the words of CIA adviser Edward Lansdale.[36] Diem, a member of the Confucian elite, found any opposition intolerable as it called into question his moral superiority as ruler. Police and army units arrested and murdered thousands, and Diem himself died in a coup in 1963. In 1960, the communists revived the southern Viet Minh under the new name of National Liberation Front (NLF), and by 1962 they controlled two-thirds of the villages in the South. To forestall a communist victory, the United States began its direct involvement, and by 1967 there were 525 000 United States troops serving in Vietnam. The resulting destruction disrupted the southern NLF, but the South Vietnam government could not survive without American military support and collapsed in 1975 when that support was withdrawn.

Ho Chi Minh had died in 1969, and the general secretary of the Vietnamese Communist Party, Le Duan, came to exercise a decisive influence over the Soviet-style Politburo. The party 'bore a striking resemblance to the elderly male Confucian oligarchy that had traditionally ruled Vietnam'. Despite its official role as 'proletarian vanguard', fewer than 10 per cent were workers, and only 17 per cent were women. Finally, during the 1980s, another aspect of the older elite culture reemerged, as younger relatives of powerful Politburo members came to occupy the strategic offices just below the Politburo.[37]

THE INSTITUTIONAL GRID

What Kind of Nationalism?

The history outlined above exercises an ongoing influence on public and private sector governance structures. In some districts individuals with personal memories of atrocities committed by the imperial powers during the conquest lived until the late twentieth century, and many with memories of the colonial period, the Japanese invasion, and the wars of independence are still alive. Not surprisingly, therefore, Southeast Asia is a region of intense nationalism and potential hostility to foreigners. Because the states of Southeast Asia are national states, and because they have frequently been intensely 'nationalistic', understanding the institutional grid requires an appreciation of the quality of nationalism. While on the one hand history and nationalist myths underpin the claims of states, on the other hand inherited social structures have limited state capacity. And, while on the one hand national states claim to represent uniform and unified peoples, on the other hand 'foreigners' can include ethnic Chinese who may in fact be fourth- or even fifth-generation residents, and the so-called 'indigenous' peoples are also deeply divided.

Nationalists insist that their nation rests on a primordial, enduring ethnic basis, a combination of race, culture, and rootedness to a particular place. Nationalist historians often project the contemporary consciousness of nationhood back into the distant past, as seen above in the case of Thailand. In Indonesia, the Japanese-sponsored language committee sponsored new histories that portrayed a glorious pre-colonial Indonesian society, then three and a half 'dark centuries' of Dutch rule punctuated by heroic resistance to Dutch oppression, and then the final triumph of a single, unified Indonesian 'nation'. They became school texts and remained standard for the next 20 years.[38] In national school systems, memory overlaps with history and becomes belief. Official myths repeated to successive cohorts of students take on a life of their own, and it is in this form that they affect the actions of individuals, as citizens, government officials, employers, or workers.

Historians and social scientists who study the phenomenon of nationalism disagree with nationalist historians, but they themselves disagree about definitions, evidence, and methods. Some scholars argue that there is a factual basis for the claim that nations possess an inherited identity. Anthony Smith believes that national identity rests on an *ethnie*, an ancient grouping of people residing in a particular area.[39] Others dispute this and argue that there is neither a single identity which must necessarily be derived from the inheritance of the past, nor a single ethnic basis for nations. Benedict Anderson believes that modern nations are 'imagined communities' that can only come into existence when there are sufficiently highly developed means of communication.[40] Liah Greenfeld insists that the creation of single 'national' identities out of previous cultural, ethnic, or regional identifications has always involved the emphasis on some elements, some of them contradictory, and the suppression of others.[41] Further, it appears that, even after the formation of a national state, the 'national' identity continues to evolve. Particularly at higher levels of economic development, affluent and educated individuals may choose to identify with the nation, but they may not.[42]

Modern nationalism has arisen in parallel to the development of industrial economies, but the relationships are disputed. Some see nationalism everywhere as a reaction to modernization and the extension of market relationships into new areas.[43] Western European historians have tended to see 'their' nationalisms as the result of economic development, and the assertion that modern economic growth, representative parliamentary governments, and nationalism were all part of a single broader process was perhaps the central tenet of the so-called 'modernization theory' that was influential in the 1950s and 1960s. In contrast, historians of Central and Eastern Europe argued that the 'latecomer' nations of those regions failed to modernize as the Western European nations had. Instead they developed 'reactive' nationalisms and adopted dictatorial forms of government. In response to the threat posed by the industrialization of Western Europe, and particularly England, they might sponsor rapid industrialization as in Germany, or they might remain locked in a condition of semi-dependency as in Italy or Russia.[44]

Partha Chatterjee has taken the approach of Central and Eastern European historians in his analysis of the emergence of nationalism in the colonial world. Drawing on the work of the Italian social thinker Antonio Gramsci, he argues that the subjection of native elites to the cultural and political 'hegemony' of imperialist domination resulted in a 'passive revolution' that led them to an essential contradiction. Nationalists in colonial societies, says Chatterjee, had to address their texts to two audiences simultaneously, 'both to "the people" who were said to constitute the nation and to the colonial masters whose claim to rule nationalism questioned'. But their messages to both audiences were in fact the same: 'To both, nationalism sought to demonstrate the falsity of the colonial claim that the backward peoples were culturally incapable of ruling themselves in the conditions of the modern world.' Therefore, on the one hand, 'nationalism denied the alleged inferiority of the colonized people', while, on the other hand, 'it also asserted that a backward nation could "modernize" itself while retaining its cultural identity'. That is, colonial nationalists insisted that they were not inferior, but at the same time also admitted that they were backward.[45]

According to Chatterjee, colonial nationalism has bridged the inconsistency in its structure in two ways. First, it asserts that the nation and the state are one and the same. Any questioning of the assertion that the 'people-nation' and the 'state-representing-the-nation' are identical is simply denied legitimacy. The state therefore is responsible for the nation's economic well-being. This defines a large role for the state, which becomes 'the principal mobiliser, planner, guarantor and legitimator of productive investment'.[46] Thailand fits Chatterjee's scheme closely. After resigning near the end of the war, Phibun Songkhram returned to power in the 1950s. He argued that there were four fundamental political institutions that played a unique role in Thailand: the monarchy, the assembly, the bureaucracy, and the military. But he emphasized the military, because only it was 'abiding and permanent', whereas the assembly could be 'abolished through various events and causes'. Comparing Thailand to Germany and Japan, Phibun argued that the military was in fact the expression of the popular will because of its unique ability to build a stronger nation.

Ironically, Phibun lost power to Sarit Thanarat, the head of the Thai army, in a coup in 1958. Sarit claimed to represent a 'Thai form of democracy'. He drew on the ideas of Wichit Wathakan, an intellectual who had served governments since the 1930s. Like Phibun, Sarit justified the appointment of military officers and bureaucrats to serve in the parliament, because, he said, 'we work with honesty, scholastic competence, and just decision-making which is not under the influence of any private party and does not have to demonstrate personal heroism for purposes of future elections'. Following Wichit, Sarit said the King was the source of Thailand's 'one national spirit', the font of spiritual and moral leadership for the nation. Comparing Thailand with Meiji Japan, Sarit viewed the army as 'the army of the King'. Significantly, however, he extended the comparison with Meiji Japan in insisting that the role of the King was passive. While the King provided spiritual and moral leadership, it was the government that played the active role of deciding policy. Thailand's state, said Sarit, consisted of three strata, the government, the bureaucracy, and the people, and it was the function of the government to make policy, of the bureaucracy to implement it, and of the people to accept it.[47]

Second, Chatterjee argues that colonial nationalism asserts that there is a privileged 'inner' quality to the national identity, inaccessible to outsiders. This defines a further large role for the state, because it is the state's responsibility to foster and protect the nation's essence. The state is therefore also responsible for the nation's morals. For example, in a speech in May 1945 to the Body to Investigate Measures for the Preparation of Indonesian

Independence, Professor Supomo, the leading judicial official on Java during the Japanese occupation and a leader in drafting the 1945 constitution, argued that Western individualism and liberalism 'invariably gave rise to imperialism and exploitation'. In contrast, he said,

> The inner spirit and spiritual structure of the Indonesian people is characterized by the ideal of the unity of life, the unity *kawulo-gusti*, that is of the outer and the inner world, or the macrocosmos and microcosmos, of the people and their leaders. All men as individuals, every group or grouping of men in a society . . . is considered to have its own place and its own obligations according to the law of nature, the whole being aimed at achieving spiritual and physical balance. . . . So it is clear that if we want to establish an Indonesian state in accordance with the characteristic features of Indonesian society, it must be based on an integralist state philosophy, on the idea of a state which is united with all its people, which transcends all groups in every field.[48]

Building on Chatterjee's analysis, we may add that, because it asserts that backward nations can modernize themselves, because it asserts that modernization must be led by the state, but also because it asserts that modernization cannot undermine the inner essential core of the national identity, colonial nationalism therefore defines a very large role for the leaders of the state. As we have seen, the imperialist powers claimed that government intervention in the economy was necessary because native peasants and artisans were 'traditional', meaning unsophisticated, backward, and irrational. As we have also seen repeatedly, this was not true. Rather, it was an ideological justification for the imperial governments to remain in control. However, it is important that this portion of imperialist ideology was frequently adopted by the new nationalist leaders, thereby becoming a justification for old elites to transmute themselves into new elites.

The leaders of Southeast Asian nations have recognized the divisions in their societies, and have concluded that it is they, the leaders, who will have to act to overcome them. Sukarno defined what he called 'guided democracy':

> In Guided Democracy the key ingredient is leadership. The Guider . . . incorporates a spoonful of so-and-so's opinions with a dash of such-and-such, always taking care to incorporate a *soupçon* of the opposition. Then he cooks it and serves his final summation with 'OK, now my dear brothers, it is like this and I hope you agree . . .' It's still democratic because everybody has given his comment.

Following the violent fall of Sukarno's government, for 30 years Soeharto used the broad powers of the presidency to maintain his 'New Order'.[49]

Recreating, and in some cases literally inventing, elements of so-called 'Javanese tradition', Soeharto identified himself with an image of the Javanese king. Power in this view centered on the person of the king. However, somewhat paradoxically, the king never had to exercise power directly. Rather, his subordinates were expected to anticipate his wishes and act on his behalf. Whether this is an accurate reflection of Javanese tradition, and whether it adequately describes Soeharto's own political methods, are debatable.[50] However, the vision appears to have widespread resonance among Indonesia's leaders. During her period as President, Sukarno's daughter Megawati Sukarnoputri, for instance, preferred to act to ratify decisions made by others, rather than herself become identified with any particular policy position.

In the Philippines, President Ferdinand Marcos identified the 'politics of dependence' as the Philippines' most intractable problem. The poor masses, he said, had come to depend on 'the benefits – jobs, handouts, help in dealing with an often lazy and corrupt bureaucracy – that they could get from the rich and the powerful in exchange for their loyalty and courteous respect'. He argued that only 'martial law' could combat these entrenched relationships. The Philippines, he said, could use martial law to build democracy, something that Westerners simply could not understand.

> ... to the Western mind, martial law by itself is outrageous. ... we in the Philippines have developed the new idea of a reform government under martial law. ... we are using it as the legal means to bring about badly needed and drastic reforms in our country. ... I believe that other democracies – especially in the poor countries – can use martial law in the same way.[51]

Marcos fell a decade later to the 'people's power' movement that placed Cory Aquino in the presidency, and his regime is now remembered as spectacularly corrupt, but we need to remember that he was elected, and overwhelmingly reelected, as a reformer who campaigned for 'rice and roads' against the weak and corrupt regime of Diosdado Macapagal, and that he did in fact disarm the private armies. Elites continue to focus on the presidency as a potential source of patronage.[52] But, at the same time, the President remains the perceived driver of reform and social change.

In Malaysia, in 2002, Prime Minister Mahathir Mohamad chided Malays for leaning on the 'crutches' of the privileges accorded to protect them.

> Unfortunately their view is that the crutches are the symbols of their superior status in the country. The sad thing is that they are not even using the crutches properly. ... There is a minority of Malays who are confident enough to think of doing away with these aids gradually, but they are a small minority.

Unfortunately, their numbers are not going to increase anytime soon and these people are generally regarded as traitors to the Malay race.[53]

Mahathir closed his speech with an injunction to Malays to change their culture, develop a 'proper work ethics' and look toward work as a reward in itself. 'They must regard achievements at work as a reward. Although there should be some financial rewards, it must not outweigh the satisfaction obtained from the result of their work.' However, the subtext, since he presumed that the majority of Malays would continue not to have a work ethic and would continue to demand the crutches of privilege, was that the preferential treatment of Malays and the guiding role of leaders such as himself would continue indefinitely.

Thailand: the Postwar Institutional Grid

The relationships among nationalist ideology, leadership, the state, and society at large can be illustrated through the Thai example. Nationalism has not brought stability, and government has been particularly unstable in Thailand. Since 1932, the country has experienced 14 revolutions, ten constitutions, and over 30 changes of administration. Periods of rule by decree have alternated with experiments in constitutional rule. Military leaders have dominated, but they have had to balance alliances among the royalist party, nobility, and senior bureaucrats. Although the forms of government responsible to parliament have generally been retained, the actual operation of government has remained in the hands of the elite. Economic growth has been rapid, but the equation of the state with the nation has remained, and so has continued dependence on foreign capital, first American and then Japanese.[54]

Thailand is a kingdom, and the king remains the ultimate repository of sovereignty and the ultimate source of power. In addition, the large extended royal family is an interest group in its own right. King Bhumibol Adulyadej personally has immense influence. He enjoys wide respect, even reverence, among ordinary Thai citizens. He also can make or break governments. Although he has generally 'reigned' and not 'ruled', he has intervened directly twice in political crisis situations. On both occasions his action forced an end to open conflict. His interventions have lasting impact. His rebuke to the army in 1992 removed the military from politics for 14 years, and the bloodless coup of 2006 came with his approval.

Conflicts within the government carried over from the prewar period, between the followers of Phibun and Pridi on the one hand, and between both groups and the royalist party on the other. In 1946, Pridi became Prime Minister. A period of cooperation between Pridi and the royalists ended when Pridi insisted on an elected Senate, rather than the appointed body favored by the royalists, and then packed the Senate with his supporters. The king was murdered in 1946 and Pridi was accused of complicity. In 1947 came a military coup, backed by royalists, demobilized soldiers, and followers of Phibun. In 1948, Phibun returned to power as Prime Minister, and despite attempted countercoups by Pridi supporters, he held office until 1957. The military–royalist government introduced a new constitution with an appointed senate, permission for military officers and civilian bureaucrats to sit in Parliament and hold cabinet office, and increased powers for the king. Regional protest in the northeast and in the south was crushed, and a number of opposition leaders were murdered, as were suspected leftists, particularly Chinese with contacts in China.

Having secured its position, the army gradually reduced the power of the royalists. Phibun encouraged the centralization of the army under Sarit Thanarat. To balance the army, Phibun also fostered the expansion of the police under Phao Siriyanond. In 1957, Phibun attempted to secure his position over these two powerful subordinates. Returning to the authoritarian approach he had taken 20 years before, he staged an election featuring himself as an Argentine-style 'Peronist' popular leader. He used Phao's police to organize his campaign. In response, Sarit and the army seized power. Phibun and Phao fled, and Sarit became Prime Minister. The coup also entrenched an alliance of royalist noble families, bureaucrats, senior army officers, and business leaders. The bureaucracy increased in size, government departments multiplied, and the annual military budget rose from US$20 million in the early 1950s to US$250 million in the early 1970s.[55]

Centralization of power in Bangkok required more direct administration of the provinces. New forestry regulations outlawed the migratory (or swidden) pattern of cultivation typical of many hilly areas. The prohibition of opium growing in 1958 destroyed another source of livelihood for rural villages. Police and military units attempted to suppress opposition, and their actions created support for the Thai Communist Party. Thai communists received support from China and Vietnam. In 1965, they announced the beginning of a guerilla war. By 1969, districts in 35 of the 71 provinces were officially designated as 'communist-infested sensitive areas'. Two large-scale assaults on communist base areas in 1972 ended disastrously.

Opposition to the military government increased in Bangkok as well, among the rising numbers of university students, but also among business leaders and other members of the elite, as economic growth slowed. In 1973, student demonstrators clashed with police and more than 100 students died. The military prepared to reassert its control by force, but the King intervened. He ordered the prime minister and his deputy to leave the country. However, the new government proved unstable. Renewed communist agitation in Bangkok, the fall of Vietnam, a confrontation with the United States over the presence of American forces in Thailand, and a reluctance of foreign investors to risk their capital in the uncertain climate, led to widespread fear of a communist coup and a resurgence of support for the conservative bureaucracy and military. The King shifted his support to the right and granted the exiled prime minister permission to return. A series of violent incidents culminated, in late 1976, in a military assault on the campus of the leftist Thammasat University in which some 1300 died. The new government pursued its opponents, all of whom were labeled communists, ruthlessly. Thousands fled to the countryside to join the insurgents, and at the time it seemed this increase in strength might bring the communists to power.[56]

The government survived the crisis, the economy recovered, and Thailand enjoyed high rates of growth through the 1980s and up to 1997.[57] Agreement with China on citizenship for Chinese in Thailand made possible a more complete assimilation of several million Chinese immigrants, a development often cited as an important background factor in the country's economic success. In the provinces a boom in cash crops led to alliances between local military commanders and wealthy individuals. Rapid growth and a proliferation of infrastructure projects provided further opportunities.[58] From 1976 to 1991, all prime ministers were army generals, but the ruling coalition divided. Periodic elections failed to produce a majority. Large numbers of successful businessmen entered political life, and they needed money to buy votes and provide patronage for supporters. Senior bureaucrats were alienated when the government removed a number of them from positions in state enterprises. Proposed cuts in the army budget opened further disputes. The resulting instability led to another military coup in 1991. Demonstrations began in April 1992 and continued into May. The army moved to suppress them, and several hundred people were killed. However, the King intervened again, demanded a halt to the violence, and in effect ordered the army to remove itself from political life.

New elections in September 1992 gave the opposition party a narrow plurality, but the distribution of seats meant that reformers and liberals centered in Bangkok could not hope to dominate, and in 1995 the more conservative provincial-based parties returned to power.[59] The instability, inefficiency, and corruption of government, and preferential treatment of favored rural districts, all alienated business leaders and the professional middle classes. Pressure for reform grew, and drafting began on a new constitution. The draft pleased the national media and urban reformers, but the political elites generally opposed it. Then the 1997 economic crisis further discredited the existing framework, and public pressure forced Parliament to adopt the new constitution.

The 1997 Constitution seemed to mark a milestone in the development of Thai political institutions. In February 2001, Thaksin Shinawatra became Prime Minister. Of Chinese descent, but also a former senior police official, he was the head of the largest information technology and telecommunications company in the country. He had used his fortune to establish his own party, Thai Rak Thai (Thais Love Thais), which ran a clever, and expensive, American-style campaign that relied on mass advertising promoting more effective economic management, transparency, and efficiency in government. Thaksin increased his majority in 2005, but disappointed observers. Reform slowed, notably in the telecommunications sector where his own firm remained dominant. The government placed its supporters in key positions, and by mid-2004 Thaksin family companies controlled more than 10 per cent of the shares on the Thai stock exchange. Police and army units killed at least 2400 accused drug dealers in urban areas and hundreds of Muslim insurgents in the south.[60]

In early 2006, the Thaksin family sold their 49.6 per cent holding in Shin Corp to Temasek, Singapore's government-owned holding company, for 73.3 billion baht (US$1.9 billion). They paid no tax, and the resulting scandal led to mass protests and to petitions to the king to intervene as he had in the early 1990s.[61] In September, army leaders overthrew the government and announced plans for yet another constitution that would include ongoing provisions for military oversight of civilian administrations.

STATE CAPACITY: THE THAI EXAMPLE

BOX 7.2   POINT AND COUNTERPOINT: THAILAND'S REGULATION OF FOREIGN INVESTMENT

The good and the bad must be clearly distinguished; negligence will lead to confusion and chaos. (Tao Zhu-gong, the Twelfth Business Lesson)

The Thai government regulates foreign investors carefully and attempts to distinguish clearly between the good and the bad. The economic activities of 'aliens' in Thailand fall under the Foreign Business Act (FBA) of 1999, administered by the Board of Investment (BOI). The FBA defines an 'alien' as follows:

- a natural person who is not of Thai nationality;
- a juristic entity that is not registered in Thailand;

- a juristic entity incorporated in Thailand with foreign share-holding accounting for one-half or more of the total number or value of shares;
- a limited partnership or ordinary registered partnership whose managing partner or manager is a foreigner.

This means that, for a firm to escape the provisions of the FBA, it must be majority-owned by Thai nationals, registered in Thailand, and have a Thai national as its managing partner or manager. Although 'in general, foreigners enjoy the same basic rights as Thai nationals', the government excludes them from a number of areas. In addition, even in areas where foreigners are permitted, 'Thai participation will frequently be required in those activities seeking permission from the BOI.' Further areas are subject to specific limitations. There are three lists. List 1 identifies areas that are strictly prohibited to aliens:

- newspaper undertakings and radio and television station undertakings;
- lowland farming, upland farming, or horticulture;
- raising animals;
- forestry and timber conversions from natural forests;
- fishing for aquatic animals in Thai waters and Thailand's Exclusive Economic Zone;
- extraction of Thai medical herbs;
- trade in and auctioning of Thai ancient objects or ancient objects of national historical value;
- making or casting Buddha images and making monks' bowls;
- dealing in land.

Areas on List 2 are prohibited to aliens unless specific permission is granted by the Commerce Ministry, by and with an appropriate Cabinet resolution. It includes the following:

- production, disposal, and sale of firearms, ammunition, gunpowder, and explosives; components of firearms, gunpowder, and explosives; armaments and military vessels, aircraft, or conveyances; all kinds of war equipment or their components;
- domestic transport by land, water, or air, inclusive of the undertaking of domestic aviation;

- dealing in antiques or objects of art and works of art, and Thai handicrafts;
- production of wood carvings;
- raising silkworms, producing Thai silk thread and weaving, or printing patterns on Thai silk textiles;
- production of Thai musical instruments;
- production of articles of gold or silver, willowware, nickel-bronze ware, or lacquer ware;
- production of crockery and terracotta ware that is Thai art or culture;
- production of sugar from sugarcane;
- salt farming inclusive of making salt from salty earth;
- making rock salt;
- mining, inclusive of stone blasting or crushing;
- timber conversions to make furniture and articles of wood.

Finally, areas on List 3 are prohibited to aliens unless permission is granted by the Director General of the Department of Commercial Registration, Ministry of Commerce, by and with the approval of the Foreign Business Board:

- rice milling and production of flour from rice and farm crops;
- fishery, limited to propagation of aquatic animals;
- forestry from replanted forests;
- production of plywood, wood veneer, chipboard, or hardboard;
- production of natural lime;
- accounting service undertakings;
- legal service undertakings;
- architectural service undertakings;
- engineering service undertakings;
- construction, except construction of things that provide basic services, both to the public with respect to public utilities or communications and which require the use of special instruments, machinery, technology or expertise in construction and a minimum capital of the alien of at least 500 million baht;
- brokerage or agency undertakings, except: trading in securities or services concerning futures trading in agricultural commodities, financial instruments, or securities; trading in or the procurement of goods or services needed for production by, or providing the services of, an enterprise in the

same group; trading, purchasing (for others) or distributing or finding domestic or overseas markets for selling goods made domestically or imports as an international trading business, with a minimum capital of the alien of at least 100 million baht; other lines of business stipulated in Ministerial Regulations;

- auctioning, except: international bidding that is not bidding in antiques, ancient objects or objects of art that are Thai works of art, handicraft or ancient objects, or of national historical value; other types of auction, as stipulated in Ministerial Regulations;
- domestic trade concerning indigenous agricultural produce or products not prohibited by any present law;
- retail trade in all kinds of goods with an aggregated minimum capital of less than 100 million baht or a minimum capital for each store of less than 20 million baht;
- wholesale trade in all kinds of goods with a minimum capital for each store of less than 100 million baht;
- advertising undertakings;
- hotel undertakings, except for hotel management services;
- tourism;
- sale of food or beverages;
- plant breeding and propagation, or plant improvement undertakings;
- all other service businesses except for service businesses prescribed in Ministerial Regulations.

An alien can engage in businesses in Lists 2 or 3 if he is a 'promoted investor' in accordance with the Investment Promotion Act, the Industrial Estate Authority of Thailand Act, or other laws. In addition, alien juristic entities allowed to engage in List 2 activities must meet the following two conditions:

- At least 40 per cent of all shares are held by Thai persons or non-alien juristic entities (this may be reduced to 25 per cent on a case-by-case basis);
- Two-fifths of the members of the Board of Directors are Thai.

Preferred foreign investors are large, as seen especially in the exceptions granted to large infrastructure projects in List 3, and the regulations are designed to bring the maximum amount of capital directly into Thailand. An alien generally must invest at least two or three million baht in their business, depending on the kind of business, although the minimum capital and time frame for bringing it into Thailand are prescribed by ministerial regulations, and may be altered, for instance in the case of re-investment.

Thai authorities have had problems in the past with foreigners evading the restrictions on investment in various ways. Under the new act, the range of fines has increased from 100 000 to 1 million baht, and a provision introduced for imprisonment for up to three years.

Source: Thailand, Board of Investment, http://www.boi.go.th/english/business/legal_issues.html#1.

As we have seen, in Southeast Asia nationalist ideology and the personal inclinations of individual leaders have emphasized the central role of the state. The Southeast Asian state has claimed, in Partha Chatterjee's phrase, to act as 'the principal mobiliser, planner, guarantor and legitimator of productive investment'. However, as we have also seen, the claims of Southeast Asian states have typically exceeded their abilities. Governments plan for economic development, but announced policies have not been implemented. Detailed regulations are published, but reliable information is difficult to obtain. Procedures appear unnecessarily complex, and 'one-stop' approval procedures can require many separate visits to several different ministries. At upper levels government motives are not transparent, while at lower levels government functions are inefficient. And yet, in a frustrating paradox, both foreign and indigenous firms must cope with the condescending and frequently arrogant attitude of government officials, who can and will delay or refuse permissions or licenses as it suits them.

Political scientists and public policy theorists have puzzled over the paradox of states that claim to be strong but lack effectiveness. Origins are important. Joel Migdal argues that a necessary condition for the emergence of a genuinely strong state is a calamity involving massive social dislocation. In addition he lists four sufficient conditions: a favorable 'world historical moment', the perception of serious external threats, an independent and technically competent bureaucracy, and skilled top leaders.[62] Structures are also important. The governance structures that frame the field of business operations in any country can be conceptualized along the three dimensions of state capacity, policy capacity, and administrative capacity. 'State capacity' refers to the government's ability to mobilize social and economic power to achieve its goals. 'Policy capacity' refers to the government's ability to marshal information and decision-making power to make intelligent choices and set strategic policy directions. 'Administrative capacity' refers to the efficient management of resources in the various processes required for delivering the outputs of government, such as public services and the equitable enforcement of regulations. The three aspects of capacity are interrelated, each supporting the other two.[63]

As we have seen above, the Second World War created both the crisis and the world historical moment for the emergence of new states, and nationalist movements threw up a number of talented charismatic leaders. However, the independent states remained dependent on the former colonial powers, for technology, for capital, and for management expertise. It is worth looking at Thailand's regulation of foreign investment in some detail, first because the stipulations reflect the concerns not only of Thai officials but of recipient countries throughout the region, and second because they embody the dilemmas of state capacity and the institutional grid across Southeast Asia.[64] Foreign investment is seen as double-edged, on the one hand as a strategic lever to accelerate development, but on the other hand as a threat that could undermine the national culture and lock the country into a state of permanent dependency. As in the other countries in the region, the Thai state has reserved certain sections of the economy to itself, and also insisted on its right to regulate and control development elsewhere in the economy.

Firstly, there is an explicit assertion that 'foreigners in Thailand derive their legal rights primarily from the domestic laws of Thailand', a statement with the weight of history behind it. Political leaders in Southeast Asia remember the imposition of extraterritoriality by the imperialist powers in the nineteenth and early twentieth centuries. In addition it is a direct challenge to those today who might like to see international regulations, notably those of the World Trade Organization, or treaty obligations such as the Free Trade Agreements between Thailand and the United States and Japan, take precedence over national regulatory regimes.

Secondly, as with other countries, this public face of Thai investment policy reflects internal political considerations. Some areas and some industries have demanded and received protection for foreign competition, notably the large number of people engaged in farming and fisheries (List 1) and small-scale retail trade (List 3). In addition, however, there is also both the concern to protect and preserve the national culture from foreign intrusion, and the strategic vision of a future more highly developed Thai economy. List 1, for instance, preserves Thai control over sources of news and information, and Thai control over sales of land. List 2 names a number of specific areas where foreigners are perceived to have an adverse effect on art and culture, customs, or native manufactures and handicrafts. It also restricts foreign participation in businesses concerning national security or safety or with an impact on natural resources and the environment. List 3 identifies the government's strategic goals for economic development by excluding foreigners from businesses in which Thais are not yet ready to compete on an equal footing.

Policy is often caught between modernizers and traditionalists, or between market reformers and those favoring state-led development. The example of Indonesia in the 1970s and 1980s, where policy reflected the shifting balance between the market orientation of the American-trained 'Berkeley mafia' and the support for strategic state enterprises and 'competitive advantage' of B.J. Habibie, the Minister of Research and Technology, has been intensively studied.[65] In the Thai case we see two sets of values in contention, an ideology of state-directed development, and Buddhist economics, a vision of self-sufficiency shared by the King, which we will look at in Chapter 9. The central government remains committed to rapid economic growth and integration into the international economy. These ideas go back to Chulalongkorn and continue to the present. But there are divisions. The army has its own interests, if not warfare and defense, then at least protecting its share of the government budget. The senior bureaucrats also have their interests. Each ministry has its own turf, and as a group these men have their power and incomes to protect. The aristocracy and the extended royal family are another power group. Industrial and financial interests form another grouping, although they are further divided by region (Bangkok v. provinces), ethnic group (Sino-Thai v. indigenous), and their relation to foreign firms (subcontractors and partners v. competitors).

Thailand's position in the world economy remains dependent. The boom beginning in the late 1980s was led by foreign investment. The emerging domestic groups often depended on foreign sources of funds, and foreign capital dominated in a number of key areas.[66] Growth depended at first on commodity exports, and then on low-end technology manufacturing, which in turn depended on low wages. But other countries now compete with Thailand in export crops such as rice, and other countries now offer lower wages. Real wages rose rapidly after 1990. The rural labor surplus had been absorbed, and the export and service sectors competed for workers.

Thailand needs to move to higher value-added production, but this will be difficult. Productivity increased very slowly during the boom. As elsewhere in Southeast Asia, the school system is poor, especially in secondary education. In 1999, the Thai government raised the number of compulsory years of schooling from six to nine and eliminated the fees previously paid by high school students, but the impact of these reforms will not be seen in the labor force for at least a decade. Growth and wealth have concentrated in Bangkok, with its legendary traffic jams. The provinces have been left behind. At the same time, politicians need to provide for their clients in the rural areas. The need for this patronage in rural districts means that elected governments often damage the interests of urban groups such as the business associations, and this has been one of the sources of political instability and the fragility of elected governments.[67]

Many believe Thailand's future success depends on the balance between the state and private capitalists. This balance is disputed. Kevin Hewison argued for instance that the shifts from direct state investment to an import substitution strategy emphasizing the private sector in the 1950s, and then towards an export-oriented strategy in the 1980s, reflected not so much changes in policy orientation as shifts in the symbiotic relationship between local capitalists and the state.[68] More positive analyses have seen Thai politics as a 'moving equilibrium' with several power centers balancing each other so none gains permanent supremacy: the military, the political parties, the king as mediating force between them, and business as an 'increasingly important participant'.[69] Since the 1970s, Thai business associations have grown to play a leading role in state–business relations. In this interpretation the associations have actively helped to shape state policies, for instance the shift to export-oriented industrialization. Some argued in the early 1990s that Thai business could force its demands on the bureaucracy, in contrast to 'developmental states' such as Japan.[70]

These background considerations lead to an ambivalent judgment of Thailand's state capacity. There is in one sense too much central control, in that resources have over the decades come to be concentrated on the prime minister. As a result the Office of the Prime Minister is an unwieldy grouping of departments and agencies rather than an effective central policy-making unit. A prime minister can force an agenda, as for instance Thaksin Shinawatra initially attempted to do in the area of information technology, but typically this came through the creation of yet another Prime Minister's department, which competed and therefore contended with existing agencies.[71]

In terms of policy capacity, the past record of Thai governments is not encouraging. Coalition cabinets have been seen as a division of the spoils of office, and ministers look more to gaining access to resources than to the quality of the advice they receive and pass on to the head of the government. A tradition of 'leaving policy to the bureaucrats' is reinforced by the power of ministries to draft legislation in their areas. The ministries are tall structures, hierarchical and exclusive. Since the 1930s, coordination has tended to come only through high-level committees that include representatives of all agencies likely to be affected by any decision. Experienced bureaucrats are adept at using such committees to delay and thereby undermine initiatives they believe will harm the interests of their home department. System-wide initiatives, for instance in the IT area, are difficult to implement.[72]

Thai administrative capacity is low. There is widespread patronage in appointments, lack of performance incentives, and over-centralization. Thai officials are only a generation removed from a time when officials lived from their positions, by extracting fees for their services rather than relying on regular salaries, and the tradition of offering gifts in return for favors from officials remains pervasive. Gifts are offered internally as well, to gain favor from superiors. The civil service is overstaffed, both by international standards and according to the government's own stated targets, but there is little incentive to reduce numbers. Senior officials exercise great power, and their power increases with the number of their subordinates. This is also important in providing opportunities for political patronage, adding another reason for those senior officials to resist reform.[73] The Office of the Civil Service Commission, which, significantly, is located in the Office of the Prime Minister, relies largely on the input of external advisors, and on a demonstration effect from pilot projects undertaken in reform-friendly ministries.[74]

Ongoing Problems

The Thai example again can be generalized. The paradoxical situation of states that claim to be strong while in fact having quite low capacity has been and remains common in the region. The continuing influence of narrow elites has remained, with the Philippines the most widely-studied example.[75] Southeast Asian states have shared a tendency for the government sector, and the numbers of government officials, to grow. Bureaucratic control over the economy and the direct involvement of civil servants in business together have caused a blurring of the boundaries between state, economy, and society, a phenomenon already identified as 'bureaucratic capitalism' in the 1980s.[76]

As in Thailand, most Southeast Asian states possess relatively large armed forces, and the military has often played an important role, not only in politics but in the economy as well. In Indonesia, local military units have involved themselves in business enterprise to supplement the inadequate budgets allocated by the central authorities. Even when legitimate, such undertakings blur the distinction between public and private. And many of the army's business activities have been less than legitimate, and some have been simply corrupt. Soeharto himself was removed from his command in 1959 for being 'a shade too energetic' in his efforts to improve his own and his division's finances by such means.[77] In mid-2002, General Endriartono insisted that the army had no option but to continue to supplement its budget through its business interests. The government, meaning then-President Megawati Sukarnoputri, explicitly approved the continuation of these operations, but Endriartono refused to make public any audited statements of the army's business activities.[78]

As argued above, nationalist ideologies have supported systems designed for strong, energetic leaders. As in the Thai case, prime ministers and presidents have driven agendas, based on their own independent policy capacity, but in the absence of strong leadership policy drifts. Since Soeharto's fall, no Indonesian president has succeeded in re-knitting the threads of the networks through which he exercised power. In the Philippines, presidents frequently draw on the advice of high-level committees outside the regular bureaucratic framework, but since the early years of the Marcos regime no president has achieved signal success in key areas such as land reform, health, education, high-level technological development, or the government's chronic financial difficulties.

In Malaysia, much of the advice given to the Prime Minister also emerges from his own office or from closely connected organizations and institutes. For two decades Mahathir Mohamad pursued his Vision 2020, a program intended to move Malaysia to the status of a highly developed country early in the twenty-first century. Mahathir's successes include a high rate of growth, rising per capita income, and a rising share of manufacturing in output and exports.[79] Nevertheless, although administrative capacity at the upper levels appears high, this conceals serious problems. Senior bureaucrats deferred to Mahathir, partly out of fear of the consequences of disobedience, but it is not clear whether his successors have established their authority to the same extent. At lower levels the bureaucracy is not efficient.

Public service reform in Malaysia, again viewed from the top, is close to international best practice, but has not touched the mass of serving officials. Under Mahathir the Implementation and Coordination Unit (ICU), located in the Prime Minister's Department, had a staff of 600 and a complex set of governing committees, the most senior one chaired by the Prime Minister personally. In the late 1990s, a new information system called PMS II was introduced as an E-Government Pilot Project to monitor expenditure. ICU staff verified the process of data entry at ministry, state, and district levels. Nevertheless, officials often failed to enter data accurately and on time. The reporting requirements increased workloads, and inadequate training, a tendency to refer problems upwards, and false reporting to cover shortcomings and escape threatened visits by inspection teams, created serious problems. The system allowed no scope for delegated authority or local initiative, and although it reported deviations from planned expenditure, it could not identify the reasons.[80]

As in Thailand, low state capacity is accompanied by both inefficiency and corruption. With the striking exception of Singapore, Transparency International's annual rankings show Southeast Asian countries to have high levels of perceived corruption. Whereas Singapore consistently scores over nine on the ten-point scale, the others range from five for Malaysia, down to two for Indonesia, one of the lowest scores in the world.[81] The fact that choice government contracts, mining concessions, or logging rights go to domestic and foreign firms with the best connections is a matter of public record. Pressures from foreign investors for quick solutions to their perceived problems play a role, for instance in the relationship between Japanese demand for wood products and unsustainable levels of logging in Southeast Asian forests.[82]

In the case of Indonesia, the World Bank estimated in the early 1990s that rainforests were being felled at a rate 50 per cent above that which might be sustainable, and that the government's inability to increase royalties – the direct result of the connections of logging interests to Soeharto – was causing a loss of potential revenue of US$500 million per year.[83] Illegal mining poses serious environmental and health dangers, but again is often supported by local military commanders.[84] Patronage networks extend across government departments and outward into the private sector. Although the prestige of government service is high, actual salaries are generally low. Low salaries also lead to inefficiency even in the absence of corruption because officials need second jobs to support themselves. With a sort of cynical optimism, Soeharto once said that, when Indonesia had reached a level of development which would permit adequate official salaries, the problem of corruption would disappear.[85] For the present, as seen in the next two chapters, the existing structures continue to frame the operation of business in the region.

FURTHER READING

The outline of Southeast Asia's historical grid is drawn largely from my own book, Frank B. Tipton, *The Rise of Asia: Economics, Society and Politics in Contemporary Asia* (Basingstoke: Macmillan, 1998), which rests on a number of other works dealing with individual countries and themes. For Thailand in particular I have relied on the excellent book by Pasuk Phongpaichit and Chris Baker, *Thailand: Economy and Politics* (Kuala Lumpur: Oxford University Press, 1995). Thongchai Winichakul, *Siam Mapped: A History of the Geo-Body of a Nation* (Honolulu: Hawaii University Press, 1994) is an important study of the role of territorial definition in the creation of a national identity.

General introductions to the region include David J. Steinberg et al., *In Search of Southeast Asia: A Modern History* (revised edn; Honolulu: University of Hawaii Press; St Leonards: Allen & Unwin, 1987); Chris Dixon, *Southeast Asia in the World Economy: A Regional Geography* (Cambridge: Cambridge University Press, 1991); D.R. SarDesai, *Southeast Asia: Past and Present* (3rd edn; Boulder: Westview, and Houndmills: Macmillan, 1994); Nicholas Tarling (ed.), *The Cambridge History of Southeast Asia*, vol. 2: *The Nineteenth and Twentieth Centuries* (Cambridge: Cambridge University Press, 1992); Garry Rodan, Kevin Hewison and Richard Robison, (eds), *The Political Economy of South-East Asia: Conflicts, Crises, and Change* (2nd edn; Melbourne: Oxford University Press, 2001).

Rajeswary Ampalavanar Brown, *Capital and Entrepreneurship in Southeast Asia* (Houndmills: Macmillan, and New York: St Martin's Press, 1994), is very good on the management grid in the colonial period.

The aftermath of the 1997 financial crisis led to numbers of studies examining the connections between political and economic structures in the region, including Tan Kong Yam (ed.), *Asian Economic Recovery: Policy Options for Growth and Stability* (Singapore: Singapore University Press, 2002); Jomo Kwame Sundaram (ed.), *Southeast Asian Paper Tigers? From Miracle to Débâcle and Beyond* (London: RoutledgeCurzon, 2003); Martin Andersson and Christer Gunnarsson (eds), *Development and Structural Change in Asia-Pacific: Globalizing Miracles or End of a Model?* (London: RoutledgeCurzon, 2003).

The paradox of 'strong' states that frequently are unable to achieve their goals is examined in Peter Dauvergne (ed.), *Weak and Strong States in Asia-Pacific Societies* (St Leonards: Allen & Unwin Australia, 1998). Peter Evans, *Embedded Autonomy: States and Industrial Transformation* (Princeton: Princeton University Press, 1995) is an important analysis of the conditions for successful government policy. The analysis of state capacity offered here follows the outline of Martin Painter, *Public Sector Challenges and Government Reforms in South East Asia* (Sydney: Research Institute for Asia and the Pacific, 2001).

NOTES

1. Winichakul (1994).
2. Steinberg et al. (1987), p. 176.
3. Bowie (1992), 797–823.
4. Batson (1980), pp. 267–302; Pasuk and Baker (1995), p. 233.
5. Tipton (1998).
6. SarDesai (1994), pp. 145–46.

7. Larkin (1982), p. 599.
8. Trocki (1992), pp. 90–91.
9. Steinberg et al. (1987), pp. 136–8, 190.
10. Elson (1994), pp. 175–7; Sutherland (1979).
11. Wallerstein (1974–89); So and Chiu (1995); Dixon (1991).
12. Landes (1998).
13. See Tipton, (1998).
14. Mitchell (1995).
15. SarDesai (1994), pp. 137–8.
16. Pasuk and Baker (1995), pp. 404–12.
17. Caoili (1988).
18. Brown (1994), ch. 3. See Drabble (1991).
19. Nørland (1991), 72–89.
20. Rooth (1993).
21. Booth (1998), pp. 220–22.
22. Hofstede and Hofstede (2005), Table 2.1.
23. Ileto (1992), pp. 197–248.
24. Batson (1980).
25. Ibid.
26. SarDesai (1994), p. 194.
27. Taylor (1980), pp. 159–90; Steinberg et al. (1987); SarDesai (1994), p. 221.
28. Reid (1980), pp. 16–32.
29. Reid (1980).
30. Akashi (1980), pp. 65–90.
31. Jomo (1986).
32. Marr (1980), pp. 125–58; Murray (1980); Luong (1992); SarDesai (1994), pp. 176–7.
33. Marr (1980).
34. Steinberg et al. (1987), p. 359; SarDesai (1994), pp. 179–81.
35. See Lewis (1995), 153–88.
36. Steinberg et al. (1987), p. 361.
37. Ibid., p. 367.
38. Reid (1980).
39. Smith (1986).
40. Anderson (1991).
41. Greenfeld (1992).
42. Tipton (2002b), pp. 146–62.
43. Gellner (1983).
44. Moore (1966, paperback 1973); Dahrendorf (1968); Brooker (1991).
45. Chatterjee (1986), p. 30.
46. Chatterjee (1986), pp. 168–9.
47. Pasuk and Baker (1995), pp. 284–5.
48. Reid (1980), p. 26. See Van Langenberg (1993), pp. 151–74.
49. Schwarz (1994); Sears (1996).
50. See Ricklefs (1993); Jenkins (1998).
51. Marcos (1978), pp. 19–20.
52. McCoy (1994).
53 'Malaysian PM laments skewed religious views and "crutches"', *The Straits Times Interactive*, 31 July 2002.
54. See Painter (2001), ch. 3.
55. SarDesai (1994), pp. 169–72; Pasuk and Baker (1995), ch. 8.
56. Pasuk and Baker (1995), ch. 9.
57. Kulick and Wilson (1992); Richards (1993), pp. 24–8.
58. Pasuk and Baker (1995), pp. 277–81, 285–8.
59. Ibid., ch. 10.
60. Jarvis (2001), pp. 297–319; 'Voters Welcome Disclosure of Graft', *Bangkok Post* 18 November 2002; Baker (2004).

61. Noon (2006).
62. Migdal (1988); Dauvergne (1998).
63. Painter (2001), p. 14.
64. See Australia, Department of Foreign Affairs and Trade, East Asia Analytical Unit (2000), ch. 4.
65. Bresnan (1993).
66. Suehiro (1989).
67. Pasuk and Piriyarangsan (1996); McVey (2000).
68. Hewison (1989).
69. Kulick and Wilson (1992), p. 3.
70. Laothamatas (1992).
71. Tipton (2002), ch. 5.
72. World Bank (2000).
73. Asian Development Bank (1998).
74. Painter (2001), ch. 3; Jarvis (2001).
75. McCoy (1994); Gutierrez and Garcia (1992).
76. Evers (1987), 666–85.
77. Schwarz (1994), p. 28.
78. Moore, M. (2002).
79. See Brookfield (1994).
80. Painter (2001), p. 150.
81. Transparency International, Global Corruption Report (including corruption perception index and bribe payers index, annual), http://www.transparency.org.
82. Dauvergne (1997).
83. Schwarz (1994), p. 140; Peluso (1992); Peluso (1996); Thompson (1996).
84. Murdoch (2000); 'The problems are piling up', *The Australian*, 2 November 2002, p. 26.
85. See Theobald (1990); Gomez (2002); Lindsay and Dick (2004).

8. Managing cash flow in the bamboo networks: overseas Chinese and the Singapore system

> Be extremely subtle, even to the point of formlessness. Be extremely mysterious, even to the point of soundlessness. Thereby you can be the director of the opponent's fate. (Sun Tzu, *The Art of War*)

> Ability to demand payment: diligence and prudence will gain a lot more for the company. (Tao Zhu-gong, the Sixth Business Principle)

The 'bamboo networks' of the overseas Chinese of Southeast Asia appear subtle and mysterious, but the behavior of Chinese firms reflects the historical grid in which they have been forced to operate. Bamboo varies, and so do the Chinese. As sojourners and settlers some migrated to the very diverse societies of Southeast Asia in the early nineteenth century. The larger numbers of late nineteenth and early twentieth-century migrants faced changed conditions under the colonial regimes. Depression, war and independence, and nationalist reactions, altered conditions again, and the new global economy is bringing further change.

However they may vary, the statistics consistently show the dominant position of the Chinese in all of the economies of Southeast Asia. The institutional grid reflects this domination. Nationalist states have both fostered and hampered Chinese business. Certain well-connected Chinese have been favored, even while the majority faced discrimination. For Chinese firms, planning and decision making, organizing, leading and controlling all necessarily reflect the problems of operating in an ethnic minority environment.

Chinese businesses have distinctive characteristics, notably in their careful management of cash flow. The ability to demand payment has been critical to their survival. They also exist in ongoing networks, though these have varied over time and among regions. Formless and soundless, bamboo networks connected by personal relationships and the Chinese private banking sector support and reinforce the distinctive tendencies of Chinese business. At the same time a new generation of Chinese business

269

leaders is adopting new techniques, sometimes driven by information technologies, and it may be that Chinese business itself will change as a result.

Singapore was both a British outpost and a Chinese city, and the Singapore 'system' reflects that historical experience. War and decolonization brought the rise of the People's Action Party (PAP), which continues to dominate. A one-party political system has been grafted onto British parliamentary and legal institutions. War and decolonization also brought expulsion from the Malaysian federation, sudden political independence, and the need to trade. It has seemed to the PAP's leaders that Singapore's economic and social structures can and must be engineered to survive in a potentially threatening international environment. Parallel to the political system, a system of large state-owned enterprises, the government-linked companies or GLCs, has been grafted onto a free trade economy open to foreign investment. Singapore's management grid, planning and decision making, organizing, leading and controlling in both the GLC sector and in the private sector reflect the continuing three-way tension between government, domestic private enterprise, and foreign firms.

THE HISTORICAL GRID: SOJOURNERS AND SETTLERS

We can begin by asking who exactly the 'overseas Chinese' are. Chinese in China, and the government of the People's Republic, tend to assume that all 'overseas Chinese' are 'sojourners' who will 'return' to China some day, for, as an old saying has it, 'fallen leaves always return to the roots'. There are of course many Chinese citizens who reside abroad. Of these, the 'compatriots' in Taiwan are the most problematic in the eyes of the Chinese government, for, as we saw in Chapter 5, their status raises the question of Taiwan's position. In addition there are 'ethnic' Chinese or persons of Chinese descent. Many of these are of mixed parentage. In general, if the mother is non-Chinese and the father is pure Chinese, then their children are regarded as Chinese. However, if the father is non-Chinese, or if there has been more than one intermarriage, then typically the children are not regarded as Chinese. This reflects the importance of the male line of descent in China, but it also is fairly typical of citizenship rules based on blood, for instance in Japan or Germany.

BOX 8.1   POINT AND COUNTERPOINT:
OVERSEAS CHINESE IN THE COLONIAL
ERA – THE RISE AND FALL OF TAN KAH
KEE

Accounts must be vigilantly checked and monitored; sloppiness and oversight will lead to stagnated capital. (Tao Zhu-gong, the Fourth Business Lesson)

Tan Kah Kee was born into business leadership. He inherited pineapple, rice, and shipping interests from his father before the First World War. He used the profits from the existing family businesses to expand into the rubber industry. However, rather than expanding horizontally in a single branch, Tan expanded vertically along the entire value chain. The result was what Rajeswary Brown calls a 'highly integrated structure' despite being spread across most of Southeast Asia and China. Plantations in Malaya, Thailand, the Dutch East Indies, and Indochina provided sheet rubber for Tan's refining mills in Singapore. The processed rubber then went into a very wide range of goods, particularly rubber shoes, but also tires for automobiles and bicycles. Construction of factories led Tan into further expansion into cement, iron, and brickworks, and he added biscuits and soap as well.

Tan's profits rose from $250 000 in 1909, to $1.6 million in 1914, and $7.8 million in 1925. By the end of the 1920s, manufacturing output had risen to between one-quarter and one-third of the firm's total turnover. Tan controlled 20 per cent of the Dutch East Indies market for manufactured rubber imports, 10 per cent in the Straits Settlements (Malaya), 15 per cent in the Philippines, and 35 per cent of the market in China. Even in the depression following the financial crisis in 1929, Tan's rubber output and shipments remained at high levels, and he continued to invest in new production facilities.

Tan was the 'single brain' behind the organization. He personally controlled investment, production, marketing, and distribution. The company remained private, and paid no dividends from 1918 to 1930. Tan ploughed his profits back into the firm to finance expansion. In addition, he relied on two further sources of funding. First, Tan borrowed from both Chinese and Western banks, especially the Singapore branch of the Hongkong Bank. He borrowed both short and long term, and some of the short-term loans were periodically rolled over so they became in effect long-term. In 1932, Tan had a total bank debt of $9.9 million, and another $3 million secured with debentures. Second, he supplemented his bank loans with extensive trade credits. In the rubber industry the accounts of producers and dealers were intertwined, and Tan was able to exploit this aspect of the business. He could make deals by obtaining credit through Chinese agents of Western banks, through suppliers, and through his own subsidiaries. In 1931, Tan's trade credits totaled $12 million. Internal transactions also helped Tan achieve expansion. Capital and assets could be shifted from one subsidiary to another, and different subsidiaries used to acquire credit in different regions from different sources.

William Hay, the manager of the Hongkong Bank in Singapore, suspected Tan's methods. He complained that Tan had no proper bookkeeping. There were no depreciation reserves or fire insurance. Land and other assets were not revalued. Nevertheless, Hay and other bankers continued to lend, on the strength of Tan's reputation and good will. But at the end of the 1920s Tan's results were mixed, and then came a net loss in 1930. In 1931, Tan reported a further net loss of $1.28 million, but also listed new rubber investments of $12.5 million.

In 1932, the company reported losses of $1.57 million, and some creditors wanted to press for liquidation. The Hongkong Bank, which had several other failures to contend with, instead led a consortium that financed a restructuring. The company became a limited company, with Tan as the 95 per cent shareholder, but also with a committee of bank representatives to deal with outstanding debts of $11.5 million. The Chinese banks' debts were taken over by the Overseas Chinese Banking Corporation. Overdrafts were covered with mortgages and the interest rate reduced. However, losses continued and by mid-1933 the firm's capital had been wiped out. Closed temporarily in 1934, the firm was liquidated in 1936.

Hay believed that Tan had spent large amounts of money on political activities in China. This was in fact true, but there were other possibly more fundamental problems. The firm was highly leveraged, and had borrowed at very high rates of interest. In boom times Tan could cover his most pressing creditors' demands, but the depression made him vulnerable. Rubber prices fluctuated widely during this difficult period, and the gyrations had caused losses for Tan. The easy availability of loans from Western banks had also made Tan incautious. And, for their part, the Western banks had been misled by Tan's reputation and strong trading position.

Expansion had occurred without effective managerial structures to control and guide it. In addition to the accounting shortcomings, Tan did not devolve responsibility to professional managers. One of the consequences was that his factories were underutilized, and their workers poorly supervised. In China, inadequate supervision meant that Tan lost large amounts of goods stolen in transit. Tan's three sons, his son-in-law Lee Kong Chian and another relative, Tan Lark Sye, had all occupied important positions, but Lee and Tan Lark Sye left because of frustration over Tan's political activities and his financial recklessness, and even this rudimentary structure collapsed. In the aftermath, Lee in fact took over a number of his father-in-law's former properties as the Hongkong Bank attempted to recoup some of its losses.

Source: Rajeswary Ampalavanar Brown, *Capital and Entrepreneurship in Southeast Asia* (Houndmills: Macmillan, and New York: St Martin's Press, 1994), ch. 6.

But there are three viewpoints here, first the objective question of where your ancestors came from, second your own self-identification, and third the definition imposed on you by the majority of people in the country where you live. When we ask about self-identification, who the overseas Chinese believe themselves to be, we receive a variety of answers. For instance, from China's perspective, the 'compatriots' in Hong Kong and Macau have now 'returned' to China, and those in Taiwan will return, the sooner the better. But, as we have seen, many Taiwanese regard themselves as 'Taiwanese' and this includes many whose families came from the mainland following the civil war. For all these people, being Taiwanese means being 'Chinese' as well, but not 'Chinese' in the sense of belonging to the People's Republic. The Taiwanese government has invested substantial resources in activities intended to reinforce its claim to a distinctive role in the preservation and transmission of 'Chinese' culture. As a result, there are two quite distinct versions of the Chinese national identity available, and it is possible for an individual quite consciously to choose one or the other.

In Southeast Asia, many people who are objectively Chinese in descent do not identify themselves as belonging to the culture of either mainland China or Taiwan. In Singapore, most consider themselves 'ethnic Chinese' rather than 'overseas Chinese'. They are Singaporean, and they regard China as a foreign country, but in addition they divide along the lines of their origins, into Hokkien, Teochiu, Cantonese, Hakka, or Hainanese.[1] In Malaysia, although some identify with mainland China or Taiwan, the majority do not, but still see themselves as distinctively Chinese, and a further group view themselves as having a Malaysian identity. In the Philippines, people of Chinese descent divide into a majority of *mestizos* who identify themselves as Filipinos, and a minority who see themselves as ethnically Chinese, but with a high degree of cultural assimilation. In Indonesia, a large majority of people of Chinese descent are Indonesian-speaking *peranakan*, and are usually Indonesian citizens. Many of these people consider themselves Indonesian. A minority are Chinese-speaking *totok*, a group that includes those who are citizens of Taiwan or the People's Republic, but that has also included some of the most prominent local Chinese business leaders, for instance Liem Sioe Liong and Mochtar Riady. In Thailand, there appears to be a relatively smooth gradation running from full assimilation and identification with Thai culture, to an identification as ethnically and culturally Chinese.[2]

Beyond the objective facts of birth and descent, and the subjective facts of self-identification, there is as well the problem of how the majority sees you. Sadly, cultural assimilation, and even intermarriage, will not prevent hostility and discrimination if the majority defines you as 'Chinese'. The tragic violence in Indonesia in 1965–66 left hundreds of thousands dead, many and perhaps most of them Chinese. Chinese suffered again in the riots of 1997–98, despite laws passed in the meantime forbidding the use of the Chinese language and forcing Chinese to adopt Indonesian names. Rioters murdered, raped, destroyed homes, and looted businesses owned by 'Chinese', and this was a shock to those who saw themselves as Indonesian. As detailed below, governments have also passed laws discriminating against Chinese, in Thailand in the 1930s, in the Philippines and Indonesia in the 1950s, and in Malaysia under the New Economic Policy introduced in 1971 following the riots in 1969. There have been additional outbursts of hostility even when the Chinese have been very highly integrated, for instance in the Philippines and Thailand in the 1960s and 1970s.

As with identity, when we ask why the Chinese came and why they stayed, we receive a variety of answers. Southeast Asia lay at the outer limits of the Chinese sphere of influence. Ralph Fitch, an English trader who reached the uplands of Thailand in 1587, reported that in Chiang Mai he had seen 'many merchants who had traveled thither from China'.[3] Some Southeast Asian states enjoyed recognition as Chinese tributaries, which allowed official trade with central and northern China in addition to the unofficial trade with the southern provinces. As we have seen, the Europeans fit themselves into this pre-existing pattern. As they extended the areas they controlled during the nineteenth century, they continued to rely on Chinese merchants to connect them with markets in China. Trade led to migration. Demand in China, and the relatively high level of Chinese technological capabilities, caused a flow of specialists who developed the assets of

Southeast Asia. Chinese miners sought gold, gems, and tin, and Chinese merchants and manufacturers dealt in industrial agricultural products, dyes and tanning materials.

Not surprisingly, the majority of migrants came from southern coastal regions of China. But though they were culturally Chinese, this was not yet the era of nationalism. They spoke different languages, and they identified primarily with their home regions, not with 'China'. There were separate organizations for people from different regions, and sometimes riots, for instance in Penang in the 1860s. Also, most of the migrants were men, and so those who did not return usually married non-Chinese women.

These migrant communities also developed distinctive characteristics, including household and kinship relations, food, clothing, and language, reflecting variations in the local environment. G. William Skinner shows the emergence of stable and distinctive social systems during the nineteenth century among the Chinese communities in the Philippines, Java, and Malaya, despite continued contact with China as well as the surrounding communities. He emphasizes the role of local political systems in shaping these communities, and in doing so anticipates some of the critique of culturalist explanations of the behavior of overseas Chinese examined below.[4]

The late nineteenth and early twentieth centuries brought a new and larger migration. Colonial regimes needed workers for mines and agricultural plantations. The dislocation and disruption caused by the decline of the Qing dynasty, especially the great rebellions of the mid-nineteenth century, pushed many to migrate. Refugee groups formed new and sometimes distinctive communities. The defeated Taiping rebels who moved into northern Vietnam, for instance, fought for the Vietnamese against the French.

The internal warfare of the warlord period, the civil war between the Nationalists and Communists, and the Japanese invasion, caused a new wave of migration out of China in the 1920s and 1930s. A much higher proportion of these were women, or complete family groups. This is generally held to have led to an increased tendency for Chinese migrants to marry other Chinese. 'Chinese' communities, for example in Thailand, may therefore have become more visible, more distinct, and possibly more separate from the surrounding society. But the depression of the 1930s also created counter-pressures. Economic decline reduced opportunities, and it also led to hostility towards migrants who were seen as competitors, with Thailand again being a paradigmatic example.

First the collapse of the Japanese empire, and then the defeat of the Nationalists and the establishment of the People's Republic, led to another new wave of migration in the late 1940s and early 1950s. As we saw in Chapter 5, migrants from mainland China played important roles in the development of trade, industry, and business structures in Hong Kong and Taiwan.

Similarly, many of the new migrants to Southeast Asia were also merchants and industrialists who had no place in the People's Republic. And, not surprisingly, many of them came from the same regions as the new migrants to Hong Kong and Taiwan and therefore had contacts among those groups.

THE INSTITUTIONAL GRID: NATIONALIST STATES AND CHINESE BUSINESS

The outline above might give the impression that there are large numbers of Chinese in Southeast Asia. However, although they are in total a substantial number of people, with the exception of Singapore they are a minority, and frequently a very small minority. Further, the history of migration indicates that they are very diverse. Nevertheless, and this is the point that has attracted the attention of all observers, they occupy a position in the economy far in excess of their numbers in the population. A range of statistics can be cited to show the dominant position of the Chinese, and some of them are summarized in Table 8.1. However, although the contrast between the small numbers of Chinese and their immense economic influence is striking and even shocking, we need to remember that the numbers depend on who is counting and what their purposes are. Governments sometimes find it genuinely difficult to count the Chinese, and sometimes governments in fact do not want to know how many Chinese there are. In these intensely nationalistic societies, the numbers of Chinese is a sensitive issue. Accordingly, the relative wealth of the Chinese is an even more sensitive issue. Some governments have found it convenient to blame 'foreigners' for their problems, and these so-called 'foreigners' included the Chinese community even where this meant persons whose grandparents or great-grandparents had settled in the country and intermarried. But, at other times, governments and Chinese businesses have shared an interest in maintaining a low profile and minimizing the role of Chinese in the economy.

As we saw in Chapter 5, by the late 1960s all the former colonies were independent countries. As we also have seen, these were nationalistic states. The new governments restricted immigration and passed quite restrictive citizenship laws, with citizenship typically seen as a privilege, not an automatic right. In the Philippines, it was not until a decree issued by President Ferdinand Marcos in 1974, as part of the move to normalize relations with China, that ethnic Chinese were allowed to apply for Filipino citizenship. Brunei restricts citizenship to those whose father is a citizen. Foreigners who apply must pass a Malay language test and another test on general knowledge, and must have lived in Brunei for 20 of the preceding 25 years. As a result most Brunei

Table 8.1   *Numbers and economic position of overseas Chinese in Southeast Asia, early 1990s*

Country	Numbers of Chinese	Percentage of total	Role in economy
Brunei	42 800	15.0	Dominant in commerce
Cambodia	200 000 to 300 000? (500 000 before 1975)	1.9 to 2.8	Dominant in commerce; 70% of industry before 1975
Indonesia	3 250 000	3.5	73% of listed share capital; 68% of top 300 conglomerate groups
Laos	50 000	1.3	Dominant in commerce and service industries
Malaysia	5 400 000	29.0	61% of listed share capital; 60% of private sector managers; overrepresented in all professions
Myanmar (Burma)	?	15 to 20?	Dominant in commerce and industry before 1962; majority of businesses created under new 'opening' policy
Philippines	1 200 000?	2.0?	50 to 60% of listed share capital; 35 per cent of sales
Singapore	2 079 000	77.0	81% of listed share capital
Thailand	5 800 000?	10.0?	81% of listed share capital; 'no class of indigenous big business entrepreneurs exists'
Vietnam	1 000 000	1.5	Before 1975, 80% of industry, 100% of wholesale and foreign trade, 50% of retail trade. Since 1986 dominant in private sector, 45% of registered private firms in 1992

Source: Australia, Department of Foreign Affairs and Trade, East Asia Analytical Unit, *Overseas Chinese Business Networks in Asia* (Canberra: EAAU, 1995). The quote regarding Thailand is on p. 78.

Chinese are 'permanent residents' who travel with Brunei identity cards, although their families may have lived in Brunei for several generations.

Nationalism waxes and wanes, and government policy varies and changes over time. The socialist governments of Burma, Cambodia, Vietnam, Laos, and also Indonesia in the 1950s and early 1960s, all discriminated against private enterprise generally. But this affected Chinese more than others, because of their prominent position in trade and industry. Today Vietnam, Cambodia, Laos, and Burma are quite friendly environments for Chinese business, although Burma remains under the control of a small military clique, and Laos is still quite closed. China attacked Vietnam in 1979, and Vietnam's socialist regime identified the Chinese as a potential internal political threat, as well as socially objectionable insofar as they were capitalists. However, having defeated the Chinese invaders, in 1982 the Vietnamese Communist Party issued a directive that said previous policies had been excessively harsh toward the Vietnam Chinese (known as *hoa*), and that they should no longer be treated as 'reactionaries'. Then came economic reform. Vietnam has been actively attempting to re-create a market economy since the beginning of the *doi moi* renovation movement in 1986. The move away from central planning has involved the extension of private ownership and opening to foreign investment. The Chinese have been actively encouraged to participate. Much of the new investment has come from the Chinese elsewhere in the region, and nearly half of the new private firms are Chinese.

Non-socialist governments' policies have ranged from acceptance, through grudging toleration, to institutionalized discrimination and brutal violence. Thailand and the Philippines have a high degree of integration and long histories of intermarriage. In the Philippines, Cardinal Jaime Sin is part Chinese. In Thailand, the eldest son of the Chirathivat family (which controls the Central Group) married a niece of the Queen in the early 1990s. Under the gradually liberalizing military regime of the 1980s, a substantial number of Sino-Thais rose to prominence in politics. Since 1988, they have led all the political parties and several have served as Prime Minister. The new constitution of 1997 opened the system even further and, as we saw in Chapter 7, Sino-Thai business leader Thaksin Shinawatra, owner of Thailand's largest telecommunications company, founded his own political party and became Prime Minister in 2001.

In both Thailand and the Philippines, it is difficult to determine the precise number of Chinese. Nevertheless, Thais and Filipinos know who is Chinese and who is not. Eduardo Cojuangco, the CEO of Philippines brewing and food processing conglomerate San Miguel, for example, was instantly identified as 'the head of the Chinese Cojuangco clan' by interviewees, and most also knew that former President Corazon Aquino belongs to a branch of the Cojuangco family as well. In both countries ethnic Chinese continue to dominate the economy, and in both countries this is an ongoing source of resentment.[5]

Both Thailand and the Philippines have histories of violence and legal discrimination against the Chinese. In the Philippines under President Ramon

Magsaysay, the government passed the Retail Trade Nationalization Law in 1954. Non-citizens who owned retail trade businesses were required to liquidate their business, either within ten years or on the death of the owner, whichever came first. Further laws restricted trade in rice and corn to Filipino citizens. Because the majority of ethnic Chinese were not Filipino citizens, and because their businesses were concentrated in wholesale and retail trade, an estimated 80 per cent of Chinese-owned businesses had to be either sold or otherwise wound up. In 1960, Republic Act No. 3018 required all alien-owned businesses in wholesale and retail trade, cultivation, and transportation to cease operation within two years, and all related mills and warehouses within three years.

However, the anti-Chinese legislation did not drive the Chinese out of the Philippines economy. In fact, leading Chinese firms found ways to benefit. Because it was so difficult to obtain Filipino citizenship, Chinese moved out of trade and into manufacturing. First in textiles and then in other branches, Chinese opened firms in the expanding industrial sector. In effect they were forced to move into the most dynamic area of the economy and, once there, they also benefited from tariffs and subsidies provided under the government's import substation policies. Parallel to the shift to manufacturing, Chinese also expanded into banking and financial services. There were four Chinese-controlled banks in the Philippines in 1956, nine in 1971, and 16 in 1974. In the early 1990s, Chinese held majority interests in ten of the 26 private commercial banks.[6]

In Thailand during the 1920s, hostility towards Chinese immigrants increased. Among the Chinese, higher numbers of female migrants provided Chinese men with marriage partners, and possibly reduced the previous tendency towards assimilation. The victory of the Nationalists in China led to a new assertiveness among these 'overseas' Chinese. In 1930, the Thai government revoked the extraterritorial privileges of Chinese immigrants. Under Phibun in the 1930s, the government closed Chinese schools and newspapers, limited immigration, and deported illegal migrants. Chinese were 'encouraged' to take Thai names. Anti-Chinese riots orchestrated by the government both reflected and intensified nationalistic resentment of this discriminated minority. As in Vietnam, Chinese were suspected of connections with the People's Republic, and many were arrested and executed. When the threat of communist insurrection passed, the government in 1973 announced a new policy of assimilation, but Chinese were generally excluded from the most senior positions in the government bureaucracy until the 1980s. Since then, as noted above, wealthy Sino-Thais have entered politics, and Sino-Thai business leaders played a large role in the business associations that have been seen as an important aspect of democratization.[7]

BOX 8.2   POINT AND COUNTERPOINT:
OVERSEAS CHINESE IN THE
NATIONALIST ERA – THE RISE, FALL
AND RISE OF LIEM SIOE LIONG AND
ANTHONY SALIM

*Unexpected events must be tackled responsibly; neglecting them will
lead to greater harm. (Tao Zhu-gong, the Eighth Business Lesson)*

Liem Sioe Liong, founder of the Salim Group, was also born into
business, though not directly into ownership like Tan Kah Kee. In
1938, the 22-year-old Liem and his brother left the Chinese
province of Fujian and moved to Java, where they joined their
uncle's peanut oil business. Liem began his own business as well,
buying cloves from farmers and selling them to cigarette makers
as a flavor additive. During the war of independence against the
Dutch, Liem supplied the Diponegoro division in central Java with
food, medicines, and military supplies. He worked with then-
Colonel Soeharto, the quartermaster of the division, and the relationship continued. When President Sukarno ordered the army to
take over Dutch companies in 1957, Liem was asked to provide
both credit and management services. He also branched out into
manufacturing, taking advantage of the tariffs introduced under the
government's import substitution program, and also avoiding the
new restrictions imposed by the government on traditional local
Chinese merchants.

    Then, following the brutal anti-Chinese violence in 1965,
General Soeharto became President. In 1968, the government
granted exclusive rights to import the popular cloves to two companies, one owned by Soeharto's brother and the other by Liem.
Liem's clove business averaged annual net revenues of more
than US$1 million from 1968 to 1980. In 1969, Liem founded PT
Bogasari Four Mill, and the government granted the new firm a
monopoly on the milling of flour imported by the National Logistics
Board. In the 1990s, Bogasari was being paid three times the world
price for its milling services. Control over flour milling led to food
processing, and the Salim Group's Indofoods became the world's
largest producer of instant noodles, next to rice the most popular
staple food in Indonesia. In 1973, Liem founded Indocement,
which profited from public works contracts, as well as the profits it
made on the difference between the government-fixed wholesale

price and the unfixed retail price of cement, sold through another firm connected with the Salim Group, PT Semen Roda Prasetya.

During the following years the Salim group expanded to become the largest conglomerate in the country, and Liem reputedly became the second wealthiest individual in Southeast Asia, behind only the Sultan of Brunei. Connections with the government remained close. In 1985, the government purchased a quarter of the shares of Indocement. In 1989, a ministerial decree allowed the firm to list on the Jakarta exchange although it had not shown a profit over the previous two years as required under exchange regulations. The government also called on Liem to manage Krakatau Steel, the country's only integrated steel plant. The firm had been losing money and could dispose of only half of its output. The government imposed tariffs and granted the firm export and import monopolies, allowing it to sell its entire capacity. In 1989, the government took over the Salim Group's 40 per cent interest in a cold rolling steel mill, which was losing money, and integrated it into Krakatau Steel. Connections with Soeharto and his family also remained close. Soeharto's cousin Sudwikatmono remained one of the central investors in the Salim Group into the 1990s. In 1989, social foundations chaired by President Soeharto bought Rp 60 billion worth of Indocement's convertible bonds, and his eldest son and eldest daughter held 17 per cent of the shares in the Salim Group's Bank Central Asia.

Bank Central Asia (BCA) began as a knitting company. Liem purchased the firm in 1957 and restructured it into a bank. Until the early 1970s it had only one branch and was not permitted to trade in foreign exchange. In 1975, Mochtar Riady was appointed president and given a 17.5 per cent shareholding. Profits from other Salim Group companies went to the bank, and Indocement's customers were solicited to pay for their purchases in cash remitted into accounts at BCA. With this inflow of capital the bank expanded its loan portfolio by lending at lower rates than other banks. The government granted its request to trade in foreign exchange, allowing it to tap overseas capital markets for further loans. By the early 1990s, it had become the largest private bank in Indonesia and had more branches than any other bank.

Despite its growth, through the 1980s the Salim Group remained under the control of a small group known as the 'Liem Investors', including Liem, two long-term associates, two of their sons, a younger cousin, and Sudwikatmono. There were few outside professional managers. Mochtar Riady, the main exception, resigned from BCA to concentrate on his own Lippo Group in 1990. Joint ventures allowed quick entry into markets, but flexibility came at the cost of inadequate coordination, identified as a key area of concern in an INSEAD case in 1993.

Change and restructuring accompanied a move outward from Indonesia, and Liem's son Anthony Salim (Liem Fung Seng) received credit from most observers. Hong Kong-based First Pacific Group, acquired in the early 1980s, became the vehicle for acquisitions in Thailand, the Philippines, Australia, the United States, Britain, and the Netherlands, where its majority-owned vehicle assembly and international trading company Hagemeyer NV had a market turnover of US$2 billion and operations in 21 countries. In 1990, the entire Salim Group was brought under a single board of directors. The group was structured into 11 divisions, each with its own steering committee and sub-divisions overseeing individual companies. From middle management downwards the group had moved toward a mix of ethnic Chinese and non-Chinese. However, the Liem family remained in control. Although First Pacific Group blandly described the Liem shareholding as 'passive', the group was in fact controlled through a Liem-owned company registered in Liberia, which in turn controlled a company registered in Bermuda, which owned the majority stake in First Pacific Group.

In 1992, Anthony Salim succeeded his father as Group Chairman, and all seemed well until 1997. The financial crisis hit Indonesia the hardest of any country. The Rupiah declined from 2430 to the U.S. dollar to a low of 17 000. In 1998, the Soeharto regime collapsed as well, and rioters burned Liem's Jakarta residence to the ground. BCA had borrowed U.S. dollars to lend to its clients, and half of its loans had gone to other Salim Group companies, well over the legal limit of 20 per cent for related party transactions. Caught by the decline in the exchange rate, BCA went bankrupt and passed under the administration of the Bank Restructuring Agency, which nationalized it. The privileges enjoyed under Soeharto were withdrawn; Bogasari, for instance, lost its monopoly on flour milling. However, Anthony Salim was able to save key portions of his empire by shifting ownership overseas. The Salim Group sold 40 per cent of Indofoods to First Pacific Group in 1999, which transferred ownership to a foreign entity, raised desperately needed cash, and yet retained control. To survive, however, Indofoods also needed the brilliant leadership of its CEO, Eva Rianti Hutapea. Appointed in 1996, she faced losses of Rp 1.2 trillion in 1997, but purchased a huge currency hedge and gained access to US$72 million. Although paid for at twice the current exchange rage, the hedge provided the insulation needed to prevent the further losses that would have sent the firm under.

Many believed that the Salim Group should have been broken up, and that the corrupt dealings under the Soeharto regime should have been punished, but, as the *Asian Wall Street Journal* put it in February 2000, 'Faced with economic crisis and worries that ethnic Chinese money might never return, Indonesia and the International Monetary Fund ultimately decided Salim Group was too important to dismantle.' Again using First Pacific Group as the vehicle, the Salim Group moved to a new phase of expansion, acquiring for instance Philippine Long Distance Telephone Co. (PLDT), the largest telephone company in the Philippines. Bogasari still enjoyed a 65 per cent share of the flour milling market in Indonesia in 2003, and Indofoods still commanded 88 per cent of the noodle market, although in fact the relationship with Bogasari appeared to have loaded Indofoods with a relatively high-cost structure. A dispute over that relationship led to conflict between Anthony Salim and Hutapea, and Hutapea resigned in December 2003.

Sources: H. Schutte, L. Forman and M. Cannizzo, 'The Salim Group', INSEAD Case 393-008-1 (1993); Y. Sato, 'The Salim Group in Indonesia: the development and behavior of the largest conglomerate in Southeast Asia', *The Developing Economies* (1993); Adam Schwarz, *A Nation In Waiting: Indonesia in the 1990s* (Boulder: Westview Press, 1994); Min Chen, *Asian Management Systems* (1995; London: International Thomson Business Press, 1997), pp. 102–4; Australia, Department of Foreign Affairs and Trade, East Asia Analytical Unit, *Overseas Chinese Business Networks in Asia* (Canberra: EAAU, 1995), pp. 163–75; 'Soeharto: patronage and its prizes', *The Sydney Morning Herald*, 30 October 1997; Bill Guerin, 'World's top noodle maker loses its bite', *Asia Times Online*, 23 December 2003.

Indonesia is the worst case of violence. As elsewhere the newly independent nation discriminated against minorities. Islamic parties pushed their long-standing agenda to redress the balance between Chinese and indigenous interests, and in addition President Sukarno's vision of a socialist community prejudiced the government against private business in general. The government nationalized foreign firms and emphasized the role of the state. In 1955, the government restricted ownership of rice mills to indigenous Indonesian citizens. The owners, nearly all ethnic Chinese, were required to transfer ownership to indigenous citizens within two years. In 1957, 15 industries were reserved for Indonesian citizens, and the Chinese owners, almost none of whom were Indonesian citizens, again were required to transfer ownership to Indonesian citizens. In 1959, 'aliens' were banned from operating businesses in rural areas. In 1960, 'aliens' were prohibited from engaging in retail trade at the local level, and the Chinese who dominated this area of business were again shut out.

As in the Philippines, the restrictions did not reduce the role of the Chinese in the economy. The capital that Chinese were forced to remove from their previous trading and food processing businesses became available for other undertakings. The government hoped to accelerate industrialization through import substitution policies. Tariffs and outright prohibitions on foreign manufactured goods, combined with preferential tax rates, access to credit from state banks, guaranteed protection from further expropriations, and sometimes monopoly privileges, all were intended to develop industries that one day might be competitive internationally. Investors, particularly when they had the support of powerful government officials, were guaranteed profits. Consequently, cash-rich and well-connected Chinese such as Liem Sioe Liong moved away from trade and into manufacturing, and their very high profits became the basis for the growth and eventual international expansion of the Salim Group and other large conglomerates.

In the early 1960s, slow growth and runaway inflation brought hardship, and the country divided politically. Chinese were resented for their economic position, but also for their connection to the People's Republic and for their role in the Indonesian Communist Party. The army and local civilians forced Chinese to leave some rural areas. In 1965, an attempted leftist coup was followed by spreading mob violence, encouraged by the army. The killing began in mid-October 1965, raged into early 1966, and continued sporadically for another year. Estimates of the total number of dead range from a low of 100 000 to over a million, but most place the number of victims between 300 000 and 400 000. Because the violence was primarily rural, and because many Chinese had already been driven out of the rural areas, the victims were not all Chinese. Nevertheless, the Chinese suffered as particular targets of hostility. At the end of 1966, Soemitro, the military commander of East Java, announced restrictions intended to obliterate the Chinese presence there: 'I didn't allow them to live in villages, I didn't want them to trade, I didn't even want them in business. No public use of the Chinese language, no Chinese books, no public speaking of Chinese, no Chinese shrines, nothing. We needed a comprehensive solution.'[8]

Soeharto emerged as the new ruler, and his so-called New Order regime lasted until the economic collapse of 1997–8. Official discrimination against the Chinese continued. The government banned the public use of the Chinese language and the import of Chinese language materials. Chinese community organizations and schools were closed. Chinese were encouraged or forced to take Indonesian names. The army contributed to the violence in 1965, played an important role in the institutionalization of discrimination, and did not defend the Chinese in 1997 and 1998. However, in the background wealthy Indonesian Chinese have benefited from contacts with powerful persons. Virtually all senior Indonesian military leaders have a Chinese business associate. As noted in Chapter 7, army units have established various enterprises to supplement their budgets, and the commanding officer's Chinese partner typically operates these businesses.[9] As seen in Box 8.2 above, at the very top, Liem Sioe Liong continued his long-time association with Soeharto, Soeharto's cousin Sudwikatmono continued as one of the 'Liem Investors' and Soeharto's children also became large investors in Salim Group undertakings.

In Malaysia, some blame the British for the continuing ethnic economic divide. The Malay states were a classic 'colonial' economy, dependent on primary product exports and with little manufacturing industry. The large firms were nearly all British, such as Harrisons and Crosfield, as seen in Chapter 7 and Box 7.1, involved in tin mining, rubber plantations, shipping and commercial services. As we have seen, the British wanted Malays to remain on their small farms, essentially self-sufficient. Indians, conceived as more or less temporary migrants, were to work as laborers on British-owned plantations. The Chinese were to provide small-scale commercial and retail sales services. As seen in Box 8.1 above, some, such as Tan Kah Kee, did far more than that.

The Malayan and Singapore Chinese communities had become more cohesive and encapsulated because of more equal sex ratios in the prewar period. As in Thailand, many began to consider themselves more 'Chinese' than before and supported China against Japan in the 1930s. Hurt by the depression, some left the urban areas and became squatters, where some adopted the communist ideology. As already noted in Chapter 7, the Japanese considered the Chinese enemies and treated them exceptionally harshly. When they captured Singapore in 1942, they raped, murdered, arrested, and executed thousands, forced the Chinese community to pay a huge indemnity to atone for 'crimes' against Japan, and forcibly settled further thousands of Chinese in the countryside to increase food production. The Chinese predominated in the Malay People Anti-Japanese Army (MPAJA) guerilla struggle, but they as well as the Japanese requisitioned food from the Malay farming villages. In the prewar period rice production only covered 40 per cent of consumption and was paid for with rubber and tin exports. Exports ceased when the Allies gained control of the sea routes, and their activities therefore reinforced Malay hostility toward the Chinese.

As we have seen in Chapter 7, the emerging Malaysian state was dominated by the United Malays National Organization (UMNO), led in the early years by Malay aristocrats. Singapore's expulsion from the federation was intended to forestall a possible non-Malay alliance that would have threatened their position. Malaysian officials adopted the definitions of 'race' imposed by the British on the very diverse Chinese, Indian, and Malay communities, because they suited the interests of Malay political leaders and conveniently glossed over the potentially dangerous divisions among 'Malays' and between the mass of Malays and the elite.[10] Nevertheless, however we balance the possible causes, it was true that, despite efforts by the government to foster Malay interests, economic inequality increased in the decade following independence. By the late 1960s, Chinese dominated all non-agricultural sectors. Chinese controlled 76 per cent of retail trade and all but one of the 16 banks (the other one was state-owned).

Malay resentment finally culminated in the riots of 1969 in Kuala Lumpur and other cities.[11] In the aftermath of the riots, the government announced the New Economic Policy, intended to reduce economic inequality between the Malays and the other ethnic communities, particularly the Chinese. The *Second Malaysia Plan 1971-1975* announced:

> the first prong is to reduce and eventually eradicate poverty, by raising income levels and increasing employment opportunities for all Malaysians, irrespective of race. The second prong aims at accelerating the process of restructuring Malaysian society to correct economic imbalance, so as to reduce and eventually eliminate the identification of race with economic function.

To build the 'first prong', the plan aimed to reduce Malaysia's dependence on primary products by encouraging labor-intensive industries that would raise the share of manufactured goods in exports. Here Malaysian officials were explicitly following what they considered the 'Japanese model' of development.

The 'second prong' became the New Economic Policy (NEP). The NEP did not expropriate Chinese, but imposed administrative regulations that required all businesses, for instance, to set aside 30 per cent of capital for Malay interests, to train Malays for all positions and especially for managerial roles, and to use Malay firms for distribution and subcontracting work. In 1972, Prime Minister Tun Razak attempted to reassure the Chinese community by emphasizing the government's fundamental belief in free private enterprise. The ongoing intervention in the economy, he said, was a short-term measure intended to make incomes more equal. The next year's mid-term review of the Second Malaysia Plan promised that 'no particular group' would experience any loss or feel any sense of deprivation as a result of NEP measures.

Despite reassurances, and the bland and neutral legal phrasing of the regulations, the prominent position of Chinese firms meant that they were the ones that would be affected. The 1974 Petroleum Development Act gave the government extensive control over firms in the petroleum and petrochemical sectors, although it was presented as a measure directed against foreign companies. The 1975 Industrial Coordination Act imposed a licensing system on manufacturing firms and gave the Minister of Trade and Industry broad powers to impose conditions in the 'national interest'. The government imposed quotas in education, employment, and access to capital to privilege Malays. Places in schools and universities were reserved for Malays, loans were made available to Malay firms, and incentive schemes encouraged non-Malay employers to favor Malays in hiring new workers. A new regional policy favored poor regions with majority Malay populations. Government leaders announced plans to reduce the proportion of Malays in agriculture, because they regarded the disproportionately large numbers of Malay farmers as both the cause and the main symptom of Malay backwardness.[12]

The NEP officially ended in 1991, but the government continued to guide development, and the discrimination in favor of Malays has remained to the present. The quota that reserved 55 per cent of public university places to Malays was finally dropped in 2003, but Chinese students continue to believe that they are discriminated against. Chinese business leaders also feel themselves at a disadvantage. In 2004, an executive in a Malaysian Chinese electronics firm said, 'We have MSC [Multimedia Supercorridor] status, but we have to just hope that any Malay company will pay us. If we sue there is just no chance that we will ever get a judgment against them.'

THE MANAGEMENT GRID: PLANNING AND DECISION MAKING, ORGANIZING, LEADING AND CONTROLLING WITHIN AN ETHNIC MINORITY ENVIRONMENT

Founders and Families

As with their origins, the business operations of the overseas Chinese can be viewed from different perspectives. Objectively, there is little dispute.[13] Overseas Chinese firms tend to be family firms, run by a patriarchal founder, and the structural implications of these factors are examined below. Two of their competitive advantages, careful management of cash flow and connections to networks of other firms, are also widely recognized. However, the definition and extent of the networks are contentious, as are the subjective motivations of overseas Chinese business people. Some argue their behavior reflects inherited Chinese and especially Confucian cultural values, but others emphasize environmental factors. Most contentious of all are predictions of the future, and this in part explains the dispute over origins and motivations. A cultural explanation would imply that change will be difficult or impossible, whereas an environmental emphasis suggests, first, that Chinese firms may not have to change drastically in order to survive, and second, that if they do need to change, it may prove quite easy.

Overseas Chinese firms are family firms, and most are small. They also are frequently highly diversified, and their diversification is often unrelated, contradicting Western management theory. However, as we have seen in the case of Qing and Nationalist China, and again in the cases of Taiwan and Hong Kong, small family firms are by no means inefficient. Indeed, they possess certain strengths that may yield substantial competitive advantages.

Planning and decision making are simplified. The boss, the founder of the firm or the patriarch of the family, makes the decisions, based on his information and understanding. He is the only one with complete information about the firm, and his knowledge of the operating environment is greater than that of anyone else in the firm. He bases decisions on his years of hands-on experience. As his experience lengthens he becomes more able to transfer knowledge across businesses, to analyze new situations based on analogy with what he has seen in the past. The decision-making style of Chinese firms appears intuitive, based on the 'gut feeling' of the boss. They typically do not rest their strategies on analysis of objective data or externally imposed metrics. Instead they rely on qualitative information, a balancing of multiple factors, and a 'holistic' process of information processing.[14]

As a result, two of the core competencies of overseas Chinese firms are rapid, action-driven decision making, and the ability to shift quickly from one area to another. Southeast Asia has been, and in a number of countries it remains, a region where reliable objective data are lacking, an 'information black hole'. Therefore an intuitive, analogical approach can be more effective than an attempt to apply quantitative models. Southeast Asia is also an area where prices and relative prices of different goods can fluctuate widely and rapidly, so the ability to move quickly out of one business and into something more immediately profitable is advantageous.[15]

However, reliance on a single person to make all the decisions loses the potential benefits of wider consultation. And, as we saw in the case of Korean *chaebol* groups in Chapter 3, this sort of boss-centered decision making style decreases in effectiveness, the more complex the decisions and the longer the time horizon. It works best when rapid decisions are needed, and when opportunities must be seized as they arise. It works much less well when long-range plans involving multiple factors are required, or when complex technical questions need to be considered. In these sorts of cases the firm requires transparent information, and free input from all those involved. The secretive nature, distrust of outside experts, and deference to the boss that typify overseas Chinese firms can become disadvantages.

Leadership reflects the central role of the boss or patriarch. As the firm grows he will appoint people he believes he can trust to oversee those things he cannot supervise personally. These will be family members, other relatives, or old employees who have become in effect honorary family members. For new employees, this means it is crucial to cultivate connections with those closer to the center of the family. The need for trust and the need to be trusted work together to create another core competency of overseas Chinese firms, the implicit and intuitive understanding of the firm's strategic orientation, which leads to flexibility and the willingness to change directions or activities quickly in response to orders from the boss.[16]

Again there is a potential weakness, however. A firm organized in this way will be particularly reluctant to hire and rely on professionals, for human resource management or for financial management, for instance. The patriarch's position, decision making style, and desire for control, mean that professional expertise constitutes a threat to his authority. The HRM function is reduced to relying on those that the boss feels he can trust. Information is only revealed to those who are trusted, and this applies to finance in particular. To reveal the firm's financial dealings, even to an employee, means revealing the family's business to an outsider. More generally, interviewees report that overseas Chinese firms dislike spending money on anything not directly and immediately related to profits. This would apply to paying professionals who the boss feels are simply duplicating functions he can perform himself, but as we saw in the case of Hong Kong firms and quality circles in Chapter 5, it can apply to new and innovative management techniques as well.

Control and financial structure also reflect the family- and boss-centered nature of the firm. If the family is the focus of interest, then the business owner, who is also the family patriarch, regards the business as the private property of the family. He will be reluctant to share ownership with others. This means he will not want to adopt a public ownership form. Among overseas Chinese firms, even large firms that are publicly listed frequently have a large fraction of shares held by the family to ensure control. They may use other means as well, such as combinations of listed and unlisted companies in the same group, cross-shareholdings, holding companies, or pyramid structures. It is not only Chinese who behave this way, as many successful Western family firms go through a traumatic period when the founding family surrenders control. However, in the context of Southeast Asia this factor may be reinforced. Public listing in a hostile environment is a risk, because it exposes the firm to scrutiny from government authorities, who may be prejudiced against Chinese.

Overseas Chinese firms are typically small in size, or if they are large they may in fact be conglomerates that group together a number of small or medium-sized firms. In either case the controlling group of managers is small, as seen in the case of the Salim Group. If the firm is small, then the immediate family, extended family, previous employer, and friends may be able to provide the necessary capital the firm might need to conclude a deal. Again, this is also typical of family firms in Western countries, but again we need to remember that, in a hostile environment, large size is a risk. In addition, overseas Chinese firms have a tendency to divide when the patriarch dies. The old tradition of division of the family inheritance among sons is now often extended to daughters as well. The division is not always harmonious. Not all siblings get along well together, and the personalized relations within the firm may mean that each child has their own clique of supporters. There are numerous examples of successful overseas Chinese firms that have failed to survive the transition to a new generation.[17]

The boss-centered management style requires less in the way of complex formal structures. In a patriarchal family firm there probably is very little 'structure' at all. In addition to the absence of professionalized HRM and financial management, most overseas Chinese firms do not have specialized departments for research and development or marketing. Instead, as they expand into new products, new industries, or new regions, they tend to rely on agents or connections with other firms rather than internalizing transaction costs. They may 'buy' technology, products, or entry into markets, but many observers have noted their failure to innovate, develop new products, or establish recognized brands.

Overseas Chinese firms do not recruit employees primarily on the basis of formal qualifications or ability. Although younger overseas Chinese report that they would not hire exclusively on the basis of *guanxi* (relationships or 'connections'), it is commonly observed that the most important means of selecting or promoting employees is trust, and most observers believe that this reflects the role of the boss and the owner family.[18] Human resource management reflects the attitude that all employees should be involved in the central business, and that their activities should be directly contributing to profits. Overseas Chinese firms typically show low levels of specialization. Jobs are not clearly specified or assigned, routine procedures are frequently not formalized, and employees may be reassigned at the whim of the patriarch.

Management by objectives in such a firm is extremely difficult. Levels of planning are not formalized, and evaluations are not transparent. Pay often depends on the patriarch's subjective evaluation of the employee. Those with good relations with the boss receive bonuses, and those without good relations receive low wages and may be harassed or 'driven' by middle managers trying to impress the patriarch. Within the firm, employees' dependence on connections means there is a tendency for cliques to form. Again, this raises problems of succession and what to do when the patriarch dies, because the patriarch's sons and daughters may have formed their own cliques.

At its best, Chinese firms are flat organizations with good internal information flows, in which each employee is capable of being redeployed on short notice, and this makes the firm flexible and efficient. At its worst, the boss may withhold crucial information, or family members may be given responsibility even if they are incompetent, and employees who are not family members will feel no loyalty to the firm. Problems have arisen in China, where workers complain that overseas Chinese managers demand loyalty and commitment, but will not extend trust in return.[19] In their home countries, overseas Chinese firms can have problems when the employees are not Chinese. These problems emerged clearly in a discussion group involving a Malaysian Chinese, with management experience in his family's firm, a non-Chinese Filipino, and a non-Chinese Malaysian. One problem is supervision, which non-Chinese employees regard as intrusive and demeaning.

Malay: 'Chinese are not that good managers. They can't leave you alone.'
Filipino: 'I had a Chinese boss, she was in my face the whole time. Nothing I did seemed right. Always checking on me, getting me to do it over. I really thought she was just trying to impress her uncle, who was the big boss.'
Malaysian Chinese: 'Yeah, ok, I have to say, we worry about Malay workers, whether they can really handle the stuff, you know.'

Promotion is another issue for the non-Chinese employees of Chinese firms.

Malay: 'No chance you get promoted if you're not Chinese.'
Filipino: 'Agree. Chinese company, there is a level you just can't go beyond. Get to a point and you have to go out on your own.'
Malaysian Chinese: 'Yeah, well, our particular company is, you know, a family company. So, there is really no role for anyone who isn't in the family, above that level. Maybe if we get bigger, things could be different . . . [pause] But it is hard to say.'

Rates of Return

The evidence presented above showing the dominance of Chinese firms of course relates primarily to relatively large, publicly listed firms. It also is badly skewed in that the totals frequently reflect the position of a very few successful groups.[20] Nevertheless, the majority of small and medium-sized overseas Chinese firms are on average apparently more successful than their indigenous counterparts and competitors. Victor Limlagen published a study of Southeast Asian Chinese firms in 1986 that demonstrated the link between their cash flow management, inventory, pricing, and profitability. Even with low prices and low gross profit margins, through careful management a firm can achieve a high rate of return on its equity.[21]

Return on the firm's equity, the ratio of gross profit to equity, is a function of the level of total assets related to equity, multiplied by the ratio of gross profits to total assets. In turn, the relation of gross profits to total assets is a function of the level of gross profits to sales, multiplied by the ratio of sales to total assets.[22] The ratio of gross profit to sales can be low. Low prices will, other things equal, increase the number of sales, which will raise the ratio of sales to assets. At every step the Chinese firms Limlagen studied had an advantage over non-Chinese firms. At the bottom line, they enjoyed a rate of return on their equity nearly 60 per cent higher than non-Chinese firms. As Limlagen decomposed this result, he found that Chinese firms were only slightly better at debt management, as the ratio of assets to equity was about equal. However, they were far better at asset management, as their ratio of gross profits to assets was half again as high as non-Chinese firms. Chinese firms' reputation for low prices was confirmed, as their ratio of gross profits to sales was substantially below non-Chinese firms. However, their turnover was extremely high, with a ratio of sales to assets that was two and a half times that of non-Chinese firms.

Achieving these results requires constant attention. It is important to keep in mind that assets are both fixed and current, and that current assets include inventory and accounts receivable. A firm can achieve a high ratio of sales to assets by reducing the amount of inventory held, and by reducing the collection period, which lowers the amount of accounts receivable. It is crucial to attain a low inventory level, but there are limits. Hold too much inventory, and you waste money. But, if you hold too little inventory, you lose sales. There are precise quantitative relationships determining the correct amount to order, and when to order.[23] Quantitative inventory control, however, is more likely to be employed by large firms. Small firms everywhere, including small Chinese firms, tend to rely on the boss's instinctive sense of 'when' and 'how much' to order. Experience counts, particularly in countries where accurate information may be unobtainable. Limlagen's Chinese firms held inventory less than a week, compared to nearly a month for non-Chinese firms.

It is also critical to attain the lowest possible collection period to reduce accounts receivable to a minimum. If you are too generous with your customers, you lose money because you are in effect making them an interest-free loan. Eventually you may also have trouble with your suppliers if you do not have the cash to cover your own purchases. But, if you are too stringent, your customers may be unable to pay, or else they may go to someone else. Again, experience counts, and success in this area leads directly to a high ratio of sales to assets. Limlagen discovered that Chinese firms had a collection period of less than a month, while non-Chinese firms had a collection period of almost two months.

Limlagen made another point about Chinese firms and their cash management, emphasized and extended by Min Chen.[24] Chinese firms were not only concerned about managing cash flow. They were also concerned about cash itself. Chinese firms emphasized cash and liquidity. Chinese viewed all assets other than cash as 'sleeping' cash. They considered it a risk to let cash sleep, because the cash might not wake up, and would be lost. The point for many Chinese firms was above all to minimize the time that their cash spent sleeping, and to maximize their total amount of cash. The implied 'cash generation cycle' is shown in Figure 8.1.

This seems counter-intuitive from the standpoint of Western management theory. An alternative 'assets and wealth generation cycle' is shown in Figure 8.2. Rather than maximizing cash holdings, the point for firms is to maximize assets. Most managers concentrate especially on the level of current assets, which includes inventory, accounts receivable, and of course cash. All should be minimized, and especially cash. Cash on hand from this perspective is not 'working' as it should be, and it certainly should be earning more than the bank rate of interest, so the point is to put cash to

(1)	Cash	
(2)	Fixed assets and inventory	
(3)	Sales	'Sleeping' cash
(4)	Accounts receivable	
(5)	Cash	

Sources: Adapted from Victor Simpaol Limlingan, *The Overseas Chinese in ASEAN: Business Strategies and Management Practices.* (Manila: Vita Development Corporation, 1986), p. 87, and Min Chen, *Asian Management Systems* (1995; London: International Thomson Business Press, 1997), p. 109.

Figure 8.1   The cash generation cycle

(1)	Fixed + current assets (including cash)
(2)	Production and/or sales
(3)	Profit
(4)	Assets

Figure 8.2   The assets and wealth generation cycle

work as quickly as possible, by investing it in fixed assets and inventory, which will lead to increased production, sales, and profit, and to increased assets at the end of the cycle.

'Sometimes,' says Chen, 'the concern over "sleeping" cash can reach absurdity.' Chinese may borrow from a bank, and then place the money on deposit at the same bank. The interest rate differential is the price paid in order to have instant access to cash. This is insurance for business purposes.[25] In addition we may add that, if you live in a hostile environment, where one of your customers might simply refuse to pay and legal recovery of the debt is difficult or impossible, or where your factory or shop might be burned down, then access to cash also becomes a form of disaster insurance.

Aside from cash serving as an insurance policy, in general access to cash is also crucial in a diversified and rapidly changing trading environment. Chinese, as emphasized by Chen, have proved themselves adept at recognizing an advantageous 'deal' and also adept at breaking a big deal down into several smaller ones. Best of all are the deals that generate continued cash flows even after the original cash has been recovered (they produce 'gravy profits'), and those that are self-financing and require no cash investment at all (they 'fry in their own fat').[26] A Chinese firm might even take a loss on one deal, concluded quickly, in order to raise cash for another, more profitable opportunity. Chinese firms, with their relatively short collection periods, can also exploit the more liberal credit terms offered by other firms. Goods obtained on 90-day credit can be sold instantly at a loss, and the cash used to finance three rounds of further sales with 30-day terms, ending with a net profit. There is of course a positive correlation of risk and return, so the higher the profit on a transaction, the higher the risk, and therefore taking a loss to finance a high profit deal is almost by definition very risky. A lot of Chinese firms have failed, but many have succeeded, combining the careful day-to-day management of their cash flows with the ability to exploit sudden opportunities.

The desire to have access to cash means that Chinese firms cultivate links with the banking system. Best of all, however, would be to have your own bank, and Chinese have established banks whenever they could. The first local bank in Singapore was established by Wong Ah Fook, who had migrated from southern China in 1854 and become a successful builder and property developer.[27] Control of a bank means a secure source of cash, and a source of capital for expansion. For a Chinese firm, being in debt to outsiders is problematic, because it gives them control. In general, Chinese firms prefer internal financing, and for the larger firms and groups, debt finance often comes from a bank connected with the group. Related party lending is of course very bad from the perspective of banking professionals, because it means the quality of the projected earnings is not subjected to sufficient scrutiny. Imprudent lending contributed to the collapse in 1997, in Indonesia and especially in the case of Bank Central Asia and the Salim Group, but also in Thailand, where finance companies had rushed to increase their loan portfolios in order to position themselves to compete for one of the new full banking licenses the government was rumored to be planning to grant.[28]

Networks

Cash flows irrigate the bamboo networks. Chinese firms have existed in webs of credit, connected by mutual obligation, trust, and the assurance that both suppliers and customers will pay on time. As in Hong Kong or Taiwan, among Southeast Asian Chinese subcontracting is often based on personal relationships, for instance former employees who have established their own businesses. A firm can respond to an opportunity by calling on its network of connections. Rapid responses reduce turnover time and collection periods. Informal, the networks rely on verbal contracts. Network relations are very flexible, but only up to a point, and that point is that an agreement to deliver goods at a fixed price, or to pay by a certain date, must be honored if the firm is going to retain its position of trust in the network.

Looking at the case of Tan Kah Kee again, we can see the risks of doing business without a supporting network. Tan borrowed to expand, but the 1929 crisis and drying up of previously plentiful sources of finance brought him down. Tan could have spread his risks by raising capital from other Chinese or bringing them in as partners. In the early 1920s, he had maintained these sorts of networks, but they had atrophied.[29] Instead, Tan insisted on sourcing rubber from only his own plantations, processing it in his own plants, and controlling his own marketing and distribution. All of this was particularly risky in an industry with very wide and sudden changes in price. Tan also insisted on selling directly in China, rather than working through networks of agents. This was also a very high-risk strategy. His market information was less good than it might have been, and he suffered serious problems in his supply chain logistics. And finally, the hostility he had created made the Chinese community unwilling to help when he fell.[30]

To avoid Tan's fate, membership in a network may be imperative. From the standpoint of the cash flow management strategy outlined above, it is obvious that, if your firm sits midway along a supply chain, and you have suppliers who expect to be paid in less than a month, then you must be able to rely on your customers to pay in less than a month as well. The question then becomes, who do you trust? Chen quotes Janet Landa, who interviewed a number of Hokkien Chinese businessmen in the Malaysian rubber industry in the early 1980s. One of her informants put it this way:

> Because of the risk involved in advancing money without security, based purely on trust, we tend to trade with those whom we trust; they are often kinsmen, friends, people from the same place in China and those who speak the same dialect . . . we find it easier to give credit to a fellow Hokkien, because there are ways of finding out the creditworthiness of that person – about his background, his associates, his ethical code, and so on.[31]

Initial contact may be through these family or other personal connections (*guanxi*), but the development of a reputation for integrity and creditworthiness (*xinyong*, the use or usefulness of trust) takes time. In the early 1990s, one of Tong Chee Kiong and Yong Pit Kee's informants, also from the Singapore rubber industry, said,

> In business, you must really do a few rounds, then you will know the guy. If you do business for so much and the price moves against him, if the guy still honours his contract, then you know that this guy is reliable up to how much, how many thousand dollars. You test him this way, slowly trust him for bigger amounts. All this therefore depends very much on the actual situation.

And another pointed to the possible consequences of not holding to a deal:

> Traditionally, the rubber circle is so small and it is getting smaller. Everybody knows everyone else. So if someone doesn't abide by *xinyong*, if you try to [to go back on your word] just once, people will spread the news, and he's finished![32]

Networks of contacts, relying on trust and reputation, allow firms to mobilize capital, share information, and minimize transaction costs by reducing the effort required to monitor performance. Parallel to Ramon Myers' analysis of firms in Qing and Nationalist China, Gordon Redding identified the use of these networks as a crucial source of strength for overseas Chinese firms.[33] In a well-known article he mapped the deals connecting Chinese groups in Hong Kong and Taiwan with Chinese groups in

Thailand, Malaysia, Singapore, the Philippines, and Indonesia in the early 1990s, another even denser set of deals tying the Sino-Thai groups in Thailand together, and a third linking Southeast Asian Chinese groups to China via their connections in Hong Kong.[34] These deals added up, for overseas Chinese were among the largest foreign investors in all the countries of Southeast Asia in the early 1990s.[35]

The firms' external relations are analogous to their internal structures. They are based on personal relationships. Credit extended on trust connects firms that have dealt with each other over time. Deals can be done, and joint ventures formed, based on these ongoing connections. Networks of contacts yield higher quality information, and control over information allows firms both to improve the services they offer their clients, and also to exclude outside competitors. Together small firms can achieve more than any of them could separately. Relationships can be extended through contacts with networks of other firms extending into other markets. These tend, not surprisingly, to be Chinese firms, possibly from the same region in China, for instance a case of separate firms in Sydney, Kuala Lumpur, and Vancouver, connected over five decades by the fact that the current heads' fathers had known each other in Shanghai before emigrating in the late 1940s.

However, as with boss- and family-centered internal structures, reliance on external connections also has disadvantages. The exclusiveness of the networks is an issue for non-Chinese, and it arose in the discussion group already quoted above:

Malay: 'No point trying to deal with Chinese companies. They don't deal with anyone else but other Chinese.'
Filipino: 'It's true in the Philippines too. Weird, because everybody is "Filipino" but some are "Chinese" too, and for them that makes the difference.'
Malaysian Chinese: 'Not true. For one thing we have to use Malay companies as suppliers because the government makes us. But, yeah, true, it is more comfortable . . . you know you will get paid.'

Promising opportunities to partner with non-Chinese firms therefore may be lost. Chinese firms also can find themselves confined to their 'home turf' because of the very specific nature of their knowledge. This of course applies most strongly to small and medium-sized firms, but reliance on family members for managerial expertise has a similar effect on large firms. The web of obligations, or prejudices of the patriarch, may hamper judgment. In many cases such as Salim Group, the 'network' of the Chinese firms includes members of the non-Chinese ruling elite, but in these relationships they are dependent on the goodwill of their powerful friends, and if this disappears so too will their competitive advantage. Finally, because they rely on trust and on unwritten agreements, Chinese firms run the risk of being "cheated" by partners who renege on commitments, particularly when they move into other regions.

Further, as we saw in Chapter 6, it is incorrect to attribute an internal quality, such as *guanxi*, to an individual or a group, such as the Chinese, and then use this quality to explain their behavior, while ignoring the influence of the social context on their actions.[36] Personal connections are important in all businesses, and connections among Chinese firms do not add up to a single all-encompassing network, as has sometimes been argued.[37] Edmund Gomez and Michael Hsiao insist that the large number of individual deals among big Chinese firms does not prove the existence of permanent networks. There is, for instance, little evidence of mergers, or of ongoing sharing of resources and information between or among family groups.[38]

Many of the deals reported between Chinese firms have failed to deliver the profits the partners hoped, and the aftermath has sometimes been acrimonious.[39] Prime Minister Lee Kwan Yew of Singapore, for instance, said in 1993 that Singapore's investments in China, such as the Suzhou Industrial Park (SIP), were examples of *guanxi*. *Guanxi*, he said, 'through the same language and culture can make up for a lack in the rule of law and the transparency of rules and regulations'. There was, he said, no need for ethnic Chinese 'to be aplogetic about wanting to maximise benefits through contacts and access to opportunities'.[40] Subsequently, however, Singapore authorities accused the Suzhou municipal government of diverting investment away from the SIP and towards its own industrial park. When the mayor of Suzhou insisted that his government had fulfilled its side of the contract with Singapore, Lee responded that he had now discovered that signing a contract on the mainland was the beginning of negotiations, not the end. 'You have to be flexible,' he said. 'We are not going to change them and they are not going to change us. But, if we want to do business in China, this is something we have to remember: it's different from doing business in other countries because they are clever people – in fact, too clever.' In the end, Singapore reduced its stake in the park to 35 per cent, and the Suzhou government took over management.[41]

Firm Competencies and Chinese Culture

Explanations for the success of overseas Chinese firms tend to emphasize either structural and historical factors, or the ongoing influence of Chinese culture. Overseas Chinese have survived in part by maintaining a low profile. Sun Tzu's advice to be subtle and mysterious appears an apt description of the overseas Chinese. But low key does not mean disappearing. No matter what their degree of assimilation, most continue to see themselves as 'Chinese'. In part this reflects their sense of identification with Chinese in other parts of the world. From a cultural perspective, to Chinese, Chinese civilization looks more sophisticated than the colonial or recently independent societies of Southeast Asia. In addition, however, even cultural identity can be in part determined by the environment, and for the overseas Chinese, identifying themselves as 'Chinese' may reflect a sense of threat from the surrounding community. In Redding's phrase, the overseas Chinese are a 'networked society' embedded in a larger and generally hostile environment.[42]

Opinion recently has shifted somewhat, away from cultural explanations and toward environmental factors. Gomez and Hsiao note the lack of systematic data on Chinese firms. There are many case studies and many individual deals, but the case studies frequently lack a comparison with non-Chinese firms, and the individual deals relate only to the activities of the small number of large groups.[43] Redding's influential work, for instance, relies on interviews with 36 managers in Hong Kong, 21 in Taiwan, 12 in Singapore, and three in Indonesia, but none in any of the other countries of Southeast Asia.[44] Nevertheless, he extended his analysis to all Chinese firms and especially to the overseas Chinese. Redding's interviewees agreed that their management style reflected Chinese and especially Confucian values. However, identification with Chinese culture does not necessarily mean familiarity with its components. As seen below, at the same time Redding was conducting his interviews, the Singapore government was unable to locate a single qualified expert in Confucian culture to design its proposed high school course, and as noted previously, a large majority of the Chinese and overseas Chinese students we surveyed had difficulty even naming the fundamental five Confucian relationships. Any direct influence of Confucian tradition must be very attenuated indeed.[45]

Chinese firms are extremely competitive, and business losses are seen as threatening the existence of the family. Again this can reflect either cultural or environmental factors. They may not be able to name the five relationships, but many overseas Chinese business people have read Sun Tzu and possibly other military classics such as *The 36 Stratagems*.[46] In interviews they often compare business to warfare. But this is possibly no more than one would expect from a migrant community. Where Chinese are a small minority, competitiveness is turned against the surrounding society. The obverse, cooperativeness with other Chinese firms, in turn often reflects kinship or regional connections based on place of origin in China. Chinese share further characteristics with other migrant groups. Migrants are self-selected.

They tend to be tough, adaptable, energetic and, of course, mobile, all qualities that will contribute to success in business.

In addition, compared to indigenous groups and to other migrant groups, Chinese in Southeast Asia tend to be well educated. Though the original migrants to Southeast Asia were not members of the Chinese elite, a long Chinese tradition supports formal education. For the overseas Chinese, this means providing advanced education for their children. For the children it means intense pressure to succeed academically. This can reflect back on their parents' firms. Already in the early 1990s there was evidence that overseas Chinese business people felt themselves at a disadvantage, compared to 'professionals' with their specialized knowledge.[47] The resulting pressure to change and adapt has intensified, as a new generation adds new levels of expertise, for instance in financial management, or whole new areas of expertise, for instance information technology.[48] Overseas Chinese make up the large majority of the 'new managers' identified by Michael Carney and Eric Gedajlovic. Often with overseas educations and frequently employing Japanese or Western management techniques, they have established new firms in telecommunications, computers, and media.[49]

Overseas Chinese firms have always confronted dilemmas of growth and success. At some point a successful firm must expand, but all the possible options require higher levels of expertise and increased risk. The firm, for instance, could move forward into mass retail sales. The resulting high volumes will yield economies of scale, but the firm will need more working capital. It might move backward into wholesaling, but this is only an option for a few of the strongest firms. It might move another step backward into production, but this requires different skills and expertise, and would involve substantial fixed capital investment. Over decades, overseas Chinese firms have tended to prefer the final option, and branch into other products. This might involve trade both ways, supplying goods to the countryside and collecting goods for sale in the urban area, and it could lead the firm to diversify into other areas, such as transportation or finance.

Globalization offers a new set of opportunities for diversification. Moving from domestic bases in the 1980s, many successful Chinese firms expanded outside their home countries. This is a way both of protecting themselves, and of gaining new fields for investment that have been or may be denied them at home as a result of state regulation and discrimination. As in the case of Salim Group, organizational structures change with expansion and movement into new areas. These changes, particularly public listing, have frequently been taken to mean that overseas Chinese firms must and will 'modernize' and become more like Western firms.[50] However, even the 'new managers' have relied on their connections with existing family business groups to finance their expansion.[51] Further, where the environment continues to be potentially hostile, and in situations where inherited ways of doing business continue to bring in profits, the older patterns seem certain to persist. At the same time, in expanding markets such as China where their inheritance may smooth their way, Chinese may adapt, and their firms may modify their strategies, to achieve competitive advantage.[52]

THE SINGAPORE 'SYSTEM'

BOX 8.3   POINT AND COUNTERPOINT: TEMASEK HOLDINGS AND THE STRENGTHS AND WEAKNESSES OF THE SINGAPORE SYSTEM

Temasek Holdings sits at the center of the Singapore system, and it exemplifies both Singapore's positive aspects and high ambitions, and its negative side and problematic position in the world. Temasek's website, like most corporate sites, is self-congratulatory:

> Born of humble roots during a turbulent and uncertain time, now Temasek's companies have survived, grown and extended their reach as leading regional and international businesses.
> Temasek is committed to building a vibrant future through successful enterprise – leveraging on the existing platforms or creating new platforms for tomorrow.
> *People, Purpose and Passion* are the key drivers for excellence in Temasek and its companies.

The site describes Temasek as 'an Asia investment company headquartered in Singapore'. Temasek sees itself as 'a pro-active, long-term investor' whose strategy is 'to invest in companies with high regional or global potential and build them into successful enterprises'. The first 'thrust' is a program of 'strategic development' through oversight and monitoring that 'pro-actively identifies business opportunities, and links the TLCs [Temasek-linked companies] with potential partners and markets'. The second thrust is 'corporate development' which ensures that TLCs 'have good quality boards and management teams'. Finally, 'capital resources management' maximizes Temasek's returns from its portfolio. The three thrusts are further characterized as 'grow (scale)', 'glow (performance)' and 'go (energy)'. In particular, the statement continues, Temasek realizes its aims through working with its fellow shareholders, regulators, and 'other market participants' in order 'to foster a fair and efficient corporate governance environment in support of a vibrant business culture'.

The first of a list of 'frequently asked questions' (FAQ), however, is, 'Is Temasek Holdings a statutory board or government agency?' The response in fact does not answer the question:

> Temasek Holdings is an investment holding company incorporated under the Singapore Companies Act. We operate strictly as a commercial entity. We are run independently by a board of directors and management team, with the key objective of maximising shareholder returns from our investments. As a shareholder, we expect our businesses to make their decisions based on commercial and economic grounds. Temasek's own decisions are also based strictly on commercial considerations.

The reason the question is not answered directly appears in the answer to the third FAQ, 'Who is Temasek's shareholder?' The answer is,

> Temasek Holdings's shareholder is the Singapore Ministry of Finance (MOF). MOF appoints Temasek's Board of Directors, and is represented on Temasek's Board. The Board of Directors provides strategic direction to Temasek's management. As with any other commercial company, Temasek submits annual performance reviews, audited financial statements, and pays dividends to our shareholder.

And the answer to the eighth FAQ, 'Where can I get a copy of Temasek's financial statements?' is:

> Temasek has been granted the status of an exempt private company. As an exempt private company we are not required to disclose financial information. In October 2004 we launched the Temasek Review, disclosing for the first time in 30 years our financial review . . . [this is] part of our on-going efforts to institutionalise Temasek's role as a long-term shareholder and an active investor.

Technically, that is, despite being responsible for publicly-owned assets that it said totaled S$90 billion (around US$53 billion) in mid-2005, because it is a company with not more than 20 members and with no shares held by other corporations (its only shareholder, the Ministry of Finance, is not legally a corporation), Temasek is required to reveal only as much information as it chooses, and for 30 years it chose to reveal nothing.

Established in 1974, Temasek took over investments previously held directly by the Ministry of Finance. Its holdings among

Singapore firms in 2005 included 63 per cent of SingTel (near-monopoly of telephone services), 100 per cent of MediaCorp (largest provider of television and radio), 28 per cent of DBS Bank (dominant in both retail and equity banking), 57 per cent of Singapore Airlines, 100 per cent of PSA International (port and harbor facilities), 55 per cent of SMRT Corporation (controls rapid transit, bus, taxi, and car rental services), 100 per cent of Singapore Power (owns and operates Singapore's electricity and gas distribution networks), 100 per cent of three power generation companies that provide 89 per cent of Singapore's electric power, SembCorp Industries (shipbuilding), and a range of property development and infrastructure firms, including 32 per cent of construction firm Keppel Corporation and 88 per cent of Wildlife Reserves Singapore, which owns and operates the Singapore Zoo.

The CEO of Temasek is Ho Ching. Appointed in 2002, she is the wife of Singapore Prime Minister Lee Hsien Loong, and the daughter-in-law of former Prime Minister Lee Kuan Yew. The chairman of Temasek's board, S. Dhanabalan, is also the chairman of DBS Group Holdings, and one of the deputy chairmen is Lim Siong Guan, the Permanent Secretary of the Ministry of Finance. Temasek's own governance therefore reflects the close overlapping interconnections among the government-linked companies that dominate the Singapore economy. It also poses the question of the extent and meaning of the privatization of state enterprises. At the same time, however, their evident desire to appear responsible and transparent has led these companies to adopt the forms of modern corporate governance, notably in Temasek's decision to publish an annual report including its aggregate financial results.

News reports have attributed Temasek's recent 'overseas push' in financial services to Ho Ching's influence. Temasek already held major stakes in two large banks in Indonesia, Bank Danamon (56 per cent) and Bank Internasional Indonesia (28 per cent), as well as 9 per cent of ICICI Bank (India), 10 per cent of Hana Bank (Korea), and a majority interest in NIB Bank (Pakistan). It had also bid for the Taiwan government's remaining 22 per cent share of the formerly state-owned Changhwa Bank. In China, Temasek had acquired a small share of the private Minsheng Bank. Then, in June 2005, Temasek paid US$1.4 billion for a 5.1 per cent stake in China Construction Bank (CCB), and in August 2005 it was reported to be negotiating to purchase approximately 5 per cent of the Bank of China (BoC) for some US$1 billion.

These investments in one sense show the flexibility and quick responses that Singapore's system makes possible. However, they have also highlighted the difficulties of definition, role, and scale that Singapore's government-linked enterprises confront. In the case of China, it was reported that the Chinese government may have previously regarded Temasek with suspicion, because of its status as an agency of the Singapore government. CCB quite deliberately chose Bank of America over Temasek as its largest foreign partner, and Royal Bank of Scotland and UBS were both reported to be considering purchases of shares of BoC about twice the size of Temasek's proposed share. Aside from the link with the Singapore government, the issue for major Chinese banks was their desire to acquire financial, banking, and above all management expertise from their foreign partners ahead of their public listings. Temasek had access to large financial resources, but did not possess the technical competencies that American or British banks could offer.

None of the Chinese holdings was large enough to exercise management influence, and this was true of other investments Temasek has made outside of Singapore, for instance its 5 per cent share of Telekom Malaysia. As noted in Chapter 7, in early 2006 Temasek's purchase of a 49.6 per cent share in Shin Corp, the family holding company of Thai Prime Minister Thaksin Shinawatra, for 73.3 billion baht (US$1.9 billion) caused mass protests in Thailand because the sellers paid no tax. Aside from the scandal, which contributed to Thaksin's downfall, here too it was not clear what role Temasek, a foreign firm whose interest was held through two Thai subsidiaries, would play in the company, although there were references to 'leveraging Temasek's global network' in working together with the Shin Corp management. Rather than the value-creating active investor role Temasek sees for itself, news articles quoted observers who suggested that these were passive 'private equity-type investments', which could and would be sold if the share prices rose high enough.

Sources: http://temasekholdings.com.sg (there are links to the websites of all the companies in which Temasek holds significant stakes); Kathrin Hille, 'Temasek tries to gazump bank bid', *The Australian*, 2 August 2005; Francesco Guerrera and Richard McGregor, 'Temasek eyes $1.3bn BoC stake', *The Australian*, 10 August 2005; Chris Noon, 'Thai PM Thaksin's son fined over Shin sale', Forbes.com, 3 March 2006; Temasek Holdings, 'Temasek-SCB led investors group acquires Shinawatra and Damapong families' stake in Shin Corp', press release, 23 January 2006.

The Historical and Institutional Grids

Singapore was a British colony, though migration made it overwhelmingly a Chinese city. As a trading center and naval base, Singapore played a key role in Britain's imperial strategy, and the fall of Singapore to the Japanese was traumatic, both to the British and, as we have seen above, and in Chapter 7, to many thousands of the city's Chinese people. Following the war Singapore became part of the British-sponsored Malaysian Federation. At the same time the rise of the People's Action Party (PAP) and its leader Lee Kwan Yew raised the possibility of uniting all the federation's non-Malay voters, a strategy that could have made Lee the leader of the federation. As we have seen, the Malay elite perceived Lee and his bloc of Chinese voters as a threat, and Singapore was expelled from the federation in 1965.

The institutional and management grids that make up the Singapore 'system' reflect this history. British influence continued in government structures. Singapore has a parliamentary government, a formally independent judiciary, a professional civil service, and widely admired corporate governance rules and regulations. However, although there are opposition parties, the PAP has remained utterly dominant, and in effect Singapore is a one-party state. An Internal Security Act allows detention without trial, and PAP leaders have used the courts to harass and hamper political opposition. The PAP uses control over residence as another lever to keep potential opposition in check. Singapore's apartment blocks are the result of a massive urban reconstruction program from the 1960s through the 1980s. The government has provided housing for nearly 90 per cent of the population. Early developments broke up Malay centers, and ethnic quotas imposed in the new blocks in 1989 to achieve 'racial balance' prevented the formation of new concentrations of Malay or Indian voters, since a district with 80 per cent Chinese is considered balanced, while one with anything over 20 per cent Malay is considered unbalanced.[53]

PAP leaders have envisaged a large role for the state to build competitive competencies in the global economy. As the Housing Development Board was transforming and modernizing Singapore's physical structure, the government also planned to maintain and enhance its human capacity. Schooling has been a priority. Singapore is small in absolute terms, and the educational inheritance left by the British was not favorable. In 1980, over 43 per cent of the population over the age of 25 had no formal schooling, compared to 20 and 23 per cent in South Korea and Taiwan, for instance. Since then, Singapore's ruthlessly competitive and rigorously meritocratic educational system has become legendary, and government scholarships have paid for elite overseas educations for the very best high school graduates.

In addition, Lee Kwan Yew and other PAP leaders believed intelligence to be genetically determined. In his National Day address in 1983, Lee asserted that intelligence is 80 per cent inherited, and said that the tendency for educated women to remain unmarried and childless would undermine Singapore's competitiveness. Although PAP leaders have consistently denied the connection, it is the relatively high birth rate of the Malay minority that worries them. Concern over the relative decline of the Chinese population has led the government to encourage educated immigrants, largely Chinese from Hong Kong, Macau, and Taiwan. 'Draconian' laws restricted the rights of Singaporeans to marry unskilled foreign workers, most of whom were non-Chinese, and required sterilization after their second child if they were granted permission. Further laws provided for the deportation of unmarried foreign workers who became pregnant and imposed punishments on their employers.[54]

Lee's comments on unmarried educated women set off the 'Great Marriage Debate'. Singapore possesses a Women's Charter passed in 1961 that prohibits polygamy and gives wives equal rights with husbands to property, divorce, and responsibility for children. The labor shortage of the 1960s caused the government to encourage employers to hire 'under-utilized' women. However, Singapore did not sign the United Nations conventions guaranteeing equal pay and treatment for female workers, and has consistently defined husbands as the head of family units. Male government employees can claim medical benefits for their dependants, but female government employees cannot, for instance. Following Lee's speech the government introduced financial incentives to encourage marriage and childbearing by university-educated women, who are disproportionately Chinese, and educational benefits including reserved places in desirable schools for their children (parallel financial incentives for less educated women to undergo sterilization proved too controversial and were dropped). A matchmaking service, the Social Development Unit, was established in 1985 to ensure that as many university-educated women as possible marry and produce children.[55]

Government leaders wanted not only intelligent citizens raised in families headed by men; they also wanted moral citizens, insulated against 'the supposedly decadent and morally corrosive values of the West'.[56] To achieve this, in 1984, the previous high school course in Civics was replaced by Religious Knowledge. Students had the option of studying Christianity, Islam, Buddhism, Hinduism, Sikhism, or Confucian ethics. The government had particular hopes for the Confucian ethics option, which was added at the insistence of Lee Kwan Yew for Chinese students, in order, he said, to give them 'a cultural ballast against the less desirable aspects of Western culture'. The course was designed with advice from Chinese-American academics such as Tu Wei-ming, because there were no suitably qualified Confucian scholars in Singapore.[57] The attempt failed. Confucian ethics did not attract students. Only 17.8 per cent of students chose the course, and although these were mostly Chinese, three-quarters of Chinese students chose not to study Confucian ethics. Further, religious belief could become the basis for opposition to government policy. In 1987, groups of both Christian and Muslim activists were expelled, and, following official inquiries that indicated a rise in religious revivalism, in 1989 the government announced that the Religious Knowledge course would be phased out and replaced by a secular moral education program, and in 1990 new laws prohibited religious groups from engaging in political activity.[58]

Government leaders also wanted their Chinese citizens to speak Mandarin. Reflecting their family backgrounds, some 40 per cent of Singaporean Chinese spoke Hokkien, around 12 per cent Teochiu, and the rest a number of other southern Chinese dialects. Mandarin was the native language of at most 1 per cent of the population. Nevertheless, the government defined Mandarin as the 'mother tongue' of Singaporean Chinese, and in 1981 required pupils to study it in school and prescribed minimum levels of proficiency for admission to tertiary education (boys were admitted with lower Mandarin scores than girls). Lee Kwan Yew said, 'The greatest value in the teaching and learning of Chinese is in the transmission of the norms of social or moral behaviour. This means principally Confucianist beliefs and ideas, of man, society, and the state.' Government leaders were also worried because large numbers of Chinese students had been taking Malay as their second language.[59] Success here was partial, for although compulsory study results in reasonable fluency in spoken Mandarin, most Singapore Chinese also communicate in one of the southern Chinese dialects, standard English, or 'Singlish', a blend of English mixed with Chinese, Malay, and Tamil syntax and phrases that the government regards with distaste and tries to ignore.

Singapore's role as a commercial center for Britain's Asian interests had led to a one-sided emphasis on re-export (or entrepôt) trade, 43 per cent of total trade and 94 per cent of exports in 1960. With independence the Singapore government adopted an import substitution policy, attempting to move the economy toward manufacturing. This changed abruptly to an emphasis on exports following ejection from the Malaysian Federation, which cut the city off from its natural hinterland. The government favored labor-intensive products in the late 1960s. Then, in the 1970s, the government decided to move to higher value added goods, and the National Wage Council deliberately increased wages and retirement contributions to discourage low-skill, labor-intensive manufacturing and lay the foundation for a 'Second Industrial Revolution'. Increased labor costs and an appreciation

of the Singapore dollar caused a severe recession in 1985. In response government leaders changed course again, turning towards the services sector.
Singapore, they now said, would become a regional services hub, supplying
financial and technical expertise to other Asian countries, as well as logistical support and subcontracting for foreign multinationals in the region.[60]

Although policy has shifted, one constant has been the encouragement
of foreign investment. The Economic Development Board (EDB) was
established in 1961 to seek out and smooth the path of foreign firms
wishing to establish themselves in Singapore. The EDB was not a planning
agency with the powers of Korea's EPB or Taiwan's CEPAD, nor has it fostered the creation of domestic technological capabilities, as MITI has in
Japan. What it has done is to provide a range of tailored benefits to foreign
firms.[61] Foreigners also have been assured of peaceful labor relations, as the
National Trade Union Congress is allied with the PAP, and the 1968
Industrial Relations (Amendment) Act banned illegal strikes. Through the
early 1990s, foreign establishments employed over half of Singapore's
manufacturing workers and produced 70 per cent of industrial output and
80 per cent of manufactured exports. In the later 1990s and early 2000s,
foreign firms tended to retain their headquarters functions in Singapore,
but locate their manufacturing in lower wage environments, which most
commonly meant in nearby Johore in Malaysia. In possibly the most spectacular case, however, the specialist contract manufacturer Flextronics
International, an American firm registered in Singapore, whose total sales
rose from US$93 million in 1993 to US$15.9 billion in 2004–5, used its
Singapore base to coordinate design and manufacturing in plants in
Mexico, Brazil, Hungary, Poland, and several locations in China.[62]

The Government-linked Company Sector

Much of the manufacturing output not produced by foreign firms has been
produced by the large state enterprise sector. In fact, until the late 1980s, the
so-called government-linked companies (GLCs) were the second leg of the
government's 'two-legged' policy, the first leg being the favored foreign
multinational firms. As the list of Temasek's interests shows, the GLCs
extend across the entire economy. In the early 1990s, the GLCs were organized into four main holding companies, Temasek Holdings controlled by
the Ministry of Finance, Ministry of National Development Holdings
(MNDH) controlled by the Ministry of National Development, Sheng-Li
Holdings (SHL, later re-named Singapore Technologies) controlled by the
Ministry of Defence, and the Hospital Corporation of Singapore, which
was formed as part of a move to privatize government hospitals in the late
1980s. Some estimates have suggested that GLCs employ over a quarter of

the labor force and produce half of Singapore's total output. Government officials dispute this, and point to the program of divestment and privatization in place since 1987, but the list of Temasek's interests also shows that government agencies hold a substantial fraction of the shares of 'privatized' firms.

The capital needs of the government sector have been met through savings mobilized through the compulsory retirement contributions made by workers to the Central Provident Fund, which in some periods has deducted as much as half of their wages. In addition, government surpluses were invested through the Government of Singapore Investment Corporation (GSIC or GIC), though GSIC has spun off its real estate and other holdings as separate companies and now reportedly concentrates more on short-term financial instruments. The Development Bank of Singapore (DBS Bank), incorporating the former postal savings system, and reportedly the largest lender in Southeast Asia, mobilized further financial resources and has served as another of the government's holding companies. Singapore's savings ratio rose from 19 per cent of GNP in 1970, to 34 per cent in 1980, peaked at 45 per cent in 1990, and has remained one of the highest in the world.

Statutory Boards and GLCs are believed to produce large surpluses, which go to the government under a law passed in 1989. This was not generally the intention, as most were formed to overcome perceived market failures, but over time the government has tended to allow those boards that produce profits to become more autonomous and to operate more like independent corporations. Boards have also multiplied as they are split into more specialized bodies. The boards have a tendency to move into profitable areas, at the expense of the private sector. The government may or may not intend this, but its desire for revenues and general encouragement of the boards' activities reinforce this tendency. Successful GLCs are now viewed as regional and global firms. Conversely, the government has closed down or sold loss-making GLCs.

Surpluses suggest that the GLCs are well-run, but exactly how well they are run is difficult to say. There is very little public information available, and especially about their financial performance. The 1984 Statutory Bodies and Government Companies (Protection of Secrecy) Act severely limited information. Parliament has oversight only of the funds of those GLCs audited by the Auditor-General. The others may appoint private auditors, but these come under the control of the government ministries that oversee the holding companies, and their reports are confidential. The holding companies, the GSIC, and the SHL companies are exempted from filing reports with the Registrar of Companies, and other vehicles, as in the case of Temasek, are exempt because of their legal structure.

The state economic development program led to the creation of an elite group of bureaucratic administrators. A pyramid of control began with the Prime Minister's cabinet and a special committee, the Directorship and Consultancy Appointments Council. The second tier was the ministries themselves, each with their own large holding companies and statutory boards, and, as in the case of Tamesek, ministerial control has continued. The small group of directors and chairmen of the holding companies typically have also occupied positions on the boards of a number of the larger individual GLCs. Finally, directors of the larger GLCs also typically sit on the boards of smaller GLCs. The number of directors increased to close to 1000 in the early 1990s, of whom some 20 served as directors of ten or more GLCs.[63]

Recruitment into the management of the GLCs is of course élitist. The government sends a select few students overseas for education each year. The best of those, and the best of the best from local institutions, then receive government appointments. But ultimately recruitment is political. High positions come only to those whose loyalty has been tested by long service. A rotation system, high salaries, and harsh punishments for corruption have worked to prevent the establishment of patronage and clientèle networks independent of the ruling PAP. Appointments do depend on personal connections, but over the years careful personal control by the group at the very top has ensured both technical competence and honesty.

The GLCs have led Singapore's expansion. The Singapore–Malaysia–Indonesia growth triangle or 'Sijori' (for Singapore, Johor in Malaysia, and Riau in Indonesia), has led to large infrastructure investments in the southern districts of Johor, and on the islands of Batam and Bintan opposite Singapore. Among others, on Bintan a $2 billion project for tourist development was a joint venture between Singapore Technologies Industrial Corporation (STIC), one of the SHL companies, and Indonesia's Salim Group. Lee Kwan Yew visited China in 1992 and then criticized Singapore for falling behind Hong Kong and Taiwan in investment in China. The rush to comply saw various GLCs commit over US$900 million in 742 projects within months. The 1993 agreement to establish the Suzhou Industrial Park (SIP) and Wuxi-Singapore Industrial Park, both in the general vicinity of Shanghai, seemed both a capstone and a base for further expansion. SIP, which was to showcase Singapore's integrated planning approach and combine high-end technology manufacturing with residential development, was celebrated as 'Singapore II' by the Singapore press. As we saw above, this proved much more difficult than imagined, but the absence of financial information makes it difficult to determine the extent of Singapore's losses.

Chinese Business and Entrepreneurship in Singapore

Singapore has a very large number of private firms, making up 90 per cent of total establishments and employing possibly half of all workers. These are 'Chinese' firms in about the same proportion as Chinese in the population. Some are large. The ten largest groups control 25 per cent of Singapore's corporate sector, but these large groups are controlled by individual families and, although they may appoint outside managers, they ensure control through pyramid structures, tightly held blocks of shares, and a preference for debt financing through banks connected with their group.[64] Most private firms are small, with an average of 34 employees compared to 212 for foreign firms in the early 1990s, for instance. Local firms have the lowest percentage of sales exported. Small and medium enterprises have very low average labor productivity, less than half that of large firms.

The relationship of private business to the state has been problematic, and reflects the desire of the elite to maintain control. At the time of their initial election victory in 1959, the PAP's leaders, Lee Kwan Yew and a small group of mostly English-educated professionals, had no military to support them, and no money or business networks to provide patronage. The education system, as noted above, was extremely poor, as was the housing supply, and Britain also left behind a corrupt and inefficient public service. The PAP's leaders managed to hold power by solving the critical problems of unemployment and housing to the satisfaction of the majority of the population. They improved education, they built new housing, and, because they did not rely on the public service for support, they had no hesitation in reforming it. A new Prevention of Corruption Act in 1960 gave the Corrupt Practices Investigation Bureau broad powers to investigate and arrest. Public sector salaries remained low through the 1970s but then rose. The prestige of government service increased and, as we saw above, the government systematically favored successive cohorts of the brightest high school students with educational scholarships followed by subsequent employment in the GLC sector and government departments.[65]

As noted in Chapter 7, Singapore today is perceived as one of the least corrupt countries in the world, but there is another aspect. Civil service reform restricted the chance of forming patronage networks outside the ruling circle. And in a parallel and related fashion, from the beginning the PAP's leaders refused to share power with the indigenous Chinese business community. For the PAP's leaders, modernization meant overcoming the 'outdated and superfluous' inheritance of traditional Chinese ways.[66] As in the Japanese case, the reformed bureaucracy became the instrument of government policy. Singapore's political elite also resembles the cases of Japan and Thailand, in that the claim to be modern and the claim that society requires their leadership, although objectively false, is a powerful force for legitimizing their continued rule. In Singapore's case the PAP leaders' attitude also reflected distrust, for Chinese business leaders had supported the opposition Socialist Front against the PAP following independence.[67]

A looming labor shortage in the mid-1970s prompted the government to direct its attention to the neglected small and medium businesses, because these were typically labor-intensive operations and if their productivity could be improved it would release labor to the more dynamic sectors of the economy. The government introduced measures to encourage them to upgrade their technologies, but small employers were also badly hurt by the increase in wages and retirement contributions imposed by the Second Industrial Revolution policy. The ensuing recession of the mid-1980s, a report that identified the 'lop-sided' development of the economy as a problem, and further difficulties as the government found there were not enough private firms able to take over the 500 or so enterprises that it wished to divest, together led to the formulation of an SME Master Plan in 1989. Programs were developed to link small firms with foreign multinationals as subcontractors, to assist them in participating in the development of the Sijori growth triangle, and to help them list on the stock exchange to raise capital.

By 1998, the government could point to 60 or more programs directly aimed at small and medium businesses, including permission to operate businesses directly from Housing Development Board apartments.[68] A new 'SME 21' plan launched in 2000 envisaged trebling the number of SMEs with sales turnover of more than S$20 million, doubling the productivity of SMEs in retailing, and quadrupling the number of e-commerce-enabled SMEs, by 2010.[69] The government subsidized studies of rags-to-riches success stories of successful Chinese entrepreneurs. Goh Keng Swee, one of the most senior figures in Singapore's economic administration, said he hoped that they would refute Max Weber's denigration of Confucianism as inimical to economic growth, and also demonstrate that 'high morality' was the basis of Chinese–Singaporean entrepreneurship.[70] As we have seen in several different contexts, the relationship of Confucianism to modern economic growth is in fact problematical and, as we will see in Chapter 9, morality has very little to do with entrepreneurship, but Singapore's leaders certainly would like to have successful businessmen. The government has continued to celebrate individuals such as Sim Wong Ho, who founded Creative Technology in 1981 and developed the Sound Blaster stereo sound card for PC computers, the de facto international standard.[71]

Patterns that Singaporean entrepreneurs share with similar groups elsewhere in the world include family support, a long-cherished ambition for independence, experience in a previous job or hobby, insight and recognition of opportunity (often accidental), and travel. Notably in the information technology sector, experience with foreign firms has often been important. Creative Technology's Sim Wong Ho, for instance, worked for a Japanese firm, and moved to California for a time. Factors specific to Singapore include a lack of capital, which is a key problem for many small firms. The high rate of contributions imposed by the Central Provident Fund limits the funds available for private investment, and for individuals may make it impossible to accumulate independent savings. Very few Singaporean entrepreneurs have been able to obtain bank loans. Many do not apply for support that they might be entitled to, because they are not convinced that the government really wants to help them, or because they do not know about the programs.[72] Those that do apply will discover that the government insists that they 'assume ownership and responsibility for their upgrading', that it has no intention of favoring them in procurement contracts, that their creditworthiness will be scrutinized by 'participating financial institutions' and that the upgrading will be provided by 'private sector training providers and consultants' and only 'partially' funded by the government.[73]

As in the case of Creative Technology, successful entrepreneurs have excellent management skills, have introduced the right product at the right time, have developed a niche, or have seen the 'new' product as an opportunity. Sim was the tenth of 12 children, an undistinguished student with a diploma in engineering from Ngee An Technical College, who set up Creative Technology in a shopping center with childhood friend Ng Kai Wa. They failed in their attempt to create a multimedia computer, but in doing so developed the prototype of the integrated sound cards that led to success. A distinctive feature of Singaporean firms in high-tech areas is a tendency to look outside Singapore and establish overseas subsidiaries or joint ventures. Henry Yeung's survey of Singapore firms expanding internationally found that a common motive was 'market reach'. They wanted to be present in all leading markets and have access to assets available within those markets, in contrast to Hong Kong firms, which were more likely to emphasize 'horizontal integration' in their decisions to invest overseas.[74] Creative Technology again is typical in establishing Creative Labs in the United States (1988), Europe (1993), and Asia (1999), and in acquiring foreign firms, for instance 3D Labs in the United Kingdom in 2002, to gain access to the professional graphics market.

Nevertheless, there are relatively few successful entrepreneurs in Singapore and, compared to other Chinese of Southeast Asia, Singaporean Chinese are unlikely to engage in entrepreneurial behavior. Yeung echoes earlier studies in concluding that 'the real private entrepreneur is missing' and that most Singaporeans 'have become contented with their job security and are less willing to take specific kinds of risks to launch new business ventures'. Lee Kuan Yew himself said in 1996, 'We have built up too comfortable a life for Singaporeans. But the people who want to be comfortable are the people who are not going to be rich. So, you've got to decide whether you want to try for the jackpot, or you just live a quiet, peaceful life.'[75] Tan Chin Nam, Permanent Secretary of the Ministry for Manpower, said in 2002, 'To thrive in the new economy we need technology. Sim is a pioneer, but more importantly he has reinvented himself. Singapore needs to reinvent itself.'[76]

Parallel to the debate over the role of Confucianism among overseas Chinese, the cultural values of Singaporeans have been blamed for their lack of entrepreneurial spirit. *Kia su* is a Hokkien phrase meaning 'afraid to lose' and indicates a perception of failure as a disgrace that brings shame to both the individual and their family. Therefore failure is to be avoided at all cost. This attitude leads, obviously, to a tendency to avoid risk, or if something is to be undertaken, to attempts to guarantee its success in advance. Lee Tsao Yuan and Linda Low 'suspect' this attitude 'is a by-product of the very strong achievement-oriented society that Singapore has become. In the drive for growth and economic success, the system has become the epitome of meritocracy. There is no room for failure'. Singapore, they argue, is 'over-pressured', and this begins at a very young age, in the educational system. The pressure to make the grade or face shame in school is followed by pressure to obtain a good job, an apartment, a car, marriage, and children. Government actions reinforce the *kia su* attitude. The government continually portrays Singapore as being balanced on a tightrope, under threat, with no margin for error. PAP leaders have been notoriously intolerant of weakness or failure. 'There is therefore little or no room to be exceptionally daring or non-conformist . . . The culture breeds risk-aversity and cautiousness right from the very start.'[77]

Singapore's independent private firms tend to be small. Even Creative Technology has only some 14 000 shareholders, almost all in Singapore, and delisted from the United States NASDAQ exchange in 2004. The 'relatively weak' private sector is 'overshadowed' by the public sector and foreign multinational firms. The statutory boards and GLCs, with access to government funding, can easily crowd out private firms, and the government skims talent through annual offers of scholarships to top students, to the point where government employment is preferred and drains talent away from the private sector.[78] As we will see in Chapter 9, there are some intriguing parallels between Singapore and the other countries of Southeast Asia. Like those other countries, Singapore is ruled by a small elite that favors its own state sector and foreign firms. The elite has manipulated economic policy in a way that has marginalized the mass of indigenous business-people, but the irony, in the Singapore case, is that the elite and the mass of businesspeople are both Chinese.

FURTHER READING

For the historical background an excellent introduction is Anthony Reid (ed.), *Sojourners and Settlers: Histories of Southeast Asia and the Chinese* (Asian Studies Association of Australia, Southeast Asia Publication Series, No. 28; St Leonards: Allen & Unwin, 1996). As noted in Chapter 7, Rajeswary Ampalavanar Brown, *Capital and Entrepreneurship in Southeast Asia* (Houndmills: Macmillan, and New York: St Martin's Press, 1994) is very good for the management grid in the colonial period, and Brown's *Chinese Big Business and the Wealth of Asian Nations* (New York: Palgrave, 2000) analyzes a number of postwar cases. There is a book-length study of Tan Kah Kee, by C.F. Yong, *Tan Kah Kee: The Making of an Overseas Chinese Legend* (Singapore: Oxford University Press, 1987).

Overseas Chinese firms began to attract attention at about the same time as economists began to notice the acceleration of economic growth in Southeast Asia. Yuan-li Wu and Chun-hsi Wu, *Economic Development in Southeast Asia: The Chinese Dimension* (Stanford: Hoover Institution Press, 1980) was among the first; Linda Y. Lim and L.A. Peter Gosling (eds), *The Chinese in Southeast Asia* (2 vols; Singapore: Maruzen Asia, 1983) contained several chapters on management, including Frederic C. Deyo, 'Chinese management practices and work commitment in comparative perspective', vol. 2, pp. 215–29. Victor Simpaol Limlingan, *The Overseas Chinese in ASEAN: Business Strategies and Management Practices* (Manila: Vita Development Corporation, 1986), emphasized the cash flow strategy of Chinese business. Popularizations included Lynn Pan, *Sons of the Yellow Emperor: The Story of the Overseas Chinese* (London: Secker & Warburg, 1990) and Murray L. Weidenbaum and Samuel Hughes, *The Bamboo Network: How Expatriate Chinese Entrepreneurs are Creating a New Economic Superpower in Asia* (New York: Martin Kessler Books, 1996).

S. Gordon Redding, *The Spirit of Chinese Capitalism* (Berlin and New York: deGruyter, 1990) is a classic and sophisticated work that emphasizes the ongoing influence of both Confucian tradition and the institutional structures of Qing (pre-1911) China. As noted above, however, its arguments rest on interviews in Hong Kong, Taiwan and Singapore, with very little direct evidence from the rest of Southeast Asia. Redding and Gilbert Y.Y. Wong, 'The psychology of Chinese organizational behavior', in

Michael Harris Bond (ed.), *The Psychology of the Chinese People* (New York: Oxford University Press, 1990), pp. 267–95, looked at the internal dynamics of Chinese firms. Subsequent work that sought to identify the characteristics of Chinese firms tended to follow Redding's lead; for instance Min Chen, *Asian Management Systems* (1995; London: International Thomson Business Press, 1997), chs 5–7. Semi-popular books for the benefit of non-Chinese managers include George T. Haley, Chin Tiong Tan and Usha C.V. Haley, *New Asian Emperors: The Overseas Chinese, Their Strategies and Competitive Advantages* (Oxford: Butterworth Heinemann, 1998), and Ming-Jer Chen, *Inside Chinese Business: A Guide for Managers Worldwide* (Cambridge: Harvard Business School Press, 2003).

Australia, Department of Foreign Affairs and Trade, East Asia Analytical Unit, *Overseas Chinese Business Networks in Asia* (Canberra: EAAU, 1995) is a comprehensive survey emphasizing, as the title indicates, the competitive advantage that Chinese firms gain from their connections with networks across the region. The EEAU study was also typical in seeing the advantages of Chinese firms as temporary and predicting that their continued success would require them to 'modernize' their structures; that is, to become more like Western firms. Ji Li, Naresh Khatri and Kevin Lim, 'Changing strategic postures of overseas Chinese firms in emerging Asian markets', *Management Decision*, **37**(5) (1999), 445–56 is an important study of the tension between culture and strategy. Although not limiting its message to Chinese firms, James K. Ho, *Cybertigers: How Companies in Asia Can Prosper from E-Commerce* (Singapore: Prentice Hall/Pearson Education Asia, 2000) is directed squarely at the sectors where they have traditionally dominated.

The 1997 crisis of course affected Chinese firms, but many of the larger groups not only survived but have continued to profit and expand. Scholarly opinion has shifted somewhat, and more recent work is skeptical of the alleged Confucian origins of overseas Chinese business practices and the reliance on *guanxi*, but without insisting that Chinese firms must modernize and Westernize to survive. See Souchou Yao, *Confucian Capitalism: Discourse, Practice and the Myth of Chinese Enterprise* (London: RoutledgeCurzon, 2002). Thomas Menkhoff and Solvay Gerke (eds), *Chinese Entrepreneurship and Asian Business Networks* (London and New York: RoutledgeCurzon, 2004), and Edmund Terrence Gomez and Hsin-Huang Michael Hsiao (eds), *Chinese Business in Southeast Asia: Contesting Cultural Explanations, Researching Entrepreneurship* (London and New York: RoutledgeCurzon, 2004) provide an excellent sampling of work in this newer vein. On the other hand, Kai-Alexander Schlevogt argues in his chapter in Menkoff and Gerke and in his book *The Art of Chinese Management* (New York: Oxford University Press, 2002) that networks remain the chief characteristic advantage of Chinese firms, and that their extension from the overseas Chinese back into China may provide the key to China's long-term development.

An excellent background study of Singapore is Linda Low, *The Political Economy of a City-state: Government-made Singapore* (Singapore: Oxford University Press, 1998). Gavin Peebles and Peter Wilson, *Economic Growth and Development in Singapore: Past and Future* (Cheltenham and Northampton: Edward Elgar, 2002) is a balanced account and good on the technical aspects of economic policy. The problems of Singapore's national identity are examined by Loong Wong, 'The invention of nationalism in Southeast Asia: some theoretical considerations of nationalism in Singapore', in Garry Trompf (ed.), *Islands and Enclaves: Nationalisms and Separatist Pressures in Island and Littoral Contexts* (New Delhi: Sterling Publishers, 1993), pp. 127–50. Chan Kwok Bun and Ng Roy Kui, 'Singapore', in Gomez and Hsiao, pp. 38–61, is very good on Singapore's private Chinese sector. Henry Wai-Chung Yeung, *Entrepreneurship and the Internationalisation of Asian Firms* (Cheltenham and Northampton: Edward Elgar, 2002) sets Singaporean firms in a comparative context.

NOTES

1. Chan and Kui (2004), p. 46.
2. Based on surveys, interviews, and discussion groups involving some 300 overseas Chinese students in the Master of Commerce degree program at the University of Sydney from 1999 to 2004, these generalizations are robust, although based on relatively small numbers in the case of Thailand. See Chapter 1, notes 15 and 18, and Chapter 6, note 130.
3. Bowie (1992), 797–823.
4. Skinner (1996), pp. 51–93.
5. Interviews, as in note 2. This contrasts with the much more optimistic picture presented in Australia, Department of Foreign Affairs and Trade, East Asia Analytical Unit (1995), pp. 65–6, 76, which asserts that the Cojaungcos are 'not normally considered as ethnic Chinese' and that in both countries prejudice is now virtually absent.
6. Australia, Department of Foreign Affairs and Trade, East Asia Analytical Unit (1995), pp. 66–7.
7. Australia, Department of Foreign Affairs and Trade, East Asia Analytical Unit (1995), pp. 74–7.
8. Schwarz (1994), pp. 20–21, 105–6.
9. Schwarz (1994).
10. Lubeck (1992), pp. 185–7.
11. Spinanger (1986); Jomo (1990).
12. Jesudason (1989).
13. Redding (1990); Menkhoff and Gerke (2004).
14. Haley (1997), 587–94; Haley, Tan and Haley (1998), pp. 113, 120–21.
15. Haley and Tan (1996), 43–55.
16. Redding (1996), pp. 310–27; Westwood (1997), 445–80.
17. Gomez and Hsiao (2004a), pp. 20–23.

18. See Redding (1990), pp. 170–71; Westwood (1997); Tong and Yong (2004), pp. 217–32. The overseas Chinese in our survey of Chinese Master of Commerce students (above, notes 2 and 5, Chapter 1, notes 15 and 18, and Chapter 6, note 130), almost all in their twenties, reported that they generally would not hire on the basis of *guanxi*, but a majority of them believed that Chinese businesses in general did operate on the basis of *guanxi*.
19. Huang (2000), p. 29.
20. Gomez and Hsiao (2004a), pp. 9–11.
21. Limlingan (1986).
22. Algebraically,

$$\frac{gross\ profit}{equity} = \frac{assets}{equity} \times \frac{gross\ profit}{assets}$$

and

$$\frac{gross\ profit}{assets} = \frac{gross\ profit}{sales} \times \frac{sales}{assets} \ .$$

23. The optimal economic order quantity (Eoq) relates annual demand D, order costs O, and holding costs H:

$$Eoq = \sqrt{\frac{2DO}{H}}$$

The reorder point (Rop) relates lead time L to demand D. See Bartol, Tein, Matthews and Martin (2003), p. 536.
24. Limlingan (1986); Chen (1997), ch. 7.
25. Chen (1995), p. 109.
26. Ibid., pp. 107–10.
27. Huen (2003).
28. McLeod (1998), pp. 33–4; Warr (1998), p. 60; Delhaise (1998).
29. In the 1990s, merchants in the Malayan rubber industry remembered that their fathers or uncles had gotten their start with Tan, but all appear to have left without maintaining connections with him. See Tong and Yong (1998), 85–6.
30. Brown (1994), ch. 6.
31. Chen (1997), p. 98, quoting Landa (1983), vol. 1, pp. 90–91.
32. Tong and Yong (1998), pp. 85–6.
33. Redding (1990), p. 53.
34. Redding (1995), 61–9.
35. Australia, Department of Foreign Affairs and Trade, East Asia Analytical Unit (1995), ch. 9.
36. Yao (2004), pp. 233–54.
37. For instance, Weidenbaum and Hughes (1996).
38. Gomez and Hsiao (2004a), p. 14.
39. Gomez and Hsiao (2004a), pp. 33–4; Haley et al. (1998), pp. 129–38.
40. Murray (1994), pp. 118–21.
41. Chua (1997); Lague (1998); see Suzhou Industrial Park, http://www.sipac.gov.cn.
42. Redding (1990), pp. 146–53.
43. Gomez and Hsiao (2004a).
44. Redding (1990), ch. 7.
45. The mainland and overseas Chinese in our survey of Chinese Master of Commerce students (above, notes 2, 5, and 18; Chapter 1, notes 15 and 18; and Chapter 6, note 130).

46. However, among our interviewees these were almost all male. Among Malaysian Chinese a few, both male and female, could name some of Tao Zhu-gong's business principles.
47. Tong and Yong (1998), pp. 89–90.
48. See Ho (2000).
49. Carney and Gedajlovic (2002), pp. 48–50.
50. For instance, Australia, Department of Foreign Affairs and Trade, East Asia Analytical Unit (2000), pp. 141–7.
51. Carney and Gedajlovic (2002), p. 49.
52. Li, Khatri and Lim (1999), 445–56.
53. A number of multi-member constituencies guarantee that a few ethnic minority representatives will be elected, but the opposition parties are unable to campaign in them effectively, because of the expense and because of the requirement to present a racially 'balanced' team. See Rahim (1998), pp. 73–80.
54. Ibid., pp. 55–6.
55. Chan (2000), pp. 39–58.
56. Rahim (1998), pp. 162–3.
57. Tu (1984); Kuo (1996), pp. 294–309, emphasizes that this is further evidence of the weakness of any inherited 'Confucian' tradition.
58. Wong and Wong (1989); Kuo (1996); Wong (1996), pp. 276–93.
59. Rahim (1998), p. 168.
60. Rodan (1989).
61. Schein (1996).
62. http://www.flextronics.com.
63. Vennewald (1994).
64. Australia, Department of Foreign Affairs and Trade, Economic Analytical Unit (2002), pp. 190–91.
65. Cheung (2003), pp. 150–53.
66. Australia, Department of Foreign Affairs and Trade, East Asia Analytical Unit (1995), p. 70.
67. Rodan (1989), p. 98; Chan and Ng (2004), p. 42.
68. Chan and Ng (2004), p. 44.
69. Hew (2004), pp. 183–4. The former Singapore Productivity and Standards Board, now known as SPRING Singapore, coordinates SME 21 initiatives. See http://www.spring.gov.sg.
70. Chan and Ngoh (1993), foreword by Goh Keng Swee, pp. viii–ix.
71. Seno (2000). See the Creative Technology website, http://www/creative.com.
72. Yuan and Low (1990), pp. 127–35, 139–40, 191–5; Hew (2004), pp. 184–5, 190–91.
73. Shanmugaratnam (2004), p. xxi. Shanmugaratnam was Senior Minister of State for Trade & Industry and Education.
74. Yeung (1999b), 88–102. The tendency to seek 'market reach' may also reflect the difficulty of competing with GLCs and foreign firms for the small pool of skilled workers, and Singapore's small size, which means that there will not be significant clusters of firms in high-technology areas.
75. Yeung (2002), pp. 99, 141.
76. Seno (2000).
77. Yuan and Low (1990), pp. 191–2.
78. Ibid., pp. 143–68.

9. Managing cultural diversity in Southeast Asia

> To perceive victory when it is known to all is not really skilful. Everyone calls victory in battle good, but it is not really good.
>
> It does not take much strength to lift a hair, it does not take sharp eyes to see the sun and moon, it does not take sharp ears to hear a thunderclap. (Sun Tzu, *The Art of War*)

> Ability to handle people: treating people with respect will gain one wide acceptance and improve the business. (Tao Zhu-gong, The Second Business Principle)

Southeast Asian societies are plural societies. All have significant minority populations, whether they are immigrant minorities such as the Chinese or Indian communities, religious minorities such as Philippine and Thai Muslims or Balinese Hindus, or indigenous ethnic minorities such as the Shan or Hmong peoples. The majority groups are also divided along regional, class, religious, and political lines. Indeed, as we have seen, the national identity of the majority is itself a construct that has been imposed from the top down and from the capital city outwards, sometimes by force.

Chapter 7 examined the institutional grid in Southeast Asia. The paradoxical contradiction between the broad powers claimed by 'strong' states and their generally low capacities can be seen at least partly as the result of an attempt by elite groups to maintain their control over diverse societies. Chapter 8 looked at the role of the Chinese and the structure of Chinese firms within that institutional grid. The paradoxical contradiction between the economic strength of the Chinese and their social vulnerability can be seen at least partly as the result of the frequent use of Chinese by elite groups to achieve their ends. These two paradoxes lead to another, the relative absence of successful firms headed by members of indigenous groups. Although it is not true for instance that there are no successful indigenous Thai businesses, or that there are no successful Malay firms, the question remains as to why there are not more.

In this chapter we look first at the problem of entrepreneurship. Anyone can lift a hair, see the sun and moon, or hear thunder, but not everyone can see a new way to achieve victory in war, or success in business. What exactly entrepreneurship is, and how entrepreneurs acquire their special abilities, are disputed topics. Entrepreneurship has been linked to modernization, and the relative frequency of entrepreneurial behavior has been attributed to differences in cultural values, and especially to the role of religion and its effect on management. This, as argued below, is too simple, but religion is one of the factors that all managers in the region must learn to balance.

Entrepreneurial or not, indigenous firms work in the historical context of nationalist reactions to Western and Japanese imperialism and the contemporary institutional grid of 'strong' states. Southeast Asia also remains a region that on balance imports its technology rather than developing new technologies. The management grid reflects the need to respond to these conditions, and one of the skills that indigenous managers need to develop is the ability to handle people. Inside the firm this means managing people from different backgrounds, and this is another way that religion influences business. In addition, people outside the firms must be managed as well, particularly those foreigners who possess advanced technologies, and even more those local personages who possess political power. Rather than achieving victory in battle, indigenous firms may find that handling people properly can allow them to achieve victory without battle.

BOX 9.1   POINT AND COUNTERPOINT: AYALA CORPORATION AND FAMILY GROUPS IN THE PHILIPPINES

People must be handled cordially; an irritable temper and bad attitude will diminish sales greatly. (Tao Zhu-gong, the Second Business Lesson)

Ayala Corporation certainly handles people cordially: 'Ayala Corporation's legacy,' announces its website,

is its adherence to the principles and ideals that wrought its existence. The Ayala tradition of excellence and integrity has run continuously through seven generations of one pioneering family aided by some of the best management talents in the country. It is among the oldest business houses in the country. From a fledgling company in 1834, it has become one of the largest, most respected, and most widely diversified conglomerates in the Philippines today.

The connection with Philippines history is intimate and ongoing:

Its support for Aguinaldo's struggle for independence found fruition with the inauguration of the republic at Malolos, Bulacan in 1899. The event was prophetic, for, almost a century later, the corporation embraced the people's cause that led to a change in the Philippine government in 1986 and, again, in 2001.

Perhaps understandably, the presentation skips over the American colonial period, a half-century during which Ayala expanded and prospered. And, although Ayala undoubtedly rejoiced when President Ferdinand Marcos fell in 1986, relations had remained cordial. The Ayala family did not belong to the inner circle of Marcos' cronies, but their assets had not been confiscated, as were for instance those of the Lopez, Aquino, or Osmeña families; they won permission to develop their property in Makati into a major business and financial center, and Enrique Zobel de Ayala served as ambassador to Great Britain. Nor did Ayala suffer greatly under President Joseph Estrada, impeached and imprisoned for corruption in 2001. Many of the millions of SMS messages repeated around the country that spread news, rumors, and especially jokes about President Estrada, credited with seriously weakening his support, spread through Ayala's mobile phone network.

Ayala Corporation's CEO is Jaime Zobel de Ayala, and according to the American-style disclosure statements his 22 million shares equal 0.13 per cent of the total. Mitsubishi holds 10.63 per cent and is listed as a 'partner' in real estate, hotels, electronics, and information technology. The largest shareholder is Mermac, Inc, with 58.15 per cent. The company's main interests include Ayala Land Inc, the 'largest and only full-line property developer' in the Philippines, Bank of the Philippine Islands, the largest bank in the Philippines by market capitalization and the second largest by assets, Globe Telecom, one of two main suppliers of digital wireless communications with a 40 per cent market share, Manila Water Company Inc, which supplies the Metro Manila East Zone, further investments in manufacturing and services in the electronics industry, dealerships for Honda and Isuzu motor vehicles, property developer Ayala International, and finally Ayala Foundation, a charitable organization. All Ayala companies 'commit to corporate social responsibility through their support of Ayala Foundation's activities in education, art and culture, and in the alleviation of poverty'.

Although taking open pride in the size and importance of its subsidiaries, Ayala Corporation's website still does not show the weight of Ayala interests in the Philippines. The Philippines has the most highly concentrated corporate holdings in Asia. In 2002, only

80 of the largest 1000 firms were publicly listed. Families controlled 48 per cent of listed firms, and the top five families controlled 43 per cent of listed company assets. The Ayala family
holdings are the largest of those five. Ayala Corporation, itself the
second largest listed company in the Philippines, was one of 48
companies that constituted the Ayala Group, according to a count
made in 2000. Mermac, Inc, the dominant shareholder in Ayala
Corporation, is wholly owned by the Ayala family. In turn the subsidiary companies of Ayala Corporation own substantial shares of
other firms in the group.

The Philippines largely escaped the 1997 financial crisis, but this
was at least partly the result of its relatively slow growth compared
to other more dynamic Asian economies. Ayala's response was a
conservative emphasis on its balance sheet, and by 1999 a
reported 30 per cent of its assets were in cash. It also absorbed
one of its competitors in the mobile telecommunications market,
bid for another bank, and spent 'millions' to increase its landholdings. The years since have been successful. In the half-year ending
in June 2005, Ayala Corporation reported earnings of a total of
PhP25 billion (around US$625 million) and profits of PhP 4.6 billion
(US$115 million). Success, however, has been limited. Outside of
the Philippines Ayala is not well known. Ayala International has
projects in Singapore, Hong Kong, Japan, and the western United
States, but Ayala's site describes it as a 'niche player'. The major
retail operations sell imported brands. None of Ayala's diverse
manufacturing operations has established a presence in export
markets, and it does not appear that any of its connections with
foreign companies has led to the creation of new technical competencies. Its size, history, and cordial relations insulate Ayala, and
it will ride with the Philippines economy, but whether it can move
to a higher trajectory remains a question.

Sources: Ayala Corporation, http://ayala.com.ph and http://www.filipinaslibrary.
org.ph; Australia, Department of Foreign Affairs and Trade, Economic Analytical
Unit, *Changing Corporate Asia: What Business Needs to Know* (2 vols. Canberra:
EAU, 2002), vol. 2, pp. 152–5; Dilip K. Das, 'Corporate punishment: disciplining
enterprise in crisis affected Asian economies', Asia Pacific Press, Australian
National University Asia Pacific School of Economics and Management Working
Papers (2000), http://apseg.anu.edu.au; David Chan-oong King, *Crony Capitalism:
Corruption and Development in South Korea and the Philippines* (Cambridge
and New York: Cambridge University Press, 2001), pp. 141–4; 'Leaders for the
Millennium: Jaime Augusto Zobel de Ayala', Asiaweek.com, http://www.asiaweek.
com/asiaweek/99/0611/cs2-1.html (1999; accessed 10 October 2005); devGazette,
the webzine of the undp Philippine country office, 10 July 2001.

BOX 9.2   POINT AND COUNTERPOINT:
          SAPURA GROUP AND MALAYSIAN
          ENTREPRENEURSHIP

Sales must be conducted at any time; procrastination and delay lead to
lost opportunities. (Tao Zhu-gong, the Tenth Business Lesson)

Sapura Holdings was incorporated in 1975. Founded by Abdul
Kadir Shamsuddin, it operated from a one-room office in Kuala
Lumpur and was named after his wife, Siti Sapura. Trained as an
electrical engineer in Britain, Abdul Kadir began his career in 1959
with Jabatan Telekom Malaysia (JTM), Malaysia's government-
owned telecommunications company, rising to head its operations
in the state of Perak. In 1971, he left JTM and joined United Motor
Works (UMW), controlled by Malaysian–Chinese businessman
Eric Chia, and there he rose in five years to become executive
chairman.
    UMW owned a company called Uniphone Works that leased
tabletop payphones to shops, but the business had been losing
money. In 1975, Abdul Kadir left UMW and purchased Uniphone
Works, using a loan of RM400 000 (around US$160 000) from
the government-owned Bank Bumiputra, and a further loan of
RM1 158 000 (US$463 000) granted by Chia. JTM had decided
to privatize its loss-making payphone service in 1975, and
Uniphone's experience in splicing and jointing phone networks
allowed it to tender successfully for a ten-year license to supply,
install, and maintain payphone services throughout Malaysia. In
1989, the license was extended for a further 15 years. Sapura also
laid cables for JTM in the 1970s, and in 1983 won a quarter-share
of an RM2.5 billion (US$1 billion) cable laying contract. In 1984,
Sapura gained control of the publicly listed firm Malayan Cables, a
backward linkage that assured its cable supply. Malayan Cables
then bought Uniphone, and Sapura was listed as a separate
telecommunications company. By the early 1990s, Abdul Kadir, as
head of both Uniphone and Sapura, had diversified into production
not only of payphones and feature mobile phones, but also PABX
exchanges and other large-scale equipment, and in addition had
won the distribution rights for Apple Computers in Malaysia,
Singapore, and Brunei.
    Sapura's cordial relations with the government aided its
success. In addition to the initial loan from Bank Bumiputra, among

other connections, Abdul Kadir served as a director of one of the holding companies controlled by UMNO, the ruling party. However, the company neither procrastinated nor delayed, and sold whenever it could find a customer. Rather than merely supplying equipment to the government, Sapura developed the capacity to manufacture and, rather than merely copying or licensing foreign designs, Sapura formed partnerships with major foreign firms including Siemens, GEC Plessy, Sumitomo, and Nokia, to enhance its own technological capabilities. Already by 1990 the firm had spent RM10 million (US$4 million) on research and development of mobile phone technology. A decline in the Malaysian currency in the late 1980s, especially relative to the Japanese yen, made its products more price competitive in international markets, and Sapura began exporting. Rather than confronting large international firms head-on, Sapura looked for niche markets, supplying for instance feature phones to ITT, Net of Japan, and Alcatel of Belgium, and by 1993 exports accounted for some 24 per cent of Sapura's total sales.

Expansion continued through the 1990s. The group's brochure and seasonal ring tones can be downloaded directly onto joint venture partner Nokia's mobile phones, and the website is heavy with inspirational slogans, such as 'Ideas do not come to those who wait. They come to those who innovate.' Sapura's interests are now widely spread. Sapura Energy includes SapuraCrest Petroleum, an offshore drilling and services company that earned profits of RM74.9 million on sales of 1.035 billion in 2004–5. STB (Sapura Technology Berhad) claims to be 'Malaysia's leading ICT company' and includes a range of hardware and software providers, although its 2004–5 results were disappointing, a loss of RM153 million on sales of 943 million. Sapura Industrial includes design and production of automotive parts and modules, and showed a modest RM8.1 million profit on sales of 143 million. In mid-2005, Sapura also secured a dealership for BMW automobiles. Sapura Resource Berhad is an educational provider that includes two tertiary-level technology and management institutions, and it also showed a small profit in 2004–5 after three years of large losses. Sapura Defence, finally, provides simulation, air traffic control, maritime electronics, and avionics systems and training. It does not report results, but is described both as 'one of the country's leading defence partners' and also as 'a recognised player in the regional defence market'.

Abdul Kadir's son Shahril Shamsuddin was educated in the United States at California Polytechnic and MIT. Shahril joined

Sapura in 1985 and, by the late 1990s, had taken over much of the group's executive responsibilities. Observers credited him with the shift in focus from telecommunications to information technology. Sapura is closely linked to Malaysia's e-government and smart school initiatives. In 2005, Shahril was appointed to the reconstituted board of the Multimedia Development Corporation (MDC), a government-owned corporation established to coordinate the provision of physical infrastructure for the Multimedia Supercorridor project and to manage relations with potential private sector participants. According to news reports, MDC had been having difficulty meeting its objectives since the puncturing of the international IT bubble in 2000. Shahril also serves as board member and treasurer of the blue ribbon Perdana Leadership Foundation headed by former Prime Minister Mahathir Mohamad.

Sapura's diversity raises the questions of management control and focus. Implicitly, the group's strategy appears to develop economies of both scale and scope through the synergies of IT applications across all divisions, but there are potential problems. Two of its interests, mobile phones and automotive components, are intensely competitive internationally. Much of the development in the IT sector is now also commodified, and also highly competitive. MDC has been described in the Malaysian press dismissively as 'another property development scheme'. The BMW dealership may be potentially important in the liberalizing automotive markets of Southeast Asia, but it is not a technological partnership such as those with foreign electronics firms. The foreign IT partnerships have been highly successful in the past, but Sapura remains either a vehicle for foreign firms to enter the Malaysian market or a supplier of products that foreign firms sell in their own markets. Large by Malaysian standards, like other Southeast Asian firms it is neither truly large nor a recognized name internationally, although its technical competencies place it in a good position for the future.

Sources: Sapura Holdings, http://www.sapura.com.my; Peter Searle, *The Riddle of Malaysian Capitalism: Rent-seekers or real capitalists?* (Sydney: Allen & Unwin, and Honolulu: University of Hawai'i Press, 1999), pp. 170–74; Edmund Terence Gomez and Jomo Kwame Sundaram, *Malaysia's Political Economy: Politics, Patronage and Profits* (Cambridge: Cambridge University Press, 1997), pp. 72–4; 'Leaders for the Millennium: Shahril Shamsuddin', Asiaweek.com, http://www. asiaweek.com/asiaweek/99/0611/cs2-1.html (1999; accessed 10 October 2005). More formally, Abdul Kadir Shamsuddin is Tan Sri Shamsuddin bin Abdul Kadir, and Shahril Shamsuddin is Datuk Shahril Shamsuddin.

THE PROBLEM OF ENTREPRENEURSHIP

Entrepreneurship and the Business Landscape in Southeast Asia

Analysis of entrepreneurship derives from the work of Austrian economist Joseph Schumpeter.[1] Entrepreneurs, said Schumpeter, are not inventers, they are innovators. They take existing ideas, factors of production, and needs, and they combine them in new ways. This might mean the introduction of a new product, the application of a new production process, the opening of a new market, the development of new sources of supply, or the reorganization of an existing industry. Their talent is not to create opportunities, but to perceive them, to envisage the existing landscape in new ways, and to see a way to change it. Their problem, however, is that they do not possess the resources to realize their vision. For that they require another figure that Schumpeter labeled the 'banker', a person or institution from which entrepreneurs can borrow the money they need to achieve their goals. Entrepreneurs take risks, but in Schumpeter's view they typically do not risk their own money, but money that they have borrowed from others.

For an entrepreneur, the business landscape in Southeast Asia can appear particularly unpromising. To begin with, it is not easy to establish and operate a business. The World Bank has assembled comparative information regarding the conditions imposed by governments on business.[2] Some of the results for Southeast Asia are given in Table 9.1, and compared to the United States. Southeast Asia confirms the World Bank's general finding that poorer countries tend to have the most restrictive laws and to regulate the most intrusively. Singapore appears to have the lightest touch, Malaysia is in the middle, and the other lower-income countries generally impose the heaviest conditions on businesses. With the exception of Singapore, starting a business is cumbersome in terms of the number of procedures, extremely time consuming, and expensive. Outside of Singapore, laws affecting the hiring and firing of workers, and those regulating conditions of employment, are also relatively restrictive. Should something go wrong, it is also complex and very expensive to enforce a contract, with the exceptions of Malaysia and again Singapore.

As we saw in Chapter 7, government officials typically believe themselves to have the right to dictate to and impose conditions on private firms. However, as we also saw, state capacity is typically low. Except for Singapore, administrative and regulatory officials are often inadequately trained and poorly paid, and corruption is a widely reported problem. There may be other agendas as well. In these ethnically diverse societies, officials may be personally prejudiced, or they may be under instructions to favor one group over another. Official policy has frequently imposed

Table 9.1   Indicators of conditions of doing business in Southeast Asia, compared to the United States, 2004

	Cambodia	Indonesia	Laos	Malaysia	Philippines	Singapore	Thailand	Vietnam	USA
Economic structure									
Population (millions)	12.3	209	5.4	23.8	78.3	4.1	61.2	79.5	285
Income (US$ per capita)	280	710	310	3540	1020	20690	1980	430	35060
Informal economy (per cent)	na	19.4	na	31.1	43.4	13.1	52.6	15.6	8.8
Starting a business									
Number of procedures	11	11	9	8	11	7	9	11	5
Time in days	94	168	198	31	59	8	42	63	4
Cost (per cent of income)	554	15	20	27	24	1.2	7	30	0.6
Minimum capital (per cent of income)	1826	302	151	0	10	0	0	0	0
Enforcing a contract									
Procedures	20	29	na	22	28	23	19	28	17
Time in days	210	225	na	270	164	50	210	120	365
Cost (per cent of income)	269	269	na	19	104	14	30	9	0.4
Indexes of flexibility in labor relations (a score of 0 means the government imposes no regulations on employers; 100 is the maximum score)									
Hiring	33	76	33	33	58	33	78	43	33
Conditions	81	53	87	26	73	26	73	77	29
Firing	49	43	44	15	50	1	30	48	5
Employment law	54	57	54	25	60	20	61	56	22

Notes: 'na' means not available; 'income' is gross national income per capita, in US dollars.
The size of the informal economy, where available, is expressed as a percentage of total gross national income. Cost is expressed as a percentage of gross national income per capita. Minimum capital is expressed as a percentage of gross national income per capita.

Source: World Bank, *Doing Business 2004: Understanding Regulation* (Washington, D.C.: World Bank and Oxford University Press, 2004).

restrictions on Chinese businesses, as we saw in Chapter 8, but Singapore's commitment to racial 'balance' in effect discriminates against the minority Malay and Indian communities, for instance. These factors compound the difficulties imposed by the complexity, cost, and rigidity of regulations.

Schumpeter's banker is absent. A point emphasized by the World Bank is the difficulty that businesses face in obtaining finance. 'Credit is as easily obtainable in Maputo or Jakarta as in London or New York. By the right people. For everyone else, obtaining credit in most developing countries involves a lot of frustration and likely rejection. Few bother.'[3] Legal systems are partly at fault. Lack of information about borrowers, restrictions on collateral, and the difficulty and expense of recovery in cases of default, all make lenders generally hesitant to grant loans, especially to small businesses or to new firms.[4] Directed lending and related-party lending further restrict the funds available. Governments have frequently directed banks to lend to government-owned enterprises, to particular economic groups such as farmers, or to particular ethnic groups such as Malays under Malaysia's New Economic Policy. Private banks have frequently been under the control of family business groups, and have catered primarily to other related firms belonging to their groups.

In addition, looming on the business horizon in all Southeast Asian countries are massive family conglomerates and government enterprises. Some of the indicators of their size and relative position are given in Table 9.2. Some government enterprises are legal monopolies. Some, as in the telecommunications industry, are now partly or wholly privatized, but remain dominant, and have branched into other areas, for instance telecoms that have moved into communications equipment and electronics. The large family conglomerates, already extremely diverse, are not at all hesitant to move into new areas once they have been identified, and they have the resources to do so. Government enterprises, including Singapore's government-linked companies, have access to state funding. Most family conglomerates own or control their own bank. Large and diverse groups, whether government-owned or private, may expand into new areas for strategic reasons, simply to establish a presence or to exclude outsiders, and these initiatives may be subsidized by other more profitable members of the group.

Foreign firms are also active and dangerous competitors. Deregulation and the opening of markets to new entrants can place indigenous firms at a disadvantage as they are forced into direct competition with stronger foreign adversaries. Further, although foreign investment is strictly regulated, as we saw in the Thai case in Chapter 7, governments also see foreign investment as a lever for development. In addition to their technological capabilities, capital resources, and management expertise, therefore, foreign

Table 9.2   Corporate structure in Southeast Asia

	Family ownership	Conglomerate structure	Financial markets	Government enterprises
Indonesia	15 families control 62% of share market capitalization	Large and diverse; 300 groups own 10 000 units across all sectors	Banks nationalized after 1997; groups prefer debt; share market capitalization less than 20% of GDP	State controls over 40% of national assets
Malaysia	Families control over 40% of listed companies	Large and diverse; often connected to state enterprises	Banks independent; market capitalization 124% of GDP, but not liquid	State owns 35% of market capitalization; state enterprises produce 10% of national output
Philippines	5 families control 42% of share market capitalization	Large and diverse; second highest level of cross share-holding in Asia, behind Japan	Groups control banks and prefer debt; only 80 of top 1000 firms are publicly listed	179 state enterprises, mostly infra-structure and finance
Singapore	10 families control 25% of corporate sector	Large private groups limited to light manufacturing, real estate, and banking	State owned banks dominant, but families control 3 of 4 listed banks; market capitalization 250% of GDP, including many foreign firms	Extent of state ownership not clear, but at least 12% of sales, 19.5% of profits, 23% of assets of largest 500 firms
Thailand	Most owners and directors from 300 to 400 elite families; 10 families	Large and diverse; holding companies control both listed and	Groups control banks, prefer debt; very thin market; 'family controlled	50 state enterprises, some with monopolies in their industries

Table 9.2 (continued)

	Family ownership	Conglomerate structure	Financial markets	Government enterprises
	control half of all corporate assets	unlisted subsidiaries	firms often list only to gain tax concessions'	
Vietnam	Private sector includes 30 000 non-state business entities, and one million households, mostly family businesses	Most private firms are small and therefore operate in only one sector	6 state owned banks hold 75% of banking sector assets	30% of GDP, 42% of industrial output; 50% of exports; 1.6 million workers, about 5% of labor force

Source: Australia, Department of Foreign Affairs and Trade, Economic Analytical Unit, *Changing Corporate Asia: What Business Needs to Know* (2 vols; Canberra: EAU, 2002).

firms may receive a range of tailored benefits as in Singapore, access to favored export processing zones as in Malaysia or the Philippines, or subsidies as in Thailand or Vietnam. In 1989, for instance, Sapura lost a large contract to supply telephones to Malaysia's government telephone company to a Taiwanese manufacturer that enjoyed tax exemptions and other benefits because of its 'pioneer' status in the Prai free trade zone near Penang. An angry Abdul Kadir Shamsuddin pleaded publicly for a 'level playing field' for local firms.[5]

A new business in a promising area therefore faces problems on at least three and possibly four fronts. Complex and costly regulations will hamper establishment and operations, even in the absence of prejudice or corruption. Finance will be difficult or impossible to obtain. Domestic competitors linked to the government sector or to large family groups will enjoy greater financial resources, and may have privileged access to government agencies. Foreign competitors will also enjoy ample funding, they may have greater technological and managerial capabilities, and they may benefit from preferential government treatment as well. In the next section we will be looking at values as a possible explanation for the absence of entrepreneurial activity in Southeast Asia, but it is as well to remember that, in the existing historical, institutional, and competitive context, even the most dedicated and energetic entrepreneur would find success difficult to achieve.

Entrepreneurship and the Role of Values

Entrepreneurs are not nice people. They are driven by their vision, and if they find a rock blocking their road, they will find a way over it or around it, or they will 'just blow the damn thing up', as one interviewee put it. Schumpeter said entrepreneurs were engaged in a process of 'creative destruction' that would drive their competitors out of business. He believed they shared a certain keenness or narrowness of vision, but little else, and he did not believe them to care much at all about their fellow human beings or the common good. Looking at the history of European development, he theorized that many entrepreneurs had been motivated by the desire to found a dynasty. Because he believed that economic progress depended on entrepreneurial initiative, he worried that, in the modern era, the rise of large bureaucratized corporations had reduced the scope for entrepreneurial activity.[6]

Schumpeter believed entrepreneurs were rare individuals. He thought most business executives were imitators, 'routine managers' who would 'swarm' into a new area, but only after a true entrepreneur had opened it up and revealed its potential. Because of the prestige attached to the label of 'entrepreneur', the definition has frequently been extended from Schumpeter's original focus on individuals and new firms. More recent formulations include innovative behavior by employees within existing firms or 'intrapreneurship', innovation by state enterprises, political entrepreneurship, social entrepreneurship, and broad aspects of culture or a generalized 'entrepreneurial mindset'. Most Southeast Asian governments have come to equate the terms 'entrepreneur' and 'independent business owner'. In effect they assume that 'entrepreneurial' businesses will be small firms owned by single individuals, and their policies to promote 'entrepreneurship' therefore are in fact policies to support the small and medium enterprise (SME) sector.[7]

Schumpeter did not consider non-Western societies systematically, but his approach implied that entrepreneurship was more common in Western societies, and most common in Northwestern Europe and the United States. As outlined in Chapter 1, in the 1950s and 1960s modernization theorists believed that every society was a balanced system in equilibrium. They viewed 'traditional' societies as essentially static, but believed that 'modern' societies had become dynamic, because rapid economic development continually forced changes in social structures. Schumpeter's theory of entrepreneurship seemed to provide an explanation for economic change. Modernization theorists argued that dissatisfied persons, individual entrepreneurs or groups of entrepreneurial individuals, had propelled change in Europe and the United States, and their actions in effect had created a society in their own image, universalist, achievement-oriented, and affectively neutral, but also more complex and more highly specialized.

Because the first societies to industrialize had been in Northwestern Europe, and because these were predominantly Protestant countries, modernization theorists also frequently adopted Max Weber's argument that Protestantism had aided the development of capitalism. And they frequently agreed with Weber that Confucianism had hampered development in China. Historians of Europe no longer argue that Protestantism caused the rise of capitalism, or that Catholicism caused Southern European backwardness and, as we have seen, many Asian scholars now reject Weber's arguments regarding Confucianism.[8] However, some countries do in fact show higher levels of inventive and entrepreneurial activity than others, and the relative importance of values, institutional structures, and historical accident remains in dispute.[9] It is therefore important to keep the arguments of Weber and the modernization theorists in mind, because very similar arguments are often used to explain the absence of entrepreneurship among the indigenous majority populations of Southeast Asia. This is particularly true with respect to Islam.

What about Islam?

As with Weber's analysis of Catholicism, from the perspective of economic development there are negative points about Islam. Muslims of course are required to conduct themselves continually in accord with Islamic principles. This could lead to fatalistic acceptance of the world as it is, because one's fate is already determined by God.[10] The dictates of Islam also involve some wasteful behavior, and some behavior that can interfere with business. One of the main requirements is regular contributions to charity, which could lower aggregate savings and reduce the capital available for investment. The obligatory daily prayers, the need to close for much of Friday, and the slowdown during Ramadan followed by excessive eating and celebrations, all have a negative impact on the flow of business. The pilgrimage to Mecca, required of all who can undertake it, is another unproductive expenditure. Restrictions on food consumption and the prohibition on alcoholic drinks remove several categories of fast-moving consumer goods from the market in Muslim countries, and add to the difficulty of processing others. The prohibition on charging interest on loans certainly interferes with what non-Muslims would see as the normal operation of financial markets.

Islam mandates a separation of males and females, based on the prohibition of contact between unmarried men and women. In some Muslim households and some Muslim societies, women may be required to dress in particular ways, and in some cases this extends to a prohibition on females appearing outside the family home unless accompanied by an adult male member of their family. In some countries public contact between unrelated men and women is prohibited. These requirements violate a number of the principles of modernization as usually conceived. They can and do interfere with the educational and employment opportunities of women. There can be perverse effects, as in the need for households in Saudi Arabia to hire drivers because women are not permitted to operate motor vehicles.

The political systems in most Islamic countries are authoritarian. Some are explicitly clerical, for instance Iran. In Southeast Asia, however, more are in a state of tension, with parties representing devout Muslims opposed to the ruling party. In these cases the governments' authoritarian tendencies arise, not from Islam, but rather from the fact that the rulers do not want to share power. In Indonesia, the divisions between leftist secular parties and Islamic parties led to conflict in the early 1960s. Following the violence in 1965–6, for 30 years President Soeharto repressed all opposition to Golkar, the government party, including Islamic parties. Since his fall in 1998, Islamic parties have re-emerged, and this poses problems for Indonesia's leaders. The support of small Islamic parties may be crucial to coalition governments, but adopting their religious policies risks alienating the broad majority of voters, and would almost certainly create difficulties with international agencies and potential foreign investors. In Malaysia, through the 1980s and 1990s, Prime Minister Mahathir Mohamad also harassed and marginalized all opponents of the United Malays National Organization (UMNO), including Islamic parties. UMNO leaders now face a two-fold dilemma. If they attempt to compete with Islamic parties by appealing directly to Malay Islamic conservatives, they will alienate their Chinese and Indian supporters. At the same time, the government has adopted the rhetoric of globalization and reliance on the market, a secular agenda that places them at odds with some devout Muslims, and which also implies less preferential treatment for Malays, divestment of the remaining state enterprises, and the end to subsidies and favoritism to former state enterprises and other firms with connections to UMNO. Damaging these interests runs the risk of driving Malay voters away from UMNO and towards the Islamic parties.[11]

As in the case of Confucianism, Islam's economic impact may depend on the specific situation. Islam does not have a strict hierarchy of teachers, and there are many varying interpretations of what is permitted or forbidden. There are wide divisions in all Muslim countries between more 'devout' and more 'secular' individuals and families. For a Muslim each person's fate is written, and nothing they can do will change it. But as with Protestantism, there is no prohibition against acquiring wealth, as long as it is done properly. Also as with Protestantism, proper behavior combined with wealth can at least suggest that a successful person is the right sort of person.

In the specific case of Islamic banking, the prohibition on interest is no barrier to profitable activity. In 2002, it was estimated that there were 150 Islamic banks worldwide, with an estimated US$200 billion in assets. Islamic banks employ two main forms of contracts. A profit-sharing contract allows an Islamic bank to lend money to a business, but, instead of charging interest on the loan, it takes a share of the profits that result from the investment. Similarly, when depositors place money in an Islamic bank, they receive a share of the profits made by the bank, not interest. A middleman or intermediary contract allows a firm to purchase goods from the bank rather than directly from the supplier. The bank may then charge a mark-up on the price, which has been negotiated previously between the firm and the supplier. In the case of major assets, the bank may manage its risk by retaining ownership through a limited liability company.[12]

Nor do other aspects of Islamic practice necessarily impede business. For those who employ Muslims, provision can be made for daily prayers, and various ways can be found to maintain the formal separation of the sexes in the workplace. A firm that caters to religious needs and consequently develops high levels of commitment among its employees will succeed. Even the pilgrimage to Mecca can become a profitable activity. Mecca is the largest tourist destination in the world, and some Islamic banks, for instance in Malaysia, specialize in savings for the pilgrimage. Therefore, similar to Meyers' argument about Confucianism, with the proper sort of institutional grid, there is no reason why Islam could not support economic growth.[13]

What about Buddhism?

Thailand is predominantly Buddhist, and Buddhism also appears problematic from an economic perspective, passive, fatalistic, and opposed to consumption. However, looked at from the opposite perspective, for a Buddhist, there are serious difficulties with mainstream Western economics, one being that it assumes human nature centers on self-interest, rationality, and utility. The assertions that individuals seek pleasure and avoid pain, that material goods bring pleasure, and that more goods are better than fewer, are assumptions, not proven facts. Suppose, however, we ask whether humans seek to maximize 'happiness' and avoid 'misery' or 'suffering'. Buddhists argue that these lie on the same continuum, and therefore, if you reduce misery, you increase happiness.

Misery results from conflict or contradiction within an individual, and the main source of such conflict occurs when a person believes that there is such a thing as a 'self' and tries to hold very tightly to it. Buddhism teaches that there is no such thing as the self. What could be perceived as the self is in fact a temporary composition of the 'five aggregates' of corporeality, feeling or sensation, perception, mental formations or volitional activities, and consciousness. But these change from one moment to the next, so the 'self' must be impermanent. Misery arises from the refusal to recognize this fact, and this leads to the three evils, desire or greed, hatred or anger, and delusion. Conversely, happiness arises from freedom from these three evils.

Clearly there is a lower level of misery that arises from being deprived of necessities, especially food. Supplying these needs obviously increases happiness. But beyond this, the delusion of the constant self leads to greed, which leads to misery. Satisfying the desires that arise from greed will not increase happiness. In fact, it will make the problem worse, firstly because greed cannot be satisfied, second because it will prevent the person from realizing the truth of their condition, and third because it will drain resources and damage the environment through unnecessary exploitation.[14]

In Thailand there has been much opposition to the government's generally 'developmentalist' approach, and much of it is based on Buddhist modes of thinking. The King has remained skeptical of the benefits of modern, Western-style economic development. In his famous birthday speech of 4 December 1997, in the depths of the Asian financial crisis, he argued that 'to be a tiger is not so important. The most important thing is that we have enough to meet our own needs, and the economic means for self-sufficiency'. He went on to define self-sufficiency:

> A self-sufficient economy does not necessarily mean that every family must grow their own food and make their own clothes, but the village or the district must produce enough to satisfy their own needs. Items produced beyond what is needed can be traded for other necessities. Nevertheless, trade should not be conducted with the too far away places to save transportation costs.

Over the years the King and members of the royal family have sponsored a number of widely publicized initiatives to make village communities self-sufficient in these terms. These measures have included local face-to-face government, credit institutions, and development based on local resources, especially agricultural projects designed to preserve the local environment.

A Buddhist would be uncomfortable working for or with a firm devoted to profit alone, with no consideration of the long-term consequences of its actions. However, the Buddhist outlook does not preclude a search for new and more effective ways of providing for human needs, appropriate technologies leading to sustainable development. The drive to reduce human misery leads directly to various forms of social and political entrepreneurship as well, new ways of organizing and disseminating solutions to common problems. Therefore, as with Islam, there is no reason why Buddhism would not support development, given an appropriate institutional framework.

THE MANAGEMENT GRID

'Ersatz' Capitalism, the State Sector, and Privatization

BOX 9.3 POINT AND COUNTERPOINT: A STATE ENTERPRISE – VIETNAM POSTS AND TELECOMMUNICATIONS CORPORATION

Do not engage in unnecessary competition. (Tao Zhu-gong, the ninth Business Pitfall)

Responsibility for governance of the Vietnamese telecommunications sector resides with the Ministry of Post, Telecommunications and Information Technology. Within the Ministry, the Department General of Posts and Telecommunications (DGPT), oversees the regulation of the sector. DGPT's powers are extensive and include policy formulation, drafting legislation, issuing licenses to operate on particular bands or frequencies, Internet management, regulation of Internet service providers, oversight of technical compliance, and the setting of sector-wide tariffs and fees.

The DGPT operates a direct service business wing, Vietnam Post and Telecommunications Corporation (VNPT). VNPT has not engaged in unnecessary competition. Until recently it enjoyed a monopoly in the provision of all telecommunications and postal services in Vietnam, including money transfers and the postal savings bank. In 1996, the government issued operating licenses to Saigon Posts and Telecommunications Service Corporation (Saigonpostal), a joint stock company in which VNPT holds a significant share. In 1997, Vietel Corporation (Vietel), a company owned by the army, was also granted licenses to operate postal and telecommunications services. The DGPT has also issued a license to Vietnam Maritime Communications and Electronics Company (VISHIPEL) to provide and operate satellite services as a land earth station operator, and to Electric Telecommunications Company (ETC), with VNPT again taking a major equity share in the company.

Under this structure, VNPT remains the dominant player, and its relationship to the DGPT ensures it a virtual monopoly on the telecommunication market, via its responsibility for the development of network infrastructure. VNPT vets foreign purchase agreements, new network systems, and proposed operating licenses. Foreign suppliers of telecommunications equipment, as well as joint venture foreign operators, are in effect compelled to deal with VNPT.

VNPT also controls an extensive array of additional companies, either directly or via equity arrangements and joint ventures. The relationships are not always clear, and the structures vary widely. The 2002 annual report of the DGPT listed some 200 subsidiary companies, equity holdings and joint venture initiatives of VNPT. These included companies established as sourcing agents for telecommunications equipment, research companies, and over 20 companies and production facilities that manufactured a nearly complete range of telecommunications equipment. There was a further group of ancillary support companies involved in construction, transport, mobile phone tower assembly, and fixed line installation. There was also another range of companies in unrelated fields such as hotels that had been developed, acquired, or added to VNPT by the government at various times.

This structure poses potential problems. VNPT's production units are small, constrained by the size of the national market, and are not internationally competitive. However, VNPT is in a position not only to direct its own orders to its subsidiaries, but also to force other firms to source their equipment from them as well. As a monopoly provider of infrastructure, VNPT has no particular motive to strive for efficiency, and because its owner, the DGPT, is also the regulatory authority, the 'market-like' tests that might be imposed by an independent regulator are absent. As a government agency, it has access to government funding, but again the relationships and returns are not transparent.

The government uses telecommunications as a convenient revenue source. In 2000, for example, VNPT reportedly passed net profits of US$1 billion directly to the central government. Vietnam has policies that envisage the rapid expansion of telecommunications as a crucial driver of economic growth. However, the temptation to maximize revenue has seen Vietnam's end-user telecommunications charges become the highest in the region. Although Vietnam's telecommunications sector is growing rapidly, it began from an almost non-existent base, and the numbers of phone lines compared to population and Internet penetration rates remain the lowest in the region. In addition, the high cost of basic telecommunications has been frequently cited as one of the major obstacles to foreign business, creating disincentives to foreign direct investment in Vietnam.

Sources: The Vietnam Posts and Telecommunications Corporation (VNPT), http://www.vnpt.com.vn; Vietnam, Department of General Posts and Telecommunications (DGPT), *Annual Report 2002* (Hanoi: DGPT, 2002); Mekong Research, 'Vietnam: telecommunications operations' (Washington, D.C.: U.S. Foreign and Commercial Services and U.S. Department of State, 1999); Nyuyen Dzung, 'Telecom Equipment and Services: Industry Sector Analysis' (Washington, D.C.: U.S. and Foreign Commercial Services and U.S. Department of State, 2002); Nghiem T. Tung, 'Telecommunications equipment: industry sector analysis, Vietnam' (Washington, D.C.: U.S. and Foreign Commercial Service and U.S. Department of State, 2002); Xinhua News Agency, 'Vietnam sets telecommunications expansion target for 2005', 19 March 2001.

It has been argued that domestic firms in Southeast Asia do not innovate or introduce advanced technologies, not because of external constraints, but because they are unwilling to do so. In the 1980s, Kunio Yoshihara described indigenous business in Southeast Asia as 'ersatz' (artificial) capitalism. He believed the most successful domestic firms were in fact rent-seeking groups, whose position depended, not on their economic efficiency, but on their contacts with government. This reflected, in Yoshihara's view, three factors. First, low levels of investment in science and technology by both government and private firms had left Southeast Asia technologically backward. Second, the low quality of government intervention in the economy had led to reliance on subsidies and to the domination of the economy by non-indigenous Chinese and friends or cronies of political leaders. Third, the absence of a strong domestic capitalist class had led to a reliance on foreign firms to provide advanced technologies. Indigenous capital remained confined largely to the tertiary sector, and indigenous industrial capital could not drive development 'because it does not have an export capability'.[15]

Yoshihara's thesis has been extensively debated.[16] Despite criticisms, into the 1990s there were aspects of the management grid in Southeast Asia that supported his arguments.[17] The state sector expanded to dominate many sectors. The number of public enterprises in Malaysia, for instance, rose from 22 in 1960 to 109 in 1970, 656 in 1980, and 1149 in 1992. The growing state sector supported UMNO's political position, but it also reflected the government's concern that there was no indigenous Malay (*bumiputra*) capitalist class. It was widely asserted by observers that these highly capital-intensive enterprises did not develop the capabilities that would have made them internationally competitive, and that they did not support broader development, compared for instance to the large state firms in Taiwan. In 1989, the Malaysian government's own mid-term review of its Fifth Malaysia Plan said, 'the performance of heavy industrial projects sponsored by the public sector was far from satisfactory. A number of these projects suffered heavy financial losses due to the sluggish domestic demand and the inability of the industries concerned to compete in international markets'.[18]

Southeast Asian state enterprises often failed to make the connection between primary products and manufacturing. Indonesia, for example, possessed large reserves of oil, but the state oil corporation, Pertamina, despite a high degree of formal control over foreign oil corporations, generally failed to develop the hoped-for backward and forward linkages with indigenous industry.[19] Operating under its own special law, Pertamina 'was controlled by its first President Director, Ibnu Sutowo, almost as a personal fiefdom, dispensing patronage and responsible only to the President'. In general, 'The history of the state enterprise sector was generally one of corruption, inefficiency and over-expansion rather than the modernizing "commanding heights" sector that it was purported to be.'[20]

Private firms also benefited from connections to influential persons. In the Indonesian case, we looked at the relations between Liem Sioe Liong, founder of the Salim Group, and President Soeharto, in Chapter 8. Bambang Trihatmodjo, Soeharto's second son, went into business in 1982 at the age of 29 with funds provided by Pertamina, and by 1994 his group included over 100 companies with assets of some US$1.4 billion. The group's greatest asset, however, was 'Bambang's ability to ride roughshod over the bureaucracy'. Soeharto and his children formed collectively 'by far the most powerful economic dynasty in the country'.[21]

In the 1980s and 1990s, B.J. Habibie, State Minister for Research and Technology, argued that, rather than relying on the 'comparative advantage' of its natural resources, Indonesia should develop 'competitive advantage' by fostering high-technology sectors as rapidly as possible.[22] As with other programs, however, Habibie's initiatives were not supported by systematic fact gathering and analysis. Instead, the pet projects of senior figures, including the automobile firm controlled by President Soeharto's children, and the aircraft manufacturer controlled by Habibie himself, received preferential treatment and subsidies regardless of their potential to improve national competitiveness.[23] A number were then abandoned as part of the price for international assistance in the aftermath of the 1997 crisis.

On the other hand, in the decades since the thesis of ersatz capitalism was propounded, several of the Southeast Asian economies have grown rapidly. The size of the government sectors has not impeded growth. Despite the problems of state capacity outlined in Chapter 7, and the criticisms of state enterprises noted above, there is a positive correlation between the size of the government sector and economic performance. In Malaysia, for two decades, Prime Minister Mahathir Mohamad pursued plans to achieve developed country status, epitomized in his 'Vision 2020' in 1991.[24] Consistently, Mahathir portrayed the introduction of high-end technology as a partnership between state agencies and an emergent private sector. As Minister for Trade and Industry in the late 1970s, he sponsored the state-owned Heavy Industries Corporation of Malaysia (HICOM) to create 'technopoles' around which new industries would grow. As Prime Minister in the 1980s, he launched a national automobile, the Proton. Originally dependent on Japanese technology, heavily subsidized, protected by tariffs and quotas, and supplied by an equally highly protected components industry, current Proton models now appear competitive in recently liberalized regional markets. Perhaps even more importantly, Malaysian auto components manufacturers appear equally well placed to compete for orders from foreign firms locating in Southeast Asia.

Malaysia's response to the 1997 crisis, especially the imposition of controls on capital flows, was widely criticized at the time, but is now seen to have been effective in minimizing the impact of the sudden decline in exchange rates.[25] Since the mid-1990s, the government has pushed the application of information and communication technologies, notably through the Multimedia Supercorridor project.[26] The National IT Agenda (NITA) defines information, knowledge, and 'technopreneurship' all working together to transform the Malaysian economy into a 'knowledge economy' and Malaysian society into a 'knowledge society'.[27] Semiconductors and electronics components are Malaysia's largest exports. They are still dominated in quantitative terms by foreign firms, and the majority of employees are still young women working for low wages, but the share of complex assemblies and complete products has risen, and so has the proportion of locally manufactured inputs.[28]

Privatization is often conceived as a simple pushing back of the border between the state sector and private enterprise, and as a progressive replacement of bureaucratic administration with modern corporate governance. However, both the motives and the outcomes of privatization have varied considerably from country to country. Privatization in Indonesia before 1998 often meant the transfer of public property to those with connections to President Soeharto and his family. Since the fall of Soeharto, privatization has been the official goal of government policy, but this has not been unproblematic:

In recent years, privatisation has not progressed as smoothly as hoped. Indeed the reverse is true. One of the main reasons is that it has been conducted in periods of crisis where political reform, institutional change and redistribution of resources are all happening at the same time.[29]

Opposition from incumbent managers and workers, weak state capacity, and a reluctance to surrender control, all have slowed privatization. Some state enterprises have been able to delay or avoid privatization altogether, as in the case of PT Semen Gresik Tbk, the largest cement company in Indonesia. Some privatized firms have been damaged by the government's inability to prevent poaching and illegal exports, as in the case of PT Tambang Timah, the world's largest tin producer.[30] In telecommunications, despite agreements on privatization imposed by international agencies as part of the price for aid following the 1997 crisis, in 2002 the government remained the majority shareholder in both Indosat (56.9 per cent) and Telkom (54.29 per cent), and also held additional special shares that would allow continued control even in the absence of a majority holding of regular shares. New laws envisaged an early end to their monopoly positions, their evolution into two full service telecoms that would compete fairly against each other and new market entrants, and a new regulatory body to ensure they did so, but the implementation of these plans remained in the very early stages in the early 2000s.[31]

Again Malaysia appears more successful, with a history of privatization extending over two decades. However, privatization has run in parallel with three other agendas, the promotion of the economic interests of ethnic Malays, maintaining the political position of UMNO and, since 1991, the pursuit of Vision 2020.[32] For example, in the case of telecommunications, Jabatan Telekom Malaysia (JTM, the Telecommunication Department of Malaysia) was the sole provider of all telecommunication services before the early 1980s. However, as we saw in Box 9.2, already in the late 1970s JTM had begun to spin off some of its ancillary services to *bumiputra* entrepreneurs such as Abdul Kadir Shamsuddin, and in the 1980s outsourced much of its network construction to private Malay firms as well. In the meantime government concerns about the need to supplement JTM's capacity laid the groundwork for further reforms, including permission for third-party and joint venture initiatives in value-added network services in 1984, radio paging services in 1985, and mobile cellular networks in 1988.

Moves to privatize JTM itself began with legislative changes in 1985, and in 1987 Syarkay Telekom Malaysia Berhad (STM), a government-owned entity, took over the operational responsibilities of JTM. In 1990, the government floated shares in STM, now renamed Telekom Malaysia Berhad

(TMB), but it did not give up control. In 2002, the government still held 70 per cent of the firm's shares, and, as in Indonesia, the government also held 'golden shares' that bestowed special rights in respect of veto power over major decisions, board membership, and financial structure. New fixed line and mobile licenses granted in the early 1990s were intended to increase competition, but the expense of creating new networks meant that, in 2000, TMB still controlled 97 per cent of the fixed lines, as well as 18.5 per cent of the mobile phone market. However, and this is the essential difference between the two cases, while Indonesia's telecommunications density remains the second lowest in the region, the percentage of Malaysians with access to phone services has risen from 1.1 in 1992 to 32.8 in 2002, behind only the city state of Singapore.[33]

Former state enterprises, and large firms in general, tend to have tall structures with multiple layers of management. At lower levels, many Southeast Asian firms also appear to be over-staffed. This may reflect the historical pattern of rule through intermediaries, as suggested in Chapter 7. It also reflects the previous history of the firms, either as government agencies or as private firms with close government connections. In both cases the government model of bureaucratic administration remains influential. Internally, leadership may also reflect what has been called the 'dialogue ideal' in Thai firms. Informal contacts between the head and subordinates allow the latter to express their sentiments and to gain a sense of the intentions of the superior. The point is not to seek substantive advice or to allow input into decisions, but rather to defuse potential conflict by reassuring subordinates that the head is concerned about them as persons.[34] In Malaysia, opportunities for such exchanges can come at 'family days' sponsored by the firm, and intended to show the firm is in effect a village *kampung* and that the head is still at heart a '*kampung boy*'.[35]

Externally, managers must also be politically astute. Some of the CEOs of Malaysian firms have in fact been 'acting as proxies for political patrons'.[36] Even where they are truly independent, privatization, ongoing government support, and the award of licenses and government contracts, all have been and continue to be subject to political influences. Jobs in these firms have been and continue to be important sources of patronage for the ruling party. The ability to handle people therefore extends outward as well as inward. As we have seen, 'strong' states insist on their right to direct development. Government officials may have become 'promoters' of business rather than 'parasites',[37] but Southeast Asia's political leaders continue to believe that they can and must exercise control over society. Managers therefore must maintain their contacts and networks among influential bureaucrats and politicians.

Small and Medium Enterprises

BOX 9.4   POINT AND COUNTERPOINT:
           GERONIMO DANGO, MAGICLIP AND
           PHILIPPINE ENTREPRENEURSHIP

Ability to articulate: eloquence can be a way of gaining fortune and
enlightening people. (Tao Zhu-gong, the eighth Business Principle)

Geronimo Dango retired from the Philippine army as a colonel. In
the early 1970s, he was working for a small company in Los
Angeles as a maintenance engineer and observed a group of
Mexican boys playing with a T-square and old ball bearings. Using
the ball bearings, they were able to hold paper to the grooved rail
of the T-square without clips, tape, or tacks. Intrigued, Dango
experimented, and he eventually developed a fastening system
incorporating these features that he patented under the name of
Magiclip. He applied the Magiclip principle to a broad range of fix-
tures, including badge holders, portable tripod easels, fixed bul-
letin boards, reading supports for computer users, drum-shaped
order wheels for restaurants, and laboratory displays for x-rays. In
1977, he was invited to return to the Philippines under the Balik-
Scientist Program that then-President Ferdinand Marcos had
established to encourage expatriate Filipino scientists and tech-
nologists to relocate to the Philippines.
   Magiclip, however, was only modestly successful. In early 2006,
its own website had apparently not been updated since 2001. A
sales contact was available via alibaba.com, a Chinese site dedicated to supporting small and medium enterprises. According to
the company information posted, the firm employed five to ten
persons. The firm indicated that its sales were 'worldwide' but did
not record any sales figures.
   Nevertheless, Dango's eloquence opened another career, as
a promoter of Philippine entrepreneurship. He founded the
Entrepreneur Society of the Philippines, and until his death in 2004
was the organization's leader. Biographical sketches emphasize the
personal sacrifices he made for the organization, and uniformly
imply that the time he spent on behalf of Filipino entrepreneurs
detracted from the time he might have otherwise had to make
Magiclip more successful. Success came in other forms. He was recognized for his efforts by a succession of Presidents, and regularly

honored at public events celebrating or encouraging Filipino entrepreneurship. When he traveled overseas, President Ferdinand Ramos presented copies of Dango's book, *Entrepreneurs: Winning the Future*, to foreign leaders.

Sources: http://www.magiclip.com; Magiclip Products Phil., INC, http://alibaba. com; Entrepreneur Society of the Philippines, http://www.entrepreneursociety. com.ph; Geronimo A. Dango, *Entrepreneurs: Winning the Future* (Manila: Entrepreneurs Institute of the Philippines, 1998).

There are of course many more small firms than large firms in every country. Geronimo Dango cited Philippine figures for 1993 that listed 224 194 businesses in the country, of which only 1154 were 'large' and 1114 'medium' in size. He estimated that small and medium firms together accounted for 55 per cent of employment, but only 28 per cent of value added.[38] The 'sadly inadequate' official statistics showed 130 935 manufacturing firms in 1999, of which 113 864 employed fewer than ten workers, and a total of 207 158 'micro' enterprises with assets of less than PhP1.5 million (around US$37 500), and another 19 261 with assets between PhP1.5 and 15 million.[39] In addition, as seen in Table 9.1, in most Southeast Asian countries there is a large 'informal' sector whose size can only be guessed at, and which appears particularly large in the Philippines.

Governments hope that innovation arising from small private firms will drive economic development. The SME sector is the origin of the group of entrepreneurial business leaders that Michael Carney and Eric Gedajlovic label the 'new managers'. Most are overseas Chinese, as noted in Chapter 8, but non-Chinese with technical education and access to capital, located in rapidly expanding sectors, fit the profile as well.[40] There have been some dramatic success stories, as in the case of Sapura Group, but in general policy does not favor small firms. In comparison, initiatives of the European Union include the 2000 SME Charter, the 2003 Green Paper, and a range of programs undertaken by member nations to support the internationalization of small firms, both within the EU and as they expand beyond the EU. In the United States, the ongoing programs of the Small Business Administration support United States SMEs in their efforts to upgrade and expand their operations. Federal and state programs guarantee loans and actively encourage educational outreach, the movement of people, and the diffusion of ideas.[41] Neither ASEAN nor its member states have developed any program comparable to those of Europe or the United States.

As in the case of Singapore, individual countries do have programs directed at small firms, but they are top-down and patronizing. Interviewees from all Southeast Asian countries report that officials assume that small businesses require direction, training, and above all regulation. In the Philippines, for instance, the Kalakalan 20 law in operation from 1989 to 1994 offered partial tax relief to small businesses, but was primarily intended to entice them to 'join the formal economy' and 'register with the relevant authorities' and was judged a failure when it did not do so. Since 1997, Philippine banks have been required to allocate credit to small businesses, but obtaining credit 'remains the main problem for SMEs despite liquidity in the banking sector' and 'the macro-economic policy environment remains biased towards large enterprises'.[42] In addition, for the leaders of small firms, the sense that they can be the targets of arbitrary exactions, or that they can fall victim to corrupt judicial decisions, makes them reluctant to expand beyond a certain size. As one Indonesian businessman was quoted as saying, 'In the past, corruption was a fixed amount, but now the cost is between nought and infinity and that's what affects most businesses because they cannot do their business plan.'[43]

Most small firms remain family concerns, and, like Geronimo Dango's Magiclip, most will not grow to be large firms. However, firms with the potential to become large face difficulties. As we have seen above, the capital market for small firms remains undeveloped. In addition, as is often said of Chinese firms, non-Chinese firms may also avoid outside finance because of the traditional values placed on the family and the fear of losing control.[44] Dango's guide for entrepreneurs, for instance, contains a section entitled 'No Partners, Please', that says, 'entrepreneurs become entrepreneurs for one simple reason: to be free. If you give that up, you stop being an entrepreneur'. His preferred mode of financing in fact bypasses the capital market entirely, and he recommends raising what he calls 'noncontrol money' from 'people you trust'.[45]

The ability to raise money from people you trust suggests that, despite the desire for complete independence, entrepreneurs in Southeast Asia, like entrepreneurs elsewhere in the world, do in fact exist in social networks. These can be personal or family connections, or they may be groups of firms in the same industry, and they can also be political. In Malaysia, the government's policies under the NEP created opportunities for a new class of Malay business owners. Where entry costs were low and technical skills not required, the numbers of firms increased rapidly. In retail trade, for instance, Malay firms rose from 3311 in 1971 to 32 800 in 1981, while Chinese firms increased from 18 957 to 55 417. Many of these new Malay firms received loans or grants from government agencies or government-controlled banks.

Family, personal, and political networks can support a firm, but they may have negative aspects as well. As we saw in Chapter 7, former Prime

Minister Mahathir himself accused Malays of leaning too heavily on the 'crutches' of government support. Patricia Sloane believes Malays have been caught between contradictory ideals fostered by the government, 'ultra-modern' in business, but also 'ultra-traditional' in obligations to the community. Her informants had established businesses with loans from government banks. They read books on Western and Japanese management styles, and they enthusiastically 'networked' with other 'virtuoso' businesspeople. However, the modern managerial rhetoric was accompanied by a belief that 'Malay entrepreneurs' should be different from the 'culture of greed' of the West. Money often went to support their 'community', to friends or family members, or to stock market speculation. They had little time for winning contracts, completing projects, or getting paid, and on balance 'they demonstrated a remarkable lack of interest and concern in running the operations they had established'. They repeatedly said, 'We'll just hire someone to run the business later.' Their dreams recreated the racial hierarchies and management through intermediaries of the colonial regime: they, the Malay owners of the firm, would handle the 'marketing', Chinese managers would 'run the business', and the workers would be Indian. Most eventually dropped out and returned to their original jobs, or their firms were taken over by the banks when the original loans could not be repaid.[46]

The Future: Ongoing Problems and Reforming Corporate Governance

Richard Doner identified several issues confronting Southeast Asian economies in the early 1990s, all relevant to the structure and operation of firms in the region.[47] First was structural adjustment and economic reform, and, as we have seen, 15 years later the problems arising from privatization and regulation remain on the agenda. Second was the conflict between the interests of upstream and downstream firms. Here the focus has shifted from the textile and clothing industries, to automobiles and electronics. Doner argued that selective government protection and subsidies could support efficient upstream producers and satisfy the demands of downstream firms, but in the current international climate governments might find his parallel suggestion of a greater role for industry organizations more feasible. Third was standardization. In this area ASEAN has made some progress, and Doner's own work on the impact of Japanese automobile firms in Southeast Asia appears prescient, as they are continuing to drive local components suppliers to higher levels of performance.[48] Fourth was excess capacity, the result of limited domestic markets and large numbers of producers, and this too is still relevant, as in the case of VNPT and the supply of telecommunications equipment in Vietnam. Fifth was investment screening, a continuing issue in all countries, which we looked at in some detail in the Thai case in Chapter 7.

Doner's last issue was infrastructure, and again this remains a problem outside the capital cities. Roads, water, and electricity supplies are marginal and sometimes nonexistent over broad areas. For the future, Southeast Asian countries lag substantially in the provision of access to telecommunications. Investment had been rising during the 1990s, and in several countries the increases had been quite substantial. However, annual telecommunications investment per person remained at low levels. Further, in the aftermath of the 1997 crisis, per capita telecommunications investment dropped, in Singapore by over one-third, and in Malaysia by two-thirds. In Thailand and the Philippines, the already low levels were cut in half. Investment recovered to something approaching previous levels in the early 2000s, but remained well behind the average for OECD countries. Much of the new investment in wealthy developed countries is to upgrade existing delivery systems, particularly to allow broadband access, necessary for the delivery of services such as call centers using video as well as voice, distance work arrangements using video conferencing, e-commerce and education applications using real time video interaction, or health services using video for consultation and diagnosis.[49]

Human capital poses some of the same problems. Outside of Vietnam and Laos, basic primary education is adequate, and virtually the entire population is literate. However, outside of Singapore, the situation is less good with respect to secondary education, and poor at the tertiary level. In the Philippines, nearly 80 per cent of primary students move on to secondary schools and about a third to tertiary study. Elsewhere in Southeast Asia, the figures range from 20 to 60 per cent for secondary education and from 5 to 20 per cent for tertiary study. There are also shortages of skilled workers in key areas such as the Thai automobile industry. As with physical infrastructure, only a large commitment of resources will make it possible to provide universal secondary education, and expanded tertiary study will require a further massive investment.[50]

Education in turn affects technological capacities. In general, foreign firms provide most new technologies. Southeast Asian commentators argue that 'technology transfer' in fact usually means 'technology dependence' because foreign firms hold local firms captive and keep them dependent. They are held at the low end of the technology spectrum, but also held to ever-higher standards of reliability, at progressively lower prices. Foreign firms impose conditions such as demanding Internet-enabled supply chain management. There are market restrictions, including outright bans on exports, and tie-in agreements requiring the purchase of machinery and intermediate products from the seller. There may be further restrictions on research and development of improvements.[51]

Finally, like all the other states of Asia, Southeast Asian governments have committed themselves to reforms in corporate governance. At the same time they have committed themselves to privatizing their remaining state enterprises. They hope that more open, transparent, and 'modern' corporate structures will make their economies more competitive. Investors and minority shareholders will feel themselves more secure. Capital will flow to the most productive areas, rather than being subject to political direction. Firms will become more efficient as their accounting and financial systems are brought up to world standard. Parallel to these changes, governments have also introduced new and stronger regulatory bodies, whose primary mission is to maintain a freely competitive environment. Enforcement of the new rules will, it is hoped, improve corporate transparency, raise the level of accountability, and make managers more fiscally prudent.[52]

These programs are in part the result of outside pressure. International agencies have pressured governments to 'open' their economies and to break the longstanding connections between government and private business.[53] In the aftermath of the 1997 financial crisis, the IMF made its assistance conditional on the adoption of reform programs. The WTO actively encouraged continuation of the reforms. The bilateral trade agreements that the United States has negotiated with several countries, such as Thailand and Singapore, have opened previously restricted markets. International agreements have imposed new and more restrictive standards on banks, and new international accounting standards require higher levels of control and more transparent reporting by firms. The IMF sponsors Reports on the Observance of Standards and Codes (ROSCs) that monitor compliance with international standards. The module on corporate governance is the responsibility of the World Bank, the Organization for Economic Cooperation and Development, and in the Asian Region, the Asian Development Bank. Some of the results are summarized in Table 9.3.

The overall impact of these changes has been significant. Some of the main features as of 2002 are outlined in Table 9.3. However, there remain considerable areas of uncertainty. From the perspective of market-oriented reformers, the reforms appear incomplete. Legal systems are often opaque and courts overburdened. The effectiveness of the new regulatory regimes remains unclear. The relations between political, military, and business leaders remain close.[54] However, from the perspective of more state-oriented economists and political scientists, the entire project of reform may be misdirected. Many of the problems discussed above cannot be

Table 9.3   Reforms in corporate governance in Southeast Asia

	Transparency	Minority rights	Creditors' rights	Compliance
Indonesia	'Poor and deteriorating' although consolidated reports required since 1999	Formal rights good, but owners appoint managers and can expropriate minorities	Formal rights good, but not enforced	Regulatory and legal systems weak; poor training and lack of resources
Malaysia	World-class reporting standards	Voting rights and independent directors	Good; formal and informal restructuring effective	Government and non-government bodies active
Philippines	Adequate standards but not enforced	Improved rules, but not enforced	Laws are sound but application is weak	Weak despite adequate laws; poor training and lack of resources
Singapore	One of three Asian countries approved by CalPERS for equity investment	Reasonable, but hindered by cross-shareholdings and pyramid structures	Good and usually well enforced	Good, except in government sector
Thailand	Improved standards since 1997, but actual reporting often poor; preference for relationship-based business	Mixed structures allow expropriation of minorities	New laws but poorly enforced; foreign banks reluctant to lend to Thai firms	Weak, with poor training of both public officials and private directors
Vietnam	Enterprise Law 2000 covers private enterprises and publicly listed state enterprises, but reporting standards low	Inadequate under current laws	Very limited under current laws; no bankruptcy law as of 2002	Legal standards inadequate; courts are not independent

Source: Australia, Department of Foreign Affairs and Trade, Economic Analytical Unit, *Changing Corporate Asia: What Business Needs to Know* (2 vols; Canberra: EAU, 2002).

addressed by formal changes in corporate governance, which are irrelevant to unincorporated firms and will not affect the operation of tightly held listed firms, for instance. In countries where most firms are small by international standards and dependent on foreign technology, simply adopting Western models may result in their being confined to follower status, dependent on decisions taken elsewhere.[55] There is substantial opposition to reform, some from those directly affected and some from more general nationalistic sentiments. As with other Asian systems, therefore, change in Southeast Asia's corporate landscape will undoubtedly continue, but at rates and in directions that will not always be predictable.

FURTHER READING

Kunio Yoshihara, *The Rise of Ersatz Capitalism in South-East Asia* (Singapore: Oxford University Press, 1988) is an influential work that emphasized the weakness of indigenous business structures in the region, particularly the links between government and business leaders and the dependence on foreign capital and technology. General works that expanded on his arguments included Walden Bello and Stephanie Rosenfeld, *Dragons in Distress: Asia's Miracle Economies in Crisis* (San Francisco: Institute for Food and Development Policy, 1990), and James Clad, *Behind the Myth: Business, Power and Money in Southeast Asia* (London: Hyman Press, 1990).

Country studies included Yoshihara's own work on the Philippines, *Philippine Industrialization: Foreign and Domestic Capital* (New York: Oxford University Press, 1985), Akira Suehiro, *Capital Accumulation and Industrial Development in Thailand* (Bangkok: Social Research Institute, 1985), and Jomo Kwame Sundaram, *A Question of Class: Capital, the State, and Uneven Development in Malaysia* (Singapore: Oxford University Press, 1986).

More recent studies critical of existing business practice have concentrated on the specific forms of corporate governance, for instance Organization for Economic Cooperation and Development, Asian Roundtable on Corporate Governance, *White Paper on Corporate Governance in Asia* (OECD, 10 June 2003) and Ho Kai Leon, (ed.), *Reforming Corporate Governance in Southeast Asia* (Singapore: Institute of Southeast Asian Studies, 2005). Governance issues also affect public agencies. Anthony B.L. Cheung and Ian Scott (eds), *Governance and Public Sector Reform in Asia: Paradigm shifts or business as usual?* (London and New York: RoutledgeCurzon, 2003) contains very good chapters on Malaysia, Thailand, Vietnam, Indonesia, and the Philippines.

352 *Asian firms*

There has also been an opposed line of interpretation, which emphasizes the achievements of indigenous capitalists within their social context, notably Richard Robison, *Indonesia and the Rise of Capital* (London: Allen and Unwin, 1986). See Ruth McVey (ed.), *Industrializing Elites in Southeast Asia* (Ithaca: Cornell University Press, 1990); Ruth McVey (ed.), *Southeast Asian Capitalists* (Cornell Southeast Asia Program; Ithaca: Cornell University Press, 1992a); Robert W. Hefner (ed.), *Market Cultures: Society and Morality in the New Asian Capitalisms* (St Leonards: Allen and Unwin, 1998). Peter Searle, *The Riddle of Malaysian Capitalism: Rent-seekers or real capitalists?* (Sydney: Allen & Unwin, and Honolulu: University of Hawai'i Press, 1999) is relevant to the entire region in detailing the different ways in which indigenous business and state enterprise can be connected, and how these can change over time.

Denis Hew and Loi Wee Nee (eds), *Entrepreneurship and SMEs in Southeast Asia* (Singapore: Institute of Southeast Asian Studies, 2004) arises from an ASEAN Roundtable conference held in 2002, and includes chapters that provide excellent introductions to the general questions of entrepreneurship as well as to various aspects of the problems of small and medium enterprise.

T.W. Lippman, *Understanding Islam* (New York: Meridian Books, 1995), and R.H. Dekmejian, *Islam in Revolution: Fundamentalism in the Arab World* (Syracuse: Syracuse University Press, 1995) are good introductions. Rob Goodfellow (ed.), *Indonesian Business Culture* (Singapore: Butterworth-Heinemann Asia, 1997), is good on Islamic business practice in a daily context. Apichai Puntasen, 'The Asian economic crisis and the crisis of analysis: a critical analysis through Buddhist economics', in Mason C. Hoadley (ed.), *Southeast Asian-Centered Economies or Economics?* (Copenhagen: Nordic Institute of Asian Studies, 1999), pp. 62–85, and Stephen J. Gould, 'The Buddhist perspective on business ethics: experiential exercises for exploration and practice', *Journal of Business Ethics* **14**(1995), 63–70, introduce Buddhist approaches to economics and management.

NOTES

1. Schumpeter (1961). For Southeast Asia in particular, see the excellent overview by Tan (2004), pp. 7–23.
2. World Bank (2004).
3. World Bank (2004), p. 55.
4. Ibid., ch. 5.
5. Searle (1999), p. 172.
6. Schumpeter (1976).
7. Tan (2004), pp. 12–13.

8. It is also worth noting that the problems of the Philippines are also not attributed to Catholicism. See for instance McCoy (1994), which argues that the pattern of Philippine politics, and the weakness of the state, arises from the general need to rely on one's family for support. The only references to religion are observations that Philippines political leaders have tried to remain on good terms with the Church.
9. Shane (1992), 29–46; Thomas and Mueller (2000), 287–302.
10. However, the same could be said of the Protestant doctrine of predestination, a point that was made during the debate over the Weber thesis in the 1960s. See Green (1973).
11. Shome (2001); Kessler (2001). See Dekmejian (1995).
12. Interest was also prohibited in medieval Europe, but there were widely practiced methods for borrowers to pay lenders for the use of funds, for instance by returning a fraction of the loan immediately to the lender.
13. Lippman (1995); Abassi, Hollman and Murrey (1990), 5–17; Youssef (2000), 513–37.
14. Puntasen (1999), pp. 62–85, summarizes the arguments of Phra Dharmapidoke (1990; in Thai). See Gould (1995), 63–70.
15. Yoshihara (1988), pp. 3, 122–31.
16. See Searle (1999), ch. 1.
17. See for instance Bello and Rosenfeld (1990); Clad (1990).
18. Gomez and Jomo (1997), pp. 31, 78.
19. Oon (1986).
20. Habir, Sebastian and Williams (2002), pp. 7, 13.
21. Schwarz (1994), pp. 141–2; see Hill (1996), ch. 6; Australia, Department of Foreign Affairs and Trade, East Asia Analytical Unit (1995), pp. 39–45.
22. See Booth (1992); Bresnan (1993).
23. 'Soeharto: patronage and its prizes', *The Sydney Morning Herald*, 30 October 1997.
24. Mohamad (1991).
25. Nesadurai (2000), 73–113; Athukorala (2001); Jomo (2001).
26. See Multimedia Development Corporation, www.mdc.my/index.html.
27. Latifah (1999), p. 3; National Information Technology Committee, http://www.nitc.org.my. See Tipton (2002a), ch. 6.
28. Lin (2004), pp. 173–94; Kanapathy (2004), pp. 131–49.
29. Habir, Sebastian and Williams (2002), p. 3.
30. Ibid., pp. 41–9.
31. Tipton, Jarvis and Welch (2003), chs 2 and 10.
32. Jomo (1995).
33. Tipton, Jarvis and Welch (2003), chs 2 and 6.
34. Thompson (1989), 323–38.
35. Sloane (1999), pp. 108–9.
36. Gomez and Jomo (1997), p. 51.
37. McVey (1992b), p. 26.
38. Dango (1998).
39. Mendoza and Llanto (2004), p. 152.
40. Carney and Gedajlovic (2002), pp. 48–50.
41. United States, National Commission on Entrepreneurship (2002).
42. Mendoza and Llanto (2004), p. 157.
43. Moore (2002).
44. For Indonesia, see Australia, Department of Foreign Affairs and Trade, Economic Analytical Unit (2002), vol. 2, pp. 93–108.
45. Dango (1998), pp. 61–2.
46. Sloane (1999), pp. 191–4. See Li (1998), pp. 147–72.
47. Doner (1991a), 818–49.
48. Doner (1991b); Tangkitvanich (2004), pp. 214–17.
49. Tipton (2002a).
50. Tipton, Jarvis and Welch (2003), ch. 5.
51. Tangkitvanich (2004).

52. See Ho (2005).
53. See Organization for Economic Cooperation and Development, Asian Roundtable on Corporate Governance (10 June 2003).
54. Australia, Department of Foreign Affairs and Trade, Economic Analytical Unit (2002).
55. Amsden (2001); Soederberg (2003), 7–27.

Appendix
Tao Zhu-gong: the Twelve Business Principles, the Twelve Business Pitfalls, and the Sixteen Business Lessons

THE TWELVE BUSINESS PRINCIPLES

1. Ability to know people: knowing the character of people will ensure the soundness of your accounts.
2. Ability to handle people: treating people with respect will gain one wide acceptance and improve the business.
3. Ability to focus on the business: forgoing the old for the new is the curse of many businesses.
4. Ability to be organized: when products are well displayed, they will attract the attention of many people.
5. Ability to be agile and flexible: hesitation and indecisiveness will end in nothing.
6. Ability to demand payment: diligence and prudence will gain a lot more for the company.
7. Ability to use and deploy people: choosing the right person for the right job will ensure that he can be trusted and depended upon.
8. Ability to articulate: eloquence can be a way of gaining fortune and enlightening people.
9. Ability to excel in purchasing: haggling over every ounce in purchasing may not reduce one's cost of capital.
10. Ability to diagnose and seize opportunities and combat threats: shrewd business practices require the ability to sell and store at the right time.
11. Ability to initiate and lead by example: comradeship and trust will emerge naturally when discipline and high standards are enforced.
12. Ability to be far-sighted: when to go for more and when to tighten or loosen depends on the situation.

THE TWELVE BUSINESS PITFALLS

1. Do not be myopic and narrow-minded.
2. Do not adore grandeur.
3. Do not be indecisive.
4. Do not be lazy.
5. Do not be stubborn.
6. Do not be overly argumentative.
7. Do not expose oneself readily.
8. Do not be greedy for credit.
9. Do not engage in unnecessary competition.
10. Do not weaken savings and surpluses.
11. Do not ignore changing business conditions.
12. Do not over-rely on current products.

THE SIXTEEN BUSINESS LESSONS

1. Diligence is needed in managing the business; laziness will destroy everything.
2. People must be handled cordially; an irritable temper and bad attitude will diminish sales greatly.
3. Prices of products must be clearly stated; ambiguity will lead to many arguments and disputes.
4. Accounts must be vigilantly checked and monitored; sloppiness and oversight will lead to stagnated capital.
5. Goods must be well organized and displayed; sloppiness will cause obsolescence and waste.
6. Prudence and care are needed to grant credit and disburse funds; carelessness will lead to many errors and loopholes.
7. Payment must be made within the agreed time; delays will lead to the loss of credibility.
8. Unexpected events must be tackled responsibly; neglecting them will lead to greater harm.
9. Resources must be used frugally; extravagance will lead to the depletion of wealth.
10. Sales must be conducted at any time; procrastination and delay lead to lost opportunities.
11. Debtors must be well scrutinized; indiscriminate lending will lead to severe erosion of capital.
12. The good and the bad must be clearly distinguished; negligence will lead to confusion and chaos.

13. Employees must be honest and upright; cunning and crooked workers will implicate the boss.
14. Goods must be carefully examined; indiscriminate and careless buying will cause prices to be lowered.
15. Financial matters must be handled judiciously; carelessness will lead to problems and woes.
16. The leader must be steady and calm; recklessness and rashness will lead to many errors and mistakes.

SOURCE

The translations are from Chow Hou Wee, *The Inspirations of Tao Zhu-gong: Modern Business Lessons from an Ancient Past* (Singapore: Prentice-Hall, 2001), pp, 7–21. Wee is Professor of Business Policy at the National University of Singapore. Tao Zhu-gong, originally known as Fan Li, lived around 500 B.C. He was an advisor to the Emperor of Yue, but he retired and became a fabulously successful businessman. Over the centuries his Twelve Business Principles, Twelve Business Pitfalls, and Sixteen Business Lessons have become established as classic texts. However, as Wee notes, the original Twelve Business Principles most likely consisted only of the first short phrases, which each consist of three Chinese characters. The following longer phrases, each of eight characters, were probably later additions, although they still date from the ancient period. The Twelve Business Pitfalls and the Sixteen Business Lessons were then added over time and appear in a mix of classical and modern Chinese. Wee analyzes each of the Twelve Business Principles in a separate chapter, along with the corresponding pitfalls and lessons, and with extensive quotations from Chinese folk sayings and other Chinese classics, especially Sun Tzu's *Art of War*. The principles are then applied to a range of modern cases, and as indicated in his title Wee believes that Tao Zhu-gong's ancient learning does indeed provide lessons for modern business executives.

Bibliography

Abassi, S.M., K.W. Hollman and J.H. Murrey (1990) 'Islamic economics: foundations and practices', *International Journal of Social Economics* **16**(5), 5–17.

Abe, M. and M. Kawakami (1997) 'A distributive comparison of enterprise size in Korea and Taiwan', *The Developing Economies* **25**(4), 382–400.

Abegglen, James C. and George Stalk Jr (1985) *Kaisha: The Japanese Corporation*, New York: Basic Books.

Adnan, Mohammed Akhyar and Rob Goodfellow (1997) 'Understanding Islam and business in Indonesia', in Rob Goodfellow (ed.), *Indonesian Business Culture*, Singapore: Butterworth-Heinemann Asia, pp. 43–76.

Akamatsu, Kaname (1962) 'A historical pattern of economic growth in developing countries', *The Developing Economies* **1**, 7–13.

Akashi Yoji (1980) 'The Japanese occupation of Malaya: interruption or transformation', in Alfred W. McCoy (ed.), *Southeast Asia Under Japanese Occupation*, Monograph Series No. 22; New Haven: Yale University Southeast Asia Studies, pp. 65–90.

Amsden, Alice H. (1985) 'The State and Taiwan's economic development', in Peter B. Evans, Dietrich Rueschemeyer and Theda Skocpol (eds), *Bringing the State Back In*, Cambridge: Cambridge University Press.

Amsden, Alice H. (1989) *Asia's Next Giant: South Korea and Late Industrialization*, Oxford: Oxford University Press.

Amsden, Alice H. (2001) *The Rise of 'the Rest': Challenges to the West from Late-Industrializing Economies*, Oxford and New York: Oxford University Press.

Anderson, Benedict (1991) *Imagined Communities: Reflections on the Origin and Spread of Nationalism*, revised edition, London: Verso.

Andersson, Martin and Christer Gunnarsson (eds) (2003) *Development and Structural Change in Asia-Pacific: Globalizing Miracles or End of a Model?*, London: RoutledgeCurzon.

Andrews-Speed, Philip, Minying Yang, Lei Shen and Shelley Cao (2003) 'The regulation of China's township and village coal mines: a study in complexity and ineffectiveness', *Journal of Cleaner Production* **11**, 185–96.

Aoki, Masahiko (ed.) (1984) *The Economic Analysis of the Japanese Firm*, Amsterdam: North Holland.

Aoki, Masahiko (1994) 'The Japanese firm as a system of attributes: a survey and research agenda', in Masahiko Aoki and Ronald Dore (eds), *The Japanese Firm: The Sources of Competitive Strength*, Oxford: Oxford University Press, pp. 11–40.

Aoki, Masahiko (2000) *Information, Corporate Governance, and Institutional Diversity: Competitiveness in Japan, the USA, and the Transitional Economies*, Tokyo, 1995; translated by Stacey Jehlik, Oxford and New York: Oxford University Press.

Aoki, Masahiko and Ronald Dore (eds) (1994) *The Japanese Firm: The Sources of Competitive Strength*, Oxford: Oxford University Press.

Aoki, Masahiko and Hugh Patrick (eds) (1994) *The Japanese Main Bank System: Its Relevance for Developing and Transforming Economies*, New York: Oxford University Press.

Arnason, Johann P. (1997) *Social Theory and Japanese Experience: The Dual Civilization*, London and New York: Kegan Paul International.

Ash, Robert (ed.) (2000) *Hong Kong in Transition: The Handover Years*, Basingstoke: Macmillan.

Asian Development Bank (1998) *Governance in Thailand: Issues and Prospects*, Manila: ADB.

Asian Development Bank (2001) *Corporate Governance and Finance in East Asia: A Study of Indonesia, Republic of Korea, Malaysia, Philippines, and Thailand*, 2 vols, Manila: ADB.

Asiaweek.com (1999) 'Leaders for the millennium: Jaime Augusto Zobel de Ayala', http://www.asiaweek.com/asiaweek/99/0611/cs 2-1.html, accessed 10 October 2005.

Asiaweek.com (1999) 'Leaders for the millennium: Shahril Shamsuddin', http://www.asiaweek.com/asiaweek/99/0611/cs 2-1.html, accessed 10 October 2005.

Athukorala, Parma-Chandra (2001) *Crisis and Recovery in Malaysia: The Role of Capital Controls*, Cheltenham UK and Northampton, MA, USA: Edward Elgar.

Aubert, Jean-Eric (1996) 'Science and technology in Korea', *OECD Observer*, No. 200 (June/July), pp. 35–9.

Australia, Department of Foreign Affairs and Trade, East Asia Analytical Unit (1995) *Overseas Chinese Business Networks in Asia*, Canberra: EAAU.

Australia, Department of Foreign Affairs and Trade, East Asia Analytical Unit (1999) *Asia's Financial Markets: Capitalising on Reform*, Canberra: EAAU.

Australia, Department of Foreign Affairs and Trade, East Asia Analytical Unit (2000) *Transforming Thailand: Choices for the New Millennium*, Canberra: EAAU.

Australia, Department of Foreign Affairs and Trade, Economic Analytical Unit (2002) *Changing Corporate Asia: What Business Needs to Know*, 2 vols, Canberra: EAU.

Backman, Michael and Charlotte Butler (2003) *Big In Asia: 25 Strategies for Business Success*, Houndmills: Palgrave-Macmillan.

Bai, Chong-en, Qiao Liu, Joe Lu, Frank M. Song and Junxi Zhang (2003) 'Corporate governance and market valuation in China', William Davidson Working Paper Number 564, The William Davidson Institute at the University of Michigan Business School, May.

Baker, Mark (2004) 'Winning streak of a politician with no time for losers', *The Sydney Morning Herald*, 2–3 July.

Bangkok Post (2002) 'Voters welcome disclosure of graft', 18 November.

Bartlett, Christopher A., Sumantra Ghoshal and Julian Birkinshaw (2004) *Transnational Management: Texts, Cases and Readings in Cross-Border Management*, 4th edn, Boston: McGraw-Hill Irwin.

Bartol, Kathryn, Margaret Tein, Graham Matthews and David Martin (2003) *Management: A Pacific Rim Focus*, enhanced edn, Boston: McGraw-Hill.

Batson, Benjamin A. (1980) 'Siam and Japan: the perils of independence', in Alfred W. McCoy (ed.), *Southeast Asia Under Japanese Occupation*, Monograph Series No. 22, New Haven: Yale University Southeast Asia Studies, pp. 267–302.

Bazerman, M.H. (1986) *Judgment in Managerial Decision Making*, New York: Wiley.

Beamish, Paul W., Allen J. Morrison, Andrew C. Inkpen and Philip M. Rosenzweig (2003) *International Management: Text and Cases*, 5th edn, Boston: McGraw-Hill.

Becker, Jasper (1996) *Hungry Ghosts: China's Secret Famine*, London: Murray.

Bedeski, Robert E. (1994) *The Transformation of South Korea: Reform and Reconstruction in the Sixth Republic Under Roh Tae Woo, 1987–1992*, London: Routledge.

Beeson, Mark (2001) 'Japan and South-East Asia; the lineaments of quasi-hegemony', in Garry Rodan, Kevin Hewison and Richard Robison (eds), *The Political Economy of South-East Asia: Conflicts, Crises, and Change*, 2nd edn, Melbourne: Oxford University Press, pp. 283–306.

Bello, Walden and Stephanie Rosenfeld (1990) *Dragons in Distress: Asia's Miracle Economies in Crisis*, San Francisco: Institute for Food and Development Policy.

Beresford, Melanie (1989) *National Unification and Economic Development in Vietnam*, New York: St Martin's Press.

Bergère, Marie-Claire (1989) *The Golden Age of the Chinese Bourgeoisie 1911–1937*, Cambridge: Cambridge University Press; French original, Paris: Flammarion, 1986.

Bersani, M.D. (1993) 'Privatization and the creation of joint stock companies in China', *Columbia Business Law Review* 3, 301–28.

Biggert, Nicole Woolsey (1990) 'Institutionalized patrimonialism in Korean business', *Comparative Social Research* 12, 113–33.

Biggert, Nicole Woolsey (1998) 'Deep finance: the organizational bases of South Korea's financial collapse', *Journal of Management Inquiry* 7(4), 310–25.

Bishop, Bernie (1997) *Foreign Direct Investment in Korea: The Role of the State*, Sydney: Ashgate.

Blackman, Carolyn (1997) *Negotiating China: Case Studies and Strategies*, St Leonards: Allen & Unwin.

Blackman, Carolyn (2000) *China Business: The Rules of the Game*, St Leonards: Allen & Unwin.

Bloomstrom, Magnus, Byron Gangnes and Sumner LaCroix (eds) (2001) *Japan's New Economy: Continuity and Change in the Twenty-First Century*, London: Oxford University Press.

Booth, Anne (ed.) (1992) *The Oil Boom and After: Indonesian Economic Policy and Performance in the Soeharto Era*, Singapore: Oxford University Press.

Booth, Anne (1998) *The Indonesian Economy in the Nineteenth and Twentieth Centuries: A History of Missed Opportunities*, Houndmills: Macmillan.

Bosco, Joseph (1992) 'The role of culture in Taiwanese family enterprises', *Chinese Business History* 3(1), 1–4.

Boston Consulting Group and Knowledge @ Wharton (2004) *China and the New Rules for Global Business*, http://knowledge.wharton.upenn.edu.

Bowie, Katherine A. (1992) 'Unraveling the myth of the subsistence economy: textile production in nineteenth-century northern Thailand', *Journal of Asian Studies* 51(4), 797–823.

Brady, Anne-Marie (2003) *Making the Foreign Serve China: Managing Foreigners in the People's Republic*, Lanham: Rowman & Littlefield.

Bresnan, John (1993) *Managing Indonesia: The Modern Political Economy*, New York: Columbia University Press.

Bridges, Brian (2001) *Korea after the Crash: The Politics of Economic Recovery*, London and New York: Routledge.

Brooker, Paul (1991) *Three Faces of Fraternalism: Nazi Germany, Fascist Italy, and Imperial Japan*, Oxford: Oxford University Press.

Brookfield, Harold (ed.) (1994) *Transformation with Industrialization in Peninsular Malaysia*, Kuala Lumpur and New York: Oxford University Press.

Brown, Rajeswary Ampalavanar (1994) *Capital and Entrepreneurship in Southeast Asia*, Houndmills: Macmillan, and New York: St Martin's Press.

Brown, Rajeswary Ampalavanar (2000) *Chinese Big Business and the Wealth of Asian Nations*, New York: Palgrave.

Bruton, Garry D., Heilin Lan and Yuan Lu (2000) 'China's township and village enterprises: Kelon's competitive edge', *Academy of Management Executive* **14**(1), 19–29.

Bruun, Ole (1988) *The Reappearance of the Family as an Economic Unit: A Sample Survey of Individual Households in Workshop Production and Crafts, Chengdu, Sijuan Province*, Copenhagen: Center for East and Southeast Asian Studies, University of Copenhagen.

Bruun, Ole (1993) *Business and Bureaucracy in a Chinese City: An Ethnography of Private Business Households in Contemporary China*, Berkeley: Institute of East Asian Studies, University of California.

Burmeister, Larry L. (1988) *Research, Realpolitik, and Development in Korea: The State and the Green Revolution*, Boulder: Westview.

Bush, Richard C. (1982) *The Politics of Cotton Textiles in Kuomintang China, 1927–1937*, New York: Garland Pub.

Business Week (1977) 'Korea Inc. – volcano with a lid on', 1 August.

Business Week Online (1999) 'Zhang Ruimin, CEO, Haier Group, China', 14 June.

Campbell, John Y. and Yasushi Hamao (1994) 'Changing patterns of corporate financing and the main bank system in Japan', in Masahiko Aoki and Hugh Patrick (eds), *The Japanese Main Bank System: Its Relevance for Developing and Transforming Economies*, New York: Oxford University Press, pp. 325–49.

Caoili, Manuel A. (1988) *The Origins of Metropolitan Manila: A Political and Social Analysis*, Quezon City: New Day Publishers.

Carney, Michael (1998) 'A management capacity constraint? Obstacles to the development of the overseas Chinese family business', *Asia Pacific Journal of Management* **15**, 137–62.

Carney, Michael and Eric Gedajlovic (2002) 'International change and firm adaptation: towards a typology of Southeast Asian corporate forms', *Asia Pacific Business Review* **8**(3), 31–60.

Castells, Manuel (1992) 'Four Asian Tigers with a dragon head: a comparative analysis of the state, economy, and society in the Asian Pacific Rim', in Richard P. Appelbaum and Jeffery Henderson (eds), *States and Development in the Asian Pacific Rim*, Newbery Park: Sage Publications, pp. 33–72.

Cauley, Jon and Todd Sandler (2001) 'Agency cost and the crisis of China's SOEs: a comment and further observations', *China Economic Review* **12**, 293–7.

Chai, J.C.H. and K.B. Chai (1994) 'Economic reforms and inequality in China', University of Queensland, Department of Economics Discussion Papers, No. 141.

Chalmers, Norma J. (1989) *Industrial Relations in Japan: The Peripheral Workforce*, London: Routledge.

Chan, Anita, Richard Madsen and Jonathan Unger (1992) *Chen Village Under Mao and Deng*, Berkeley: University of California Press.

Chan, Jasmine S. (2000) 'The status of women in a patriarchal state: the case of Singapore', in Louise Edwards and Mina Roces (eds), *Women in Asia*, St Leonards: Allen & Unwin, pp. 39–58.

Chan, Kwok Bun and Claire Chiang Sie Ngoh (1993) *Stepping Out: The Making of Chinese Entrepreneurs*, Singapore: Institute for Advanced Studies, National University of Singapore, and New York: Prentice-Hall.

Chan, Kwok Bun and Ng Roy Kui (2004) 'Singapore', in Edmund T. Gomez and Hsin-Huang Michael Hsiao (eds), *Chinese Business in Southeast Asia: Contesting Cultural Explanations, Researching Entrepreneurship*, London and New York: RoutledgeCurzon, pp. 38–61.

Chan, V.L. (1998) *Economic Growth and Foreign Direct Investment in Taiwan's Manufacturing Industries*, Taipei: Academia Sinica.

Chandler, Alfred D. Jr (1966) *Strategy and Structure: Chapters in the History of the American Industrial Enterprise*, New York: Anchor Books.

Chandler, Alfred D. Jr (1990) *Scale and Scope: The Dynamics of Industrial Capitalism*, Cambridge: Harvard University Press.

Chang, C.C. (1992) 'The development of Taiwan's personal computer industry', in N.T. Wang (ed.), *Taiwan's Enterprises in Global Perspective*, Armonk: M.E. Sharpe, pp. 193–214.

Chang, Sea-Jin (2003) *Financial Crisis and Transformation of Korean Business Groups: The Rise and Fall of Chaebols*, Cambridge and New York: Cambridge University Press.

Chang, Sea-Jin and Ung-Hwan Choi (1988) 'Strategy, structure and performance of Korean business groups: a transactions cost approach', *Journal of Industrial Economics* 37(2), 141–58.

Chatterjee, Partha (1986) *Nationalist Thought and the Colonial World: A Derivative Discourse*, London: Zed Books.

Chen, Aimin (1998) 'Inertia in reforming China's state-owned enterprises: the case of Chongqing', *World Development* 26, 479–95.

Chen, H.M. and T.J. Chen (1998) 'Foreign direct investment as a strategic linkage', *Thunderbird International Business Review* 40(1), 13–30.

Chen, H.M. and T.J. Chen (1998) 'Network linkages and location choice in foreign direct investment', *Journal of International Business Studies* 29(3), 445–68.

Chen, J. (1999) *Chinese Law: Towards an Understanding of Chinese Law, Its Nature and Development*, The Hague: Kluwer Law International.

Chen, Min (1997) *Asian Management Systems*; 1995; London: International Thomson Business Press.

Chen, Ming-Jer (2003) *Inside Chinese Business: A Guide for Managers Worldwide*, Cambridge: Harvard Business School Press.

Chen, Z.X., A.S. Tsui and J.L. Farh (2002) 'Loyalty to supervisor versus organizational commitment: relationship with the performance of Chinese employees', *Journal of Occupational and Organizational Psychology*, **75**, 339–56.

Cheng, Chung-ying (1989) 'Totality and mutuality: Confucian ethics and economic development', in Chung-Hua Institution for Economic Research, *Conference on Confucianism and Economic Development in East Asia, May 29–31 1989*, Chung-Hua Institution for Economic Research, Conference Series No. 13, Taipei: Chung-Hua Institution for Economic Research.

Cheng, Chu-yuan (1989) 'The doctrine of people's welfare: the Taiwan experience and its implications for the Third World', in Chu-yuan Cheng (ed.), *Sun Yat-sen's Doctrine in the Modern World*, Boulder: Westview Press.

Cheng, Linsun (2003) *Banking in Modern China: Entrepreneurs, Professional Managers, and the Development of Chinese Banks, 1897–1937*, New York: Cambridge University Press.

Cheng, Lucie and Ping-chun Hsiung (1992) 'Women, export-oriented growth, and the state: the case of Taiwan', in Richard P. Appelbaum and Jeffery Henderson (eds), *States and Development in the Asian Pacific Rim*, Newbury Park: Sage Publications, pp. 233–66.

Cheng, Yak-shing, Wong Marn-heong and Christopher Findlay (1998) 'Singapore and Hong Kong', in Ross H. McLeod and Ross Garnaut (eds), *East Asia in Crisis: From Being a Miracle to Needing One?*, London and New York: Routledge, pp. 162–78.

Cheung, Anthony B.L. (2003) 'Public service reform in Singapore: reinventing government in a global age', in Anthony B.L. Cheung and Ian Scott (eds), *Governance and Public Sector Reform in Asia: Paradigm Shifts or Business as Usual?*, London and New York: RoutledgeCurzon, pp. 138–62.

Cheung Anthony B.L. and Ian Scott (eds) (2003) *Governance and Public Sector Reform in Asia: Paradigm Shifts or Business as Usual?*, London and New York: RoutledgeCurzon.

Child, John, Yanni Yan and Yuan Lu (1997) 'Ownership and control in Sino-foreign joint ventures', in Paul W. Beamish and J. Peter Killing, *Cooperative Strategies: Asian-Pacific Perspectives*, San Francisco: New Lexington Press.

Chiu, W.C.K. and C.W. Ng (1999) 'Women-friendly HRM and organizational commitment: a study among women and men of organizations in Hong Kong', *Journal of Occupational and Organizational Psychology* 72, 485–502.

Cho, Y.H. and J. Yoon (2002) ' "The origin and function of dynamic collectivism: an analysis of Korean corporate culture" ', in Chris Rowley, Tae Won Sohn and Johngseok Bae (eds), *Managing Korean Business: Organization, Culture, Human Resources and Change*, London: Cass, pp. 70–88.

Choe, Heungsik and Bong-Soo Lee (2003) 'Korean bank governance reform after the Asian financial crisis', *Pacific Basin Finance Journal* 11, 483–508.

Chon, Soohyun (1992) 'Political economy of regional development in Korea', in Richard P. Appelbaum and Jeffrey Henderson (eds), *States and Development in the Asian Pacific Rim*, Newbury Park: Sage Publications, pp. 150–75.

Chong, Florence (2004) 'Banks to break China's fall in "soft landing" ', *The Australian*, 16 June.

Chu, Chin-ning (1995) *The Asian Mind Game: A Westerner's Survival Manual*, Australian Edition, St Ives: Stealth Publications.

Chu, W.W. (1994) 'Import substitution and export-led growth: a study of Taiwan's petrochemical industry', *World Development* 22(5), 781–94.

Chu, W.W. and M.C. Tsai (1992) *Linkage and Uneven Growth: A Study of Taiwan's Man-Made Fiber Industry*, Taipei: Academia Sinica.

Chua, Lee Hoong (1997) 'SM Lee unhappy over Suzhou park progress', *The Straits Times*, weekly edn, 6 December.

Chuang, Y.C. and C.M. Lin (1999) 'Foreign direct investment, R&D, and spillover efficiency: evidence from Taiwan's manufacturing firms', *Journal of Development Studies* 35(4), 117–37.

Chung, Kae H., Hak Chong Lee and Ku Hyun Jung (1997) *Korean Management: Global Strategy and Cultural Transformation*, Berlin and New York: W. de Gruyter.

Clad, James (1990) *Behind the Myth: Business, Power and Money in Southeast Asia*, London: Hyman Press.

Claessens, S. and S. Djankov (1999) 'Publicly listed East Asian corporates: growth, financing and risks', Working Paper, Washington, D.C.: World Bank.

Claessens, S. and L. Lang (1999) 'East Asian corporates: growth, financing and risks over the last decade', Working Paper, Washington, D.C.: World Bank.

Coble, Parks M. (1980) *The Shanghai Capitalists and the Nationalist Government, 1927–1937*, Harvard East Asian Monographs 94, Cambridge: Harvard University Council on East Asian Studies.

Cochran, Sherman (1980) *Big Business in China: Sino-Foreign Rivalry in the Cigarette Industry, 1890–1930*, Cambridge: Harvard University Press.

Cole, Robert E. (1994) 'Different quality paradigms and their implications for organizational learning', in Masahiko Aoki and Ronald Dore (eds), *The Japanese Firm: The Sources of Competitive Strength*, Oxford: Oxford University Press.

Coleman, Samuel (1999) *Japanese Science from the Inside*, London: Routledge.

Crawford, Robert (2000) 'China's Haier Group: growth through acquisitions', INSEAD, Case 300-129-1.

Crotty, Jim and Kang-Kook Lee (2001) 'Korea's neoliberal restructuring: miracle or disaster?', *Dollars and Sense*, July/August.

Cumings, Bruce (1987) 'The origins and development of the Northeast Asian political economy: industrial sectors, product cycles, and political consequences', in Frederic Deyo (ed.), *The Political Economy of the New Asian Industrialism*, Ithaca: Cornell University Press.

Cumings, Bruce (1998) 'The Korean crisis and the end of "Late" development', *New Left Review*, September/October, 43–72.

Dahrendorf, Ralf (1968) *Society and Democracy in Germany*, London: Weidenfeld & Nicolson.

Dango, Geronimo A. (1998) *Entrepreneurs: Winning the Future*, Manila: Entrepreneurs Institute of the Philippines.

Das, Dilip K. (2000) 'Corporate punishment: disciplining enterprise in crisis affected Asian economies', Asia Pacific Press, Australian National University Asia Pacific School of Economics and Management Working Papers, http://apseg.anu.edu.au.

Dauvergne, Peter (1997) *Shadows in the Forest: Japan and the Politics of Timber in Southeast Asia*, Cambridge: MIT Press.

Dauvergne, Peter (ed.) (1998) *Weak and Strong States in Asia-Pacific Societies*, St Leonards: Allen & Unwin.

Dekmejian, R.H. (1995) *Islam in Revolution: Fundamentalism in the Arab World*, Syracuse: Syracuse University Press.

Delhaise, Philippe F. (1998) *Asia in Crisis: The Implosion of the Banking and Finance Systems*, Singapore: John Wiley and Sons.

Denoon Donald et al. (1997) *Multicultural Japan: Paleolithic to Postmodern*, Cambridge: Cambridge University Press.

Deyo, Frederic C. (1983) 'Chinese management practices and work commitment in comparative perspective', in Linda Y. Lim and L.A. Peter Gosling (eds), *The Chinese in Southeast Asia*, 2 vols, Singapore: Maruzen Asia, vol. 2, pp. 215–29.

Deyo, Frederic C. (1989) *Beneath the Miracle: Labor Subordination in the New Asian Industrialism*, Berkeley: University of California Press.

Dixon, Chris (1991) *Southeast Asia in the World Economy: A Regional Geography*, Cambridge: Cambridge University Press.

Doner, Richard F. (1991a) 'Approaches to the politics of economic growth in Southeast Asia', *Journal of Asian Studies* **50**(4), 818–49.

Doner, Richard F. (1991b) *Driving a Bargain: Automobile Industrialization and Japanese Firms in Southeast Asia*, Berkeley: University of California Press.

Dore, Ronald P. (1986) *Flexible Rigidities: Industrial Policy and Structural Adjustment in the Japanese Economy*, Stanford: Stanford University Press.

Dore, Ronald P. (2001) 'Reform? The dubious benefits of marketisation', in Craig Freedman (ed.), *Economic Reform in Japan: Can the Japanese Change?*, Cheltenham, UK and Northampton, MA, USA: Edward Elgar, in Association with the Centre for Japanese Economic Studies, Macquarie University.

Drabble, John H. (1991) *Malayan Rubber: The Interwar Years*, Houndmills: Macmillan.

Duckett, Jane (2000) 'Bureaucrats in business, Chinese style: the lessons of market reform and state entrepreneurialism in the People's Republic of China', *World Development* **29**(1), 23–37.

Duerden, Charles (2003) 'Korea, where the smart money goes', *Korea Trade and Investment* **21**(2) (March–April), 22–6.

Dyer, Geoff (2005) 'Baosteel dissenter beaten in carve-up', *The Australian*, 16 August.

Dzung, Nyuyen (2002) 'Telecom equipment and services: industry sector analysis', Washington, D.C.: U.S. and Foreign Commercial Services and U.S. Department of State.

Eckert, Carter J. (1991) *Offspring of Empire: The Koch'ang Kims and the Colonial Origins of Korean Capitalism, 1876–1945*, Seattle: University of Washington Press.

Eckert, Carter J., Ki-baik Lee, Young Ick Lew, Michael Robinson and Edward W. Wagner (1990) *Korea Old and New: A History*, Cambridge: Harvard University Press.

Edwards, Louise and Mina Roces (eds) (2000) *Women in Asia*, St Leonards: Allen & Unwin.

Elson, Robert E. (1994) *Village Java Under the Cultivation System, 1830–70*, Sydney: Allen & Unwin.

Evans, Peter (1995) *Embedded Autonomy: States and Industrial Transformation*, Princeton: Princeton University Press.

Evers, Hans-Dieter (1987) 'The bureaucratization of Southeast Asia', *Comparative Studies in Society and History* **29**(4), 666–85.

Fairbank, John K. (1992) *China: A New History*, Cambridge: Harvard University Press.

Fama, E.F. (1980) 'Agency costs and the theory of the firm', *Journal of Political Economy* **88**(2), 288–307.

Far Eastern Economic Review (2003) 'China's state-owned enterprises reform', 20 February.

Faure, David (1991) 'A note on the lineage in business', *Chinese Business History* **1**(2), 1–3.

Fewsmith, Joseph (1985) *Party, State, and Local Elites in Republican China: Merchant Organizations and Politics in Shanghai, 1890–1930*, Honolulu: University of Hawaii Press.

Fewsmith, Joseph (2001) *China since Tiananmen: The Politics of Transition*, Cambridge and New York: Cambridge University Press.

Fields, K.J. (1995) *Enterprise and the State in Korea and Taiwan*, Ithaca: Cornell University Press.

Fifield, Anna (2004) 'Move on foreigners in Korean banks', *The Australian*, 30 November.

Fingleton, Eamonn (1995) *Blindside: Why Japan is Still On Track to Overtake the U.S. by the Year 2000*, Boston: Houghton Mifflin.

Flannery, Russell (2001) 'China goes global', *Forbes*, 8 June.

Freedman, Craig (ed.) (2001) *Economic Reform in Japan: Can the Japanese Change?*, Cheltenham, UK and Northampton, MA, USA: Edward Elgar, in Association with the Centre for Japanese Economic Studies, Macquarie University, Australia.

Freedman, Craig and Alex Blair (2003) 'Flawed assumptions – Japanese corporate governance and its relation to macroeconomic policy', CJES Research Papers, No. 2003-2, September, Centre for Japanese Economic Studies, Macquarie University.

Friedman, Edward, Paul Pickowicz, Mark Selden and Kay A. Johnson (1991) *Chinese Village, Socialist State*, New Haven: Yale University Press.

Fruin, Mark (1992) *The Japanese Enterprise System: Competitive Strategies and Cooperative Structures*, Oxford: Oxford University Press.

Gagliardi, Gary (2000) *The Art of War – Plus – The Art of Management*, Seattle: Clearbridge Publishing.

Galenson, Walter (ed.) (1979) *Economic Growth and Structural Change in Taiwan*, Ithaca: Cornell University Press.

Galenson Walter and Konosuke Odaka (1976) 'The Japanese labor market', in Hugh Patrick and Henry Rosovsky (eds), *Asia's New Giant: How the Japanese Economy Works*, Washington, D.C.: The Brookings Institution, pp. 587–672.

Gapinski, J.H. and D.L. Western (1999) 'A tiger in the land of the panda: growth prospects for Hong Kong under reversion to China', in T.T. Fu, C.J. Huang and C.A. Knox-Lowell (eds), *Efficiency and Productivity*

Growth in the Asia-Pacific Region, Cheltenham, UK and Northampton, MA, USA: Edward Elgar, pp. 149–70.

Gardella, Robert (1992) 'Squaring accounts: commercial bookkeeping methods and capitalist rationalism in late Qing and Republican China', *Journal of Asian Studies* **51**(2), 317–39.

Gareffi, G. (1993) 'The organization of buyer-driven global commodity chains: how US retail networks shape overseas production', in G. Gareffi and M. Korzeniewicz (eds), *Commodity Chains and Global Capitalism*, Westport: Greenwood Press, pp. 95–122.

Garnaut, Ross and Ligang Song (1999) *China: Twenty Years of Reform*, Canberra: Asia Pacific Press.

Garnaut, Ross and Ligang Song (eds) (2004) *China's Third Economic Transformation: The Rise of the Private Economy*, London and New York: RoutledgeCurzon.

Garnaut, Ross and Yiping Huang (2001) *Growth without Miracles: Readings on the Chinese Economy in the Era of Reform*, Oxford: Oxford University Press.

Garnaut, Ross, Ligang Song, Yang Yao and Xiaolu Wang (2001) *Private Enterprise in China*, Canberra: Asian Pacific Press, and Beijing: China Center for Economic Research. Some sections appeared in 2000 in International Finance Corporation, *China's Emerging Private Enterprise*.

Gellner, Ernest (1983) *Nations and Nationalism*, Ithaca: Cornell University Press.

Gerlach, Michael L. (1992a) *Alliance Capitalism: The Social Organization of Japanese Business*, Berkeley: University of California Press.

Gerlach, Michael L. (1992b) 'Twilight of the *Keiretsu*? A critical assessment', *Journal of Japanese Studies* **18**(1), 79–118.

Gold, Thomas B. (1986) *State and Society in the Taiwan Miracle*, Armonk: M.E. Sharpe.

Gold, Thomas B. (1988) 'Colonial origins of Taiwanese capitalism', in Edwin A. Winkler and Susan Greenhalgh (eds), *Contending Approaches to the Political Economy of Taiwan*, Armonk: M.E. Sharpe, pp. 101–17.

Gold, Thomas B. (1996) 'Civil society in Taiwan: the Confucian dimension', in Tu Wei-ming (ed.), *Confucian Traditions and East Asian Modernity: Moral Education and Economic Culture in Japan and the Four Mini-Dragons*, Cambridge: Harvard University Press, pp. 244–58.

Gomez, Edmund T. (ed.) (2002) *Political Business in Asia*, London and New York: Routledge.

Gomez, Edmund T. and Hsin-Huang Michael Hsiao (2004a) 'Introduction: Chinese business research in Southeast Asia', in Edmund T. Gomez and Hsin-Huang Michael Hsiao (eds), *Chinese Business in Southeast Asia:*

Contesting Cultural Explanations, Researching Entrepreneurship, London and New York: RoutledgeCurzon, pp. 1–37.

Gomez, Edmund T. and Hsin-Huang Michael Hsiao (eds) (2004b) *Chinese Business in Southeast Asia: Contesting Cultural Explanations, Researching Entrepreneurship*, London and New York: RoutledgeCurzon.

Gomez, Edmund T. and Jomo Kwame Sundaram (1997) *Malaysia's Political Economy: Politics, Patronage and Profits*, Cambridge: Cambridge University Press.

Goodfellow, Rob (ed.) (1997) *Indonesian Business Culture*, Singapore: Butterworth–Heinemann Asia.

Goodman, David S.G. (1994) *Deng Xiaoping and the Chinese Revolution: A Political Biography*, London: Routledge.

Goodman, David S.G. (2005) 'Exiled by definition: the Salar and economic activism in Northwest China', *Asian Studies Review* **29**, 325–43.

Gordon, Andrew (1985) *The Evolution of Labor Relations in Japan: Heavy Industry, 1853–1955*, Harvard University Council on East Asian Studies, Harvard East Asian Monographs 117, Cambridge: Harvard University Press.

Gould, Stephen J. (1995) 'The Buddhist perspective on business ethics: experiential exercises for exploration and practice', *Journal of Business Ethics* **14**, 63–70.

Gragert, Edwin H. (1994) *Landownership under Colonial Rule: Korea's Japanese Experience, 1900–1935*, Honolulu: University of Hawaii Press.

Green, Robert W. (ed.) (1973) *Protestantism, Capitalism, and Social Science: The Weber Thesis Controversy*, 2nd edn, Lexington: D.C. Heath and Company.

Greenfeld, Liah (1992) *Nationalism: Five Roads to Modernity*, Cambridge: Harvard University Press.

Grewal, Bhajan, Lan Xue, Peter Sheehan and Fiona Sun (eds) (2004) *China's Future in the Knowledge Economy: Engaging the New World*, Melbourne: Centre for Strategic Studies, Victoria University, and Tsinghau University Press.

Griffith, Samuel B. (trans.) (1971), *Sun Tzu: The Art of War*, Oxford: Oxford University Press.

Groves, T., Y. Hong, J. McMillan and B. Naughton (1994) 'Autonomy and incentives in Chinese state enterprises', *Quarterly Journal of Economics* **109**(1), 183–209.

Groves, T., Y. Hong, J. McMillan and B. Naughton (1995) 'China's evolving managerial labor market', *Journal of Political Economy* **103**(4), 873–92.

Guerin, Bill (2003) 'World's top noodle maker loses its bite', *Asia Times Online*, 23 December.

Guerrera, Francesco (2005) 'The price of good governance: billions at risk if CCB shuns a Wall St listing', *The Australian*, 26 January.

Guerrera, Francesco and Richard McGregor (2004) 'Goldman scales Great Wall of China but rivals left guessing: China says it's a one-off deal', *The Australian*, 11 August.

Guerrera, Francesco and Richard McGregor (2005) 'Temasek eyes $1.3bn BoC stake', *The Australian*, 10 August.

Gutierrez, E.I. Torrente and N. Garcia (1992) *All in the Family: A Study of Elites and Power Relations in the Philippines*, Quezon City: Ateneo Center for Social Policy and Public Affairs.

Habir, Ahmad D., Eugene Sebastian and Leslie Williams (eds) (2002) *Governance and Privatisation in Indonesia*, Sydney: Research Institute for Asia and the Pacific, and The Indonesian Institute for Management Development.

Haggard, Stephan (2000) *The Political Economy of the Asian Financial Crisis*, Washington, D.C.: Institute for International Economics.

Haggard, Stephan, Byung-Kook Kim and Chung-in Moon (1991) 'The transition to export-led growth in Korea: 1954–1966', *Journal of Asian Studies* **50**(4), 850–73.

Haggard, Stephan, Wonhyuk Lim and Euysung Kim (eds) (2003) *Economic Crisis and Corporate Restructuring in Korea: Reforming the Chaebol*, Cambridge and New York: Cambridge University Press.

Haley, George T. (1997) 'A strategic perspective on overseas Chinese networks' decision making', *Management Decision* **35**(8), 587–94.

Haley, George T. and Chin Tiong Tan (1996) 'The black hole of South East Asia: strategic decision making in an informational void', *Management Decision* **34**(9), 43–55.

Haley, George T., Chin Tiong Tan and Usha C.V. Haley (1998) *New Asian Emperors: The Overseas Chinese, Their Strategies and Competitive Advantages*, Oxford: Butterworth Heinemann.

Hall, Peter and David Soskice (eds) (2001) *Varieties of Capitalism: The Institutional Foundations of Comparative Advantage*, New York: Oxford University Press.

Hamilton, Gary G. (1984) 'Patriarchalism in Imperial China and Western Europe: a revision of Weber's sociology of domination', *Theory and Society* **13**, 411–32.

Hamilton, Gary G. (1996) 'Competition and organization: a reexamination of Chinese business practices', *Journal of Asian Business* **12**(1), 7–20.

Hamilton, Gary G. and Robert C. Feenstra (1995) 'Varieties of hierarchies and markets: an introduction', *Industrial and Corporate Change* **4**(1), 75–97.

Hampson, Sasha (2000) 'Rhetoric or reality? Contesting definitions of women in Korea', in Louise Edwards and Mina Roces (eds), *Women in Asia*, St Leonards: Allen & Unwin, pp. 170–87.

Harvard Business School (1997) *Daewoo's Globalization: Uz-Daewoo Auto Project*, Cambridge: Harvard Business School.

Hatch, Walter and Kozo Yamamura (1996) *Asia in Japan's Embrace: Building a Regional Production Alliance*, Cambridge: Cambridge University Press.

Hattori, Tamio (1989) 'Japanese Zaibatsu and Korean Chaebol', in Kae H. Chung and Hak Chong Lee (eds), *Korean Managerial Dynamics*, New York: Praeger.

Hefner, Robert W. (ed.) (1998) *Market Cultures: Society and Morality in the New Asian Capitalisms*, St Leonards: Allen & Unwin.

Hein, Laura E. (1993) 'Growth versus success: Japan's economic policy in historical perspective', in Andrew Gordon (ed.), *Postwar Japan as History*, Berkeley and Los Angeles: University of California Press, pp. 99–122.

Hemple, Paul S. and Ching-yen Daphne Chang (2002) 'Reconciling traditional Chinese management with high-tech Taiwan', *Human Resource Management Journal* 12(1), 77–95.

Herold, Lars (2002) *Building a Market Economy in North Korea and Vietnam: Key Lessons from the Chinese, Russian, and German Experiences*, dissertation, University of Sydney, 2002; Aachen: Shaker Verlag.

Hew, Denis (2004) 'SME policies and SME linkage development in Singapore', in Denis Hew and Loi Wee Nee (eds), *Entrepreneurship and SMEs in Southeast Asia*, Singapore: Institute of Southeast Asian Studies, pp. 175–205.

Hew, Denis and Loi Wee Nee (eds) (2004) *Entrepreneurship and SMEs in Southeast Asia*, Singapore: Institute of Southeast Asian Studies.

Hewison, Kevin (1989) *Bankers and Bureaucrats: Capital and the Role of the State in Thailand*, Yale University Southeast Asia Studies, Monograph Series No. 34, New Haven: Yale University Press.

Hill, Charles W.L. (2005) *International Business: Competing in the Global Marketplace*, 5th edn, Boston: McGraw-Hill Irwin.

Hill, Charles W.L. and Gareth R. Jones (1998) *Strategic Management Theory: An Integrated Approach*, 4th edn, Boston and New York: Houghton Mifflin.

Hill, Hal (1990) 'Foreign investment and East Asian economic development: a survey', *Asian-Pacific Economic Literature* 4(2), 21–58.

Hill, Hal (1994) 'ASEAN economic development: an analytical survey – the state of the field', *Journal of Asian Studies* 53(3), 832–66.

Hill, Hal (1996) *The Indonesian Economy since 1966: Southeast Asia's Emerging Giant*, Cambridge: Cambridge University Press.

Hille, Kathrin (2005) 'Temasek tries to gazump bank bid', *The Australian*, 2 August.

Ho, James K. (2000) *Cybertigers: How Companies in Asia Can Prosper from E-Commerce*, Singapore: Prentice-Hall/Pearson Education Asia.

Ho, Kai Leon (ed.) (2005) *Reforming Corporate Governance in Southeast Asia*, Singapore: Institute of Southeast Asian Studies.

Ho, Samuel P.S. (1978) *Economic Development of Taiwan, 1860–1970*, New Haven: Yale University Press.

Ho, Samuel P.S. (1984) 'Colonialism and development: Korea, Taiwan, and Kwantung', in Ramon H. Myers and Mark R. Peattie (eds), *The Japanese Colonial Empire, 1895–1945*, Princeton: Princeton University Press, pp. 347–98.

Ho, Samuel P.S. (1994) *Rural China in Transition: Non-Agricultural Development in Rural Jiangsu, 1978–1990*, Oxford: Clarendon Press.

Hobday, Michael (1995) *Innovation in East Asia: The Challenge to Japan*, Aldershot, UK and Brookfield, USA: Edward Elgar.

Hofstede, Geert H. (1994) 'Cultural constraints in management theories', *International Review of Strategic Management* **5**, 27–48.

Hofstede, Geert H. (2001) *Culture's Consequences: Comparing Values, Behaviors, Institutions and Organizations across Nations*, 2nd edn, Thousand Oaks: Sage Publications; first edition, 1980.

Hofstede, Geert H. and Michael H. Bond (1988) 'The Confucius connection: from cultural roots to economic growth', *Organizational Dynamics* **16**(4), 5–21.

Hofstede, Geert H. and Gert Jan Hofstede (2005) *Cultures and Organizations: Software of the Mind*, revised and expanded 2nd edn, New York: McGraw-Hill.

Hogan, W.T. (1994) *Steel in the 21st Century*, New York: Lexington Press.

Holz, Carsten A. (2002) 'Long live China's state-owned enterprises: deflating the myth of poor financial performance', *Journal of Asian Economics* **13**, 493–529.

Holz, Carsten A. (2003) *China's Industrial State-Owned Enterprises: Between Profitability and Bankruptcy*, Singapore: World Scientific Publishing.

Hong Kong, Hong Kong Productivity Council, http://www.hkpc.org.

Hsu, Cho-yun (1980) *Han Agriculture: The Formation of Early Chinese Agrarian Economy (206 B.C. – A.D. 220)*, Seattle: University of Washington Press.

Hsu, Immanuel C.Y. (2000) *The Rise of Modern China*, 6th edn; New York and Oxford: Oxford University Press; first edn 1970.

Huang, Cen (2000) 'The myth of labour relations in overseas Chinese enterprises', *IIAS Newsletter*, No. 21 (February), p. 29.

Huang, Philip C.C. (1985) *The Peasant Economy and Social Change in
North China*, Stanford: Stanford University Press.

Huang, Philip C.C. (1990) *The Peasant Family and Rural Development in
the Yangtzi Delta, 1350–1988*, Stanford: Stanford University Press.

Huang, Yiping (2001) *China's Last Steps Across the River: Enterprise and
Banking Reforms*, Canberra: Asia Pacific Press, Australian National
University.

Huang, Quanyu, Joseph W. Leonard and Chen Tong (1997) *Business
Decision Making in China*, New York: Howarth Press.

Huber, Thomas M. (1994) *Strategic Economy in Japan*, Boulder: Westview
Press.

Huen, Patricia Lim Pui (2003) *Wong Ah Fook: Immigrant, Builder and
Entrepreneur*, Singapore: Institute of Southeast Asian Studies.

Hwang, Y.D. (1991) *The Rise of a New World Economic Power: Postwar
Taiwan*, Westport: Greenwood Press.

Hynson, Larry M. (1990) *Doing Business with South Korea*, New York:
Quorum Books.

Ibison, David (2005) 'New Daimler may dump Mitsubishi', *The Australian*,
2 August.

Il, Sakong (1993) *Korea in the World Economy*, Washington, D.C.: Institute
for International Economics.

Ileto, Reynoldo (1992) 'Religion and anti-colonial movements', in
Nicholas Tarling (ed.), *The Cambridge History of Southeast Asia*,
vol. 2; *The Nineteenth and Twentieth Centuries*, Cambridge: Cambridge
University Press, pp. 197–248.

Ip, Po-Keung (2003) 'Business ethics and a state-owned enterprise in
China', *Business Ethics: A European Review* 12(1), 64–77.

Ishikawa, Kaoru (1990) *Introduction to Quality Control*, Tokyo: 3A
Corporation.

Isobe, Takehiko, Shige Makino and Anthony Goerzen (2006) 'Financial performance and membership in Japanese Keiretsu', Association of Japanese
Business Studies 19th Annual Conference, Beijing, China, 22–3 July.

Jackson, Gregory (2003) 'Corporate governance in Germany and Japan:
liberalization pressures and responses during the 1990s', in Kozo
Yamamura and Wolfgang Streeck (eds), *The End of Diversity? Prospects
for German and Japanese Capitalism*, Ithaca and London: Cornell
University Press, pp. 261–305.

Jacobs, J. Bruce (1976) 'The cultural bases of factional alignment and division in a rural Taiwanese township', *Journal of Asian Studies* 36(1),
79–97.

Jacoby, Neil H. (1966) *U.S. Aid to Taiwan: A Study of Foreign Aid, Self-Help, and Development*, New York: Frederick A. Praeger.

Janelli, Roger L. and Dawnhee Yim (1995) *Making Capitalism: The Social and Cultural Construction of a South Korean Conglomerate*, Stanford: Stanford University Press.

Jarvis, Darryl S.L. (2001) 'Problems and prospects in Thaksin's Thailand: an interim assessment', *Asian Survey* **42**(2) (April/March), 297–319.

Jefferson, Gary H. and Thomas G. Rawski (1994) 'Enterprise reform in Chinese industry', *Journal of Economic Perspectives* **8**(2), 47–70.

Jenkins, David (1998) 'Javanese king or classic dictator?', *The Sydney Morning Herald*, 22 May.

Jesudason, James V. (1989) *Ethnicity and the Economy: The State, Chinese Business and Multinationals in Malaysia*, Singapore and New York: Oxford University Press.

Jiang, Xiaoli (2001) 'A case study of organisational culture and ideological issues in a joint venture in China', *Journal of Enterprising Culture* **9**(3), 313–30.

Johnson, Chalmers (1982) *MITI and the Japanese Miracle: The Growth of Industrial Policy, 1925–1975*, Stanford: Stanford University Press.

Johnson, Chalmers (1987) 'Political institutions and economic performance: the government–business relationship in Japan, South Korea, and Taiwan', in Frederic C. Deyo (ed.), *The Political Economy of the New Asian Industrialism*, Ithaca: Cornell University Press, pp. 136–64.

Jomo, Kwame Sundaram (1986) *A Question of Class: Capital, the State, and Uneven Development in Malaysia*, Singapore: Oxford University Press.

Jomo, Kwame Sundaram (1990) *Growth and Structural Change in the Malaysian Economy*, New York: St Martin's Press.

Jomo, Kwame Sundaram (ed.) (1994) *Japan and Malaysian Development: In the Shadow of the Rising Sun*, London: Routledge.

Jomo, Kwame Sundaram (ed.) (1995) *Privatizing Malaysia: Rents, Rhetoric, Realities*, Boulder and London: Westview Press.

Jomo, Kwame Sundaram (2001) *Malaysian Eclipse: Economic Crisis and Recovery*, London: Zed Books.

Jomo, Kwame Sundaram (ed.) (2003) *Southeast Asian Paper Tigers? From Miracle to Débâcle and Beyond*, London: RoutledgeCurzon.

Jones, Leroy and Il Sakong (1980) *Government, Business, and Entrepreneurship in Economic Development: The Korean Case*, Cambridge: Harvard University Press.

Joseph, William A., Christine P.W. Wong and David Zweig (eds) (1991) *New Perspectives on the Cultural Revolution*, Cambridge: Council on East Asian Studies, Harvard University.

Juhn, Daniel Sungil (1973) 'The development of Korean entrepreneurship', in Andrew C. Nahm (ed.), *Korea Under Japanese Colonial Rule: Studies of the Policy and Techniques of Japanese Colonialism*, The Center for Korean Studies, Institute of International and Area Studies, Western Michigan University.

Jung, K.H. (1989) 'Business–government relations in Korea', in K.H. Chung and H.C Lee (eds), *Korean Managerial Dynamics*, New York: Praeger.

Kahn, Herman (1971) *The Emerging Japanese Superstate: Challenge and Response*, Englewood Cliffs: Prentice-Hall.

Kanapathy, Vijayakumari (2004) 'Entrepreneurship in Malaysia's electronics industry: the role of SMEs', in Denis Hew and Loi Wee Nee (eds), *Entrepreneurship and SMEs in Southeast Asia*, Singapore: Institute of Southeast Asian Studies, pp. 131–49.

Kang, Chul-kyu (1997) 'Diversification process and the ownership structure of Samsung Chaebol', in T. Shiba and M. Shimotani (eds), *Beyond the Firm*, Oxford: Oxford University Press.

Kaplan, Steven N. (1994) 'Top executive rewards and firm performance: a comparison of Japan and the United States', *Journal of Political Economy* **102**(3), 510–46.

Kaplan Steven N. and Bernadette A. Minton (1994) 'Appointments of outsiders to Japanese boards: determinants and implications for managers', *Journal of Financial Economics* **36**(2), 225–58.

Kaplinsky, Raphael (1997) 'Technique with system: the spread of Japanese management techniques to developing countries', *World Development* **25**(5), 681–94.

Kaplinsky, Raphael and Anne Posthuma (1994) *Easternization: The Spread of Japanese Management Techniques in Developing Countries*, Essex: Frank Cass.

Katz, Richard (1998) *Japan: The System that Soured*, Armonk: M.E. Sharpe.

Kaur, Amarjit (ed.) (2004) *Women Workers in Industrialising Asia: Costed, Not Valued*, Houndmills: Palgrave Macmillan.

Kawai, Masahiro and Shinji Takaji (2004) 'Japan's official development assistance: recent issues and future directions', *Journal of International Development* **16**, 255–80.

Kessler, Clive (2001) 'Some thoughts on Islam and "September 11" on Malaysia', Globalization and Malaysia's Place in the Region, Malaysia Society of Australia, 12th Biennial Colloquium, University of Sydney, 8–9 November.

Khoo, Khen-tor (1997) *Sun Tzu & Management*, Malaysia: Pelanduk Publications.

Kim, Choong Soon (1992) *The Culture of Korean Industry: An Ethnography of Poongsan Corporation*, Tucson: University of Arizona Press.

King, Ambrose Y.C. (1996) 'State Confucianism and its transformation: the restructuring of the state–society relation in Taiwan', in Tu Wei-ming (ed.), *Confucian Traditions and East Asian Modernity: Moral Education and Economic Culture in Japan and the Four Mini-Dragons*, Cambridge: Harvard University Press, pp. 228–43.

King, David Chan-oong (2001) *Crony Capitalism: Corruption and Development in South Korea and the Philippines*, Cambridge and New York: Cambridge University Press.

Kirby, William C. (1995) 'China unincorporated: company law and business enterprise in twentieth-century China', *Journal of Asian Studies* **54**(1), 43–63.

Kirk, Donald (2000) *Korean Dynasty: Hyundai and Chung Ju Yung*, Hong Kong: Asia; first published Armonk: M.E. Sharpe, 1994.

Kirkbride, Paul S. and Sara F.Y. Yang (1993) 'From Kyoto to Kowloon: cultural barriers to the transference of quality circles from Japan to Hong Kong', *Asia Pacific Journal of Human Resources* **32**(2), 100–111.

Kojima, Kiyoshi (1978) *Direct Foreign Investment: A Japanese Model of Multinational Business Operations*, London: Croom Helm, and New York: Praeger.

Kojima, Kiyoshi (1985) 'Japanese and American direct investment in Asia: a comparative analysis', *Hitotsubashi Journal of Economics* **26**(1), 1–35.

Kraar, Louis (2003) 'Wanted', *Fortune* (Europe), **147**(2), 3 February.

Kratoska, Paul and Ben Batson (1992) 'Nationalism and modernist reform', in Nicholas Tarling (ed.), *The Cambridge History of Southeast Asia*, vol. 2: *The Nineteenth and Twentieth Centuries*, Cambridge: Cambridge University Press, pp. 257–324.

Krause, Donald G. (1996) *Sun Tzu: The Art of War for Executives*, London: Nicholas Brealey Publishing.

Krause, Donald G. (1999) *The Book of Five Rings for Executives: Musashi's Classic Book of Competitive Tactics*, London: Nicholas Brealey Publishing.

Krueger, Anne O. (1995) 'East Asian experience and endogenous growth theory', in T. Ito and A.O. Krueger (eds), *Growth Theory in the Light of East Asian Experience*, Chicago: University of Chicago Press, pp. 9–36.

Ku, Y.W. (1997) *Welfare Capitalism in Taiwan – State, Economy, and Social Policy*, New York: St Martin's Press.

Kulick, Elliott and Dick Wilson (1992) *Thailand's Turn: Profile of a New Dragon*, New York: St Martin's Press.

Kuo, Eddie C.Y. (1996) 'Confucianism as political discourse in Singapore', in Tu Wei-ming (ed.), *Confucian Traditions and East Asian Modernity:*

Moral Education and Economic Culture in Japan and the Four Mini-Dragons, Cambridge: Harvard University Press, pp. 294–309.

Kuo, Shirley W.Y. and Christina Y. Liu (1998) 'Taiwan', in Ross H. McLeod and Ross Garnaut (eds), *East Asia in Crisis: From Being A Miracle to Needing One?*, London and New York: Routledge, pp. 179–88.

Kwon, O. Yul (2000) 'The Korean financial crisis: implications for international business in Korea', *Asian Studies Review* **24**(1), 24–51.

Kwon, Seung-Ho and Michael O'Donnell (1999) 'Repression and struggle: the state, the Chaebol and independent unions in Korea', *Journal of Industrial Relations* **41**(2), 272–94.

Kwon, Seung-Ho and Michael O'Donnell (2001) *The Chaebol and Labour in Korea: The Development of Management Strategy in Hyundai*, London and New York: Routledge.

Lague, David (1998) 'China "shenanigans" over $30bn plan for clone city miffs Lee', *The Sydney Morning Herald*, 21 March.

Lai, Tse-han, Ramon H. Myers and Wei Wou (1991) *A Tragic Beginning: The Taiwan Uprising of February 28, 1947*, Stanford: Stanford University Press.

Landa, Janet T. (1983) 'The political economy of the ethnicity and entre-preneurship in a plural society', in Linda Y.C. Lim and L.A. Peter Gosling (eds), *The Chinese in Southeast Asia*, 2 vols, Singapore: Maruzen Asia, vol. 1, pp. 86–116.

Landes, David S. (1998) *The Wealth and Poverty of Nations*, London: Little Brown & Company.

Laothamatas, Anek (1992) *Business Associations and the New Political Economy of Thailand: From Bureaucratic Polity to Liberal Corporatism*, Boulder: Westview.

Lardy, Nicholas R. (1983) *Agriculture in China's Modern Economic Development*, Cambridge: Cambridge University Press.

Lardy, Nicholas R. (1991) *Foreign Trade and Economic Reform in China, 1978–1990*, Cambridge: Cambridge University Press.

Lardy, Nicholas R. (1998) *China's Unfinished Economic Revolution*, Washington D.C.: The Brookings Institution.

Larkin, John A. (1982) 'Philippine history reconsidered: a socioeconomic perspective', *American Historical Review* **87**, 595–628.

Lasserre, Philippe and Hellmut Schuette (1999) *Strategies for Asia Pacific: Beyond the Crisis*, South Yarra: Macmillan Education.

Latifah, Wan (1999) 'The NITC/MIMOS Berhad K-economy advanced paper', NITC/MIMOS BERHAD, Kuala Lumpur, June, http://www.nitc.org.my.

Lau, L.J. (1999) 'The sources of East Asian economic growth', in Gustav Ranis et al. (eds), *The Political Economy of Comparative Development into the 21st Century*, Cheltenham, UK and Northampton, MA, USA: Edward Elgar, pp. 45–76.

Lavely, William, James Lee and Feng Wang (1990) 'Chinese demography: the state of the field', *Journal of Asian Studies* **49**, 813.

Lee, Chang-Jae (2003) 'A hub in the making', *Korea Trade and Investment* **21**(4) (July–August), 8–12.

Lee, Ching Kwan (1998) *Gender and the South China Miracle: Two Worlds of Factory Women*, Berkeley: University of California Press.

Lee, Chi-Wen Jevons (2001) 'Financial restructuring of state owned enterprises in China: the case of Shanghai Sunve Pharmaceutical Corporation', *Accounting, Organizations and Society* **26**, 673–89.

Lee, Dong Gull (2003) 'The restructuring of Daewoo', in Stephan Haggard, Wonhyuk Lim and Euysung Kim (eds), *Economic Crisis and Corporate Restructuring in Korea: Reforming the Chaebol*, Cambridge and New York: Cambridge University Press.

Lee, Hak-Chong (1998–99) 'Transformation of employment practices in Korean businesses', *International Studies of Management and Organization* **28**(4), Winter, 26–39.

Lee, Keun (1996) 'An assessment of state sector reform in China: viability of "Legal Person Socialism"', *Journal of Asia Pacific Economies* **1**(1), 105–21.

Lee, Sang M. and Sangjin Yoo (1987) 'The K-type management: a driving force of Korean prosperity', *Management International Review* **27**(4), 68–77.

Lee, Young (1999) 'Wages and employment in China's SOEs, 1980–1994: corporatization, market development, and insider forces', *Journal of Comparative Economics* **21**, 702–29.

Leibfritz, Willi and Deborah Roseveare (1995) 'Ageing populations and government budgets', *The OECD Observer*, No. 197, pp. 33–7.

Lewis, James I. (1995) 'The French colonial service and the issues of reform, 1944–8', *Contemporary European History* **4**(2), 153–88.

Leyden, Peter, Peter Schartz and Joel Hyatt (2000) *The Long Boom: A Future History of the World 1980–2020*, London: Texere.

Li, Ji, Naresh Khatri and Kevin Lim (1999) 'Changing strategic postures of overseas Chinese firms in emerging Asian markets', *Management Decision* **37**(5), 445–56.

Li, K.T. (1988) *The Evolution of Policy behind Taiwan's Development Success*, New Haven: Yale University Press.

Li, Tanya Murray (1998) 'Constituting capitalist culture: the Singapore Malay problem and entrepreneurship reconsidered', in Robert W. Hefner (ed.), *Market Cultures: Society and Morality in the New Asian Capitalisms*, St Leonards: Allen & Unwin, pp. 147–72.

Lillrank, Paul (1995) 'The transfer of management innovations from Japan', *Organization Studies* **16**(6), 971–89.

Lim, Linda Y. and L.A. Peter Gosling (eds) (1983) *The Chinese in Southeast Asia*, 2 vols, Singapore: Maruzen Asia.

Lim, Timothy C. (1994) 'Explaining development in South Korea and East Asia', *Korean Studies* **18**, 171–202.

Lim, Wonhyuk, Stephan Haggard and Euysung Kim (2003) 'Introduction: the political economy of corporate restructuring', in Stephan Haggard, Wonhyuk Lim and Euysung Kim (eds), *Economic Crisis and Corporate Restructuring in Korea: Reforming the Chaebol*, Cambridge and New York: Cambridge University Press.

Lim, Youngil (1999) *Technology and Productivity: The Korean Way of Learning and Catching Up*, Cambridge: MIT Press.

Limlingan, Victor Simpaol (1986) *The Overseas Chinese in ASEAN: Business Strategies and Management Practices*, Manila: Vita Development Corporation.

Lin, C.Y. (1973) *Industrialization in Taiwan*, New York: Praeger.

Lin, Vivian (2004) 'Women workers and health: semiconductor industry in Singapore and Malaysia', in Amarjit Kaur (ed.), *Women Workers in Industrialising Asia: Costed, Not Valued*, Houndmills: Palgrave Macmillan, pp. 173–94.

Lincoln, James R., Michael Gerlach and Christina L. Ahmadijian (1996) 'Keiretsu networks and corporate performance in Japan', *American Sociological Review* **61**(1), 67–88.

Lindsay, Tim and Howard Dick (eds) (2004) *Corruption in Asia: Rethinking the Governance Paradigm*, Annandale: Federation Press.

Lippman, T.W. (1995) *Understanding Islam*, New York: Meridian Books.

Liu, Ya-Ling (1992) 'Reform from below: the private economy and local politics in the rural industrialization of Wenzhou', *China Quarterly* **130**, 293–316.

Lo, Dic (1999) 'Reappraising the performance of China's state-owned enterprises, 1980–1996', *Cambridge Journal of Economics* **23**, 693–718.

Low, Linda (1998) *The Political Economy of a City-state: Government-made Singapore*, Singapore: Oxford University Press.

Lu, Y. and J. Child (1996) 'Decentralization of decision making in China's state enterprises', in D.H. Brown and R. Porter (eds), *Management Issues in China: Domestic Enterprises*, London: Routledge.

Lubeck, Paul M. (1992) 'Malaysian industrialization, ethnic divisions, and the NIC model: the limits of replication', in Richard P. Appelbaum and Jeffery Henderson (eds), *States and Development in the Asian Pacific Rim*, Newbury Park: Sage Publications, pp. 176–98.

Lui, Tai-lok and Stephen W.K. Chiu (1996) 'Merchants, small employers and a non-interventionist state: Hong Kong as a case of unorganized late industrialization', in John Borrego, Alejandro Alvarez Bejar and K.S. Jomo (eds), *Capital, the State, and Late Industrialization: Comparative Perspectives on the Pacific Rim*, Boulder: Westview Press, pp. 221–46.

Luo, Yadong (1997) 'Guanxi: principles, philosophies, and implications', *Human Systems Management* **16**, 43–51.

Luo, Yadong (2000) *Partnering with Chinese Firms: Lessons for International Managers*, Aldershot: Ashgate.

Luong, Hy V. (1992) *Revolution in the Village: Tradition and Transformation in North Vietnam, 1925–1988*, Honolulu: University of Hawaii Press.

Maddison, Angus (1982) *Phases of Capitalist Development*, Oxford: Oxford University Press.

Maddison, Angus (1995) *Monitoring the World Economy 1820–1992*, Development Centre Studies, Paris: Organization for Economic Cooperation and Development (OECD).

Magnier, Mark (2001) 'The octopus emperor who watched his house of cards collapse', *The Sydney Morning Herald*, 8 May; *Los Angeles Times* report.

Malaysia, Multimedia Development Corporation, www.mdc.my/index.html.

Malaysia, National Information Technology Council, Secretariat (2000) 'Access and equity: benchmarking for progress', discussion paper presented at the InfoSoc Malaysia 2000, Kuala Lumpur, 17 May, http://www.nitc.org.my.

Mann, Susan (1987) *Local Merchants and the Chinese Bureaucracy, 1750–1950*, Stanford: Stanford University Press.

Mao, Tse-tung [Mao Zedong] (1939) 'The Chinese Revolution and the Chinese Communist Party', in Mao Tse-tung, *Selected Works*, 5 vols, New York: International Publishers, 1954, vol. 3, pp. 72–101.

Mao, Tse-tung [Mao Zedong] (1966) *Quotations from Chairman Mao Tse-tung*, Peking: Foreign Languages Press.

Marcos, Ferdinand (1978) *Revolution from the Center: How the Philippines Is Using Martial Law to Build a New Society*, Hong Kong: Raya.

Marr, David G. (1980) 'World War II and the Vietnamese Revolution', in Alfred W. McCoy (ed.), *Southeast Asia Under Japanese Occupation*, Monograph Series No. 22, New Haven: Yale University Southeast Asia Studies, pp. 125–58.

Mason, R. Hal (1980) 'A comment on Professor Kojima's "Japanese type versus American type of technology transfer"', *Hitotsubashi Journal of Economics* **20**(2), 42–52.

Mathews, John A. (2002) *Dragon Multinational: A New Model for Global Growth*, New York: Oxford University Press.

Mathews, John A. and Dong-Sung Cho (2000) *Tiger Technology: The Creation of a Semiconductor Industry in East Asia*, Cambridge: Cambridge University Press.

McClelland, David (1961) *The Achieving Society*, New York: Irvington.

McCormack, Gavan (1996) *The Emptiness of Japanese Affluence*, New York: M.E. Sharpe.

McCoy, Alfred W. (ed.) (1994) *An Anarchy of Families: State and Family in the Philippines*, Madison: Center for Southeast Asian Studies, University of Wisconsin–Madison.

McDonald, Hamish (2003) 'Made in China', *Sydney Morning Herald*, 18–19 October.

McDonald, Hamish (2004a) 'Entrepreneur seen as guiding light for China's neglected farmers', *Sydney Morning Herald*, 10–11 January.

McDonald, Hamish (2004b) 'China's workforce shunning poorly paid factory jobs', *Sydney Morning Herald*, 26 August.

McLeod, Ross H. (1998) 'Indonesia', in Ross H. McLeod and Ross Garnaut (eds), *East Asia in Crisis: From Being a Miracle to Needing One?*, London and New York: Routledge, pp. 31–48.

McLeod, Ross H. and Ross Garnaut (eds) (1998) *East Asia in Crisis: From Being a Miracle to Needing One?*, London and New York: Routledge.

McNamara, Dennis L. (1990) *The Colonial Origins of Korean Enterprise, 1910–1945*, Cambridge and New York: Cambridge University Press.

McNamara, Dennis (1992) 'State and concentration in Korea's first republic', *Modern Asian Studies* **26**(4), 701–18.

McNeilly, Mark (2000) *Sun Tzu and the Art of Business: Six Strategic Principles for Managers*, new edn; Oxford: Oxford University Press.

McVey, Ruth (ed.) (1990) *Industrializing Elites in Southeast Asia*, Ithaca: Cornell University Press.

McVey, Ruth (ed.) (1992a) *Southeast Asian Capitalists*, Cornell Southeast Asia Program, Ithaca: Cornell University Press.

McVey, Ruth (1992b) 'The materialization of the Southeast Asian entrepreneur', in Ruth McVey (ed.), *Southeast Asian Capitalists*, Cornell Southeast Asia Program; Ithaca: Cornell University Press, pp. 7–34.

McVey, Ruth (ed.) (2000) *Money and Power in Provincial Thailand*, Honolulu: University of Hawaii Press.

Mekong Research (1999) 'Vietnam: telecommunications operations', Washington, D.C.: U.S. Foreign and Commercial Services and U.S. Department of State.

Mendoza, Brenda and Gilberto Llanto (2004) 'Government's role in developing entrepreneurship and SMEs in the Philippines', in Denis Hew and

Loi Wee Nee (eds), *Entrepreneurship and SMEs in Southeast Asia*, Singapore: Institute of Southeast Asian Studies, pp. 150–74.

Meng, X. and F.C. Perkins (1998) 'Wage determination differences between Chinese state and non-state firms', *Asian Economic Journal* **12**, 295–316.

Menkhoff, Thomas and Solvay Gerke (eds) (2004) *Chinese Entrepreneurship and Asian Business Networks*, London and New York: RoutledgeCurzon.

Meyer, Marshall W. and Xiaohui Lu (2003) 'Managing indefinite boundaries: the strategy and structure of a Chinese business firm', Department of Management, The Wharton School, July.

Michaelson, Gerald A. (2001) *Sun Tzu: The Art of War for Managers; 50 Strategic Rules*, Avon: Adams Media Corporation.

Migdal, Joel S. (1988) *Strong Societies and Weak States: State–Society Relations and State Capabilities in the Third World*, Princeton: Princeton University Press.

Mitchell, B.R. (1995) *International Historical Statistics: Africa, Asia & Oceania 1750–1988*, 2nd rev. edn, Houndmills: Macmillan, and New York: Stockton Press.

Mitchell, Richard H. (1996) *Political Bribery in Japan*, Honolulu: University of Hawaii Press.

Miwa, Yoshiro, Kiyohiko G. Nishimura and J. Mark Ramseyer (eds) (2002) *Distribution in Japan*, Oxford: Oxford University Press.

Mo, Jongryn and Chung-in Moon (2003) 'Business–government relations under Kim Dae-Jung', in Stephan Haggard, Wonhyuk Lim and Euysung Kim (eds), *Economic Crisis and Corporate Restructuring in Korea: Reforming the Chaebol*, Cambridge and New York: Cambridge University Press.

Mock, Noh Hee (1989) 'The development of Korean trade and investment in the PRC', *Korea in World Affairs* **13**(3), 421–39.

Mohamad, Mahathir (1991) *Malaysia: The Way Forward*, Kuala Lumpur: Malaysian Business Council.

Moore, Barrington (1966) *Social Origins of Dictatorship and Democracy: Lord and Peasant in the Making of the Modern World*, Harmondsworth: Penguin; paperback edition 1973.

Moore, Matthew (2002) 'Indonesia's new military chief hopes to be hammer of Aceh', *The Sydney Morning Herald*, 30 August–1 September.

Morden, T. and D. Bowles (1998) 'Management in South Korea: a review', *Management Decision* **36**(5), 316–30.

Morita, Akio, with Edwin M. Reingold and Mitsuko Shimomura (1986) *Made in Japan: Akio Morita and Sony*, New York: Dutton.

Morris-Suzuki, Tessa (1994) *The Technological Transformation of Japan: From the Seventeenth to the Twenty-First Century*, Cambridge: Cambridge University Press.

Moskowitz, Karl (1982) 'Korean development and Korean studies – a review article', *Journal of Asian Studies* **42**, 63–90.

Mulgan, Aurelia George (2002) *Japan's Failed Revolution: Koizumi and the Politics of Economic Reform*, Canberra: Asia Pacific Press at the Australian National University.

Murdoch, Lindsay (2000) 'Digging their own graves', *The Age*, 1 July.

Murray, Geoffrey (1994) *Doing Business in China: The Last Great Market*, St Leonards: Allen & Unwin.

Murray, Martin J. (1980) *The Development of Capitalism in Indochina (1870–1940)*, Berkeley: University of California Press.

Myers, Ramon H. (1980) *The Chinese Economy: Past and Present*, Belmont: Wadsworth.

Myers, Ramon H. (1989) 'Confucianism and economic development: Mainland China, Hong Kong and Taiwan', in Chung-Hua Institution for Economic Research, *Conference on Confucianism and Economic Development in East Asia, May 29–31 1989*, Chung-Hua Institution for Economic Research, Conference Series No. 13, Taipei: Chung-Hua Institution for Economic Research, pp. 282–304.

Myrdal, Jan (1984) *Return to a Chinese Village*, New York: Pantheon.

Nakata, Hiroko (2004) 'METI considers hostile-takeover defenses – Government fears an increase in foreign acquisitions of Japanese firms', *The Japan Times*, 7 October.

Naughton, Barry (1994) 'Chinese institutional innovation and privatization from below', *AEA Papers and Proceedings* **84**(2), 266–70.

Naughton, Barry (1995) *Growing Out of the Plan: Chinese Economic Reform 1978–1993*, Cambridge: Cambridge University Press.

Nee, Victor and Sijin Su (1990) 'Institutional change and economic growth in China: the view from the villages', *Journal of Asian Studies* **49**, 3–25.

Needham, Kirsty (2004) 'China tough nut to crack: banker', *The West Australian*, 4 February; *Sydney Morning Herald* report.

Nesadurai, Helen E.S. (2000) 'In defence of national economic autonomy? Malaysia's response to the financial crisis', *Pacific Review* **13**(1), 73–113.

Nestor, W. (1991) *Japanese Neo-Mercantilism*, Basingstoke: Macmillan.

Nezu, Risaburo (2000) 'Carlos Ghosn: cost controller or *keiretsu* killer?' *OECD Observer*, No. 220 (April), pp. 17–19.

Ngai, Pun (2004) 'Engendering Chinese modernity: the sexual politics of *Dagongmei* in a dormitory labour regime', *Asian Studies Review* **28**(2), 151–65.

Noguchi, Yukio (1994) 'The "bubble" and economic policies in the 1980s', *Journal of Japanese Studies* **20**(2), 291–330.

Nolan, Peter and Dong Furen (eds) (1990) *Market Forces in China: Competition and Small Business – the Wenzhou Debate*, London: Zed Books.

Nolan, Peter and Wang Xiaoqiang (1999) 'Beyond privatization: institutional innovation and growth in China's large state-owned enterprises', *World Development* **27**(1), 169–200.

Nolan, Peter, Peter Sutherland and Wu Qing (2001) *China and the Global Business Revolution*, London and New York: Palgrave.

Nonaka, Ikujiro and Hirotaka Takeuchi (1995) *The Knowledge-Creating Company: How Japanese Companies Create the Dynamics of Innovation*, New York: Oxford University Press.

Noon, Chris (2006) 'Thai PM Thaksin's son fined over Shin sale', Forbes.com, 3 March.

Nørland, Irene (1991) 'The French Empire, the colonial state in Vietnam, and economic policy: 1885–1940', *Australian Economic History Review* **31**(1), 72–89.

Numazaki, I. (1986) 'Networks of Taiwanese big business', *Modern China* **12**(4), 487–534.

Numazaki, I. (1997) 'The Laoban-led development of business enterprises in Taiwan: an analysis of the Chinese entrepreneurship', *Developing Economies* **34**(4), 485–508.

O'Brien, Kevin (1994) 'Implementing political reform in China's villages', *Australian Journal of Chinese Affairs* **32**(July), 51–3.

O'Connor, Neale G., Chee W. Chow and Anne Wu (2004) 'The adoption of "Western" management accounting/controls in China's state-owned enterprises during economic transition', *Accounting, Organizations and Society* **29**, 349–75.

Ogura, Shinji (2002) *Banking, the State and Industrial Promotion in Developing Japan*, New York: Palgrave Macmillan.

Oi, Jean C. (1989) *State and Peasant in Contemporary China: The Political Economy of Village Government*, Berkeley: University of California Press.

Oi, Jean C. (1992) 'Fiscal reform and the economic foundations of local state corporatism in China', *World Politics* **45**(1), 99–126.

Oi, Jean C. (1998) 'The evolution of local state corporatism', in Andrew Walder (ed.), *Zouping in Transition*, Cambridge: Harvard University Press, pp. 35–61.

Oi, Jean C. (1999) *Rural China Takes Off: Institutional Foundations of Economic Reform*, Berkeley: University of California Press.

Okabe, Mitsuaki (2002) *Cross Shareholdings in Japan: A New Unified Perspective of the Economic System*, Cheltenham, UK and Northampton, MA, USA: Edward Elgar.

Oon, Khong Cho (1986) *The Politics of Oil in Indonesia: Foreign Company–Host Government Relations*, Cambridge: Cambridge University Press.

Organization for Economic Cooperation and Development, Asian Roundtable on Corporate Governance (2003) *White Paper on Corporate Governance in Asia*, Paris: OECD, 10 June.

Organization for Economic Cooperation and Development, Development Assistance Committee (2004) *Peer Review: Japan*, Paris: OECD.

Ozaki, Robert (1991) *Human Capitalism: The Japanese Enterprise System as a World Model*, New York: Penguin Books.

Painter, Martin (2001) *Public Sector Challenges and Government Reforms in South East Asia*, Sydney: Research Institute for Asia and the Pacific.

Pan, Lynn (1990) *Sons of the Yellow Emperor: The Story of the Overseas Chinese*, London: Secker & Warburg.

Panitchpakdi, Supachai and Mark L. Clifford (2002) *China and the WTO: Changing China, Changing the World*, Singapore: John Wiley & Sons.

Park, Albert and Minggao Shen (2003) 'Joint liability lending and the rise and fall of China's township and village enterprises', *Journal of Development Economics* **71**, 497–531.

Park, Kyung Suh (2003) 'Bank-led corporate restructuring', in Stephan Haggard, Wonhyuk Lim and Euysung Kim (eds), *Economic Crisis and Corporate Restructuring in Korea: Reforming the Chaebol*, Cambridge and New York: Cambridge University Press.

Park, Y.C. (1991) 'The development of financial institutions and the role of government in credit allocation', in L.J. Cho and Y.H. Kim (eds), *Economic Development in the Republic of Korea*, Honolulu: University of Hawaii Press.

Parsons, Talcott (1954) *The Social System*, Glencoe: The Free Press.

Parsons, Talcott and Neil J. Smelser (1956) *Economy and Society: A Study in the Integration of Economic & Social Theory*, London: Routledge & Kegan Paul.

Pascale, Richard and Thomas P. Rohlen (1983) 'The Mazda turnaround', *Journal of Japanese Studies* **9**(2), 219–64.

Pasuk, Phongpaichit (1990) *The New Wave of Japanese Investment in ASEAN*, Singapore: Institute of Southeast Asian Studies.

Pasuk, Phongpaichit and Chris Baker (1995) *Thailand: Economy and Politics*, Kuala Lumpur: Oxford University Press.

Pasuk, Phongpaichit and Sungsidh Piriyarangsan (1996) *Corruption and Democracy in Thailand*, Thailand: Silkworm Books.

Patrick, Hugh and Henry Rosovsky (eds) (1976) *Asia's New Giant: How the Japanese Economy Works*, Washington, D.C.: The Brookings Institution.

Peebles, Gavin and Peter Wilson (2002) *Economic Growth and Development in Singapore: Past and Future*, Cheltenham, UK and Northampton, MA, USA: Edward Elgar.

388 *Asian firms*

Pei, Xiaolin (1996) 'Township–village enterprises, local governments and rural communities: the Chinese village as a firm during economic transition', *Economics of Transition* **4**(1), 43–66.

Peluso, Nancy Lee (1992) *Rich Forests, Poor People: Resource Control and Resistance in Java*, Berkeley: University of California Press.

Peluso, Nancy Lee (1996) *Borneo in Transition: People, Forests, Conservation, and Development*, Kuala Lumpur and New York: Oxford University Press.

Peng, Yusheng (2001) 'Chinese village and townships as industrial corporations: ownership, governance, and market discipline', *American Journal of Sociology* **106**(5), 1338–70.

Perkins, Dwight H. (1969) *Agricultural Development in China, 1368–1968*, Chicago: Aldine Pub. Co.

Perkins, Dwight H. (1983) 'Research on the economy of the People's Republic of China: a survey of the field', *Journal of Asian Studies* **52**, 345–72.

Perkins, Dwight H. (1986) *China: Asia's Next Giant?*, Seattle: University of Washington Press.

Perkins, F.C. (1996) 'Productivity, performance, and priorities for the reform of China's state-owned enterprises', *Journal of Development Studies* **32**(3), 414–44.

Perotti, Enrico C., Laisiang Sun and Liang Zou (1999) 'State-owned versus township enterprises in China', *Comparative Economic Studies* **41**(2–3), 151–79.

Perris, Kristen (1993) 'Local initiative and national reform: the Wenzhou model of development', *China Quarterly* **134**(June), 242–63.

Pesek, William Jr (2004) 'Daiei another day: Zombie firm should unnerve investors', *The Japan Times*, 18 October, Bloomberg report.

Phatak, Arvind V., Rabi S. Bhagat and Roger I. Kashlak (2005) *International Management: Managing in a Diverse and Dynamic Global Environment*, Boston: McGraw-Hill Irwin.

Porter, Michael E. (1998) *The Competitive Advantage of Nations*, updated edn, Houndmills: Macmillan.

Porter, Michael E., Hirotaka Takeuchi and Mariko Sakakibara (2000) *Can Japan Compete?*, Houndmills: Macmillan.

Pun, Ngai (2004) 'Engendering Chinese modernity: the sexual politics of *Dagongmei* in a dormitory labour regime', *Asian Studies Review* **28**(2), 151–65.

Puntasen, Apichai (1999) 'The Asian economic crisis and the crisis of analysis: a critical analysis through Buddhist economics', in Mason C. Hoadley (ed.), *Southeast Asian-Centered Economies or Economics?*, Copenhagen: Nordic Institute of Asian Studies, pp. 62–85.

Rabushka, Alvin (1979) *Hong Kong: A Study in Economic Freedom*, Chicago: University of Chicago Press.

Rahim, Lily Z. (1998) *The Singapore Dilemma: The Political and Educational Marginality of the Malay Community*, Kuala Lumpur: Oxford University Press.

Ranis, Gustav (ed.) (1992) *Taiwan: From a Developing to a Mature Economy*, Boulder: Westview Press.

Rawski, Thomas G. (1989) *Economic Growth in Prewar China*, Berkeley: University of California Press.

Redding, S. Gordon (1990) *The Spirit of Chinese Capitalism*, Berlin and New York: Walter deGruyter.

Redding, S. Gordon (1995) 'Overseas Chinese networks: understanding the enigma', *Long Range Planning* **28**(1), 61–9.

Redding, S. Gordon (1996) 'Societal transformation and the contribution of authority relations and cooperation norms in overseas Chinese business', in Wei-ming Tu (ed.), *Confucian Traditions in East Asian Modernity*, Cambridge: Harvard University Press, pp. 310–27.

Redding, S. Gordon and Michael Ng (1982) 'The role of "face" in the organizational perception of Chinese managers', *Organization Studies* **3**(3), 201–19.

Redding, S. Gordon and Gilbert Y.Y. Wong (1990) 'The psychology of Chinese organizational behavior', in Michael Harris Bond (ed.), *The Psychology of the Chinese People*, New York: Oxford University Press, pp. 267–95.

Reid, Anthony (1980) 'Indonesia: from briefcase to Samurai sword', in Alfred W. McCoy (ed.), *Southeast Asia Under Japanese Occupation*, Monograph Series No. 22, New Haven: Yale University Southeast Asia Studies, pp. 16–32.

Reid, Anthony (ed.) (1996) *Sojourners and Settlers: Histories of Southeast Asia and the Chinese*, Asian Studies Association of Australia, Southeast Asia Publication Series, No. 28, St Leonards: Allen & Unwin.

Rhee, Whee Yung, Bruce Ross-Larson and Garry Pursell (1984) *Korea's Competitive Edge: Managing Entry Into World Markets*, Baltimore and London: Johns Hopkins University Press for the World Bank.

Richards, Anne (1993) 'Korea, Taiwan and Thailand: trade liberalisation and economic growth', *OECD Observer*, No. 184, pp. 24–8.

Richards, Anne (1994) 'Hong Kong, Singapore, Malaysia and the Fruits of Free Trade', *OECD Observer*, No. 185, pp. 29–33.

Richards, M.D. (1986) *Setting Strategic Goals and Objectives*, St Paul: West.

Ricklefs, M.C. (1993) *A History of Modern Indonesia since c. 1300*, 2nd edn, Houndmills: Macmillan.

Roberts, Glenda S. (1994) *Staying on the Line: Blue-Collar Women in Contemporary Japan*, Honolulu: University of Hawaii Press.

Robinson, Kathryn (2000) 'Indonesian women: from *Orde Baru* to *Reformasi*', in Louise Edwards and Mina Roces (eds), *Women in Asia*, St Leonards: Allen & Unwin, pp. 139–69.

Robinson, Michael E. (1991) 'Perceptions of Confucianism in twentieth-century Korea', in Gilbert Rozman (ed.), *The East Asian Region: Confucian Heritage and Its Modern Adaptation*, Princeton: Princeton University Press.

Robison, Richard (1986) *Indonesia and the Rise of Capital*, London: Allen & Unwin.

Rodan, Garry (1989) *The Political Economy of Singapore's Industrialization: National State and International Capital*, New York: St Martin's Press.

Rodan, Garry, Kevin Hewison and Richard Robison (eds) (2001) *The Political Economy of South-East Asia: Conflicts, Crises, and Change*, 2nd edn, Melbourne: Oxford University Press.

Rooth, Tim (1993) *British Protectionism and the International Economy: Overseas Commercial Policy in the 1930s*, Cambridge: Cambridge University Press.

Rowe, William T. (1984) *Hankow: Commerce and Society in a Chinese City, 1796–1889*, Stanford: Stanford University Press.

Rowley, Chris (2002) 'South Korean management in transition', in Malcolm Warner (ed.), *Managing Across Cultures*, London: Thomson, pp. 178–92.

Rowley, Chris, Tae Won Sohn and Johngseok Bae (eds) (2002) *Managing Korean Business: Organization, Culture, Human Resources and Change*, London: Cass.

Ruigrok, W. and R. Van Tulder (1995) *The Logic of International Restructuring*, London: Routledge.

Saich, Tony (2004) *Governance and Politics of China*, 2nd edn, Houndmills and New York: Palgrave.

Sakakibara, Eisuke (1993) *Beyond Capitalism: The Japanese Model of Market Economics*, Lanham: University Press of America.

SarDesai, D.R. (1994) *Southeast Asia: Past and Present*, 3rd edn, Boulder: Westview, and Houndmills: Macmillan.

Sargeson, Sally (1996) 'Localising globalisation: industrial relations in a Chinese joint-venture factory', Communications With/In Asia, 20th Anniversary Conference, Asian Studies Association of Australia, Latrobe University.

Sargeson, Sally (1999) *Reworking China's Proletariat*, New York: St Martin's Press.

Sato, Y. (1993) 'The Salim Group in Indonesia: the development and behavior of the largest conglomerate in Southeast Asia', *The Developing Economies* **29**, 110–25.

Schein, Edgar H. (1996) *Strategic Pragmatism: The Culture of Singapore's Economic Development Board*, Cambridge: MIT Press.

Schenk, Catherine (2001) *Hong Kong as an International Financial Centre: Emergence and Development, 1945–65*, London: Routledge.

Schlevogt, Kai-Alexander (2002) *The Art of Chinese Management*, New York: Oxford University Press.

Schlevogt, Kai-Alexander (2004) 'Chinese entrepreneurship and resilient national development: how "Web-based Management" can help the growth of China's multiple ownership economy', in Thomas Menkhoff and Solvay Gerke (eds), *Chinese Entrepreneurship and Asian Business Networks*, London and New York: RoutledgeCurzon, pp. 84–99.

Schrade, Ulrike (1994) 'Understanding corporate governance in Japan: do classical concepts apply?', *Industrial and Corporate Change* **3**(2), 300–325.

Schumpeter, Joseph A. (1934) *The Theory of Economic Development*, New York: Oxford University Press; paperback edition 1961.

Schumpeter, Joseph A. (1943) *Capitalism, Socialism, and Democracy*, 5th edn, London: Allen & Unwin; paperback edition 1976.

Schutte, H., L. Forman and M. Cannizzo (1993) 'The Salim Group', INSEAD Case 393–008–1.

Schwarz, Adam (1994) *A Nation In Waiting: Indonesia in the 1990s*, Boulder: Westview Press.

Searle, Peter (1999) *The Riddle of Malaysian Capitalism: Rent-seekers or real capitalists?*, Sydney: Allen & Unwin, and Honolulu: University of Hawaii Press.

Sears, Laurie J. (ed.) (1996) *Fantasizing the Feminine in Indonesia*, Durham and London: Duke University Press.

Selmer, Jan (2002) 'Coping strategies applied by Western vs overseas Chinese business expatriates in China', *International Journal of Human Resource Management* **13**(1), 19–34.

Seno, Alexandra A. (2000) 'Creative's Genius', *Asiaweek* **26**(38).

Shane, S.A. (1992) 'Why do some societies invent more than others?', *Journal of Business Venturing* **7**, 29–46.

Shanmugaratnam, Tharman (2004) 'Foreword – SMEs: a new role in economic growth strategies', in Denis Hew and Loi Wee Nee (eds), *Entrepreneurship and SMEs in Southeast Asia*, Singapore: Institute of Southeast Asian Studies, pp. xv–xxv.

Shih, Stan (2001) *Growing Global: A Corporate Vision Masterclass*, New York: John Wiley & Sons.

Shimada, Haruo (1994) *Japan's 'Guest Workers': Issues and Public Policies*, Tokyo: University of Tokyo Press.

Shirozu, N. (1999) 'Nissan shakes Japan's economic structure', *The Wall Street Journal*, Interactive Edition, 19 October.

Shome Tony (2001) 'Reconstructing the racial and religious divide: oblique change in socio-economic policy in Malaysia', Globalization and Malaysia's Place in the Region, Malaysia Society of Australia, 12th Biennial Colloquium, University of Sydney, 8–9 November.

Short, Philip (2000) *Mao: A Life*, New York: Henry Holt.

Silverthorne, Sean (2004) 'What it takes to succeed in China', Working Knowledge, Harvard Business School, April, http://hbswk.hbs.edu.

Skinner, G. William (1964–5) 'Marketing and social structure in rural China' (3 parts), *Journal of Asian Studies* 24, 3–43, 195–228, 363–99.

Skinner, G. William (1977) 'Cities and the hierarchy of local systems', in G. William Skinner (ed.), *The City in Late Imperial China*, Stanford: Stanford University Press, pp. 275–351.

Skinner, G. William (1977) 'Regional urbanization in nineteenth-century China', in G. William Skinner (ed.), *The City in Late Imperial China*, Stanford: Stanford University Press, pp. 211–52.

Skinner, G. William (1996) 'Creolized Chinese societies in Southeast Asia', in Anthony Reid (ed.), *Sojourners and Settlers: Histories of Southeast Asia and the Chinese*, St Leonards: Allen & Unwin, pp. 51–93.

Sloane, Patricia (1999) *Islam, Modernity and Entrepreneurship among the Malays*, Houndmills: Macmillan.

Smith, Anthony D. (1986) *The Ethnic Origins of Nations*, Oxford: Blackwell.

Smith, Heather (1998) 'Korea', in Ross H. McLeod and Ross Garnaut (eds), *East Asia in Crisis: From Being a Miracle to Needing One?*, London and New York: Routledge, pp. 66–84.

Smyth, Russell, Jianguo Wang and Quek Lee Kang (2000) 'Efficiency, performance and changing corporate governance in China's township–village enterprises since the 1990s', *Asian-Pacific Economic Literature* 14(1), 30–41.

So, Alvin Y. and Stephan W.K. Chiu (1995) *East Asia and the World Economy*, Thousand Oaks: Sage Publications.

Soederberg, Susanne (2003) 'The promotion of "Anglo-American" corporate governance in the South: who benefits from the new international standard?', *Third World Quarterly* 24(1), 7–27.

Sohn, Chan-Hyun (1997) 'The emerging WTO and new trade issues: Korea's role and priorities', in Korea Economic Institute of America (ed.), *The Emerging WTO System and Perspectives from East Asia*, Ann Arbor: KEIA, pp. 211–38.

Solinger, Dorothy (1999) *Contesting Citizenship in Urban China: Peasant Migrants, the State, and the Logic of the Market*, Berkeley: University of California Press.

Solomon, Jill, Aris Solomon and Chang-Young Park (2002) 'The evolving role of institutional investors in South Korean corporate governance: some empirical evidence', *Institutional Investors* **10**(3), 211–24.

Song, Byung-Nak (1994) *The Rise of the Korean Economy*, updated edn, Hong Kong: Oxford University Press.

Song, Ligang (1998) 'China', in Ross H. McLeod and Ross Garnaut (eds), *East Asia in Crisis: From Being a Miracle to Needing One?*, London and New York: Routledge, pp. 105–19.

Spear, Steven and H. Kent Bowen (1999) 'Decoding the DNA of the Toyota production system', *Harvard Business Review*, September/October, pp. 97–106.

Spinanger, Dean (1986) *Industrialization Policies and Economic Development in Malaysia*, Singapore: Oxford University Press.

Steers, Richard M. (1999) *Made in Korea: Chung Ju Yung and the Rise of Hyundai*, New York: Routledge.

Steers, Richard M., Yoo Keun Shin and Gerardo R. Ungson (1989) *The Chaebol: Korea's New Industrial Might*, New York: Harper & Row, Ballinger Division.

Steinberg, David J. et al. (1987) *In Search of Southeast Asia: A Modern History*, rev. edn, Honolulu: University of Hawaii Press, and St Leonards: Allen & Unwin.

Stevens, Barrie (1996) 'China enters the 21st century', *OECD Observer*, No. 201 (August/September), pp. 28–32.

Stockwin, J.A.A. (1999) *Governing Japan: Divided Politics in a Major Economy*, Oxford: Blackwell.

Studwell, Joe (2002) *The China Dream: The Elusive Quest for the Greatest Untapped Market on Earth*, London: Profile Books.

Suehiro, Akira (1985) *Capital Accumulation and Industrial Development in Thailand*, Bangkok: Social Research Institute.

Suehiro, Akira (1989) *Capital Accumulation in Thailand, 1855–1985*, Tokyo: The Centre for East Asian Cultural Studies.

Sun, Haishun (1996) 'Macroeconomic impact of direct foreign investment in China 1979–93', Working Papers in Economics, No. 232, Department of Economics, University of Sydney.

Sun, Haishun and Frank B. Tipton (1998) 'A comparative analysis of the characteristics of foreign investment in China, 1979–1995', *Journal of Developing Areas* **32**(2), 159–86.

Sung, Wook Joh and Euysung Kim (2003) 'Corporate governance and performance in the 1990s', in Stephan Haggard, Wonhyuk Lim and Euysung

Kim (eds), *Economic Crisis and Corporate Restructuring in Korea: Reforming the Chaebol*, Cambridge and New York: Cambridge University Press.

Sutherland, Heather (1979) *The Making of a Bureaucratic Elite: The Colonial Transformation of the Javanese Priyayi*, Asian Studies Association of Australia, Southeast Asian Publications Series, No. 2, Singapore: Heinemann.

Tan, Kong Yam (ed.) (2002) *Asian Economic Recovery: Policy Options for Growth and Stability*, Singapore: Singapore University Press.

Tan, Wee Liang (2004) 'Entrepreneurship development: the necessary conditions', in Denis Hew and Loi Wee Nee (eds), *Entrepreneurship and SMEs in Southeast Asia*, Singapore: Institute of Southeast Asian Studies, pp. 7–23.

Tangkitvanich, Samkiat (2004) 'SME development in Thailand's automotive industry', in Denis Hew and Loi Wee Nee (eds), *Entrepreneurship and SMEs in Southeast Asia*, Singapore: Institute of Southeast Asian Studies, pp. 206–20.

Tannenbaum R. and W.H. Schmidt (1973) 'How to choose a leadership pattern', *Harvard Business Review*, May–June, pp. 162–80.

Tarling, Nicholas (ed.) (1992) *The Cambridge History of Southeast Asia*, vol. 2: *The Nineteenth and Twentieth Centuries*, Cambridge: Cambridge University Press.

Taylor, Alex (2004) 'Shanghai Auto wants to be the world's next great car company', *Fortune*, 4 October.

Taylor, Bill (2001) 'Labor management in Japanese manufacturing plants in China', *International Journal of Human Resource Management* 12(4), 601–20.

Taylor, Robert H. (1980) 'Burma in the Anti-Fascist War', in Alfred W. McCoy (ed.), *Southeast Asia Under Japanese Occupation*, Monograph Series No. 22, New Haven: Yale University Southeast Asia Studies, pp. 159–90.

Tellzen, Roland (2005) 'Flat panel helps to end flatline charts', *The Australian*, 1 November.

Temasek Holdings (2006) 'Temasek-SCB led investors group acquires Shinawatra and Damapong families' stake in Shin Corp.', Press release, 23 January, http://temasekholdings.com.sg.

The Australian (2002) 'The problems are piling up', 2 November.

The Australian (2003) 'Samsung makes China shift', 15 October, www.australianIT.com.au.

The Australian (2005) 'Twin daggers to cut a brand in Taiwan', 30 August, *The Economist* report.

The Australian (2005) 'Beijing rolls dice in huge banking gamble', 1 November, *The Economist* report.

The Economist (2000) 'Chronology of Mitsubishi complaints cover-up', 25 March.

The Economist (2000) 'Mitsubishi runs out of gas', 25 March.

The Economist (2004) 'Fools rush in', 7 August.

The Japan Times (2004) 'Firms look to protect sensitive technology at home', 14 October, Kyodo report.

The Straits Times Interactive (2002) 'Malaysian PM laments skewed religious views and "crutches" ', 31 July.

The Sydney Morning Herald (1997) 'Soeharto: patronage and its prizes', 30 October.

The Sydney Morning Herald (1998) 'Sex harassment case costs car maker $58m', 3 June, Bloomberg, Associated Press reports.

The Sydney Morning Herald (1999) 'Loans ease Daewoo jitters', 27 July, Bloomberg Report.

The Sydney Morning Herald (1999) 'Daewoo hints of more to come', 18 August, *Los Angeles Times* Report.

Thelen, Kathleen and Ikuo Kume (2003) 'The future of nationally embedded capitalism: industrial relations in Germany and Japan', in Kozo Yamamura and Wolfgang Streeck (eds), *The End of Diversity? Prospects for German and Japanese Capitalism*, Ithaca and London: Cornell University Press.

Theobald, R. (1990) *Corruption, Development, and Underdevelopment*, Basingstoke: Macmillan.

Thomas, A.S. and S.L. Mueller (2000) 'The case for comparative entrepreneurship', *Journal of International Business Studies* **31**(2), 287–302.

Thompson, A.G. (1989) 'Cross-cultural management of labour in a Thai environment', *Asia-Pacific Journal of Management* **6**(2), 323–38.

Thompson, Herb (1996) 'Deforestation and non-sustainable wood production', Murdoch University, Department of Economics Working Papers, No. 152.

Tipton, Elise K. (2000) 'Being women in Japan 1970–2000', in Louise Edwards and Mina Roces (eds), *Women in Asia*, St Leonards: Allen & Unwin, pp. 208–28.

Tipton, Elise K. (2002) *Modern Japan: A Social and Political History*, London and New York: Routledge.

Tipton, Frank B. (1998) *The Rise of Asia: Economics, Society and Politics in Contemporary Asia*, Basingstoke: Macmillan.

Tipton, Frank B. (2002a) *Alleviating the Digital Divide: Policy Recommendations – Malaysia, Thailand, The Philippines, Vietnam*, Sydney: Research Institute for Asia and the Pacific.

Tipton, Frank B. (2002b) 'Japanese nationalism in comparative perspective', in Sandra Wilson (ed.), *Nation and Nationalism in Japan*, London: RoutledgeCurzon, pp. 146–62.

Tipton, Frank B. and David Hundt (2006) 'Japanese ODA and economic development in South Korea', in Bill Pritchard (ed.), _Japanese Official Development Assistance within the Asian Region_, Sydney: Research Institute for Asia and the Pacific.

Tipton, Frank B., Darryl Jarvis and Anthony Welch (2003) _Redefining the Borders Between Public and Private in Southeast Asia: Malaysia, Philippines, Vietnam, Thailand and Indonesia. Financial Sector, Telecommunications, Information and Communications Technologies, Higher Education_, Sydney: Research Institute for Asia and the Pacific.

Tong, Chee Kiong and Yong Pit Kee (1998) 'Guanxi bases, Xinyong and Chinese business', _British Journal of Sociology_ **49**(1), 76–96.

Tong, Chee Kiong and Yong Pit Kee (2004) 'Personalism and paternalism in Chinese business', in Thomas Menkhoff and Solvay Gerke (eds), _Chinese Entrepreneurship and Asian Business Networks_, London and New York: RoutledgeCurzon, pp. 217–32.

Torrente, E.I. Gutierrez and N. Garcia (1992) _All in the Family: A Study of Elites and Power Relations in the Philippines_, Quezon City: Ateneo Center for Social Policy and Public Affairs.

Transparency International, Global Corruption Report, http://www.transparency.org.

Trevor, Malcolm (2001) _Japan: Restless Competitor. The Pursuit of Economic Nationalism_, Richmond: Curzon Press.

Trocki, Carl A. (1992) 'Political structures in the nineteenth and early twentieth centuries', in Nicholas Tarling (ed.), _The Cambridge History of Southeast Asia_, vol. 2: _The Nineteenth and Twentieth Centuries_, Cambridge: Cambridge University Press, pp. 79–130.

Tsai, Kellee (2002) _Back-Alley Banking: Private Entrepreneurs in China_, Ithaca: Cornell University Press.

Tsurumi, E. Patricia (1990) _Factory Girls: Women in the Thread Mills of Meiji Japan_, Princeton: Princeton University Press.

Tsuchiya, Moriaki and Yoshinobu Konomi (1997) _Shaping the Future of Japanese Management: New Leadership to Overcome the Impending Crisis_, Tokyo: LTCB International Library Foundation.

Tu, Howard S., Seung Yong Kim and Sherry E. Sullivan (2002) 'Global strategy lessons from Japanese and Korean business groups', _Business Horizons_, March/April, pp. 39–46.

Tu, Wei-ming (1984) _Confucian Ethics Today: The Singapore Challenge_, Singapore: Federal Publications.

Tu, Wei-ming (1989) 'The Confucian dimension in the East Asian development model', in Chung-Hua Institution for Economic Research, _Conference on Confucianism and Economic Development in East Asia_,

May 29–31 1989; Chung-Hua Institution for Economic Research, Conference Series No. 13. Taipei: Chung-Hua Institution for Economic Research, pp. 71–110.

Tu, Wei-ming (ed.) (1996) *Confucian Traditions and East Asian Modernity: Moral Education and Economic Culture in Japan and the Four Mini-Dragons*, Cambridge: Harvard University Press.

Tung, Nghiem T. (2002) 'Telecommunications equipment: industry sector analysis, Vietnam', Washington, D.C.: U.S. and Foreign Commercial Service and the U.S. Department of State.

Tylecote, Andrew (1993) *The Long Wave and the World Economy: The Current Crisis in Historical Perspective*, London: Routledge.

Unger, Jonathan (1994) 'Rich man, poor man: the making of new classes in the countryside', in D.G.S. Goodman and B. Hooper (eds), *China's Quiet Revolution: New Interactions between State and Society*, London: Longman Cheshire, pp. 43–63.

Unger, Jonathan (1999) 'The rise of private business in a rural Chinese district: the emerging characteristics of entrepreneurship in the PRC', Working Paper No. 90, January, Asia Research Centre, Murdoch University.

Unger, Jonathan and Anita Chan (1999) 'Inheritors of the boom: private enterprise and the role of government in a rural South China township', Working Paper No. 89, January, Asia Research Centre, Murdoch University.

United States, National Commission on Entrepreneurship (2002) *American Formula for Growth: Federal Policy and the Entrepreneurial Economy, 1858–1998*, Washington, D.C.: NCE.

Van Langenberg, Michael (1993) 'Importing nationalism: the case of Indonesia', in Garry Trompf (ed.), *Islands and Enclaves: Nationalisms and Separatist Pressures in Island and Littoral Contexts*, New Delhi: Sterling Publishers, pp. 151–74.

Vennewald, Werner (1994) 'Technocrats in the state enterprise system of Singapore', Working Paper No. 32, Asia Research Centre, Murdoch University.

Vertinsky, I., D.K. Tse, D.A. Wehrung and K. Lee (1990) 'Organization design and management norms: a comparative study of managers' perceptions in the People's Republic of China, Hong Kong, and Canada', *Journal of Management* **16**(4), 853–67.

Vietnam, Department of General Posts and Telecommunications (2002) *Annual Report 2002*, Hanoi: DGPT.

Vitols, Sigurt (2003) 'From banks to markets: the political economy of liberalization of the German and Japanese financial systems', in Kozo Yamamura and Wolfgang Streeck (eds), *The End of Diversity? Prospects for German and Japanese Capitalism*, Ithaca and London: Cornell University Press.

Vogel, Ezra F. (1979) *Japan as Number One: Lessons for America*, Cambridge: Harvard University Press.

Wachman, Alan M. (1994) *Taiwan: National Identity and Democratization. Taiwan in the Modern World*, Armonk and London: M.E. Sharpe.

Wade, Robert (1990) *Governing the Market: Economic Theory and the Role of Government in East Asian Industrialization*, Princeton: Princeton University Press.

Wade, Robert (1993) 'Managing trade: Taiwan and South Korea as challenges to economics and political science', *Comparative Politics* **25**(2), 147–68.

Walder, Andrew G. (1995) 'Local governments as industrial firms: an organizational analysis of China's transitional economy', *American Journal of Sociology* **101**(2), 263–301.

Wallerstein, Immanuel (1974–89) *The Modern World System*, 3 vols, New York: Academic Books.

Wallich, Henry C. and Mable I. Wallich (1976) 'Banking and finance', in Hugh Patrick and Henry Rosovsky (eds), *Asia's New Giant: How the Japanese Economy Works*, Washington, D.C.: The Brookings Institution, pp. 249–316.

Wang, Annie (2004) 'Holding up half the sky. Five Chinese women: some are smart, rich, and running the show; others just want a piece of the booming economy', *Fortune*, 4 October.

Wank, David L. (1999) *Commodifying Communism: Business, Trust and Politics in a Chinese City*, Cambridge: Cambridge University Press.

Waring, Marilyn (1988) *If Women Counted: A New Feminist Economics*, San Francisco: Harper & Row.

Warner, Malcolm (ed.) (2003) *Culture and Management in Asia*, London: RoutledgeCurzon.

Warr, Peter G. (1998) 'Thailand', in Ross H. McLeod and Ross Garnaut (eds). *East Asia in Crisis: From Being a Miracle to Needing One?*, London and New York: Routledge, pp. 49–65.

Watson, James (1982) 'Chinese kinship reconsidered: anthropological perspectives on historical research', *China Quarterly* **92**, 589–622.

Watson, Rubie S. (1985) *Inequality Among Brothers*, Cambridge: Cambridge University Press.

Weber, Max (1904–5) *The Protestant Ethic and the Spirit of Capitalism*, trans. Talcott Parsons, New York: Charles Scribner's Sons, 1958.

Weber, Max (1920–21) *The Religion of China*, trans. H.H. Gerth, Glencoe: The Free Press, 1951.

Wedeman, Andrew Hall (2003) *From Mao to Market: Rent Seeking, Local Protectionism, and Marketization in China*, Cambridge and New York: Cambridge University Press.

Wee, Chow Hou (2001) *The Inspirations of Tao Zhu-gong: Modern Business Lessons from an Ancient Past*, Singapore: Prentice-Hall.

Weidenbaum, Murray L. and Samuel Hughes (1996) *The Bamboo Network: How Expatriate Chinese Entrepreneurs are Creating a New Economic Superpower in Asia*, New York: Martin Kessler Books.

Weiss, Linda (1995) 'Governed interdependence: rethinking the government–business relationship in East Asia', *Pacific Review* **8**(4), 589–616.

Weiss, Linda (1998) *The Myth of the Powerless State: Governing the Economy in a Global Era*, Cambridge: Polity Press.

Weiss, Linda and John M. Hobson (1995) *States and Economic Development: A Comparative Historical Analysis*, Cambridge: Polity Press.

Westwood, Robert (1997) 'Harmony and patriarchy: the cultural basis for "paternalistic headship" among the overseas Chinese', *Organization Studies* **18**(3), 445–80.

White, Gordon (1993) *Riding the Tiger: The Politics of Economic Reform in Post-Mao China*, Houndmills: Macmillan.

Whiting, Susan H. (2001) *Power and Wealth in Rural China: The Political Economy of Institutional Change*, New York: Cambridge University Press.

Whitley, Richard D. (1992a) *Business Systems in East Asia: Firms, Markets, and Societies*, London: Sage.

Whitley, Richard D. (ed.) (1992b) *European Business Systems: Firms and Markets in their National Contexts*, London: Sage.

Whitley, Richard D. (1999) *Divergent Capitalisms: The Social Structuring and Change of Business Systems*, Oxford: Oxford University Press.

Whitley, Richard D. (2005) *Changing Capitalisms? Internationalization, Institutional Change, and Systems of Economic Organization*, Oxford: Oxford University Press.

Wing, Thye (1999) 'The real reasons for China's growth', *China Journal* **41**, 115–37.

Winichakul, Thongchai (1994) *Siam Mapped: A History of the Geo-Body of a Nation*, Honolulu: Hawaii University Press.

Winn, Jane Kaufmann (1992) 'Law and the underground economy in Taiwan', *Chinese Business History* **3**(1), 1–8.

Wolferen, Karel van (1989) *The Enigma of Japanese Power: People and Politics in a Stateless Nation*, New York: Alfred A. Knopf.

Wong, John (1996) 'Promoting Confucianism for socioeconomic development', in Tu Wei-ming (ed.), *Confucian Traditions and East*

Asian Modernity: Moral Education and Economic Culture in Japan and the Four Mini-Dragons, Cambridge: Harvard University Press, pp. 276–93.

Wong, John and Aline Wong (1989) 'Confucian values as a social framework for Singapore's economic development', in Chung-Hua Institution for Economic Research, *Conference on Confucianism and Economic Development in East Asia, May 29–31 1989*, Conference Series No. 13, Taipei.

Wong, Loong (1993) 'The invention of nationalism in Southeast Asia: some theoretical considerations of nationalism in Singapore', in Garry Trompf (ed.), *Islands and Enclaves: Nationalisms and Separatist Pressures in Island and Littoral Contexts*, New Delhi: Sterling Publishers, pp. 127–50.

Wong, Siu-lun (1988) *Emigrant Entrepreneurs: Shanghai Industrialists in Hong Kong*, Hong Kong: Oxford University Press.

Woo, Jung-en (1991) *Race to the Swift: State and Finance in Korean Industrialization*, New York: Columbia University Press.

World Bank (1993) *The East Asian Miracle: Economic Growth and Public Policy*, Oxford and New York: Oxford University Press.

World Bank (1995) *Bureaucrats in Business*, New York: Oxford University Press.

World Bank (1996) *The Chinese Economy: Fighting Inflation, Deepening Reform*, Washington D.C.: World Bank.

World Bank (2000) *Thailand: Public Finance in Transition*.

World Bank (2004) *Doing Business 2004: Understanding Regulation*, Washington, D.C.: World Bank and Oxford University Press.

Worm, V. (1997) *Vikings and Mandarins: Sino-Scandinavian Business Cooperation in Cross-Cultural Settings*, Copenhagen: Copenhagen Business School Press.

Woronoff, John (1991) *Japan as Anything but Number One*, New York: Macmillan.

Wright, Tim (1984) *Coal Mining in China's Economy and Society, 1895–1937*, Cambridge: Cambridge University Press.

Wright, Tim (1994) 'China: what will happen after Deng?', *Asiaview* 4(3), 1–2; Asia Research Centre, Murdoch University.

Wu, Chen-Fong (2001) 'The study of global business ethics of Taiwanese enterprises in East Asia: identifying Taiwanese enterprises in Mainland China, Vietnam and Indonesia as targets', *Journal of Business Ethics* 33, 151–65.

Wu, Yuan-li and Chun-hsi Wu (1980) *Economic Development in Southeast Asia: The Chinese Dimension*, Stanford: Hoover Institution Press.

Xinhua News Agency (2001) 'Vietnam sets telecommunications expansion target for 2005', 19 March.

Xue, L. (1997) 'Promoting industrial R&D and high-tech development through science parks: the Taiwan experience and its implications for developing countries', *International Journal of Technology Management*, Special issue on R&D management **13**(7–8), 744–61.

Yamamura, Kozo and Wolfgang Streeck (eds) (2003) *The End of Diversity? Prospects for German and Japanese Capitalism*, Ithaca and London: Cornell University Press.

Yang, Mayfair (1994) *Gifts, Favors, and Banquets: The Art of Social Relationships in China*, Ithaca: Cornell University Press.

Yao, Souchou (2002) *Confucian Capitalism: Discourse, Practice and the Myth of Chinese Enterprise*, London: RoutledgeCurzon.

Yao, Souchou (2004) 'Guanxi: sentiment, performance and the trading of words', in Thomas Menkhoff and Solvay Gerke (eds), *Chinese Entrepreneurship and Asian Business Networks*, London and New York: RoutledgeCurzon, pp. 233–54.

Yeung, Henry Wai-Chung (1998) *Transnational Corporations and Business Networks: Hong Kong Firms in the ASEAN Region*, London and New York: Routledge.

Yeung, Henry Wai-Chung (ed.) (1999a) *The Globalization of Business Firms from Emerging Economies*, Cheltenham, UK and Northampton, MA, USA: Edward Elgar.

Yeung, Henry Wai-Chung (1999b) 'The internationalization of ethnic Chinese business firms from Southeast Asia: strategies, processes, and competitive advantage', *International Journal of Urban and Regional Research* **23**(1), 88–102.

Yeung, Henry Wai-Chung (2002) *Entrepreneurship and the Internationalisation of Asian Firms*, Cheltenham, UK and Northampton, MA, USA: Edward Elgar.

Yonekura, Seiichiro (1994) *The Japanese Iron and Steel Industry, 1850–1990: Continuity and Discontinuity*, Houndmills: Macmillan.

Yong, C.F. (1987) *Tan Kah Kee: The Making of an Overseas Chinese Legend*, Singapore: Oxford University Press.

Yoo, Keun Shin (1998–9) 'The traits and leadership styles of CEOs in Korean companies', *International Studies of Management and Organization* **28**(4) (Winter), 40–48.

Yoshihara, Kunio (1985) *Philippine Industrialization: Foreign and Domestic Capital*, New York: Oxford University Press.

Yoshihara, Kunio (1988) *The Rise of Ersatz Capitalism in South-East Asia*, Singapore: Oxford University Press.

Yoshino, Kosaku (1992) *Cultural Nationalism in Contemporary Japan: A Sociological Inquiry*, London: Routledge.

Youngson, A.J. (1982) *Hong Kong: Economic Growth and Policy*, Hong Kong: Oxford University Press.

Youssef, D.A. (2000) 'Organizational commitment as a mediator of the relationship between Islamic work ethic and attitudes toward organizational change', *Human Relations*, **53**(4), 513–37.

Yuan, Lee Tsao and Linda Low (1990) *Local Entrepreneurship in Singapore: Private and State*, Singapore: Times Academic Press.

Zeng, Ming and Peter J. Williamson (2003) 'The hidden dragons', *Harvard Business Review*, October, pp. 92–9.

Zhou, Mi and Xiaoming Wang (2000) 'Agency cost and the crisis of China's SOE', *China Economic Review* **11**, 297–317.

Index

Xie Qihua 213
Xiqiao village 217
  private textile firms, case study 194–6

Yamamura, Kozo 58, 59
Yang, Mayfair 216
Yao, Souchou 217
Yasuda group 31, 32
Yawata Steel Works 30
Yeung, Henry Wai-Chung 156–7, 158, 313
Yin, K.Y. 144
Yoo, Keun Shin 89
Yoshihara, Kunio 339

Yoshihasa, Ojimi 36–7
Yuan, Lee Tsao 314

zaibatsu 30–33, 34, 138
  chaebol comparison 88, 89–90
  expansion 32
  labour relations 33
  structure 31, 32
Zeng, Ming 208
Zhang Ruimin 212, 213
  and Haier Group, case study 206–9
Zhou Enlai 167–8
zombie corporations 55–6